No Turning Back

No Turning Back

The Peacetime Revolutions of
Post-War Britain

PAUL ADDISON

OXFORD
UNIVERSITY PRESS

OXFORD

UNIVERSITY PRESS

Great Clarendon Street, Oxford OX2 6DP

Oxford University Press is a department of the University of Oxford.
It furthers the University's objective of excellence in research, scholarship,
and education by publishing worldwide in

Oxford New York

Auckland Cape Town Dar es Salaam Hong Kong Karachi
Kuala Lumpur Madrid Melbourne Mexico City Nairobi
New Delhi Shanghai Taipei Toronto

With offices in

Argentina Austria Brazil Chile Czech Republic France Greece
Guatemala Hungary Italy Japan Poland Portugal Singapore
South Korea Switzerland Thailand Turkey Ukraine Vietnam

Oxford is a registered trade mark of Oxford University Press
in the UK and in certain other countries

Published in the United States
by Oxford University Press Inc., New York

© Paul Addison 2010

The moral rights of the author have been asserted
Database right Oxford University Press (maker)

First published 2010

British Library Cataloguing in Publication Data

Data available

Library of Congress Cataloging in Publication Data
Library of Congress Control Number: 2010925606

Typeset by SPI Publisher Services, Pondicherry, India
Printed in Great Britain
on acid-free paper by
Clays Ltd., St Ives plc

ISBN 978–0–19–219267–7

1 3 5 7 9 10 8 6 4 2

For Rosy

Acknowledgements

My thanks are due first of all to the editorial staff of Oxford University Press for the patient support and encouragement they have given to a laggardly author. I am grateful in particular to Catherine Clarke, Luciana O'Flaherty, and Matthew Cotton for constructive criticism and advice. I have had the good fortune of knowing that I could rely at all times on the guidance and friendship of my agent, Bruce Hunter of David Higham Associates. Special thanks are also due to Mr John Gilmour, Professor Keith Robbins, and Professor Peter Hennessy, for reading and commenting on a draft of the book. Without their intervention it would have many more faults than it does, but they are not in any way responsible for the faults that remain. I am very grateful to Zoe Spilberg for picture research, to Connie Roberston for copyright research and clearances, and to Susan Beer for copy-editing.

In the School of History, Classics and Archaeology at the University of Edinburgh, and its predecessor the Department of History, I have enjoyed the best of historical company for the better part of a lifetime, and I must ask colleagues and former students to forgive me if I do not express my gratitude to them all individually: the list would certainly be a long one. In recent years I have had a new academic home at the Centre for the Study of the Two World Wars, and although this is not a book about war it would be incomplete without a warm word of thanks to colleagues with whom it has been a pleasure to work: Professor Jim McMillan, Dr Jeremy Crang, Dr David Stafford, and Ms Yvonne McEwen.

My greatest debt, as ever, is to my wife Rosy, my sons James and Michael, and their two grannies, Cath and Pauline.

Paul Addison
University of Edinburgh
Centre for the Study of the Two World Wars
February 2010

Contents

List of Illustrations

List of Graphs and Maps

Graphs

Maps

Introduction

This is a book about the changing character of Britain between the end of the Second World War and the start of the twenty-first century. It can best be described as social history in a broad sense that encompasses politics and government as well as the many topics that are usually thought of as 'social': standards of living, social class, race relations, sex and marriage and so on. Much has been written about these things in recent years, and I have been able to draw freely on the findings of academics and commentators without whose guidance I would certainly have gone astray. I have tried to acknowledge my debt to them in the text as well as the source references. That said, this is also a book with a more personal dimension.

Among the illustrations is a photograph of form Lower Five Modern at King Edward VI Grammar School, Lichfield, in May 1957. There I am at the age of fourteen, third from the left in the front row. At the centre of the group is Mr A. R. Handley, known as 'Tommy' after the comedian Tommy Handley, the star of ITMA: the war was still a very recent event. 'Tommy', one of nature's Tories, was one of two inspiring history teachers by whom I had the good fortune to be taught: the other, Carl Emery ('Caje') had been a conscientious objector during the war and taught us that history was all about the class struggle. I am happy to say that the school still flourishes, though it ceased long ago to be a single sex grammar school and is now a co-educational comprehensive. For me the photo is not only a record of my classmates but a snapshot of a conservative world on the brink of many transformations.

Would I, if I could, put the clock back to Britain as it was in 1957? Hardly: the gains we have made since then outweigh the losses. I have to admit, however, that the passage of time has left me with a sense of disorientation I can never quite suppress. At some barely conscious level of my imagination the England of which I was a part in the late 1950s is forever the norm, and almost everything that has happened since a puzzling deviation. Much as I like to think of myself as fully adult, I know that somewhere at the back of my mind lurks a schoolboy forever putting up his hand to ask why smoking is banned in the cinema, or why passengers on the railways are referred to as 'customers', or why so many couples live together without getting married.

Historians used to argue that Britain was transformed in the first half of the twentieth century by the social upheavals of the two world wars. With the advantage of a longer perspective we can see that the comparative peace and growing prosperity of the second half of the century were more powerful solvents of tradition than the Battle of the Somme or the Blitz. There is no denying the importance of the two main domestic consequences of the war: full employment and the welfare state. But the war had conservative as well as radical effects, entrenching British attitudes and delaying the advance of consumer society. By the later 1950s the profound conservatism of British institutions was indeed a recurrent theme of social commentators. They, however, imagined that Britain could be modernized by incremental change and enlightened experiments in state intervention. They were mistaken: they had been drifting all the time towards the rapids.

An economy based mainly on manufacturing was transformed into an economy founded mainly on finance, services, and the housing market. A predominantly working-class society evolved into a predominantly middle-class one. The social democratic state of the mid-twentieth century, with its mixed economy, full employment, and strong trade unions, mutated under Mrs Thatcher into a neo-liberal state, founded on privatization and market forces. There were sweeping changes too in social values and behaviour. Much of the sexual morality preached, if not always practised, in the past was dismantled in favour of a more permissive society. The traditional division of labour between the sexes was challenged by feminists, and more significantly perhaps by women who would never have described themselves as such. The notion of the British as a homogeneous white nation was gradually supplanted by the idea of a multiracial and multicultural Britain.

This is not to imply that everything changed. The fundamentals of a capitalist economy and a parliamentary system were never seriously in doubt. The British remained a comparatively tolerant and orderly people, and Britain one of the best countries in which to live. The readiness of people to wait patiently in queues, the stoicism with which travellers greeted the news of trains delayed or flights cancelled, the continuing attachment of the public to the monarchy and the welfare state, all bore witness to a certain continuity of values. The tendency, none the less, was for the ties and constraints that had bound society together in the 1940s and 1950s to loosen. By the end of the twentieth century the direction of change was clear. In many ways society was becoming more liberal: more individualist, more tolerant of diversity, more committed to racial and sexual equality, but the role of the state was more of a paradox. The state had freed up sexual morality in the 1960s, liberated market forces in the 1980s, and granted a measure of self-government to Scotland and Wales at the turn of the century. But if the state was relaxing its control in some areas, it was tightening it in others.

In juggling these topics I have been torn between a thematic and a chronological approach and opted for a compromise between the two. As readers will see, the book is divided into three main periods—1945 to 1957, 1957 to 1974, and 1974 to 1997, with an epilogue on the more recent past. Each of the main periods is subdivided into chapters exploring four specific themes: the role of the state in economic and social affairs, standards of living and social class, gender, sexual morality and the family, and questions of national identity. In concentrating on these themes I have deliberately left out almost everything else, though it is never easy to know exactly where to draw the line. Apart from occasional references, for example, Northern Ireland is omitted on the grounds that although it was a part of the United Kingdom, it was such a hybrid of British and Irish history that it has to be treated as a separate subject. As one historian puts it: 'The Ulster political culture and social mood were so utterly distinct from that of the rest of the United Kingdom that it hardly related to the governability or peaceableness of British life in general.'[1]

The three main chronological divisions represent cycles of change in political history and are quite arbitrary in relation to the other themes, each of which had its own narratives and turning-points. If I have given pride of place to the role of Whitehall and Westminster it is because they were of such great importance in shaping the lives of the British, and managing or mismanaging their affairs. Writing in the eighteenth

century Samuel Johnson doubted whether the actions of rulers were of
any great consequence for the happiness of the ruled:

> How small of all that human hearts endure
> That part which laws or kings can cause or cure!
> Still to ourselves in every place confined
> Our own felicity we make or find.

He was writing at a time when the role of government was strictly limited, but even then it was of crucial importance in establishing the
peace, prosperity, and order that made the pursuit of happiness possible. In the twentieth century governments became agencies of great
power and potential in economic and social affairs. Dr Johnson would
surely have changed his mind if he could have witnessed the activities
of the British state on the home front during the Second World War.
'Never before and never since', writes Peter Hennessy, 'has a British
government taken so great and so intrusive a range of powers over the
lives of its citizens—where they worked, what they did in uniform or
"civvies", what they ate, what they wore, what they could read in the
newspapers, what they could hear on the wireless sets.'[2]

The British had given up most of their liberties for the duration of the
war. It remained to be seen how far they would recover them when
peace returned. The first phase of post-war British history was a time of
cross-currents in which a momentum in favour of social reform encountered a momentum in favour of the restoration of pre-war ways of life.

PART I

The Aftermath of War
1945–1957

1

The Gentleman in Whitehall

In the Members' Lobby of the House of Commons stand four imposing statues of British prime ministers. Flanking one entrance are the two great war leaders, Lloyd George and Churchill: flanking the other, the leaders of the two peacetime administrations that did most to change the face of Britain after 1945: Clement Attlee and Margaret Thatcher. In redefining the role and purpose of government they changed the character of British society, though not always in the way they hoped or intended.

As professional politicians both 'Clem' and 'Maggie' were well versed in the arts of compromise and manoeuvre, but their politics were grounded in strong and simple convictions formed early in life. This was a feature of Attlee's personality that commanded the respect of the young Margaret Roberts. 'Of Clement Attlee', she wrote, 'I was an admirer. He was a serious man and a patriot. Quite contrary to the general tendency of politicians in the 1990s, he was all substance and no show. His was a genuinely radical and reforming government. The 1945 Labour manifesto was in fact a very left-wing document. That is clearer now than it was then.'[1]

At the zenith of her fortunes in the mid-1980s Mrs Thatcher was a political giant who towered over the Conservative party and imposed on the Cabinet her own personal brand of politics: 'Thatcherism'. No one, however, was less likely to inspire a cult of personality than Attlee. Even as Prime Minister he could pass unnoticed in a crowd. Once when he was changing trains at Baker Street a woman approached him and said: 'Have you ever been told you look just like Mr Attlee?' 'Frequently', he replied.[2] The least charismatic of personalities and the most uninspiring of speakers, he had risen to the top through hard work, steady application to the most unglamorous of political tasks, and a large measure of luck. Never under the illusion that he possessed even a grain or two of the personal magnetism that enabled a Lloyd George or a Churchill to dominate or captivate others, he was a modest, self-effacing character, true to the service ethic of the high-minded Victorian professional class from which he sprang. 'Always a mistake', he remarked, 'to think you are larger than you are.'³ Attlee thought of himself as the representative of his party, and served it as loyally as he had once served his school and his regiment. Most of all, he shared its sense of historical mission.

'When I was a young barrister just down from Oxford', he wrote in 1937, 'I engaged in various forms of social work in East London. The condition of the people of that area as I saw them at close quarters led me to study their causes and to reconsider the assumptions of the social class to which I belonged. I became an enthusiastic convert to Socialism...I have never lost my early enthusiasm. I have never doubted that the Labour Party, whatever faults or failings it may have, is the only practical instrument in this country for the attainment of a new order of society.'⁴ It was clear to Attlee what was wrong with Britain, and how it could be put right. 'The evils that Capitalism brings', he wrote, 'differ in intensity in different countries, but, the root cause of the trouble once discerned, the remedy is seen to be the same by thoughtful men and women. The cause is the private ownership of the means of life; the remedy is public ownership.'⁵

The Labour Party was notorious for its doctrinal disputes, but Attlee's words expressed a common faith that bound the party together. It was restated in *Let Us Face the Future*, the 1945 election manifesto. Voters were warned against the machinations of 'Big Business' in alliance with the Conservatives, whose aim was to 'sweep away public controls, simply in order to give profiteering interests and the privileged rich an entirely free hand to plunder the rest of the nation as shamelessly as they did in the 1920s'. Labour would therefore maintain control of private industry. There must be 'no more dole queues in order to let the Czars of big business remain kings in their castles'. The great liberal economist John Maynard Keynes had argued that mass unemployment could be prevented, and capitalism preserved, by measures to stimulate demand during a recession. But although the manifesto included a Keynesian pledge to maintain a high level of purchasing power in the economy, the main emphasis was on economic planning and public ownership. Labour promised to 'plan from the ground up—giving an appropriate place to constructive enterprise and private endeavour in the national plan'. The Bank of England, coal, gas, electricity, railways, canals, and road services, and the iron and steel industry, were to be nationalized. Nor was that all. 'Labour', the manifesto added, 'believes in land nationalization and will work towards it.' In social policy the party pledged itself to press ahead with a vigorous housing programme, but without committing itself to a numerical target. The school-leaving age was to be raised from fourteen to sixteen 'at the earliest possible moment' and there were brief pledges on town and country planning, social insurance, and the National Health Service.[6]

In the 1960s and 1970s historians used to argue that the Attlee governments were so moderate as to be scarcely socialist at all, but with the rise of New Labour in the 1990s the ideological character of Old Labour stood out more boldly in retrospect. But if they travelled some distance along the road to socialism, the Attlee governments never reached their destination. Once they had nationalized 20 per cent of the economy and created the welfare state, they had fulfilled their manifesto promises and were uncertain of the next step. The uncertainty increased in February 1950, when Attlee called another general election and Labour's overall majority in the House was reduced to five. They fell from office with the New Jerusalem still under construction, but enough of it in place to serve as the foundation of a new political settlement.

After Labour's defeat in the general election of October 1951, it was a settlement revised by the Conservatives. Although they were pragmatic enough to accept much of Labour's welfare state and mixed economy, they also changed the mix by giving more scope to market forces. The ultimate outcome of Labour's victory in 1945 was therefore one that Attlee and his party had never intended: a makeshift social democracy based on expediency rather than principle.

It was a classic case of muddling through, but compromise ought not be mistaken for continuity. In the 1937 edition of his book *The Socialist Case*, the economist Douglas Jay had argued that the necessities of life should be subject to planned distribution by the state. 'Housewives as a whole', he wrote, 'cannot be trusted to buy all the right things, where nutrition and health are concerned. This is really no more than an extension of the principle according to which the housewife herself would not trust a child of four to select the week's provisions. For in the case of nutrition and health, just as in the case of education, the gentleman in

Whitehall really does know better what is good for people than the people know themselves.'[7,8] One of the most significant differences between the Britain of 1935 and the Britain of 1955 was the extent of state intervention in society. Politicians were now expected to tackle social and economic problems that Baldwin or Chamberlain would have left to sort themselves out, or devolved to local authorities. Governments wrestled ceaselessly with the Five Giants encountered by Beveridge on the road to reconstruction—Ignorance, Idleness, Want, Squalor, and Disease. It was a task that Conservatives, in general, approached with greater reluctance than Labour, but also with the aim of showing how much better they could do it.

The Socialist Moment

For Labour, 1945 was the best of times at which to come to power, and the worst. The Party itself was much the same political animal as it had been in 1939, but the war had greatly improved its fortunes. Attlee, Bevin, Cripps, Dalton, and Morrison had all served an apprenticeship to power as ministers in the Churchill Coalition. In varying degrees all had been involved in the organization of the war economy. All had taken part in the debates and discussions in Whitehall, in the aftermath of the Beveridge Report of December 1942, over post-war reconstruction. In social policy they also had extensive preparations to guide them in the shape of White Papers on national insurance and the national health service, the Education Act of 1944, and the Family Allowances Act of 1945. On taking office in July 1945, they had the great advantage of knowing who was who and what was what in Whitehall.

In the 1930s Labour politicians had spoken of the need for comprehensive economic planning, but with little idea of how the machinery of planning could be created. In 1945 they inherited a comprehensive system of economic controls which had been created in order to maximize the nation's war potential. Under the Emergency Powers Acts of 1939 and 1940, the government was granted sweeping powers over people and property which it exercised through Defence Regulations which had the force of law. While some of the regulations were designed to restrict civil liberties, others gave the government direct administrative control over the economy. From the point of view of the general public the most familiar type of control was the rationing of consumer goods, but there were several others: price controls, building licences, controls over investment, raw material allocations, import controls, controls over labour, and controls over the production and design of goods.[9] As the 1944 White Paper on Employment Policy explained, the most urgent economic problem after the war would not be unemployment but shortages. Labour and Conservative ministers agreed that in order to prevent inflation, and also to ensure that jobs were available for demobilized servicemen, it would be essential to retain a framework of economic controls during the period of transition from war to peace.

The 'command economy' of the war years resembled socialism and was welcomed by the party as a rehearsal for the real thing. The stupendous increases achieved in industrial output, the elimination of unemployment, and the general acceptance of food rationing as fair and effective all tended to strengthen the case for state intervention in the minds of 'the great and the good', the public-spirited professionals who served on advisory committees and Royal Commissions, or as temporary civil servants in wartime. This helps to explain why Labour took office with a large measure of sympathy and support from the leader-writers of *The Times*, the *Manchester Guardian*, and *The Economist*. Along with greater respectability, the war brought Labour greater popularity. The Conservatives suffered from their reputation as the 'guilty men' who allegedly had failed to rearm Britain in the 1930s, and no less as the party suspected of obstructing the implementation of the Beveridge Report with its promise of social security for all. When the results of the general election were announced on 26 July 1945 they revealed a sweeping victory for Labour with an overall majority of 146 in the House of Commons. The parliamentary numbers, however, gave an exaggerated impression of the party's popularity. 48.3 per cent of the electorate voted Labour but the party won more than 60 per cent of the seats in the House.

Having showered Labour with blessings that created a mood of euphoria in the party, fortune added a curse. The war had inflicted grievous bodily harm on Britain's earnings from exports and overseas investments. From 1942 onwards the yawning gap between imports and exports was filled by Lend-Lease supplies from the United States, but following the surrender of Japan in August 1945 Lend-Lease was abruptly terminated by President Truman. A hastily and painfully negotiated American loan approved by Congress in 1946 gave the British a breathing-space but a further period of austerity was unavoidable. In order to minimize imports, maximize exports, and prevent inflation, it was essential to hold down consumption and continue the rationing of essential goods in short supply.

Between 1945 and 1950 exports increased in volume by 77 per cent while imports were restricted to an increase of only 14.5 per cent, and consumption held down to a rise of 6 per cent. In a Europe devastated by war, Britain was setting the pace in economic recovery and the output of British industry in 1951 was as great as that of West Germany and France combined.[10] It was a creditable performance but the life of the Attlee governments was repeatedly punctuated by economic crises. In the fuel crisis of February and March 1947, a largely self-inflicted disaster, snow and freezing temperatures halted the movement of coal from the pits to the power stations, electricity supplies had to be cut and factories closed down. Two million people were thrown temporarily out of work. A second major setback occurred in July 1947, when the government, in compliance with the conditions attached to the loan agreement, carried out its promise to make sterling freely convertible into other currencies. As holders of sterling rushed to exchange their pounds for dollars, the Treasury's gold and dollar reserves drained away, and convertibility had to be suspended. Shaken to the core by the crisis Attlee and his colleagues were compelled to introduce a fresh round of austerity. In 1948–9 payments of $1,500 million from the United States under the Marshall Aid programme gave some relief but a second balance of payments crisis blew up in the summer of 1949 and the Chancellor of the Exchequer, Sir Stafford Cripps, was forced to announce a devaluation of the pound in September. Another round of cuts in public spending followed. No sooner was recovery achieved, than it was undermined again by the outbreak of the Korean war in June 1950 and the government's decision to embark on a large-scale programme of rearmament further delayed economic recovery. All things considered it is not surprising that consumer spending only increased by about one per cent per annum between 1945 and 1951.

Liberty and Controls

In his book *The Road to Serfdom*, published in 1944, the great free market liberal Friedrich Hayek, Professor of Economics at the LSE, warned that centralized economic planning was incompatible with liberty and bound to result in a totalitarian state. Churchill made a crude attempt to popularize the argument in the opening broadcast of the general election campaign. A socialist government, he predicted, would eventually be obliged to fall back on 'some sort of Gestapo, no doubt very humanely directed in the first instance'. Only crackpots repeated the claim but Labour's opponents hammered home the argument that socialism was not only inefficient but hostile to freedom. Though sometimes applied to the nationalization programme or aspects of social policy, the argument hinged on the future of wartime controls over the economy.

Within three weeks of taking office in 1945, Attlee and his Cabinet were confronted by the celebrated memorandum in which Keynes analysed Britain's financial situation and warned that it faced a 'financial Dunkirk'. On 16 August, with Keynes's paper before them, they took a bold decision. The Coalition had agreed that wartime emergency powers over the economy, which were due to expire in February 1946, should be extended for a further period of two years. The Labour Cabinet decided to extend the period to five years and a bill to this effect, the Supplies and Services (Transitional Powers) Bill, was passed in October. The Act authorized the government to retain many of the wartime emergency powers for broadly defined peacetime purposes. As Neil Rollings explains: 'Regulations could be used to secure sufficient supplies essential to the well-being of the community or to ensure their equitable distribution, to facilitate demobilization, to assist the readjustment of industry to peacetime requirements, to assist in relief of other countries and to control prices.'[11] Among the key Defence Regulations retained by Labour the most important were Defence Regulation 55, which provided sweeping powers over the control and allocation of goods and services, 55AB, which enabled the government to fix prices, and 62, which gave the government the right to determine the use of agricultural land. The practical effect was that the government continued to operate wartime controls over imports, the allocation of raw materials, building licences, prices, and of course rationing.

Since Parliament was sovereign and could make whatever laws it pleased, Attlee and his colleagues were within their constitutional rights but *The Economist* was worried:

Nothing could illustrate more vividly the change that has come over British public life than the comparative ease with which the Supplies and Services (Transitional Powers) Bill passed through its Committee stage in the Commons on Monday. A war has just ended during which the government was given, as an unfortunate necessity, complete and arbitrary powers over the life, liberty and property of every citizen; and its ending is a signal less for withdrawing these extraordinary and altogether unprecedented powers than for extending them still further—extending them, what is more, not on a year-to-year basis as in wartime but for a certain period of five years.... Not only do Defence Regulations which permit the seizing of any property or undertaking, the search of any premises, the conscription of the person or property of any individual, and the suspension of any law, remain in full force, but they can be 'adapted'—whatever that means—in any way the government decides to meet the new purposes of reconstruction.[12]

The inclusion of the word 'transitional' in the Supplies and Services Act implied that economic controls would only be retained as long as there was an emergency, but there was an ambiguity in Labour attitudes. The party was also committed to a planned economy, and as Cairncross writes, 'hardly any member of the government was sure what it meant except perhaps the continuation of physical controls'.[13]

In the short term the most important reason for the retention of economic controls was the persistence of shortages and the need to prevent inflation, but they were also important in boosting the export drive. When the production of motor vehicles resumed, the government employed its control over supplies of steel to compel manufacturers to export the bulk of their output.[14] When the pottery trade was re-started the President of the Board of Trade, Sir Stafford Cripps, ruled that only plain white china should be available at home: coloured and decorated china must be reserved for export.

The machinery of control necessitated a large bureaucracy and a formidable amount of paperwork: as in the war years industry and agriculture were swathed in red tape. *The Times* complained in December 1945 of the complexity of the procedure for obtaining building licences:

A business requiring a building licence must first get some Ministry to agree that it is the responsible authority. Sometimes the control is clear—any steel-maker or machine-tool maker knows that he works under a trade control which is itself under the Ministry of Supply, but sometimes the matter is open to real doubt and the identification of the controlling Ministry, including the persuasion of that Ministry to acknowledge its responsibility, takes a long time. If the project is eventually agreed to concern the Ministry of Supply approach must then be made to the regional controller of the Ministry of Supply, who may or may not refer to headquarters and may or may not make an investigation of his own. If and when that hurdle is cleared the case goes to the regional board and thence to the Board of Trade. Those two authorities satisfied, reference is next to the distribution of industries committee; on this the Ministry of Town and Country Planning is represented and usually wishes to refer to headquarters, which has usually to consult the Ministry of Transport, Ministry of Agriculture, and others who might be interested. If the passage of the project is piloted safely so far, it will go to 'Panel A', on which are represented all Ministries who might be concerned, which, after suitable inquiry, will send it back to the original sponsoring Ministry for inspection by the Controller of Building and Construction in that Ministry, who will then send the case on to the Ministry of Works. Thence it will go to the Ministry's regional office, which, if all has been well so far, will issue a building licence.[15]

There were many expressions of anxiety over the regulation of everyday life by an over-mighty bureaucracy. In September 1947 the Archbishop of York, Dr Garbett, who had recently been carving out a role for himself as a globe-trotting anti-communist, declared that planning in Britain was in danger of being carried to such an extent

that it may presently deprive the individual citizen of freedom, responsibility and initiative. I question if it is really necessary when we are crying out for labour to employ an army of 570,000 clerks and secretaries in the Civil Service to keep the law-abiding citizen in order. I question if it is necessary to send out a constant stream of forms with long lists of interrogations while at the same time paper for the use of the Press is drastically restricted... Gradually, almost imperceptibly, these permits and restrictions, few of them of themselves of great importance, wind themselves round the farmer, the builder, the industrialist, the man of business, until he finds he has lost all freedom and is in the position of Gulliver bound by the strings of Lilliput.[16]

The economist John Jewkes, an opponent of centralized planning, described the detail of control as incredible:

The Board of Trade finds time to fix maximum prices for haircuts...
Boxes containing fragments of wedding cake sent to friends abroad are
emptied and sent on empty because the export of confectionery is prohibited. The government seeks to impose an order preventing a house-
holder from decorating his own house, without getting a licence, if the
cost of raw materials plus the estimated cost of his own labour comes to
more than £10 [£228]. Strong protests forced the government to
exclude the cost of labour but not to drop the control. The owners of
private gardens, are prohibited, except under licence, to bottle fruit and
sell it to the public.[17]

One of the inevitable consequences of this proliferation of regulations
was the problem of enforcement. In the main the government relied on
moral exhortation, but coercion was employed as a back-up. Every year
from 1946 to 1949 officials of the Ministry of Food launched more than
20,000 successful prosecutions against black-market operators for
offences such as overcharging or illegal sales. In order to suppress a
flourishing black market in the sale of commercial petrol to private
motorists, petrol intended for commercial purposes was dyed red, and
stringent penalties imposed on offenders. Garage owners found with
red petrol in pumps intended for private motorists were deprived of all
petrol supplies for twelve months, and private motorists caught with red
petrol in the tank forfeited their licence for twelve months. Conservatives, with Churchill's 'gestapo' speech echoing in their minds, warned
of the danger to civil liberties.[18]

In response to the convertibility crisis of August 1947 the government equipped itself with even more extensive powers. The Supplies
and Services (Extended Purposes) Act authorized ministers to employ
the Defence Regulations for promoting productivity, regulating imports
and exports and 'generally for ensuring that the whole resources of the
community are available for use, and are used, in a manner best calculated to serve the interests of the community'. Churchill described the
bill as 'a blank cheque for totalitarian government'.[19]

No sane observer imagined that Attlee and his colleagues intended
to turn Britain into a totalitarian state, but the continued existence of
sweeping and arbitrary powers was against the grain of British political
culture and gave rise to genuine unease. In Fleet Street, the *Observer*
remarked, newspapers that had previously been broadly sympathetic to
the government—*The Times*, the *Manchester Guardian*, the *News Chronicle*

and the *Daily Mirror*, were all opposed to the new legislation. 'To hand such powers to a Cabinet which obviously does not know how it will use them', the *Observer* commented, 'is a grotesque surrender of democratic rights which is being strongly and justly challenged.'[20] George Orwell was distressed when American critics interpreted his novel *1984* (1949), with its nightmare vision of a totalitarian Britain of the future, as an attack on the Labour government. But although Orwell described the book as a parody, he did acknowledge something like it might happen. As he explained in a press release concocted with his publisher, Frederick Warburg:

> Members of the present British government, from Mr Attlee and Sir Stafford Cripps down to Aneurin Bevan, will *never* willingly sell the pass to the enemy, and in general the older men, nurtured in a Liberal tradition, are safe, but the younger generation is suspect and the seeds of totalitarian thought are probably widespread among them.[21]

Arguably the Labour Party contained its own built-in safeguard against totalitarianism—a trade union movement rooted in the culture of Victorian liberalism, hostile to state control, and wedded to the doctrine of 'free collective bargaining'. After the convertibility crisis of 1947 the Ministry of Labour issued a Control of Engagements Order under Defence Regulation 58A, entitling officials to compel an applicant for employment into essential work. In 1948 a total of twenty-nine directions were issued.[22]

With hindsight we can see that the anxieties expressed by Orwell were exaggerated by the sinister light of the Cold War, and the fear that one by one the nations of Europe would succumb to communism. But the battering the government received from liberal opinion, not to mention bankers and industrialists, helps to explain their retreat from a command economy.[23] The government's economic advisers were themselves divided between the protagonists of two different types of planning: 'Gosplanners' (Gosplan being the Soviet state committee for economic planning) who argued for plans based on physical controls, and 'Thermostatters' who advocated a combination of demand management along Keynesian lines, and the selective use of controls.[24] While therefore the politicians talked of planning, the question of the form that planning should take remained unresolved. Nor was there any machinery of planning until the spring of 1947, when a Central

Economic Planning staff was established under Cripps at the Board of Trade.

It was Cripps who at last introduced some coherence into Labour's economic policies. When he succeeded Dalton as Chancellor of the Exchequer in November 1947 he took the planning staff with him to the Treasury, and steered the government towards a Keynesian version of socialism.[25] In 1946, 94 per cent of the fifteen most important raw materials were allocated by Whitehall to industry; by 1950 the figure was 47 per cent.[26] In November 1948 Harold Wilson, the President of the Board of Trade, abolished a multitude of commodity controls in two well-publicized 'bonfires' in November 1948 and March 1949. While the Board of Trade issued 2,580,000 licences and permits in 1947, by 1949 the total was down to 1,118,000. Over the same period the number of officials administering the controls fell from 14,200 to 10,450.[27]

Under Cripps 'planning' now hinged more and more on the use of the budget to regulate demand, but the restoration of market forces was far from complete when Labour fell from office in 1951. At that point the government was still directly buying in almost three-quarters of imported food and more than half of imported manufactures.[28] Nor were the rising generation of Labour politicians—Hugh Gaitskell, Harold Wilson, Douglas Jay—prepared to put all their eggs in the Keynesian basket. Fearful always that a slump was around the corner, they planned to retain a nucleus of controls, in particular controls over imports and prices, on a permanent basis. Rather than rely on a renewal of emergency powers, they proposed an Economic and Employment Bill to enshrine controls on a permanent basis.

When the bill was discussed by the Cabinet in July 1950, some apprehension was expressed on the grounds that 'it would bring into sharper focus the extent of the powers which the government was already exercising: this was less obvious now, when the existing powers were scattered among numerous emergency statutes and regulations dating from the war and immediately thereafter.'[29] Redrafted as the 'Full Employment Bill', it would have enabled the government to retain permanent powers over production, prices, building, and the allocation of raw materials. Announced in February 1951, it was condemned by R. A. Butler for the Conservatives as 'the Reichstag method of governing'. It was then dropped from the government's programme, ostensibly in order to prevent confusion between its proposals for peacetime controls, and the emergency powers necessitated by rearmament and the Korean war.[30] Perhaps, however, it was not confusion the government feared, but a renewed focus on the issue of arbitrary powers. In the absence of legislation, Attlee and his ministers continued to administer economic controls under wartime Defence Regulations, which were extended for a further period of twelve months. Of the 687 Defence Regulations in existence on VE-Day, no fewer than 215, filling many volumes of statutory instruments, remained.[31] It was ironic that the practice of democratic socialism should have relied so heavily upon *droit administratif.*

One other legacy of the wartime emergency was the national identity card which had been issued to every man, woman, and child in the autumn of 1939. A simple document giving details of name, date of birth, and address—there was no photograph or fingerprint—it had to be produced if a policeman demanded proof of identity, and also served various administrative purposes such as the distribution of ration books. In spite of the fact that the war was over, there were still occasions when officials, and the police, required members of the public to produce their national identity cards. Ever alert to the dangers of administrative despotism *The Economist* protested: 'If it is asked why there should be any objection to people being asked for their identity numbers, the answer is that national registration and identity cards were part of the emergency legislation of war. They have no place in peacetime England, and no Minister has ever given a satisfactory explanation why they are still necessary in the semi-peace of today.'[32] The issue was put to the test in December 1950 when police constable Harold Muckle stopped a car driven by Clarence Willcock in Ballards Lane, and asked him to produce his national identity card. Willcock, a fervent Liberal, refused to do so and was convicted of breaking the law, but appealed to the High Court which gave him an absolute discharge in June 1951. Lord Chief Justice Goddard said: 'To use Acts of Parliament, passed for particular purposes during war, in times when the war is past, except that technically a state of war exists, tends to turn law-abiding subjects into lawbreakers.'[33] The implication was that if the government wanted a system of national identity cards in peacetime, they ought to introduce fresh legislation. Whether Labour would have done this if they had returned to power in 1951 we cannot say. As with economic controls, the use of emergency powers during the transition from war to peace enabled the government to postpone difficult and almost certainly controversial decisions about the future role of the state. In the event, identity cards were abolished by the Churchill government in 1952.

On and Off the Ration

As far as the general public was concerned, the most familiar aspect of economic controls was the rationing of consumer goods—chiefly basic foods, clothing, furniture, and petrol. The Conservatives liked to allege that socialists believed in rationing for its own sake. 'The queues of housewives outside the shops', Churchill declared in 1949, 'are the essence of socialism and the restrictive system by which it and its parasites hope to live.' In a broadcast of 1950 he invented the term 'Queuetopia' to describe Britain under socialist rule.[34]

In fact there is little or nothing to suggest that Labour ministers ever saw rationing as anything more than a temporary expedient, essential if inflation was to be avoided, and staple products fairly distributed. But while they could always fall back on the claim that rationing ensured fair shares, reductions in the ration were bound to be unpopular. The most sensitive area, because it affected virtually the whole population every day of the week, was food rationing. Although British farmers had greatly increased their output during the war, the British were still dependent on imports for a substantial part of the nutrition they needed. The war, however, had created a world food shortage. Millions in Europe and the Indian subcontinent were on the verge of starvation. The United States was the one great power with abundant food supplies, but the British were chronically short of dollars.

With fresh eggs in such short supply, powdered egg, which had first been imported from the United States in 1942, had become remarkably popular. There was a terrific row in February 1946 when the Minister of Food, Sir Ben Smith, announced that supplies of dried egg from the United States were to be suspended in order to save dollars. There were howls of complaint. If dollars had to be saved, why not cut supplies of tobacco or Hollywood movies? The recently formed British Housewives' League, of which more will be said in the next chapter, organized an impressive protest rally. 'We are under-fed, under-washed, and over-controlled', a Liverpool housewife complained.[35] When the

Cabinet discussed the import programme a few days later ministers were clearly rattled. Supplies of dried egg were restored, but this time on the ration under the points system. On 3 March 1946 the weekly ration of fats was reduced from eight ounces to seven; on 26 May the cheese ration was cut from three to two ounces a week. The following day Sir Ben Smith resigned, and it was left to his successor John Strachey, to announce on 31 May that from July bread would be rationed for the first time in British history.

This was a precautionary measure introduced in response to forecasts, which proved to be overly pessimistic, of a world-wide shortage of wheat. Petitions from housewives against bread rationing poured in, but it went ahead and proved to be something of an anti-climax.[36] The quantities of bread allowed under the ration were generous and there was no reduction in the amount of bread consumed. Two years later in July 1948 bread rationing was quietly abandoned, and other de-rationing measures followed:

De-rationing under Labour 1948–51

Sept. 1948	Footwear and children's clothes
Dec. 1948	Jam
Apr. 1949	Furniture
Apr. 1949	Sweets (rationing *reintroduced* August 1949)
May 1949	Clothes
May 1950	Petrol; Points rationing of 'inessential' foods
Sept. 1950	Soap

'In total', writes Christopher Dow, 'consumer rationing—even at its height, in 1947 and 1948—applied to less than a third of consumers' expenditure. When clothes and furniture—and also bread, potatoes, and preserves—were taken off the ration in 1948–9, the proportion fell to a mere twelve per cent or so. Thus even by 1949, rationing can hardly have been much of a restraint on consumption in total.'[37]

By the time the Conservatives returned to office in October 1951 it was clearly only a matter of time before rationing was abolished altogether. As Ina Zweiniger-Bargielowska has pointed out, the key policy difference between the parties was that the Conservatives were prepared to de-ration even if prices rose as a result, while Labour were reluctant to de-ration until supply was sufficient to ensure that prices would remain stable.[38]

This was not the only dividing line between the parties over the rising tide of consumer demand. There was a discernible puritanism in Labour's preference for collective social provision over personal consumption, and an appeal to materialism in the Conservative rhetoric of tax-cutting and setting the people free. An illuminating episode occurred in the autumn of 1947 when controversy broke out over the length of women's skirts. After the angular, utilitarian styles of the war years, designed to economize on the quantity of materials required in the manufacture of women's clothes, Christian Dior had launched in Paris a romantic counter-revolution featuring curves, bustles, wasp-waists, and long swirling skirts. In Britain, where cloth was in short supply and clothing still rationed, the government was perturbed by signs of a growing demand among women for the longer skirts associated with the 'New Look'. From the Whitehall point of view the case against the lowering of the hemline was that it would be 'wasteful', diverting raw materials that could have been employed in the production of a larger number of skirts. Sir Stafford Cripps, the President of the Board of Trade, appealed to the British Guild of Creative Designers for their co-operation in keeping shorter length skirts popular in Britain. 'The shorter the skirt the better', he told a gathering of clothing manufacturers in September 1947, while prudently adding: 'there must be some limits introduced by other considerations.' Dior's hemlines descended to somewhere between eight and twelve inches from the ground. Board of Trade officials hoped to ensure that skirts for the home market had hemlines above the 'mid-calf' level of fourteen inches above the ground.[39]

Women featured prominently on both sides of the argument. *Vogue* magazine rejoiced in the lengthening of skirts, as did Anne Scott-James, the editor of *Harper's Bazaar*: 'Sir Stafford Cripps', she warned, 'cannot halt the world march of fashion. He has the choice of encouraging our manufacturers to keep up with fashion or of forcing England to trail behind, an isolated pocket of dowdiness.' Jill Craigie, a socialist and documentary film maker, deplored the trend as anti-social and suggested that if British film directors refused to dress their stars in the new styles, 'there is some chance that this wasteful move will die a natural death'. At the annual Labour party conference the redoubtable Mrs Bessie Braddock condemned the long skirt as 'the ridiculous whim of idle people'. Alex Meynell, a Board of Trade official (and Labour supporter), held a press conference for women journalists at which she was heckled for urging women to count their blessings and resist changes in fashion. Shortly afterwards there arrived on her desk a package containing a fig-leaf with a sales leaflet explaining that by wearing this new style of dress 'people will save cloth, button, pins, needles and also manpower'.[40] In the end fashion carried all before it, with longer skirts prevailing in spite of the government.

A few years after Labour's fall from office in 1951 a Labour supporter, meeting Attlee at a party, plucked up the courage to ask whether he ever thought that Labour had imposed an unnecessary degree of austerity on the country. 'Wondered about that myself, a dozen times', Attlee replied. 'But I think when we saw the real state the country was in at the end of the war, the finances, the economy, the railways, the housing stock, we all went into a blue funk. Scared the pants off us, as the Americans would say. Austerity and more austerity seemed the only way out. You're asking were we too heavy on the brake? Yes, I think we got it wrong there.'[41]

Commanding Heights

While the wartime state was dismantled, a new post-war state was under construction. Labour politicians often spoke before 1945 of the need to capture 'the commanding heights of the economy', a phrase originally coined by Lenin.[42] They assumed, more as a matter of faith than logic, that the nationalization of industry would deliver the commanding heights into their hands. Once in power they began by nationalizing the Bank of England, but as the Bank was already subject to government direction this made very little difference. The key change was the transfer of fuel and transport to the state. The coal industry, which at that time supplied 90 per cent of Britain's energy requirements, and gas, which provided another 8 per cent, were nationalized. So were the supply and distribution of electricity. The railways and canals, along with the ports and long-distance road haulage were all taken into public ownership as divisions of the British Transport Commission, which had the authority to fix freight charges and passenger fares, and was under instructions to pursue that will o' the wisp of post-war planning, an integrated transport policy.

There were also pragmatic reasons for the nationalization of particular industries. Coal was notorious for a toxic history of conflict between the colliery companies and the miners, and the technical backwardness of the industry had once again been exposed by disappointing production figures during the war. The Reid Report of 1945, the outcome of an enquiry by senior mining engineers commissioned by the Coalition government, concluded that it had fallen behind the Ruhr, the Netherlands, and Poland in productivity, and put the technical case for the reorganization of the industry. 'Even had the Conservatives been elected in 1945', writes Martin Chick, 'it seems probable that coal mining would have been nationalized.'[43] The railway companies had been in financial difficulties before the war and by 1945 there were railway stations encrusted with soot which had never had a lick of paint in years. 'Bridges, tunnels and buildings had also been allowed to decay', writes Christian Wolmar, 'while many locomotives were at the end of their useful lives.' 10 per cent of carriages were still lit by gas.[44] The case for capital investment in the coal mines and the railways was unanswerable and since the only likely source of capital was the taxpayer, an increase in state control was inevitable no matter which party was in power.

As the nationalization bills marched triumphantly through Parliament it seemed that Britain was destined to become a land in which large-scale enterprise was all in the hands of the state. As John Parker, a young Labour MP who had been Secretary of the Fabian Society during the Second World War, wrote in 1947: 'Although it is not very clear as to which industries are next likely to be tackled following the completion of the present nationalization programme, there is a strong case for believing that the working of a planned economy, particularly if the traditional democratic liberties are to be preserved, will lead to a fairly rapid extension of national ownership for the simple reason that it is much easier to plan the nationalized than the non-nationalized sectors of national life. Wherever a particular private industry does not fit into the working of the national plan, or where it is in the hands of a monopoly or of one or two big capitalists, there will be a clear case for taking over that industry or group of firms.'[45]

This proved to be a false dawn. The conversion of industries into public corporations aroused little enthusiasm among the workers they employed or among the general public. The railwaymen and the miners had campaigned long and hard for public ownership but when it arrived, with the same managers in charge and working conditions initially much the same, it proved to be something of an anti-climax. On the political level the nationalization programme had only just begun when the economic troubles of 1947 precipitated a crisis of confidence in the Cabinet and the Labour Party. Hitherto it had been carried through as an act of faith in an ideological goal which had commanded universal acceptance. Now the party began to divide into traditional socialists who retained their belief in nationalization as an end in itself, and revisionists who argued that nationalization should only be introduced where it could be justified in terms of improving the economic efficiency of the industry concerned. By far the most contentious of the candidates for nationalization was iron and steel, the only manufacturing industry on Labour's shopping-list, and according to its defenders an example of capitalism at its most efficient. It was only after agonizing debates within the Cabinet that it was decided to go ahead with legislation which eventually became law, after a ferocious party political battle with the Conservatives and the rejection of the bill by the House of Lords. The bill eventually became law in 1951, but by this time there was no consensus within the party over future measures of nationalization and very little enthusiasm in the Cabinet for extending the shopping list.[46]

Hence after six years in office the Labour Party had brought into being a greatly expanded public sector employing more than two million people:

Employees of nationalized industries in 1951

Industry	Numbers employed
Inland transport*	888,100
Coal	780,000
Iron and steel	292,000
Electricity	181,900
Gas	148,000
Airways	24,900

* Including 599,000 on the railways.
Source: Terry Gourvish, 'The Rise (and Fall?) of State-Owned Enterprise' in Terry Gourvish and Alan O'Day (eds.), *Britain Since 1945* (1991), p. 113.

The ideological debate over nationalization distracted attention from a key element of continuity in industrial policy. 'Before 1914', writes Julian Greaves

> the state had laid down general ground rules on how business conducted its affairs, but had taken little interest in the competitive make-up of industries, firm sizes, and structuring technology choices, forms of management control, or the implications thereof for efficiency and profitability. These issues were considered best left to individual businessmen operating through the invisible hand of the market. Yet, by the 1920s, the vocabulary of mergers, cartels, trade associations and (to a lesser degree) scientific management abounded in ministerial speeches and official reports. By the 1930s intervention in the conduct of major industries was commonplace.[47]

Nationalization was in part a means of accelerating a process that had already been taking place: the amalgamation of smaller units into larger organizations. In 1921 the number of railway companies had been reduced from 130 to the 'Big Four': the London and North Eastern, London Midland and Scottish, Great Western, and Southern. Labour merged all four, and the Thomas Cook travel agency of which they were joint owners, to form British Railways. The nationalization of gas and electricity involved the merging of numerous private and municipal enterprises into monopolies. The National Coal Board took possession of about 1,500 collieries which had been owned by more than 800 firms and individuals. Along with the collieries themselves came 21,000 pit ponies, 'colliery coke ovens and manufactured fuel plants...coal preparation plants, colliery offices and workshops, colliery electricity plants, colliery railways, and canal wharves and their loading and storage facilities, colliery merchanting property, welfare institutes such as colliery institutes, baths, and canteens...'[48] The new nationalized industries took their place alongside other great corporations like ICI, created from the merger of four companies in 1926, and the British Motor Corporation, formed in 1952 from the amalgamation of the Austin and Morris motor companies.

Although the various state corporations were separately managed and independent up to a point, they were all subject to Treasury control and hence to the economic policies of the government. The government, therefore, was now in a position to exercise much greater leverage than it had in wartime over the general level of wages and salaries. This helps to explain why the government, as part of its anti-inflationary strategy, introduced in 1948 the previously untried device of a notion of an incomes policy. Embracing both the public and the private sectors, the policy was voluntary and rested on the support of the TUC, which endorsed it in 1948 and 1949, but turned against it in 1950 on the grounds that prices were now outstripping wages.

The nationalized industries soon acquired a reputation as inefficient, loss-making organizations which had to be repeatedly subsidized by the taxpayer. But, as Alec Cairncross writes, this was largely a consequence of government policies, rather than inefficiencies within the industries themselves: 'On the one hand they had been obliged to hold down prices for long periods as part of the government's fight against inflation; on the other hand they had been obliged to maintain output (e.g. in coal mining and rail transport) in places and at levels that were plainly unremunerative. The resulting losses did not necessarily reflect on their efficiency; but they did point to the vulnerability of the nationalized industries to government pressure that could be attacked as misconceived.'[49]

The most important single objective of Labour policy was full employment. Fortunately for Attlee and his colleagues this had already been achieved as a result of the war, though it would not have been possible to maintain it without the economic life-lines provided by the United States. For Labour, however, employment policy also had a crucial regional dimension. Between the wars, mass unemployment had been concentrated in certain areas of the country, especially those heavily dependent on a single declining industry. During the war the Coalition had introduced a form of regional employment policy by directing government contracts to the pre-war depressed areas. The Coalition government's Distribution of Industry Act of 1945 was in effect a mandate for the post-war continuation of a policy essential to the objective of full employment. The Act defined certain parts of the country as 'development areas' and gave the Board the power to forbid a manufacturer from extending a factory by more than 5,000 feet without an industrial development certificate. In this way employers could be compelled to locate new factories or plant in the development areas, and in order to give them an incentive to do so the Board also provided them with a building licence entitling them to the necessary labour and materials. Only 10 per cent of the population lived in the development areas, but they received 50 per cent of all building investment between 1945 and 1947.[50]

Town and Country

The faith of socialists in economic planning dovetailed with a no less strongly held belief in the planning of the environment: town and country planning as it was usually called. Once again it was the story of a socialist vision that faded, but left behind it a more interventionist state.

This was a sphere in which Labour's objectives overlapped with those of the town and country planning movement, a loose coalition of social reformers, public-sector architects and local government officials, which campaigned for comprehensive controls over the use of urban and rural land. Prior to 1939 the use to which land was put had been determined mainly by market forces. The powers of local authorities were very limited and only three per cent of the land was effectively subject to planning permission. The town and country planners, however, seized the opportunity presented by the blitz to campaign for radical change. A Ministry of Town and Country Planning was set up in 1943. The Town and Country Planning Act of 1944 gave local authorities powers of compulsory purchase and planning in areas which had been devastated in the blitz. A Coalition White Paper of 1944, *Control of Land Use*, accepted the principle that no land should be developed without planning permission. Beyond this, the divide between a Labour Party committed to environmental planning, and a Conservative party committed to a free market in land, prevented agreement.

The *Greater London Plan* of 1944, commissioned by the government from Professor Patrick Abercrombie, epitomized the ideals of the dominant school of thought within the planning movement. Based on the assumption that London was overcrowded, the plan proposed that a million people should be dispersed from the inner city and the suburbs into the countryside. With the density of the urban population reduced, residential districts would be separated out from industry and roads carrying heavy traffic and planned as neighbourhood units of between 6,000 and 10,000 people, each with its share of civic amenities: schools, health centres, libraries, and so on. In order to prevent 'urban sprawl' and 'ribbon development'—the building of factories and housing estates along main roads into the countryside—London would be encircled by a Green Belt, an area of countryside in which new housing and industrial development were forbidden. In an outer circle beyond the Green Belt eight new towns housing 300,000 people would be built. Like the neighbourhood units, they were to be planned as communities.[51]

Attlee's Minister of Town and Country Planning, Lewis Silkin, was an able politician who succeeded in translating parts of the planning agenda into legislation. His New Towns Act of 1946 gave him the power to designate the sites of new towns and set up Development Corporations to plan them. Of the fourteen towns he designated, eight were to be satellite towns of London: Basildon, Bracknell, Crawley, Harlow, Hatfield, Hemel Hempstead, Stevenage, and Welwyn Garden City. The other six were Cwmbran in south Wales, Corby in the Midlands, Peterlee and Newton Aycliffe in the north-east, East Kilbride in the west of Scotland, and Glenrothes in the east. When Labour fell from office in 1951 the new towns were scarcely more than building sites, leaving them vulnerable to a Conservative economy campaign. They might indeed have withered away but for the strong support they received from the incoming Minister of Housing, Harold Macmillan, who obtained increased funding for them from the Treasury. The new towns were to grow quietly through the 1950s, an unobtrusive feature of the post-war consensus.

Town planning in general failed to live up to the expectations raised by planners themselves during the war. Silkin's Town and Country Planning Act of 1947 imposed an obligation on the planning authorities to produce development plans not just for blitzed or slum areas but for areas as a whole, and gave them increased powers of compulsory purchase. The most socialist feature of the Act, intended to ensure that no landowner benefited from the granting of permission to develop, was a provision vesting the ownership of all development rights—that is, the increase in value due to planning permission—in the state. The somewhat predictable consequence was that landowners were deterred from seeking planning permission by the knowledge that the whole of any consequent increase in value would be appropriated by the government. The subsequent development of urban areas rarely lived up to the vistas the propagandists for planning had conjured up during the war. So intense was the demand for housing in the late 1940s and early

1950s, and so great the shortage of capital for anything but the most urgent priorities, that the building of homes took precedence over the planned development of neighbourhoods. Even in the heavily blitzed cities, which had been empowered to plan boldly by legislation specifically for their benefit in 1944, plans for radical reconstruction were in most cases conspicuous by their absence.[52]

Labour's footprints were to be seen in the countryside as well as the towns. The balance of payments crisis, and the importance of ensuring adequate food supplies in the event of another great war, convinced the government that farmers should continue to receive, in return for their co-operation in the fulfilment of production targets, the guaranteed prices introduced during the war. Under the Agriculture Act of 1947 an annual farm review fixed prices in advance for about two-thirds of all agricultural produce. In effect farmers were guaranteed a level of future profits that encouraged them to invest in new buildings or machinery. 'Throughout the land', writes Kenneth Morgan, 'from the wheat fields of East Anglia, through the horticultural stronghold of the Vale of Evesham, and the hop fields of Herefordshire, to the hill farms of rural Wales, Cumberland, and the Scottish Highlands, farmers after 1945 experienced a growing prosperity...'[53] In April 1950 Stanley Evans, a junior minister at the Ministry of Food, committed a *faux pas* by complaining in a speech that the farmers were 'feather-bedded' at the expense of the taxpayer. Having blurted out the truth he was compelled to resign.

For Labour, the countryside was both a source of food and an oasis of leisure and recreation for weary townsfolk. A White Paper written by John Dower, and published by the Coalition government in May 1945, had recommended the creation of National Parks with two main objectives in mind: firstly that 'the characteristic beauty of the landscape shall be preserved' and secondly 'that the visiting public shall have ample access and facilities within it for open-air recreation and the enjoyment of its beauty'. Dower, a self-taught architect, and advocate of National Parks since the 1930s, was almost literally wedded to rural England. He had married Pauline Trevelyan, daughter of the socialist baronet and Northumberland landowner Sir Charles Trevelyan, and taken up the life of a country gentleman. After intense bureaucratic wrangling the National Park and Access to the Countryside Act of 1949 set up the National Parks Commission with a mandate to select and define the areas concerned. In its first annual report, which designated the Lake District, Snowdonia, and the Peak District as the first three National Parks, the Commission accepted that some economic development would have to be allowed. 'But we also recognize', the report continued, 'that it may prove vital to this nation's economy, expressed in terms of the improved physique and mental poise of our people, that these great areas of open and unspoilt countryside shall be preserved as a national heritage.'[54] Here again was the civilized, paternal voice of the gentleman in Whitehall, though the eleven members of the Commission did include one woman—John Dower's widow Pauline.

The League against Cruel Sports had hoped to persuade the Labour government to ban fox-hunting in the National Parks. This had never been the intention of Dower, a sometime Master of Foxhounds himself, and was never likely to appeal to a government which had formed a strong working alliance with the farmers. The popularity of fox-hunting in some mining communities was another significant factor in the equation. In January 1949 two private member's bills banning hunting were successful in the ballot for parliamentary time. The Cabinet concluded that the case against hunting

> was greatly exaggerated. These pursuits formed part of the traditional life of the countryside and could not be regarded simply as amusements of the aristocracy...If the House of Commons were to pass these bills, they would almost certainly be rejected by the House of Lords, and the government might again be placed in the embarrassing position in which they had found themselves on the question of capital punishment, where the Lords appeared to show a better judgement of public opinion than the Commons.

The government ensured that the first of the two bills, which would have banned the hunting of deer, otters, and badgers, and made hare and rabbit coursing illegal, was decisively defeated in the Commons. The second bill, for the abolition of fox-hunting, was then withdrawn. All in all the Attlee governments, which had won fifty rural seats in 1945, were as supportive of the countryside as they were of the industrial areas.[55]

As with the New Towns, the National Parks continued to develop and flourish under the Conservatives after 1951. By 1957 there were ten National Parks with a total area of 5,200 square miles, and the Commission was deeply engaged in negotiations over a large number of planning issues. The Conservatives also added one important element to the programme of rural conservation. In August 1955 Churchill's son-in-law, Duncan Sandys, the Minister of Housing, issued a circular to the planning authorities requesting them all to include Green Belts in their development plans.

Cradle to Grave

According to the opinion polls, the issue voters rated as the most important in 1945 was housing. The war had brought a halt to the slum clearance programme of the 1930s, leaving parts of the housing stock sunk in Dickensian squalor. Very few new homes had been built during the war but about half a million had been destroyed or made uninhabitable by air attack, and a quarter of a million severely damaged. The freezing of rents at 1939 levels, and the scarcity of building materials, had deterred landlords in the private sector from repairing and maintaining their properties. An unexpected wartime boom in marriage and the birth-rate, coinciding with the impending demobilization of five million men and women from the armed forces, widened the gap between supply and demand. Young couples, with or without children of their own, were compelled to live as lodgers in bed-sitting rooms or with relatives. In the spring and summer of 1946 the more desperate set up home as squatters in former army and air force camps, where many of them were to remain for two or three years. Although the occupation of the camps was illegal, the press and public opinion were sympathetic to the squatters and the government made no attempt to evict them.

When the Labour government was formed, Attlee entrusted both housing and health to Aneurin Bevan, the Minister of Health. The son of a Welsh miner, Bevan had fought his way out of poverty through the eloquence of his tongue, the passion of his political convictions, and the charisma of one of nature's aristocrats. During the Second World War he was the only MP whose oratory could match that of Churchill, and the only politician who consistently attacked Churchill as a war leader. His early experiences had bred in him a bitter class consciousness which occasionally found expression as when he described the Conservative party in 1947 as 'lower than vermin'. In both housing and health he was an egalitarian who believed in levelling the working class up, which also meant levelling the middle class down.

In 1945 only one-third of the population owned their own home. Only one in ten lived in one of the council houses built by local authorities between the wars. More than half, including most manual workers, lived in private rented accommodation. In urban areas they were typically housed, close to the industries that employed them, in back-to-back terraces one room deep. Toilets, placed in courtyards behind the terraces, were shared between a number of families. In the poorest areas conditions were aggravated by overcrowding. 'In 1935', writes John Stevenson, 'it was estimated that approximately 12 per cent of the population lived at a density of more than two persons per room, in what was officially regarded as overcrowded conditions. London had one of the worst problems...almost half the families in Islington, Finsbury, and Shoreditch were living at a level of three or more families per house, which usually consisted of four or five small rooms. In Finsbury 60 per cent of families were living in one or two rooms; Stepney had over 50,000 people living two or more to a room, while 16,000 lived three or more to a room.'[56] Glasgow, with its massive tenement blocks, was notorious for its overcrowded conditions, but there were problem areas in almost every major town or city, and the cottages of rural England, however picturesque they might appear with roses round the door, were often the most lacking in amenities.

Bevan believed that the working classes deserved the same quality of life as the middle classes, and that only the state could provide it. His housing policy was based on the pre-war method of Exchequer subsidies to local authorities, which drew up and commissioned their own housing programmes. The subsidies were more generous than before the war, and much was left to the initiative of the local authorities, but there were strong elements of compulsion by central government. Bevan used the government's control over building licences to ensure that four out of five houses built were in the public sector. As an emergency measure following the convertibility crisis of August 1947, all work on private housing was forbidden and only resumed in June 1948. To ensure that the priority for new council housing was enforced, strict limits were maintained on the amount that anyone was allowed to spend without a licence on repairs to a single property: £2 [=£46] in any one month, or £10 [=£228] over a period of six months.[57]

Bevan put quality before quantity. He scorned as 'rabbit-hutches' the prefabricated homes ('prefabs') which the previous government had authorized as a temporary expedient, and concentrated on the construction of two-storey, semi-detached brick-built homes, with gardens at the front and back. In place of the pre-war minimum standard of 750 square feet for a three-bedroom home, he imposed a requirement of 900 feet. He insisted that every house should have an upstairs as well as a downstairs toilet and was outraged when his successor as Minister of Housing, Hugh Dalton, did away with the requirement in 1951. In London and some other cities the local authorities devoted part of the housing budget to blocks of low-rise flats, but there were no high-rise flats or tower blocks between 1945 and 1951. The Bevan housing estate was a communal, public sector version of the 'Tudorbethan' villas which the middle classes had built between the wars. Bevan himself hoped that public sector housing would be socially mixed and available to middle-class as well as working-class tenants. In practice the tests of social need applied by local authorities tended to restrict the council estates to manual workers.

The main problem with Bevan's housing programme was the snail's pace at which it moved. Not only were building materials and labour in short supply, but the procedures involved were highly bureaucratic, involving a number of Whitehall departments as well as a multitude of local authorities. To Bevan's frustration the housing programme was also a prime target, in moments of economic crisis, for cuts in the government's investment programme. Almost a million new homes were built between 1945 and 1951—807,000 by local authorities and 180,000 for private owners[58]—but the Coalition had estimated that three to four million were needed in order to fulfil the government's aim of a separate home for every family.

In the 1951 Census it was decided to find out what proportion of households had all four of the following facilities: piped water, cooking stove, water closet, and fixed bath. The answer was 52 per cent, another measure of the vast extent of the problem of levelling up the whole of the housing stock to the standards at which Bevan aimed. Overcrowding was worst of all in Glasgow, where just over 50 per cent of the city's housing stock consisted of only one or two rooms, compared with a figure of 5.5 per cent for greater London.[59] Most working-class people still lived in rented Victorian housing, much of it badly built, or in

lodgings. The Conservatives, meanwhile, kept up a running fire of criticism and pledged themselves at the annual party conference in 1950 to
build 300,000 houses a year, a figure the Labour government had never
achieved. Under Bevan the council estate became a more familiar feature of life in Britain, but his socialist vision of public sector housing was
never to be realized.

In 1944 the Coalition government had promised a National Health
Service in which medical, dental, and opthalmic services would be
available, free of charge at the point of delivery, to the whole population. But no such health service could be established without the agreement of the medical profession and the local authorities. When Labour
took office in 1945 negotiations with the British Medical Association,
which represented the general practitioners, had reached a stalemate,
and the role of the local authorities was uncertain. It was Bevan who
resolved the problems. His most radical stroke was the nationalization
of the hospitals, transferring to the state the ownership of both the voluntary hospitals, which had previously raised their own funds through
fees and flag days, and the municipal hospitals, which had been financed
out of the local rates. Henceforth there was a unified hospital service,
organized by region. But the socialist objective of a single health authority in charge of all medical services was thwarted. Bevan accepted that
there would have to be three authorities working side by side: in effect,
the regional hospital boards, the general practitioners, and the local
authority health services. Although the local authorities lost their hospitals they were empowered to build and equip health centres, maternity
and child welfare centres and old people's homes, an ambitious remit.
The health centre, where general practitioners would operate in a group
practice under the same roof as various clinical services was intended to
be one of the key elements in the National Health Service.

The initial hostility of the BMA to Bevan's proposals for the NHS
was driven mainly by the fear that they would deprive general practitioners of their professional independence. A fully socialist health service would indeed have transformed both general practitioners and
hospital consultants into full-time salaried employees of the state. As they
would never have signed up to the NHS on these terms, Bevan opted
for compromise. Firstly he struck a deal with the consultants enabling
them to continue lucrative private work in NHS hospitals. Secondly he
offered the BMA an arrangement whereby general practitioners were

to be paid through a combination of a basic salary and capitation fees. After much harrumphing and threats of non co-operation, the BMA accepted the arrangement. An amending Act in 1949 guaranteed that full-time salaried service was ruled out.

Although Labour did not nationalize the drug companies, health was now in large part a nationalized industry. The numbers employed in 1949 in the Hospital Service alone for England and Wales were as follows:

Doctors and dentists	11,900
Professional and technical	12,500
Administrative and clerical	23,800
Nurses and midwives	148,900
Domestic staff	128,300
Total	225,400

Source: Charles Webster, *The Health Services since the War Vol. I: Problems of Health Care: The National Health Service before 1957* (1988), p. 300.

The method by which this vast new organization was paid for was one of the most radical aspects of the scheme. National insurance contributions accounted for only a fraction. The rest was financed out of general taxation, thus ensuring that the higher income groups contributed a larger share of their earnings than the less well paid. More nearly than any other aspect of the welfare state, the NHS bore out the principle 'to each according to his needs, from each according to his abilities'.

In the 'bad old days' of 1938 more than twenty million people, 43 per cent of the population, were covered by National Health Insurance, which entitled workers in employment up to a certain income level to the services of a general practitioner, but not to hospital or specialist treatment. Their dependants—usually wives and children—lacked insurance cover and had to pay the doctor's bills, though doctors often reduced their fees for the benefit of poorer families. The upper and middle classes, who were excluded from National Insurance, were expected to pay in full for the services of their own 'family doctor'. The poor were treated free of charge in the voluntary hospitals, but the middle and upper classes were generally expected to pay a part of the cost. Local authority hospitals also charged for treatment on a means-tested basis, though the costs were heavily subsidized. Then of course there were fees to be paid to dentists and opticians. The inevitable consequence of this patchwork system was that people, including middle-class people on modest incomes, were often deterred from seeking treatment in order to avoid the bills. At midnight on 5 July 1948 the deterrents were abolished. It is no wonder that long queues formed outside doctors' surgeries. The entire range of medical, dental, and opthalmic services was now free at the point of demand. No greater blessing was ever bestowed on the British people by statute, but even so it had its limitations. The NHS gave the state something very close to a monopoly of health care and hence the power to determine the amount that should be spent on it. In effect the Treasury and the Cabinet determined the overall level of expenditure and the doctors decided, on the basis of their clinical judgement, how it should be distributed among their patients. The doctors drove a hard bargain with the government over their salaries, and the public drove a hard bargain in its own way by insisting that health care should, as far as possible, be free at the point of delivery. Whether from deference to the medical profession, or gratitude for the fact that they no longer had to pay, the public at this stage seems to have been fairly uncritical of the quality of the services it was receiving. Meanwhile the Treasury strove constantly to restrict the growth of public expenditure. Although therefore the NHS was a shining example of 'fair shares for all', the consequences for the overall level of investment in health care were ambiguous. Was it a method of ensuring that additional resources were channelled into the improvement of medical services, or a method of rationing and restricting expenditure on health?

When the National Health Service bill was drawn up, the estimated annual expenditure was £134m. During the first year of the new service, the actual expenditure was £275m, rising to £352m in 1949/50 and £464m in 1950/1.[60] The unexpectedly high level of popular demand, the expansion of staff numbers and the rising cost of the drugs bill all contributed to the increase. Bevan was inclined to regard it as a sign of progress, but there was great alarm in the Treasury, which embarked on a long-drawn out campaign to contain health expenditure. This eventually resulted in the Cabinet crisis of April 1951 when Bevan (by this time Minister of Labour) resigned in protest against the imposition by the Chancellor, Hugh Gaitskell, of charges for teeth and spectacles.

As long as the government struggled to restrain spending on the NHS, the building of new hospitals was almost out of the question. The 'age of austerity' necessitated the rationing of investment as well as consumption, with manufacturing industry as the top priority, housing a close second, and health lagging far behind. This was despite the fact that many of the 2,700 hospitals inherited by the NHS were obsolete and the former Poor Law hospitals, as surveyors reported at the time, 'dark, old, devoid of modern sanitary conveniences, death-traps in the case of fire; and in short unfit for the Nursing of Chronic Sick or any other form of Sick Person'.[61] Surveys during the Second World War estimated that £500m in capital expenditure was needed to replace obsolete buildings and facilities but during the first six years of the National Health Service (1948–54) capital investment in the hospitals averaged £7m per year, compared with £35m in 1938–9.

The National Health Service gave all patients equality of access to medical services. What it could not do was eliminate the social inequalities in health associated with variations in housing, standards of living, lifestyle, and levels of education: with differences, in other words, of social class. Thirty years after the foundation of the NHS a historian of the health services could write:

> It is indeed striking that in the 1970s the gap between the upper and lower social classes in terms of mortality experience was two or three times as large in the early 1930s. Most major causes of death are now two to three times as common among social classes IV and V as among classes I and II, and the overall death rate was by the early 1970s 50 per cent higher among the lower than among the upper classes.[62]

A random sample of the British population in 1980 revealed, to no one's great surprise, that the upper classes were taller than the middle classes, and the middle classes taller than the working classes. On average young men in social classes I and II stood 3.2 cm higher than their counterparts in classes IV and V. The differences among women were similar.[63]

Like the NHS, education also tended to mould itself around existing social contours. The Attlee governments' goal was to implement the 1944 Education Act, which instructed the local education authorities to organize a separate level of secondary schooling for all pupils over the age of eleven, abolished fees in the grammar schools, and provided for the raising of the school-leaving age to fifteen. This was not simply to be a reorganization on paper. The ideal was to emancipate pupils and staff from the cramped quarters and crumbling buildings characteristic of so many elementary schools between the wars. Regulations set out by the Ministry of Education in March 1945 laid down new standards for school premises and buildings. Every primary and secondary school was to have a playing field. Every secondary school was to have an assembly hall, dining room, gymnasium, library, and a room for arts and crafts. Minimum requirements were laid down for the size of classrooms, playgrounds, and sites.[64]

In practice, buildings and facilities could only be provided when circumstances permitted and capital investment in education was strictly limited during the first post-war decade. The Attlee governments restricted new school building to three categories: the replacement of schools destroyed in the blitz, schools for new housing estates, and extra primary schools to cater for the increased infant population resulting from the wartime 'baby boom'. They were pledged by their manifesto to raise the school-leaving age but the Cabinet hesitated and considered postponement. In the event the decision was made to raise the age to fifteen from 1 April 1947. The urgent need for extra accommodation was met largely through the manufacture of prefabricated huts with concrete floors and walls and corrugated roofs. In an operation known as HORSA—the Hutting Operation for the Raising of the School-Leaving Age—the components were packed into boxes, delivered to the school site, and assembled on the spot. By September 1948 HORSA had provided 3,583 extra classrooms. On paper there was no such thing any more as an 'elementary school', but no magic wand could produce separate secondary school buildings overnight. In January 1952 more than 5,000 all-age elementary schools, mainly in the countryside, survived in all but name.

The 1944 Education Act did not specify the type of secondary education to be provided but left the decision to local authorities, subject to the approval of the Ministry. This left the door open for the creation of comprehensive (or as they were referred to at the time, 'multilateral' or 'common') schools, in which pupils of all aptitudes and abilities would be taught under the same roof. The annual conference of the Labour Party had passed a resolution in favour of multilateral secondary schools in 1942, but opinion in the party was divided. Many Labour politicians and activists welcomed the abolition of grammar school fees as a means of opening them up to the brightest working-class children. Among them were Attlee's two ministers of education, Ellen Wilkinson, herself an ex-grammar school pupil, and George Tomlinson. They pressed the local authorities to adopt the 'tripartite' system of grammar, technical, and modern schools recommended by Sir Cyril Norwood, a classics scholar and former headmaster of Harrow, in a report published in 1943. The Norwood theory, if it deserves to be called that, was that children could be classified on the basis of tests at the age of eleven or twelve into one of three different kinds of mind, and allocated accordingly to the appropriate type of school and curriculum: the child with academic ability to the grammar school, the child with technical aptitude to the technical school, the child who was best at practical or concrete tasks to a 'secondary modern'. In practice this meant retaining the grammar schools, upgrading and re-labelling some of the existing elementary schools as secondary moderns, and promising to increase the small number of technical schools already established.

Educational policy was the most important gap in Labour's egalitarianism. The grammar school/secondary modern divide tended to mirror rather than modify the class structure. An expansion in the number of technical schools would have done more to create ladders of opportunity for working-class pupils and might also have been of great value to manufacturing industry, but the great majority of local authorities opted for a bipartite system of grammars and secondary moderns. By January 1949 there were over 3,000 secondary modern schools in England and Wales, and 1,229 grammar schools, but only 310 technical schools, a *reduction* in the number Labour had inherited in 1945. Nor was there much sign of the comprehensive revolution that was yet to come. In 1950 there were only ten comprehensive schools in England and Wales. Labour ministers paid lip service to the concept of 'parity of esteem' between the grammar schools and the secondary moderns, but the 30 per cent of pupils who passed the eleven-plus and entered a grammar school received almost half of the expenditure allocated to secondary schools as a whole.[65]

The Labour government had no intention of abolishing the 'public' schools—the fee-paying private schools to which only the upper classes and the more prosperous middle classes could afford to send their children. The fact that 23 per cent of the Labour MPs elected in 1945 were themselves from public schools, as of course was the Prime Minister, goes some way to explaining the situation. But Labour ministers of education did hope to build a bridge between the private and public sectors by following up the proposals of the Fleming Report of 1944, which recommended that the public schools should make up to 25 per cent of their places available to children awarded scholarships by local education authorities. Sensing that they were under pressure to democratize, the public schools in 1948 offered 580 places to the local education authorities. Only 155 were taken up: the cost of maintaining a pupil at public school was so high that local education authorities preferred to spend the money on better provision for state pupils. The Fleming proposals withered on the vine but not before they had served their purpose, which was to ensure the survival of the public schools. Now indeed that middle-class parents could no longer get their children into a grammar school simply by paying a fee, demand for a public school education was likely to increase. The Headmaster of Christ's Hospital, H. L. O. Flecker—a formidable personality, well known to boys of the school for outbursts of screaming, uncontrollable rage—added the insidious argument that academic standards in the grammar schools were in decline.[66]

The Attlee governments never intended to carry through a social revolution, but no previous government had employed the power of the state so consistently for the benefit of manual workers. In his first post-war budget, Hugh Dalton reduced the standard rate of income tax from 50p to 45p in the pound, but there were no more cuts after that and Labour retained the highly redistributive system of personal taxation which had been introduced during the war. This meant the continuation of historically high levels of income tax on middle-class incomes, which at that time ranged from about £750 to £2,000 a year [=£19,433 to £51,900] coupled with surtax at even higher levels on incomes above £2,000, and increased death duties on inherited wealth. In 1946 Dalton raised the death duties on estates worth £21,500 [=£661,725] or more to 75 per cent.[67]

The Conservative Turn

In almost every sphere of social and economic policy, the architecture of the post-war state had been shaped by the Attlee governments.

But how much of their work would survive a change of government and a prolonged spell of Conservative rule? While still in Opposition the Conservatives signalled that they would accept much of Labour's welfare state, and the nationalization of the railways, fuel, and power, as irreversible. But they were also pledged to cut public expenditure and restore market forces. No one could be sure exactly what they would do and they probably did not know themselves. But although they won the general election of October 1951, their overall majority was only fifteen and it was noticeable that Labour had won more votes nationally than the Conservatives. The result suggested that moderation might be the best policy.

The new Prime Minister was Winston Churchill, the war hero of 1939–45. At the age of seventy-seven he could look back over a life of high adventure that spanned the historical abyss between the battle of Omdurman and the atom bomb. On his return to 10 Downing Street his first priority was the renewal of the Anglo-American 'special relationship' and his last great mission, to which he now devoted most of his remaining energies, was to halt the nuclear arms race through personal negotiations with the leaders of the Soviet Union. In social and economic affairs Churchill employed the broad brush of rhetoric, leaving the nuts and bolts to others, but there was no doubt of the general direction in which he wanted to Britain to move. His policy, as he explained late one night at Chequers, consisted of 'houses and meat and not being scuppered', and his slogan was 'set the people free'—free, that is, from rationing and economic controls.[68] Part of his agenda was libertarian, but he was also a pragmatist seeking to win working-class votes from Labour. Nor was this all that he brought to the domestic political scene. Churchill had shown during the war that he could endure physical hardship, but his love of champagne, brandy, and outsize cigars, his passion for the race-course, his luxurious holidays in sunny climes, even the vivid colours of his paintings, had always stood out in gaudy relief against the backcloth of austerity. Like Charles II returning from his travels in 1660, his arrival foreshadowed the end of a puritan era.

A gut anti-socialist in more ways than one, Churchill believed in the rights of the stomach and had never taken kindly to ration books or the Ministry of Food. Having always lunched and dined well, however, he had only a vague idea of the extent and character of food rationing. When he came to examine the figures he was puzzled and asked the Minister of Food, Gwilym Lloyd George, to arrange for a scale model to be made displaying the individual ration. Harold Macmillan has described the scene:

> This exhibit duly appeared on a large tin dish—a painted piece of meat, a little heap of sugar and the rest. The Prime Minister looked at it with some satisfaction.
>
> 'Not a bad meal', he said, 'Not a bad meal.'
>
> 'But these', cried the Minister, 'are not rations for a meal or for a day. They are for a week.'
>
> 'A week!' was the outraged reply. 'Then the people are starving. It must be remedied.'[69]

Unfortunately for Churchill, the Conservatives had taken office in the midst of a balance of payments crisis caused by the effects of the Korean War on world commodity prices, and the massive and unsustainable rearmament programme which the Attlee governments had set in motion. The government was compelled for a year or two to maintain or reinstate controls, the meat ration had to be cut below the wartime level, and for much of 1952 the cheese ration was one ounce per person per week. The Chancellor of the Exchequer, R. A. Butler, attempted without success to persuade the Cabinet to float the pound, a remedy that carried with it a high risk of mass unemployment, and would have put an end to Churchill's strategy of outflanking Labour. In 1953 the government's fortunes changed as the terms of trade improved, shortages eased, and the work of dismantling the command economy resumed. In a landmark speech of October 1954 the Chancellor of the Exchequer, R. A. Butler, prophesied that the British standard of living would be doubled in the next twenty-five years. By the end of 1955 *The Economist* was marvelling at a year which had seen industrial output rise by six per cent and remarked on 'a splurge of consumer durables' with the motor car in the lead and furniture, television, and radio next in order of importance.[70] With some exceptions, controls over imports, raw materials, and prices were abandoned between 1952 and 1955. Much to Churchill's satisfaction, food rationing followed suit:

De-rationing under the Conservatives

Oct. 1952	Cooked gammon, ham; tea
Feb. 1953	Chocolates and sweets
Sept. 1953	Sugar
May 1954	Cheese
July 1954	Meat

The Ministry of Food was finally abolished in October 1954.

With the waning of controls, the remaining Defence Regulations were dismantled. Even Conservative ministers, however, were reluctant to abandon all their powers and it took Acts of Parliament in 1959 and 1964 to sweep the remaining handful of regulations away.[71] Petrol rationing was briefly reintroduced under Defence Regulation 55 during the Suez crisis of 1956, and it was not until 1958 that coal rationing was ended. Of the wartime command economy, only exchange controls survived until they were finally abolished by the Thatcher government in 1979.

While scrapping wartime controls, the Churchill government absorbed much of the new post-war settlement. The denationalization of steel proved to be a slow and cumbrous process and a large measure of state control was retained through an Iron and Steel Board, created in 1953. Plans to denationalize long-distance road haulage by selling off the fleet of lorries owned by British Road Services were hindered by the reluctance of private investors to buy them, and British Road Services vehicles continued to be a familiar sight on the roads.[72]

Apart from this the nationalized sector remained intact, though various attempts were made to reorganize the administrative structures. Britain's railways had suffered from under-investment between the wars, when they were privately owned. The nationalization of the railways in 1948 was intended to change all that but owing to the post-war squeeze on capital investment, and the acute shortage of steel, most of the expenditure on the railways was absorbed by essential repairs like the replacement of station roofs that were about to collapse. The rolling stock of steam locomotives, coaches, and freight wagons was ageing at a rate faster than it was being replaced. 'Except on the crack trains', observed *Time* magazine in January 1955, 'cars are dirty, creaky, ramshackle and old, though also comfortable in a musty, antimacassar way.'[73] Britain had the 'Flying Scot' but there were no electrified main lines and it was not until 1956 that plans to introduce them were approved.[74] The antiquated character of the network was affectionately mocked in *Punch* by the cartoonist Rowland Emmett's 'Far Twittering and Oysterperch Railway'.

The decade after the war was the heyday of the bicycle, the motorbicycle, the bus, and the train. In a misconceived burst of modernization, the tramlines which had been laid down in the late nineteenth century were torn up everywhere except in Blackpool. The last tram ran in Oldham in 1946, in London in 1952, in Edinburgh in 1956. Whether privately owned like the Midland Red in the West Midlands, or run by London Transport, bus services boomed. The roads, however, suffered neglect. A plan for a network of motorways was announced in 1947 but repeatedly delayed. The first post-war road programme was a small-scale affair in which £2m was devoted between 1952 and 1954 to the elimination of accident black spots.[75] The first section of motorway, the eight-mile Preston by-pass, was only completed in 1958. So little was spent on the roads by the Attlee and Churchill governments that in 1955 they 'still presented a picture of traffic struggling along narrow, twisty defiles in town and country alike, and bottlenecked at river crossings and estuaries by medieval bridges, or the wait for intermittent ferries'.[76]

Given their greater faith in market forces, the Conservatives were more reluctant than Labour to compel employers to establish new factories in the development areas, but they could also argue that there was less need to do so. In July 1957 the unemployment level for Great Britain as a whole was 1.2 per cent; for Scotland 2.3 per cent, for Wales 2 per cent, for North-West England 1.4 per cent, and for the North of England 1.3 per cent.[77] These were minor variations compared with the picture for the 1930s and compatible with the party's continuing commitment to the maintenance of 'full employment'. More surprisingly was the continuity in fiscal policy. There was no repeat of the 'taxpayers' revolt' which had followed the First World War. Some ministers called for radical changes in the tax system to benefit the middle classes but, as Martin Daunton writes, 'more cautious members of the government believed it was not politically feasible to roll back the fiscal structure created during the war and confirmed by the Attlee administration... The Conservatives achieved little change in the structure of indirect taxes or in the balance between direct and indirect taxes between 1951 and 1964.'[78]

The Conservatives, of course, had a more distant relationship with the trade unions than Labour, which had been founded by the unions and was still largely financed by them. But here too there was much continuity. Churchill was keen to maintain cordial relations with the TUC and also to avoid industrial disputes. As Minister of Labour he appointed his old friend Walter Monckton, a wealthy, Whiggish lawyer. 'Winston's riding orders to me', wrote Monckton in his memoirs, 'were that the Labour Party had foretold great industrial troubles if the Conservatives were elected, and he looked to me to do my best to preserve industrial peace.'[79] The government, therefore, adopted a position of neutrality in industrial disputes, referring them if necessary to an independent court of enquiry 'that invariably split the difference or backed the trade union's demands'.[80] In 1954 the chairman of the Conservative Party, Lord Woolton, told the party's annual conference: 'Since the party came to power we have been gratefully impressed by the statesmanlike way in which so many trade union leaders have sought to gain their legitimate ends. There is no reason why Conservatism and trade unionism should not walk hand in hand.'[81] By the time Churchill was succeeded by Eden in April 1955, industrial relations were deteriorating, and the Cabinet considered the idea of legislation to impose statutory strike ballots on the unions, but in the end agreed to rely on persuasion and consultation with the TUC.

When the Conservatives first arrived in office they were determined to make substantial cuts in expenditure on the National Health Service. Harry Crookshank, the new Minister of Health, contemplated 'hotel' charges for accommodation in hospital, charges for hospital appliances and so on. In the course of ministerial discussions the proposed cuts were whittled away, leaving him with minor economies which were then attacked by backbench Conservative MPs. R. A. Butler, the Chancellor of the Exchequer, introduced prescription charges in his first budget, but the NHS was already so popular that politicians hardly dare lay hands on it. In May 1952 Churchill decided to replace Crookshank with Ian Macleod, who was not only the son of a doctor but had been a strong supporter of the National Health Service ever since 1945. When in 1952 the Treasury mounted a renewed attack on the NHS budget the Cabinet set up a genuinely independent enquiry into the cost of the service under a Cambridge economist, Claude Guillebaud. Much to the frustration of Treasury officials, the Committee proceeded at a snail's pace, enabling Macleod to fend off all demands for retrenchment in the meantime. When it did report, in January 1956, the Committee delivered a knock-out blow to the Treasury. No additional charges or economies were possible, it concluded, and more needed to be spent on the NHS. The major problem, they argued, was the continuing lack of capital investment in the hospitals. The myth of an extravagant and wasteful service was destroyed and, as its official historian writes, the

NHS was now 'protected by a broad consensus, embracing all social classes, both political parties, all but an eccentric fringe of the medical profession, and all others employed in the service'.[82]

Though the Conservatives were unable to slash the budget for the NHS they were nevertheless determined to cut social expenditure. Food subsidies were abolished in 1952 with the exception of a reduced subsidy on bread, which lingered on until 1956, and a modest subsidy on milk, which ended in 1962.[83] Education was the sacrificial lamb, freely offered up by the new Minister of Education, Florence Horsbrugh, who at once ordered cuts in expenditure and restrictions on new buildings. Even she, however, was excelled in her zeal for economy by the Chancellor of the Exchequer, R. A. Butler, the author of the 1944 Education Act, who now began to hack away at the flesh of his own great reform. He pressed the Ministry of Education to charge fees for all secondary school pupils, and tried to undermine the new school-leaving age by giving pupils permission to leave at the age of fourteen. These ominous demands hovered over the schools until October 1954, when Churchill appointed David Eccles to succeed Horsbrugh. Eccles, a strong character with a genuine enthusiasm for education, took advantage of the improving financial situation to halt and eventually reverse the cuts.[84] It was late in the day. Even at the end of the 1950s some state pupils were still being taught in prefabricated huts, or next door to primary pupils in elementary school buildings.

For the Conservatives, as for Labour, the main social priority was housing. At the annual party conference in Blackpool in October 1950 Lord Woolton succumbed to a demand from the floor and pledged the next Conservative government to build 300,000 new homes a year. It was a rash promise, certain to make huge demands on scarce resources of manpower, timber, and steel. Nor had it yet been decided whether the houses would be built mainly by the private or mainly by the public sector. The issue was still unresolved when Churchill returned to office and entrusted the task of fulfilling the pledge to Harold Macmillan. Having appointed him, Churchill also gave him robust support against the inevitable demands of the Treasury for a scaling back of the programme.

With Macmillan in charge 'the political objective of achieving the pledge took clear precedence over ideological and economic goals'.[85] Given the fact that the two main political parties were so evenly matched electorally, and competing for working-class votes, it would have been foolish at least in the short term for the Conservatives to have abandoned Labour's programme of Exchequer-subsidized council housing. Macmillan, however, revised it, increasing the proportion of licences for private building from one in five to one in two, and abolishing building licences altogether in 1954. At the same time he accelerated the production of council houses by reducing them in size—though they still had three bedrooms—and substituting terraced for semi-detached housing. Quick off the mark, with a flair for publicity, Macmillan declared the first of the new 'People's Houses' open at Desford in Leicestershire in January 1952. They had been built, reported Pathe News, in twelve weeks at a cost of £1,000 [=£22,780] each. The hot water system was fuelled by a coal fire, the bedrooms had fitted cupboards, and a serving hatch from the kitchen gave on to the dining room. 'Women', the commentator explained, 'will find their work has been made as simple as possible.'[86]

Macmillan achieved and indeed surpassed his target of 300,000 houses a year in 1952, 1953, and 1954 and in doing so staked a strong claim to the future leadership of his party. But the council house programme was a temporary expedient intended to fulfil a political promise and relieve the housing shortage. By 1953 Macmillan had formulated a long-term policy that was far more in sympathy with Conservative philosophy and the aspirations of the party's rank and file. The overall aim was to replace the state with private enterprise as the main driving force. Subsidized state housing was to be reserved in future for the replacement of homes removed by slum clearance, a return to the policies of the 1930s. Whether owner-occupiers, tenants of private landlords, or tenants of local authorities, 'the majority of people must pay the full cost of the accommodation they occupy'. Above all, home ownership should be encouraged 'as part of our general policy of a property owning democracy'.[87] By 1956 Conservative housing policy had reverted to the practice of the 1930s, with the private sector as the main provider of new housing, and public sector housing reserved for categories of tenant with special needs.

For almost a decade after the war, governments ensured that housing and factories had the first claim on building materials, but the abolition of building licences in 1954 gave property developers the chance to get planning permission for offices and shops. Meanwhile the Town and

Country Planning Acts of 1953 and 1954 abolished Labour's 100 per cent charge on the increased development value of land, though they still allowed local authorities to purchase land compulsorily at the existing use value—a price, that is, below the level it would have obtained in a free market. With land in short supply due to the demand for housing and the restrictions imposed by green belts around the urban areas, and a relatively free market restored, the price of land began to rise rapidly and property speculators moved in. 'Free or rigged or both', wrote Harry Hopkins, 'the Market took over again, confirming that bizarre scale of values which placed on a teacher a fraction of the monetary valuation of the producer of some deodorant or laxative's invitation to neurosis. By the late 1950s it was the Property Kings—the Cottons, the Clores, the Samuels and the rest—and the speculators' values they represented who made the pace and the headlines, not the architects and the planners—the Gibberds and the Spences and the Aslins, the Holfords and Abercrombies—and the values they represented.'[88]

In 1950 a report on the future of broadcasting under the chairmanship of William Beveridge had predictably recommended that the BBC should retain its monopoly of both radio and television. The Churchill government's Television Act of 1954 broke the Corporation's television monopoly and opened the medium up to commercial companies financed by the revenue from advertising, and regulated by an Independent Television Authority. The decision was hotly opposed by Labour, and also by many of the 'great and the good', on the grounds that the BBC monopoly ensured the maintenance of high cultural standards, but from the moment commercial television began transmitting in the London area on 22 September 1955 it proved highly popular and profitable.

If the welfare state of the 1940s had given people what the government thought they needed, market forces enabled them—under the seductive influence of the advertising industry—to choose what they wanted. Even so, the state remained a much more important presence on the scene than it had between the wars. Graph 1.1, which tracks government expenditure as a proportion of Gross Domestic Product through the twentieth century, shows how, after its wartime peak, government spending never returned to its pre-war level—a repeat of the pattern also seen after the First World War.

The higher level of expenditure after the war was partly due to an increase in the cost of defence. The Attlee governments spent much

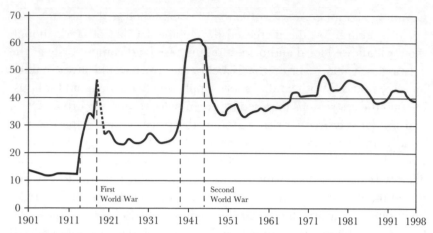

Graph 1.1 Government spending as a proportion of GDP 1901–98.

Source: Social Trends 2000, Figure 5.31, p. 100.

more on the armed forces than the governments of Stanley Baldwin had. Over the long run, however, social and economic policy were the main factors driving the growth of public spending. If the primary purpose of the 'warfare state' was to protect the British from a perceived Soviet threat, the welfare state and the mixed economy were intended to provide them with defences of a different kind.

They were the social equivalent of the Maginot Line, a chain of fortresses designed to protect the public in general, and the working classes in particular, from the consequences of another great slump. At first sight the measures taken by the Conservatives to liberalize the economy after 1951 appear to anticipate the introduction of free market policies by the Thatcher governments after 1979, but the deregulation of 1951–5 was far more limited in scope. For the time being, at least, the Maginot Line was intact.

2

Fair Shares for All

The first few years after the war are remembered as a drab period of rationing and shortages: the 'age of austerity'. Then, at some point in the 1950s, a transition occurred to a more prosperous era characterized by a restoration of choice and variety in the shops, and the arrival of a television set in almost every home: the 'age of affluence'. There is, admittedly, scope for some argument about the dates. The 'age of austerity' is sometimes equated with the Labour governments of 1945–51, and the 'age of affluence' with the Conservative governments of 1951–64, but this is too neatly political. Rationing and shortages were a consequence of the mobilization of Britain for war and the term 'austerity' was first introduced into general circulation by Sir Stafford Cripps in 1942. The rationing of food continued until 1954, a date which is perhaps the best benchmark of the end of austerity, but the idea of 'affluence' was popularized by the Canadian-American economist J. K. Galbraith, whose book *The Affluent Society* was published in 1958.

'Austerity' and 'affluence' were highly evocative terms, but what exactly did they mean? Just how austere, for example, *was* the 'age of austerity'? Subconsciously it is hard for us to avoid comparisons with the present day. For us a world without home computers, mobile phones, DVDs, and a hundred and one other articles we take for granted, could hardly be anything but austere. The living standards of the so-called age of affluence appear almost as constrained as they had been in the age of spam and powdered eggs. The benchmarks by which people measured their experiences at the time were, of course, very different, and the contrasts between the late 1940s and the late 1950s much more striking.

'Austerity' and 'affluence' affected everybody but some sections of society benefited more than others. For all those who had experienced long-term unemployment in the 1930s, 'austerity' meant work for all and a substantial rise in income. Manual workers in general enjoyed a higher income in real terms. Large sections of the middle classes, however, experienced the austerity years as a period of relative deprivation that lingered on into the 1950s. And as Ina Zweiniger-Bargielowska writes, 'women were most directly affected by austerity while men primarily benefited from full employment and higher earnings'.[1] The majority of women were housewives for whom household management, shopping, cooking, and child care were all rendered more difficult by the scarcity of items in the shops. From this it would seem to follow that 'affluence' was emancipating for women, but this is a conclusion feminist historians have been reluctant to draw.

Out of Austerity

Levels of civilian consumption were substantially reduced during the war by rationing, restrictions on the output of goods, and increased taxation. In consequence overall consumer spending fell by about 16 per cent between 1939 and 1945. The biggest falls were in spending on motoring (95%), electrical and other household goods (51%), personal effects (37%), and clothing and footwear (34%). Expenditure on food fell by 11 per cent,[2] which may sound a comparatively modest reduction, but in June 1945 the weekly food ration per person per week was frugal to say the least:

> 1s 2d worth of meat (approx. 540 grams or 1 lb 3 oz)
> 3 oz bacon and ham
> 8 oz sugar
> 2/3 oz tea on alternative weeks
> 2 oz butter
> 2 oz cheese
> 8 oz in total of butter, margarine, and cooking fats
> 4 oz jam (exchangeable for sugar)
> 1 egg per fortnight
> 2½ pints liquid milk
> 12 oz sweets per month

Sources: Ina Zweiniger-Bargieloska, *Austerity in Britain: Rationing, Controls and Consumption 1939–1945* (Oxford, 2000), pp. 34–5; R. J. Hammond, *Food Vol. I: The Growth of Policy* (1951), pp. 402–3.

One of the ironies of the 'age of austerity' is the fact that so few people were short of money: it was consumer goods that were lacking. Mass-Observation made a special study of the state of panel members' wardrobes in 1941 and again in 1947. The war years, M-O reported,

> brought men a larger collection of sports jackets, leather jerkins, shorts, dyed uniforms, and trousers fit only for gardening, but too good to be discarded. It cut them down heavily on underclothes, dress suits, old suits, ties, hats, handkerchiefs, and dressing gowns. It also gave them demobilization suits which only one in four of middle-class men approve of though more may wear them. One in three feels his wardrobe needs complete replenishment.
>
> Shortages in women's clothes stocks are a little less obvious, though underclothes, gloves, stockings, shoes and handkerchiefs stocks are considerably lower in 1947 than in 1941. To some extent, female clothes stocks have also changed their character: there are more blouses, skirts and jackets hanging in the 1947 wardrobe, and rather fewer dresses and evening dresses. Women mention much more frequently than men, that they are 'sick to death' of their present clothes...[3]

In 1950 expenditure per head on clothing and footwear was still running at below pre-war levels. Hence the persistence of the 'make-do-and-mend' culture of the war years.

According to the opinion polls, food shortages topped the list of popular grievances in the late 1940s. When a government survey asked a sample of the population in 1948 whether or not they felt they were getting sufficient food to stay in good health, 55 per cent answered 'no'. In strictly nutritional terms food rationing posed few if any problems for health, though there was a worrying phase in 1946–7 when average levels of food consumption fell for a time below the estimated calorie requirements of a working-class household.[4] Conversely it is sometimes argued that by restricting their consumption of fat, and ensuring their intake of proteins, rationing actually made people healthier. There was usually no shortage of fresh fruit or vegetables, which were never rationed. Nor were rabbits, pigeons, or poultry, though chickens were in short supply and regarded as something of a luxury. Scots could take comfort from the fact that the haggis, being made from offal, was never on the ration. Nor were ration coupons needed for a meal in a restaurant or factory canteen. As the economist and economic historian Alec

Cairncross points out, more than half of what consumers spent on food was not subject to rationing at any time.[5]

Then again there was always the black market, which flourished with a roaring trade in items such as tinned salmon. Farmers and shopkeepers often sold goods illegally but it was the 'spiv', the street trader one step ahead of the police, who attracted the most attention. When the first peacetime Christmas arrived, a reporter for Pathe News was unable to find a turkey for sale at the controlled price. 'Business was brisk in the black market', the Pathe commentator remarked. 'Very often the turkey passed through quite a few hands—all with sticky fingers.'[6] Branded in wartime as a criminal, the spiv came to be regarded in peacetime as a benefactor. The comedian Arthur English turned him into a loveable comic character of the music hall.

The trouble was that austerity went on and on. A Gallup poll reported in the spring of 1948 that 42 per cent wanted to emigrate.[7] Nor was this mere talk. Between 1946 and 1950 about 720,000 people set off in search of a new life overseas, in most cases within the spacious bounds of the Commonwealth and Empire.[8] The most popular destination was Australia, a land of sunshine and opportunity free of many of the snobberies and status anxieties of Britain, with the additional incentive of a subsidized passage by sea, paid for by the Australian government, through the Mediterranean, the Suez Canal, and the Indian Ocean.

For those who stayed on in 'Pudding Island' (the novelist Lawrence Durrell's term for Britain), the prospects began to brighten in the early 1950s. One of the contrasts between the periods of 'austerity' and 'affluence' is to be seen in Graph 2.1, which tracks the rate at which new homes were built and demonstrates the acceleration in completions, rivalling the great housing boom of the 1930s, that followed the return of the Conservatives to office in 1951. A similar pattern of acceleration in the early 1950s can be seen in the figures for disposable income.[9]

As B. C. Roberts, a lecturer in trade unions studies at the LSE, observed in 1954, housing was already acting as a powerful stimulus to consumption and hence to wage demands:

Many workers have altered the pattern of their spending to fit in with their relatively affluent circumstances. Perhaps more than two million television sets and large numbers of other consumer durables such as washing machines, vacuum cleaners and other appliances for the home have been bought by wage earners during the past two or three years. Each year over a quarter of a million new houses have to be furnished by wage earners, many of whom may have little or no furniture of their own. There must, therefore, be a considerable weight of hire purchase debt on the backs of large numbers of work-people. This may well be no bad thing, as it should encourage a desire to increase earnings; on the other hand a slight dip in real income, such as that which took place in 1952, will arouse fears and alarms.[10]

The consumer boom that began to take off around 1953 was marked by some increase in spending on food, drink, and tobacco, accompanied by a much more rapid expansion in the sales of furniture, refrigerators, and television sets. Sales of motor cycles took off after the abolition of petrol rationing in 1950, and the number of new cars registered rose above the pre-war level for the first time in 1953.[11] The decision to televise the Coronation of Elizabeth II gave an enormous boost to sales of television sets, which began to rise months in advance of the event. For decades people had been able to enjoy moving pictures of spectacular events in the cinema, and the cinema still had some advantages over television: colour and the big screen. But whether it was the Coronation, a Cup Final, or a Test Match, cinema could never match the excitement of an event transmitted live to your own home. The broadcast of

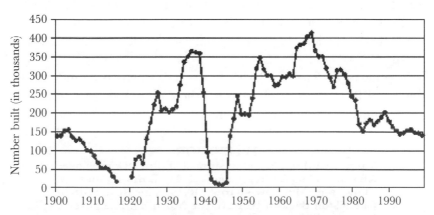

Graph 2.1 New dwellings built in Great Britain 1900–98.

Source: Joe Hicks and Graham Allen, *A Century of Change: Trends in UK Statistics since 1900*, House of Commons Research Paper 99/111 (1999), p. 12.

the Coronation itself (2 June 1953), with Richard Dimbleby's hushed and reverent commentary, attracted a peak audience of over twenty million.

The rise of television was the single most sweeping change in mass consumption in the 1950s. Embracing more and more of the population, it came as close to transcending social class as any leisure activity could:

Percentage of the population with a TV in the home

	%
1950	4.3
1955	39.8
1960	81.8

Source: A. H. Halsey (ed.), *Trends in British Society since 1900* (1972), p. 552.

Television created enormous excitement, generating huge audiences and making household names of a galaxy of presenters and performers. By our standards, however, it was still in a rudimentary state of development. Programmes were in black-and-white, and most television screens twelve or fourteen inches wide. Until 1955 there was only one channel, monopolized by the BBC. There were no programmes in the morning, and the hour between 5 pm and 6 pm was reserved for children's programmes in conformity with 'Children's Hour' on the wireless. Transmission then ceased for an hour or more, an interlude known as 'the toddlers' truce' intended to allow the parents of young children to put them to bed. By 10.30 or 11 pm it was time for the service to close down.

Turning to *The Times* for 3 May 1952—a date chosen at random—we find the BBC television schedule for the day tucked away in a short paragraph at the bottom of a column:

TELEVISION
5 p.m., Children's Television. 8, Film: "Comet over Africa." 8.30, Arthur Askey. 8.45, Emrys Jones, in "Love and Mr. Lewisham." 10.15, The Rev. Wilfrid Garlick on Back to Work in the Morning. 10.25, News (sound only).

This added up to less than four hours' broadcasting.

Moving on, we come to *The Times* for 3 May 1957, by which time the BBC had a formidable competitor in commercial television. (Of the three regional television listings only one is shown below.) Hours of broadcasting were longer, the 'toddler's truce' had vanished, and the BBC schedule included the first British TV soap opera, *The Grove Family*.

TELEVISION
2 p.m., Lawn Tennis. Hard Court Championships of Great Britain. 3 (approx.), Mainly for Women. 3.15, Lawn Tennis. 3.45, Watch with Mother. 4, Lawn Tennis. 5, Children's Television. 5.57, Weather. 6, News and Sports News. 6.5, To-night. 6.35, Gardening Club. 6.55, The Grove Family. 7.15, News. 7.20, Behind the Headlines. 7.30, Up for the Cup (McDonald Hobley). 8.15, Association Football—England v. Young England (second half). 9, Half the World Away—2: Hong Kong. 9.30, Canadian Television Theatre—"Passport to Yesterday," by Enid Rollins. 10.20, Report from America. Weather Gone Wild. 10.45, News and Weather.

I.T.A.
ASSOCIATED REDIFFUSION
12.43 p.m., Thought for the Day. 12.45–1.30, "Lunch Box." 4.45, "Jolly Good Time." 5.45, Time, News, and Weather. 6, "Cross Talk." 6.30, The Adventures of Robin Hood. 6.58, News Flash. 7, "Emergency—Ward 10" (Episode 22). 7.30, "Take Your Pick." 8, Dragnet Series—"The Big New Years." 8.30, Jack Hylton presents Flanagan and Allen, in "Together Again." 9, "This Week." 9.30, Alfred Hitchcock presents "Back for Christmas." 10, Under Fire. 10.15, Palais Party, from Hammersmith Palais. 10.46, Time, News, and Weather. 11, Epilogue.

By the end of 1957, 72 per cent of viewers were choosing to watch commercial television instead of the BBC and, as the Conservatives had hoped, ITV gave a powerful boost to consumerism. Between 1956 and 1958 expenditure on TV advertising rose from £13m in 1956 to £48m.[12] In the view of Mary Ingham it was particularly important in overcoming the conservatism of housewives: 'What commercial television did...was persuade people of the advantages of new ways of doing things by showing them a live demonstration.'[13]

To the extent that the affluence of the 1950s was widespread, it did not extend much beyond the purchase, very often on credit, of goods and furnishings for the home. In 1960 only 29 per cent of households possessed a car.[14] But the sense of growing abundance probably owed as much to the proliferation of inexpensive items that *felt* like luxuries after a decade of scarcity: Babycham (1952); Bird's Eye Fish Fingers (1955); Kellogg's Frosties and Sugar Puffs (1956); sliced white bread from Mother's Pride and Sunblest (1956).[15] Shopping habits were also beginning to change. Curiously it was not one of the commercial chains that pioneered the concept of the supermarket in Britain, but the Co-op, which experimented with it during the war and opened the first fully self-service store in Southsea in 1948. They were soon overtaken by Tesco and Sainsbury's, with thirty-five stores between them by 1951. Gradually the term 'self-service' was replaced by 'supermarket', but the principle was the same. No longer did the customer have to wait at the counter for an assistant to take an order and collect the relevant items from the shelves. Now the customer helped herself (most shoppers were women), put the items to be purchased in a wire basket, intended to discourage stealing, and paid for them at the check-out. By 1961 there were 571 supermarkets in Britain, but there was still a long way to go before they ousted the grocer, the butcher, and the fishmonger from the high street.[16]

During the war years, hedonism was out of key with the moral austerity of the times. With peace restored, the cavaliers began to challenge the puritans and roll back the frontiers of restraint. We have already come across the New Look. The male equivalent was the American Look, introduced in 1946 by the London-based retailer, Cecil Gee. It consisted, in the words of Mark Woodhouse, of 'double-breasted lounge suits, pleated trousers with deep turn-ups, colourful shirts, hand-painted ties, a trilby hat and two-tone shoes'. The American Look, which became the trade mark of the spiv, proved very popular with young working-class males, and later evolved into the uniform of the Teddy Boy.

The British were notorious for their lack of skill in cookery and their taste for brown Windsor soup, boiled cabbage, and steamed puddings. Both during and after the war the Ministry of Food did its best to raise culinary standards with recipes and cookery hints, but the objectives were severely practical: to encourage the consumption of foodstuffs the Ministry had purchased. The home front was no place for gourmets or connoisseurs but they began to re-appear in the late 1940s. Prominent among them was the socialist, Raymond Postgate.

With the aid of a team of volunteers who reported on the quality of food served in restaurants and hotels, he organized and edited the annual *Good Food Guide*, the first edition of which was published in 1950. At about the same time Elizabeth David, the daughter of a Tory MP, began her own rebellion against the monotony of British fare. Having discovered Mediterranean food in the course of a passionate love-affair in the first year of the war, and subsequently lived in Athens and Cairo, she was homesick for warmer climes and found relief in writing down descriptions of Mediterranean and Middle Eastern cookery. 'Even to write words like apricot, olives and butter, rice and lemons, oil and almonds produced assuagement', she wrote. 'I came to realize that in the England of 1947, those were dirty words that I was putting down.'[17] *A Book of Mediterranean Food* (1950) and *French Country Cooking* (1951) were the first of a series of classic works intended to persuade the English that cookery should be an art and food a pleasure.

The Working Man's Britain

In the mid-twentieth century about two-thirds of the population of Britain consisted of manual workers and their families. They were extremely diverse, a multitude of communities and cultures distinguished from one another by region, culture, occupation, and degree of skill. The stereotypical image of the working man was of the worker in large-scale manufacturing industry, which was indeed still one of the main pillars of the economy, accounting for 32.1 per cent of GDP in 1960.[18] But four of the six largest occupations—transport and communications, building and contracting, distributive trades, and coal mining—were non-factory trades and there were still nearly 900,000 agricultural workers in 1948.[19] As Gary Runciman writes:

> The shop floor and the assembly line are integral to both the experience and the image of the mid-twentieth century British working class. But what about the building site, the brewery, the delivery van, the ship's hold, the bus, the dairy farm, the gas works, the storeroom, the municipal garden, the hospital kitchen, the railway line, the bakery, the timber yard, the car park, the furniture repair shop, the laboratory, the lock gate, the post office, the garage, or the fairground?[20]

The proportion of manual workers in the population was in fact in long-term decline, as the table shows:

Manual workers as a percentage of the employed population

	1911	1921	1931	1951
Skilled	30.6	28.8	26.7	24.9
Semi-skilled	34.4	29.0	28.8	27.2
Unskilled	9.6	14.2	14.8	12.0
All manual	74.6	72.0	70.3	64.2

Source: Duncan Gallie, 'The Labour Force' in A. H. Halsey and Josephine Webb (eds.), *Twentieth-Century British Social Trends* (2000), p. 288.

Contemporaries seem not to have noticed: they expected the machine age to continue indefinitely, with new technologies replacing the old, and manual labour as indispensable as ever.

The middle classes, meanwhile, had been gradually increasing in numbers. There were, for example, 36,000 doctors in 1951 compared with 26,000 in 1931, and 19,689 solicitors as against 15,777 twenty years before. It was the newer professions—scientists, engineers, and civil servants in particular—who spearheaded the expansion of the middle classes. Increasingly it was middle-class professionals who organized and ran both the private and the public sectors. Nevertheless middle-class Britain remained, as it had been in Victorian times, an archipelago of little islands in a working-class ocean. Pessimists feared that the waters were rising and would soon engulf the inhabitants.

They also believed, with good reason, that a change in the social balance had occurred. In February 1945 the journalist J. L. Hodson, a close observer of industrial Britain, attempted to weigh up the social consequences of the war:

> The working-classes, feeling their power, have often shown some ruthlessness, manifested by bus drivers refusing to stop at halts, transport workers striking on Christmas Day, coal-miners refusing sometimes to do a decent day's work…Whether, however, it is right to include this uprising of the workers, this mild revolt against society, as part of the debit side I'm not sure. I used to be appalled by the apathy of the workers in our old distressed areas, feeling that if they expressed themselves with more energy, were more intolerant of abuses, and readier to take some action, the monstrous condition of affairs would be remedied all the faster.[21]

Hodson's contemporary verdict has been confirmed by historians. The period from 1938 to 1951, writes Ross McKibbin,

> is notable for the virtual disappearance of unemployment and for a redistribution of national income which much favoured the working class... An index of manual workers' earnings in 1937 and 1939 set against the higher professions shows how disproportionately well the manual working class did. In 1949 the average earnings of a manual worker were 241 per cent of their 1937 level; those of a member of the higher professions 188 per cent.[22]

The primary explanation was full employment. The 'age of austerity' was a period in which British industry was booming. Boosted by the temporary absence of competition from Germany and Japan, and restrictions on consumption at home, exports were making a spectacular recovery. Order books were full and overseas customers queueing up for British products. 'In 1953', Correlli Barnett reminds us. 'Britain was building 36.6 per cent of the global shipping tonnage under construction—nearly three and a half times as much as Germany, her nearest rival... The industry's existing order book, at 5.8 million gross tons, was more than four times its annual output.'[23]

Employers were hungry for labour. Workers and their trade unions took advantage of their enhanced bargaining power. No sooner were the VE celebrations over in 1945 than they began to claim the peace dividend of a shorter working week. Within a year or two national agreements established a five-day week of 45 hours as the standard. Saturday working, which had been common in between the wars, was phased out, and the benefits of the change were hailed by the Chief Inspector of Factories in his annual report for 1947:

> Its popularity with the work people is great: the opportunities it gives to women to shop on Saturday morning when all the best foodstuffs are displayed in the shops, the freedom for men and boys to attend sports meetings, even at a distance, or to follow other spare-time occupations, and the long break from work each week, combine to make it the most valued advance of modern times.[24]

Hodson reported anecdotal evidence of a general relaxation of effort on the part of workers. In June 1947 a works manager told him: 'Some jobs in my department take two and a half times as long as pre-war. Mid-morning I find men with feet up and reading the paper.

The amount of scrapped stuff is as much in a month as it used to be in six.'[25]

Coal was still the source of more than 90 per cent of the nation's heat and energy supplies, both domestic and industrial. When the industry was nationalized in 1947 the National Coal Board invested heavily in the modernization of the pits and ambitious plans were drawn up to expand the labour force by recruiting young men. Average cash earnings per week more than doubled from £6.65 in 1947 to £14.52 in 1957, an increase ahead of the curve for the average increase in wages over the period,[26] but the recruitment campaigns never achieved their targets. In conditions of full employment there were too many attractive alternatives to going down the mine.[27] Between 1948 and 1955 the number of men employed in engineering, shipbuilding, and electrical goods increased by 1,776,000 to 2,020,000, a rise of 14 per cent. In clothing the numbers employed rose by 6.8 per cent, in textiles by 7 per cent, in chemical and allied trades by 14.8 per cent, in paper and printing by 17 per cent, in food, drink, and tobacco by 21 per cent.[28]

In 1955 BBC Television sent the reporter and presenter Robert Reid to revisit the Lancashire industrial town of Salford, which he had known well in the 1930s. 'Very little seemed to have changed', he reported. 'I found the same grim backs and the same drab fronts. The same houses but twenty years older and that much worse. The housewives still keep up the old tradition of brownstoning the front steps. And you can still buy a hot cooked meal at the shop around the corner.' The black-and-white images of rows of terraced houses, covered with grime from the smoke of factory chimneys, could have been taken from a documentary film of the 1930s.[29] Yet some things were different. Salford had been the setting for Walter Greenwood's novel *Love on the Dole* (1933). By 1955 there was virtually full employment in Salford and everywhere else in Britain.

The high status and esteem enjoyed by the trade unions was a distinguishing feature of the 1940s and 1950s. The total membership of the unions had risen rapidly from 6,298,000 in 1939 to 9,363,000 in 1948, after which it grew slowly to 9,829,000 in 1957. The Trades Union Congress, to which the great majority of unions were affiliated, was a massively respectable presence in public life. With their status already boosted by their participation in the war effort, the unions reinforced their patriotic credentials as bastions of democracy in the battle against communism. The fact that some trade unions, notably the Electrical Trades Union and the Fire Brigades Union, were under Communist control, while others, like the giant Transport and General Workers Union, contained a minority of Communist officials, served only to increase the importance of the right-wing trade union leaders who dominated the General Council of the TUC. The 'big three' were Arthur Deakin, General Secretary of the Transport and General Workers Union from 1946 to 1955, Will Lawther, President of the National Union of Mineworkers from 1939 to 1954, and Tom Williamson, General Secretary of the General and Municipal Workers from 1946 to 1962. Pursuing a strategy of co-operation with employers and government, they were familiar figures in Whitehall and proud of the fact that the unions were represented, by 1949, on sixty government committees. 'We have an open door', declared Arthur Deakin, 'in relation to all State Departments.'[30]

The leaders of the TUC were firm believers in the solidarity of organized labour. They themselves gave strong support to the Attlee governments, which they regarded as the political wing of the labour movement. At the same time they expected their members to abide by the decisions reached, and the settlements negotiated, by elected union officials. The TUC maintained a policy of strong opposition to unofficial strikes, augmented from 1948 onwards by the onset of the Cold War, and the convenient allegation that unofficial disputes were the work of communist agitators. Between 1948 and 1950 they accepted the government's call for a voluntary wage freeze, and generally speaking their members complied. But there were some tensions between official union leaders and the 'rank and file', and in the case of the dockers solidarity repeatedly broke down. The leaders of the Transport and General Workers Union, whose membership of more than a million included 80,000 dockers, were proud of the part they had played in the setting up of the National Dock Labour Scheme of 1947. A consolidation of wartime reforms introduced by Bevin, the scheme outlawed the tradition of casual labour in the docks, and secured for all dockers security of employment, minimum wages, and a closed shop. The dockers, however, had become accustomed to the system of casual labour, and learned how to turn it to their advantage under conditions of full employment. The outcome was a series of unofficial strikes in the docks in 1945, 1948, 1949, 1950, and 1951. The Transport and General Workers Union condemned the strikes and supported the government, which on seven occasions sent troops into the docks to load and unload supplies.[31]

The trade union movement was a broadly based but loosely organized coalition, riven at times by internal conflicts. The trade union leaders themselves were atypical figures among the working classes, committee men devoted to their branch meetings, rule books, and conference procedures. Most trade union members played no part in the unions beyond paying a subscription, nor was adherence to the Labour Party anything like universal among manual workers. In 1945, it has been estimated, about 9.2 million manual workers voted Labour, but another 4.4 million voted Conservative.[32] Part of the explanation lies in the realm of gender. Women were less likely than men to be employees or trade unionists and hence less likely to see the world as divided into 'Them' and 'Us': employers and managers on one side, workers on the other. They were therefore more open to the appeals of the Conservative party. 'While Labour obtained a small lead among women in 1945', writes Ina Zweiniger-Bargielowska, 'from 1951 onwards there was a strong female preference for the Conservative party. By contrast, men continued to favour the Labour party and if women had been disenfranchised Labour would have won every general election in the period.'[33]

If full employment was the primary cause of the rise in working-class incomes, and trade unionism a contributory factor, social policy also played a part by mitigating poverty. In the third of his famous studies of social conditions in York, published in 1951, Seebohm Rowntree concluded that only 4.6 per cent of working-class households were in poverty compared with 31.1 per cent in 1936. He and his colleague Lavers also calculated that, but for the improvements which had been made to welfare provision since 1936, 24.7 per cent of households would have been in poverty. Rowntree and Lavers were subsequently criticized for setting the poverty line too low, but there is always room for disagreement over the definition of poverty. More recently economic historians have shown, by re-examining their original data, that even on their own definition they underestimated the extent of poverty and overestimated the impact of social policy. If they had applied their own criteria accurately, they would have concluded that

11.8 per cent of households were still in poverty instead of 4.6 per cent, and that welfare reforms had reduced poverty by 9.8 per cent rather than 20.1 per cent. But even with these modifications it is clear that poverty had fallen sharply, and that social policy had made a substantial contribution.[34]

In many respects working *men* had never had it so good as in the 'age of austerity'. They too were affected by the scarcity of goods in the shops, but it was women who bore most of the burden as they struggled with the shopping, the cooking, and the housework. Nor was there a shortage of male-dominated leisure activities on which workers could spend their cash. Smoking, for example, was predominantly a male habit: in 1949, 81 per cent of men smoked but only 39 per cent of women.[35] The pub, the race track, the greyhound racing stadium, the football or cricket ground, were never exclusively masculine territory, but women were in a minority. Spectator sports were booming with professional football attracting over 41 million spectators in 1948–9.[36]

The Plight of the Middle Class

'It would be a fair guess', reported *The Economist* in 1955, 'to say that three-quarters of the men who wore morning dress at Ascot this week were not wearing their own clothes.' They had hired them, in other words, from Moss Bros.[37] Intended, perhaps, as a reflection on the democratization of Britain, it was a comment redolent of that highly sensitive nose for distinctions of class and status for which the English, rather more than the Scots and the Welsh, were renowned. That consciousness of social gradations seems to have survived 'the people's war' with very little modification. When, for example, first-class cricket was resumed after 1945, the distinction between 'gentlemen' and players was restored with it. Gentlemen were amateurs who received only their expenses, players professionals who made a living out of the game. On scorecards and scoreboards the names of amateurs appeared with their initials before their name, professionals with their initials after. Tradition dictated that the captain of a county side, and a captain of England, must normally be an amateur, though exceptions were sometimes tolerated. The distinction between gentlemen and players was beginning to weaken after 1945, but was only abolished in 1963.[38] The novelist Nancy Mitford caused a great buzz of excitement in the press in 1955 when she published an article in *Encounter* on the difference between upper-class ('U') and non-upper-class ('Non-U') speech. The discovery that the upper class spoke of their 'false teeth' while the rest of the population talked of their 'dentures' caused so much interest that she expanded the article into one of the best-selling books of 1956, *Noblesse Oblige*.[39] In 1961 the headquarters of British Railways, that monument to the socialism of the Attlee years, had five different canteens and messes to reflect the various grades of employee.[40]

While status distinctions exercised as much fascination as ever, economic differentials had narrowed and the middle classes had lost some of the economic and political advantages they had enjoyed before the war. The figures below, compiled by Guy Routh, show in startling fashion how income differentials between the classes narrowed sharply between the late 1930s and the mid-1950s. The flat base line represents the average income of the unskilled worker; the other lines are all relative to it. The figures say nothing about the distribution of property or other forms of wealth, which remained extremely unequal. But they do show how pre-tax incomes were compressed between the late 1930s and the mid-1950s, with the higher professionals (including of course the administrative class of the civil service) experiencing the sharpest relative decline (see Graph 2.2).

The most likely explanation of these figures is the transition from the mass unemployment of the 1930s, a decade in which the unemployment rate never fell below ten per cent, to the full employment and labour shortages of the 1940s. Between 1942 and 1963 it tended to fluctuate somewhere between one and two per cent and only rose above 2.5 per cent once, during the fuel crisis of the bleak midwinter of 1947. Shortages of labour, accompanied by an increase in the strength and bargaining power of the trade unions, pushed up wages faster than salaries, a trend exacerbated by inflation.

In wartime the relative decline of middle-class living standards was enveloped in the general ethos of stoicism and solidarity in the face of hardship: Hitler was to blame. With peace restored, however, the spectacle of a Labour government with a huge parliamentary majority, supported by a trade union movement more powerful than ever before, revealed a new and unwelcome state of affairs. It was not long before

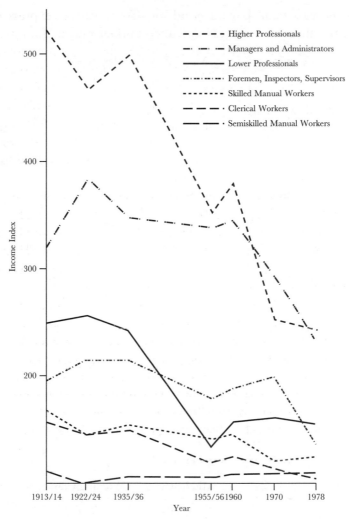

Graph 2.2 Occupational position and income of men in Great Britain 1913–78. (100 = average income of unskilled worker.)

Source: Guy Routh, *Occupation and Pay in Great Britain 1906–1979* (London, 1980), p. 127.

sections of the middle class began to complain that they were under attack, and their fortunes in decline. Anxieties of this kind, which drove the British Medical Association's campaign against Bevan, and prompted housewives to band together in the British Housewives' League to protest against rationing, were often exaggerated but expressed with great conviction. When Gallup asked voters in 1951 what the two main parties stood for, Conservatives expressed their views of Labour's objectives in no uncertain terms:

Headmaster's wife:	'More money for less work.'
Hospital nurse:	'They encourage the workers not to do a fair day's work.'
Wife of a railway official:	'The five-day week.'
Commercial traveller:	'Giving the working classes power they are not fitted to use.'
Solicitor's wife:	'They say social security but I think class warfare.'
Engineering technician:	'Class hatred, revenge, and grab.'
Farmer's wife:	'Class hatred.'
Salesman's wife:	'Class warfare.'
Accountant:	'Complete subversion of the middle and upper classes.'
Butcher's wife:	'To keep down the people with money.'
Solicitor:	'For the elevation of one class of people to the detriment of others.'
Woman clerk:	'Bringing up the working class and pulling down the other.'
Managing director:	'Fair shares for all if they are working people.'

Why such angst? Two sets of statistics help to illuminate the situation. The first, compiled by the British Medical Association, shows how nutritional standards had been levelled down since the 1930s:

Calorie intake per head per day

	Middle Class	Working Class
1936–7	3,158	2,557
1945	2,402	2,375
1950	2,506	2,468

Protein intake per head per day in grams

	Middle Class	Working Class
1936–7	89.33	69.60
1945	77.00	76.00
1950	78.75	77.20

Source: Ina Zweiniger-Bargielowska, *Austerity in Britain: Rationing, Controls and Consumption 1939–1945* (Oxford, 2000), p. 45.

Middle-class earnings were still, of course, significantly higher than those of manual workers. In 1948 market researchers estimated that the average income of a working-class family was £8 [=£182] per week, the average income of a middle-class family £20.15s [=£463] per week. Direct taxation, however clawed back 23 per cent of middle-class income but only five per cent of working-class income. Furthermore the costs of the basic essentials of food, rent, and clothing, which accounted for 47 per cent of working-class expenditure, but only 30 per cent of middle-class budgets, were controlled or subsidized by the state.[41] Although the middle classes still retained a margin of advantage, that was hardly the point: it was the sense of deprivation by comparison with the pre-war years that really hurt. 'We are losing more of the things that made life gracious in the past', wrote a female Mass-Observer. 'We have already given up a resident maid, changing our clothes three or four times a week, and, by degrees, keeping open house for our friends.'[42]

According to John Bonham's estimates, 66 per cent of the more well-to-do businessmen, and 58 per cent of higher professionals, voted Conservative in the general election of 1945, as against the 10 per cent and 15 per cent respectively who voted Labour. Among lesser business people and the lower professionals, about one in three voted Labour, but the Conservatives still enjoyed a substantial lead. As Bonham also showed, the effect of six years of austerity and Labour rule was to shift the middle classes still further to the right. In all six of the categories into which he divided the business and professional vote, support for the Conservatives increased between 1945 and 1951. This was due partly to middle-class defections from Labour, and partly to the fact that the Liberal party, which had put up candidates in 475 seats in the general election of 1950, could only field 109 in 1951. Where there was no Liberal candidate, former Liberal voters tended to vote Conservative.[43]

The Labour Party claimed to be a party of workers 'by hand and by brain', a phrase which in theory included managers, administrators, and even the self-employed: everyone, in fact, except 'Big Business'. But socialists undoubtedly gave priority to the welfare of manual workers, a fact of which the Minister of Fuel and Power, Emanuel Shinwell, boasted in May 1947: 'We know that the organized workers of this country are our friends. As for the rest, they don't matter a tinker's cuss.'[44] In an effort to counteract the unfortunate effects such remarks were likely to have on the middle classes, a significant minority of whom had voted Labour in 1945, Herbert Morrison expressed his sympathy for 'the so-called middle class which has, for some time past, been experiencing a painful and difficult reduction in their living standards . . . Many Labour MPs represent middle-class constituencies, and it is important if we are to maintain the Government, that we should retain that support.' Morrison, however, could offer them only psychological rewards. Labour's policy, he promised, would in time offer every worker, by hand or by brain, 'opportunities of service, of achievement, of personal satisfaction, and of joyful co-operative work, such as we have never known before'.[45]

Conciliatory words had little effect. 'If the middle class is, as used to be said, the backbone of the country, then Great Britain is rapidly becoming invertebrate', wrote *The Economist* in January 1948. 'Both as compared to the wage-earner and the profit-maker, the salariat have in fact lost ground out of all proportion to the general fall in national wealth. . . . from almost every relevant action that the government has taken there might be deduced a desire to hit the professional man harder than the plutocrat.'[46] The economist Graham Hutton, in a radio talk of June 1948, explained: 'The well-to-do and better off, the middle classes, have taken the biggest material cuts and sacrifices, as persons or households. The less well-to-do have had their material standards raised.'[47] There were three main reasons, argued the popular weekly magazine *Picture Post*, for the relative decline in middle-class fortunes: income tax at 45p in the £, the failure of salaries, fees, and income from investment to keep up with rising prices, and the introduction of universal social services.[48]

The Labour Party's general election manifesto of 1950 claimed that the Attlee government's social legislation 'has benefited *all* sections of the community, including members of the middle classes. Hundreds of thousands of middle-class and professional families have been relieved of one of their worst anxieties—the fear of the sudden illness, the expensive operation, the doctors' crippling bills.'[49] But even the veteran social reformer William Beveridge bewailed the fact that egalitarianism had gone so far:

Abolition of poverty by levelling up incomes has been part of our social policy for many years. In the past ten years there has been added to this a tremendous levelling down as well, mainly by taxation to pay for wars

and their consequences and preparation for fresh wars. It is not possible
for anyone in Britain who earns more than a very small income to avoid
paying substantial sums in income tax. It is not possible for anyone,
however hard and well he works, to enjoy the kind of income or to make
the savings for old age that were easy when I was a young man.[50]

The return of the Conservatives to office in 1951 appears to have made
little difference to this sense of relative deprivation. At the highest levels,
Conservative rule was patrician. Churchill, Eden, and Douglas-Home
were all from the landed aristocracy, and Macmillan had married into
the family of the dukes of Devonshire. The 1950s witnessed an Indian
summer of the aristocracy and a revival in the fortunes of the English
country house. In *Brideshead Revisited* (1945), Evelyn Waugh had lamented
its destruction at the hands of a philistine democracy but in a preface to
a second edition of the book in 1959 he conceded that much of it was 'a
panegyric preached over an empty coffin'. With the aid of the National
Trust and the opening of country houses to the public, the landed aristocracy had staged a recovery, and high society was to be seen again in
most of its old haunts. 'Not only the Eton and Harrow match', writes
Gary Runciman, 'but Ascot, Henley, Cowes, Glyndebourne, and even
Queen Charlotte's ball re-emerged much as before; property values
recovered, share prices boomed; the *Tatler's* photographer was back in
attendance at society weddings and hunt balls; winter holidays could be
taken once more in St Moritz or in the Caribbean.'[51]

This very conspicuous display of affluence at the top did nothing to
alleviate a continuing sense of relative deprivation among the middle
classes. The Conservatives, complained *The Times* in February 1956,
had done too little for them. The lower middle classes were menaced by
inflation, the upper middle classes by high levels of taxation. The salary
of a Whitehall Permanent Secretary, the paper claimed, was in 1956
worth only 44 per cent of its value in 1935. Four successive Conservative
budgets 'with little relief for the middle class anywhere and practically
none for its upper regions has left a feeling of hopelessness. If relief is not
given by a Conservative government, will it ever be given?'[52] It was an
almost unchallenged assumption of the post-war settlement that the
most wealthy should be subject to steeply progressive rates of taxation,
In 1967 the Managing Director of Jaguar cars, Sir William Lyons, paid
£83,000 [=£853,240] in tax on a salary of £100,000 [=£1,028,000]

and Sir Paul Chambers, the head of ICI, paid £39,000 [=£400,920] in tax on a salary of £50,000 [=£514,000].[53] *The Economist*, which compiled detailed statistics comparing the salaries of various grades of civil servant and teacher in 1938 and 1956, calculated that in order to maintain their pre-war purchasing power salaries needed to have multiplied by a factor of three. The figures demonstrated that in most occupations the increase was substantially less.[54]

Apart from progressive taxation and the effects of inflation a third enemy of the middle classes was coming into view: trade unionism. A Gallup poll of 1956 recorded that one in three clerical workers interviewed about recent strikes 'gave answers which clearly demonstrated their conception of the working class and trade unionism as a threatening and dangerous force which should be repressed'.[55] Possibly because the leadership of the Conservative party remained in the hands of patricians who were more interested in placating the working classes than championing the middle classes, no action was taken to clip the wings of the trade unions. When Harold Macmillan succeeded Anthony Eden as Prime Minister in January 1957, he was urged by one of his ministers to remove the bitterness felt by the middle classes by allowing them 'to keep a somewhat larger share of the money that they earn by their skill and enterprise'. The following month he wrote to Michael Fraser, the head of the Conservative Research Department: 'I am always hearing about the Middle Classes. What is it they really want? Can you put it down on a sheet of notepaper and then I will see whether we can give it to them.' Fraser replied that what they wanted was something no government could give them, a return to the comfortable standards of life they had known before the war, which had since fallen drastically 'both absolutely and/or in relation to the rapidly rising standards of the manual workers'.[56] As late as 1961, when the Conservatives lost the Orpington by-election, Macmillan described the swing against them as 'a revolt of the middle class or lower middle class, who resent the vastly improved condition of the working classes and are envious of the apparent prosperity and luxury of the rich'.[57] Not much sympathy there for Orpington Man.

The Kitchen Front

Austerity imposed a disproportionately heavy burden on the housewife. As a general rule it was housewives who did the shopping and the cooking and who stood almost every day, in all weathers, in the queues which had become a familiar feature of life in the war years. One day in June 1945 Mrs Irene Lovelock, a parson's wife from Selhurst in south-east London, set out to queue for fish and potatoes. 'That morning made me fume', she wrote,

> There were the usual queues but they seemed more pathetic than usual. There seemed more poor old women standing in the rain and the cold; more mothers with babies in prams and toddlers hanging on their skirts, more ill-looking and pregnant women. Potatoes were in very short supply and one old-age pensioner told me she had stood for hours only to be told when her turn came that she couldn't have any unless she bought peas as well. "Peas are a shilling a pound. How can I afford them?" That started me off. This is England. The country which fought alone for freedom. These are her women, that the world should honour, treated like sheep, lined up for miserable scraps of food and often exploited and insulted by thoughtless shopkeepers enjoying the whip hand.

Mrs Lovelock was an unlikely rebel who had never addressed a public meeting in her life. Now her patience had snapped. She organized a meeting in the parish hall to protest against queuing and the behaviour of shopkeepers. When the story was picked up by the *London Evening News* scores of letters of support began to arrive at the vicarage, and she was filmed in her back garden by Pathe News. When she was commissioned to write an article for the *Sunday Express*, her comments on shopkeepers prompted the arrival on her doorstep the following morning of three angry butchers, 'one very large, one medium, and one very small'. When they stormed at her she exclaimed: 'I won't be bullied!' Nor would she. On 18 July at a meeting in the vicarage drawing-room Mrs Lovelock and a small group of supporters founded the British Housewives League. The next day she addressed a meeting of over a thousand women, with a well-known Labour politician and feminist, Dr Edith Summerskill, in the chair.[58]

In June 1945 Britain was still at war with Japan, but as far as most people were concerned the war had ended on VE-Day, 8 May. Mrs Lovelock's revolt was one of the first signs of impatience with the persistence of wartime conditions, and the harbinger of many others. Nor was the reaction against the home front simply a matter of impatience with rationing and austerity. The British had given up most of their personal liberties during the war and it was only a matter of time before they demanded some or all of them back. The drive to remove state controls and restore liberty was one of the most important shaping factors as Britain emerged from the war.

When Mrs Lovelock went to the polls to vote in the first post-war general election, on 5 July 1945, she voted Labour. 'I did so', she wrote,

> because I hoped that a Labour government would give the ordinary man and woman a square deal. The memory of the huge numbers unemployed before the war and the failure of Conservatives and Coalitions to deal with the problem led me at any rate to think that Labour might be able to tackle it. Many of us had taken too little interest in politics in the past and felt we ought, at this first election for a long time, not to hesitate to vote Labour even if it meant certain controls rather than be satisfied with the state of affairs in 1938 years before.[59]

Mrs Lovelock soon repented of her decision. Convinced that Labour's policies were based on an unholy alliance between tyrannical bureaucrats and the feckless poor, she led the British Housewives League in a more and more strident campaign against rationing that was to continue throughout the period of the Labour government and into the first years of Conservative rule. Nor were Mrs Lovelock and her supporters exceptional in their exasperation with rations and shortages. In 1946 an investigator for Mass-Observation[60] joined a queue of thirty outside a baker's shop in London:

> 'I've been queueing ever since eight o'clock this morning, what with one thing and another', says F40D. 'I'm about done for. I'd like to take that Attlee and all the rest of them and put them on top of a bonfire in Hyde Park and BURN them.' 'And I'd 'elp yer', says F65D. 'Same 'ere', say several other angry women.[61]

The main hardship inflicted by food rationing was the physical stress it imposed on women, many of whom were already suffering from fatigue as a result of the war years. But the monotony of the diet was also frustrating. In her diary entry for Mass-Observation in May 1947, Maggie Joy Blunt, a middle-class woman in her thirties, describes the pangs of hunger induced by a collection of pre-war recipes:

> Oh those pre-war days! June says that when she hears good, unobtainable food discussed now her mouth waters so much she actually dribbles.

Foie gras with whipped cream and hardboiled egg set in aspic with green peas. Pineapple cream made with real fruit. Strawberry meringue pudding made with white of six eggs... Lobster mixed with mushrooms and cream. Chicken soaked in milk and herbs for twenty-four hours before cooking. A special sauce of raisins, apple, banana, curry, and cider to serve with white fish. Veal cutlets rolled in beaten eggs and grated cheese and grilled. Kidneys cooked with white wine. Pears baked in honey and butter and served with tinned cherries and lemon juice. Asparagus. I'm dribbling, too, now.[62]

For housewives the burden began to ease with the ending of rationing in the early 1950s, and the arrival in the kitchen of the fridge and the washing-machine. Taking into account the full and equal access that women now enjoyed to medical services, and the growing opportunities for part-time employment outside the home, there is much to suggest a marked improvement in their fortunes. Nevertheless the affluence of the 1950s was so intimately bound up with woman's role in the home that it tended to confirm rather than challenge traditional expectations. If there was a measure of greater equality between the classes in post-war Britain, there was also a measure of greater equality between the sexes, but in both cases the changes were modest.

3

Victorian Values

In the 1940s as in Victorian times, the British public were never short of advice on moral issues. Churchmen, Members of Parliament, judges, chief constables, head teachers, and newspaper columnists had no hesitation in proclaiming the rules that should guide men and women in their daily lives. This is not to imply that they always agreed with one another. There were passionate debates, for example, over capital punishment and the divorce laws. But men and women in public life were in the habit of exercising moral authority, and where issues of sexual morality were concerned the attitudes they expressed were in the main conservative.

They were also apprehensive: fearful that traditional conceptions of right and wrong were under attack and standards of behaviour slipping. They pointed to the effects of the war, which disrupted family life by separating husbands from wives and parents from children. The presence of American, Canadian, Polish, and other foreign soldiers led to numerous affairs with British women and accusations that teenage girls were hanging around army camps and prostituting themselves. The divorce rate and the illegitimacy rate began to rise. The constant upheavals of wartime life created more opportunities for crime and the imposition of rationing led to a flourishing black market. As always, the anxieties of the authorities tended to focus on young people and the rising statistics for juvenile delinquency, readily interpreted as evidence of a general moral decline.

There were certainly flourishing sub-cultures where the writ of respectable morality did not run: a criminal underworld, a homosexual underworld, a Fitzrovian bohemia of artists, writers, and groupies, an upper-class fast set that had never given a damn for convention. But the mass of respectable society, both middle and working class, subscribed to a broad moral consensus. Heterosexual sex was the norm, marital fidelity the ideal, and a man and a woman who lived together without getting married were said to be 'living in sin'. Advice on birth control was available from the Family Planning Association but its constitution forbade it to supply contraceptives to the unmarried. Divorce was only possible where it could be proved that a husband or wife had committed a 'matrimonial offence' which branded them as the 'guilty party'. There was still a stigma attached and the term 'divorcee' conjured up scandalous associations. Unmarried mothers were made to feel a sense of shame and their children defined by law as illegitimate. Abortion was illegal except where the health of the mother was seriously at risk. Homosexuality—by which contemporaries almost always meant *male* homosexuality—was at best lamented as a type of psychological illness, at worst condemned as a wicked perversion. All homosexual acts were criminal offences punishable by a prison sentence. Whatever might have happened during the war, peacetime Britain was a morally conservative society in which both men and women were under pressure to conform, but women were the cornerstone of the system.

Telling Right from Wrong

In the immediate post-war years discussions of the physical aspects of sex were still generally taboo, though some schools provided occasional classes in sex education, and adults could turn to the works of Marie Stopes or Dr Eustace Chesser.[1] There was no lack of sex in fiction but it was usually presented in a stylized fashion, with the physical realities airbrushed out. The BBC, the theatre, and the cinema collaborated in maintaining 'standards of public decency'. Topics like abortion or homosexuality were occasionally alluded to but never openly addressed. Adultery was often portrayed, but the rules of conventional morality required that it should be exposed as an evil for which retribution was inevitable. Better still, as in the film *Brief Encounter* (1945), a man and a woman, both married to others, could be shown as triumphing over the temptations of adultery. Language too was heavily censored. No one ever said 'fuck!' in the war movies of the period. At the BBC comedians were subject to a strict code laid down in the *BBC Variety Programmes Policy Guide for Writers and Producers*, compiled in the second half of 1948. The ripe humour of the music-halls was bowdlerized and the following topics forbidden:

Jokes about—

Lavatories
Effeminacy in men
Immorality of any kind

Suggestive references to—

Honeymoon couples
Chambermaids
Fig leaves
Prostitution
Ladies' underwear, e.g. winter draws on
Animal habits, e.g. rabbits
Lodgers
Commercial travellers

Extreme care should be taken in dealing with references to or jokes about—

Pre-natal influences (e.g. 'His mother was frightened by a donkey')
Marital fidelity.[2]

Under the Obscene Publications Act of 1857 novels as well as magazines could be prosecuted for 'tending to corrupt' the morals of readers. Between January 1950 and December 1953, magistrates in Britain issued more than 1,500 orders for the destruction of works of fiction discovered by the police on sale in bookshops. Most were 'soft porn' but they included classics by Bocaccio, Flaubert, Balzac, and Zola.[3] In 1954 Donald McGill, a prolific artist whose saucy postcards (fat man in tight swimming costume: 'I can't see my little Willie!') had been delighting holiday-makers since the 1920s, was prosecuted for obscenity and fined £50 [=£871].[4] The stage too was subject to control. The Lord Chamberlain, a member of the royal household, had the power to ban or censor any play written since the days of Walpole's premiership in the eighteenth century and 'the list of writers whose plays had at one time or another been banned was startling'.[5]

Churchmen still felt called upon to denounce the state of public morals and indeed the licentiousness of the theatre. In its annual report for 1948 the Public Morality Council, a body on which the Anglican, Roman Catholic, and nonconformist churches were all represented, launched an attack on the staging of Restoration comedy:

Many of these plays are decadent in theme, bawdy in character, and indecent throughout. They were considered unfit for public presentation at the time they were written, and yet they are now being produced by some of the companies that are being excused entertainment tax and given financial support from public money. At a time when indifference to religion and such slackness in morals as must have an incalculably harmful effect on the whole community are visible on every hand, it must be manifest that to give toleration to such plays, which hold that religion is contemptible or morality absurd, is a policy alien to the long tradition of all that is best in our country.[6]

The journalist J. L. Hodson, one of the most balanced and informative observers of his times, wrote pessimistically in December 1948:

Disrespect for authority is rife. Unofficial strikes are notorious. Gambling has spread like wildfire. Children, while physically bonnier, are often materialistic and cynical. They are sometimes harder to teach nowadays because they are distracted by radio, films, and football pools. Churches grow emptier and dog tracks more crowded. We are, I think, a less honest and moral people.[7]

Under the Attlee government Victorian values continued to prevail, though they were sometimes challenged. Many Labour backbenchers were disappointed when the Home Secretary, James Chuter Ede, introduced a Criminal Justice Bill with no provision for the suspension or abolition of corporal punishment. When the MP Sidney Silverman proposed an amendment suspending capital punishment for a period of five years, a Labour revolt led to the defeat of the government by 245 votes to 222. The House of Lords, however, struck out the amendment and under strong pressure from the government the rebel MPs backed down. The chief executioner, Albert Pierrepoint, continued in the post he had inherited in 1946 from his uncle Thomas.[8] In 1950 he hanged Timothy Evans, a psychologically disordered character convicted of the murder of his baby daughter on the evidence of John Christie, his neighbour in an upstairs flat. Another three years were to pass before Christie was unmasked as a serial killer and necrophiliac who had murdered Evans's wife, and almost certainly murdered the baby as well.

Another backbench initiative in favour of the reform of the divorce laws resulted only in the setting up of a Royal Commission, a tried and tested method of procrastination. With the exception of some of the Labour Party's Young Turks, Labour politicians were stolid figures of conventional outlook. In 1950 the party's head of research, Michael Young, commissioned from Labour lawyers a report on law reform with a view to including some of its proposals in the forthcoming manifesto. As he recalled ten years later:

> The report when it arrived contained a large number of well-reasoned proposals for reform, such as abolishing the 'crime' of homosexuality, modernizing the divorce laws, removing censorship of plays and films, and abolishing capital punishment. The members of the [Policy] Committee were acutely embarrassed. Far from considering the proposals on their merits, they showed concern only that no word should ever get out that such a dangerous report had been received.[9]

Labour politicians no doubt took into account the attitudes of the respectable working classes who had always formed the backbone of the party. Impervious though most of them were to the moral injunctions of the 'great and the good', their attitudes towards homosexuality or capital punishment were generally conservative, and their views of heterosexuality were far from permissive.

It was still conventional to describe Britain as 'a Christian country' and in a broad sense this was accurate. Adherents of non-Christian religions were comparatively few. The total Jewish population of the United Kingdom was estimated at about 450,000.[10] Hindus, Moslems, and Buddhists were present but must have totalled only a few thousand in all. Atheists and agnostics were prominent in the intellectual world, but the British public retained a residual attachment to Christianity. About three-quarters of all babies were baptized and about 70 per cent of couples got married in church. 81 per cent of British people said that they believed in the existence of God, 68 per cent in Jesus as the son of God, and 49 per cent in life after death.[11] In everyday life the theological implications of various types of Christian belief were of little or no interest to most people, but a secularized Christianity lived on as a generally accepted code of ethics. 'Ask any half-dozen working-class people what they understand by religion', wrote Richard Hoggart, 'and very easily, but not meaninglessly, they will be likely to answer with one of these phrases':

'doing good'
'common decency'
'helping lame dogs'
'being kind'
'doing unto others as y'would be done unto'
'we're 'ere to 'elp one another'
''elping y'neighbour'
'learning to know right from wrong'
'decent living'.[12]

The majority of people were not regular church attenders but substantial minorities were. A survey in 1947 showed that 11 per cent of men and 18 per cent of women claimed to go to church every week, while another 18 per cent of men and 26 per cent of women claimed to attend with a frequency varying from once every three weeks to once every two months. More surprisingly, research commissioned by the *People* newspaper in 1951 indicated that the young went to church more frequently than the middle-aged or the elderly, a reversal of the pattern we have come to expect. Nor was there much variation in attendance by social class: contrary to the widely held belief that manual workers had long since abandoned organized religion, they were no less likely to attend church than the middle or upper classes.[13] In their study of Bethnal Green in the mid-1950s, Michael Young and Peter Willmot found that whether or not they were regular churchgoers, working-class women kept up the tradition of 'churching': in theory a service of thanksgiving for the birth of a child, in practice a ritual based on superstition and the belief that a woman needed to be cleansed after childbirth. Out of 45 wives in their sample, all except four were churched after the latest birth of a child.[14]

Statistics of church membership are highly problematical, since every denomination had its own definition of membership and method of counting. Allowing for the fact that the figures are only approximations, the membership of the main Christian denominations in England, Scotland, and Wales was as follows in 1950:

Roman Catholic	3,557,059
Church of England	2,958,840
Church of Scotland	1,271,247
Presbyterian and Congregationalist	781,812

Methodist	744,815
Baptist	337,203
Church in Wales	182,000
Scottish Episcopalian	108,502

Together they come to a total of 9,941,478 or 26 per cent of a total adult population for Great Britain of 37,828,000.[15]

When all the evidence is taken into the reckoning, Britain in the aftermath of war was by no means a secular society, or one in which religion was losing ground. Indeed some historians argue, with Richard Weight, that Protestantism was experiencing a revival between 1945 and 1960. The Coronation, after all, was a religious, and emphatically Protestant, ceremony. The following year the American evangelist Billy Graham preached to audiences totalling 1.75 million in the course of a three-month London 'crusade', followed by a Scottish tour in 1955 that attracted another 1.2 million. Literary Anglicanism lived on in the work of Dorothy L. Sayers, Rose Macaulay, and C. S. Lewis, whose *Chronicles of Narnia* were published between 1950 and 1956.[16]

This is not to imply that the British in general conformed to a Christian code of conduct or ever had done. Men and women live happily enough with contradictions between the rules they profess to live by, and their own transgressions, without ever questioning the validity of the rules, a state of confusion too readily dismissed as hypocrisy. Homosexuals, for example, were sometimes ashamed of their sexual orientation, though unable to repress it. There were of course social sets in which conventional morality was regarded as strictly for ordinary people. Provided they were discrete, and managed to avoid exposure in the courts, the rule-breakers could live much as they pleased. If the novels of Evelyn Waugh and Anthony Powell, the diaries of Alfred Duff Cooper, or the private lives of the Prince of Wales and his circle are any guide, the fast set in high society between the wars operated their own permissive society behind closed doors. The Bloomsbury Group invented a morality of their own in which love, whether marital, extramarital, hetero- or homosexual, was elevated into the supreme goal. But these were exclusive metropolitan circles in a society in which the moral tone was set by the respectable, church-going classes of the provinces: Anglican, Methodist, Presbyterian, and so on.

Marriage and the Family

At the heart of the moral order were the institutions of marriage and the family; at the heart of marriage and the family, the division of roles between the sexes. Husbands were breadwinners whose duty was to provide for their wives and children. Wives were expected to make and manage a home and take care of the children. The Archbishop of Canterbury, Geoffrey Fisher, told a meeting of the Mothers' Union—an Anglican women's organization dedicated to the support of motherhood—that at least three children were needed to make a real family.[17]

In a biological sense, married women were already partially emancipated by the mid-twentieth century. In the 1890s half of all working-class couples had between seven and fifteen children, and the typical working-class wife could expect to go though ten pregnancies. In the decades since then the practice of restricting family size had spread through all social classes and by the 1940s the average number of children per family was two. It is possible that the most commonly used method of birth control in the 1940s was still *coitus interruptus*, but a range of artificial devices was already available: the condom for men, the douche, spermicidal jellies, and the cap for women.[18] Although the Roman Catholic Church was firmly opposed to contraceptive devices on doctrinal grounds, none of the Protestant Churches opposed it. The Anglican Church contented itself with opposing the selling of condoms in slot machines outside shops.[19]

As the social policy expert Richard Titmuss pointed out in a lecture in 1952, the reduction in family size had already produced liberating consequences for married women:

> At the beginning of this century, the expectation of life of a woman aged twenty was forty-six years. Approximately one-third of this life expectancy was to be devoted to the physiological and emotional experiences of childbearing and maternal care in infancy. Today, the expectation of life of a woman aged twenty is fifty-five years. Of this longer expectation only about seven per cent of the years to be lived will be concerned with childbearing and maternal care in infancy.[20]

Up until the Second World War wives were generally expected to devote themselves full-time to home and family. It was conventional for women who were young and single to go out to work, but in many occupations such as schoolteaching or work as a telephone operator, a 'marriage bar' was enforced, and women compelled to give up work when they married. If wives did go out to work it was usually on a plea of dire necessity, but in 1931 only ten per cent of married women were in paid employment. During the Second World War, however, the demands of war production resulted in an expansion of fifty per cent in the female labour force, and a relaxation of the restrictions on the employment of married women. Marriage bars were temporarily suspended, and by 1943–4 the government was encouraging married women to take up part-time employment, and providing local authority nurseries where mothers could leave their children during working hours. This marked the beginning of a trend, sustained by the buoyant demand for labour after the war, for married women to seek employment outside the home. The Royal Commission on Population, reporting in 1949, welcomed the trend:

> It is clear that women today are not prepared to accept, as most women in Victorian times accepted, a married life of continuous preoccupation with housework and the care of children and that the more independent status and wider interests of women today, which are part of the ideals of the community, are not reconcilable with repeated and excessive childbearing.

The Commission recommended that measures should be taken to make it easier for women to combine their domestic role with outside activities.[21]

In the decade after 1945 marriage bars were gradually abandoned and the percentage of married women going out to work rose to 21.7 per cent in 1951, and 45.4 per cent in 1961.[22] In their book *Women's Two Roles* (1956), Alva Myrdal and Viola Klein advised women to work up to the birth of their first child and again after their children had finished school: during this phase of their lives even part-time work was to be avoided.[23] 'Women increasingly worked until the birth of their first child,' writes Dolly Smith Wilson, 'took a few years off and returned to work when the children were older, most commonly when the youngest child entered school.'[24] From a twenty-first-century viewpoint this was a minor revolution but in the context of the time it was a notable shift that gave rise to much debate, entangled with fears about the loosening of family ties.

Although more and more married women were employed outside the home, the work was mainly part-time and except for the virtual disappearance of domestic servants, the occupational pattern of women's employment was little changed from the 1930s: 'Most women remained concentrated in lower status, poorly paid white collar, service and industrial occupations... The number in professional jobs rose only slowly. By 1961 there were still only 8,340 female medical practitioners (15% of the profession) and 1,031 women in the whole legal profession (3.5%); 1,580 were surveyors and architects (2.3%), and there were twenty-five women MPs.'[25] In the 1950s and 1960s, educational opportunities for girls were still restricted by the notion that women should be educated in domestic skills while boys were taught woodwork or physics. Fewer girls than boys took 'A' levels, and women students were heavily outnumbered by men in the universities.[26]

The desire for the restoration of normality was evident in the clothes people wore. In the 1950s men and women dressed much as they had in the Thirties. Women wore dresses, or blouses and skirts. Men wore suits or a sports jacket with flannel trousers, shirts and ties, and more often than not a cap or hat. The advertisements and magazine covers of the period expressed a longing to restore home and family as havens of peace and security after the disruptions of war. Housewives, usually depicted as young and pretty, worked happily in the kitchen with children playing around them. Husbands came home after a hard day's work to find the table laid for an enticing meal. In July or August the family went on holiday to the seaside, father perhaps discarding his jacket and relaxing in a deck chair in collar and tie, while mother and children built sandcastles or explored rock pools. At Christmas, extended families gathered together and listened to the King's speech on the wireless. Love and warmth were all around in this idealized picture, the British equivalent of the America portrayed by Norman Rockwell on the covers of the *Saturday Evening Post*.

Feminist historians argue that it was particularly misleading about the role of women who, they argue, were increasingly subject to a 'double burden'. While working part-time, and sometimes full-time outside the home, they were still expected to undertake the no less exacting tasks of housework and childcare. 'Modern labour saving devices', wrote Alva Myrdal and Viola Klein in 1956, 'seem to have raised standards of housekeeping rather than reduced the time spent on housework.'[27] Some sociologists maintained that a new type of 'companionate' marriage was emerging in which there was greater equality between husband and wife, with husbands increasingly helping with the housework. It was true that jobs like decorating or plumbing or putting up shelves had long been regarded as 'men's work', and continued to be so. But 'housework'—cooking, cleaning, washing and ironing, and childcare—had long been classified as 'women's work' and here too there was little change. Surveys demonstrated that although most husbands *helped* around the house it was wives who did most of the work. So deeply ingrained were the concepts of men's and women's work that there were wives in the 1940s and 1950s who refused to allow husbands to undertake housework, on the grounds that they would prove incompetent or show themselves up as 'cissies'. It was only when large numbers of wives began to go out to work that women began to resent the traditional division of labour.[28]

Surveys measuring the amount of time spent on housework suggest that the burden had certainly increased for middle-class women, no doubt as a result of the decline of domestic service or other paid help in the home:

Average number of minutes per day devoted to housework by women

	UK female working class	UK female middle class	UK males
1937	480	235	n/a
1961	440	440	19

Source: Thane, 'Women since 1945', p. 401.

The equal rights feminism of the previous century lived on in a low-key campaign by women's organizations in favour of equal pay, and a Royal Commission on the subject was appointed in 1945. The Commissioners concluded that although there were persuasive arguments in principle for equal pay, implementation would be damaging to the economy. This enabled the Labour governments of 1945–51 to ignore the issue, with the result that between the early 1950s and the mid-1960s women's pay actually *fell* to an average of 59 per cent of male earnings. The only concession was the decision of the Conservative government in 1955 to introduce equal pay into the civil service, local government, and teaching, over the next six years. The equal pay campaign, however, was quite compatible with the view that women with young children should stay at home. 'On the whole', writes Jane Lewis, 'post-war feminists accepted that women's most vital task was motherhood.'

Assumptions of this kind were most visible in the educational system. The 1944 Education Act was intended to mitigate inequalities of class but not to erode distinctions of gender. In his *Education for Girls* (1948), John Newsom, the county education officer for Hertfordshire, accepted that the most academically able girls should receive the same education as boys. Otherwise he argued that there should be more emphasis in the education of girls on home-making and domestic skills. 'The future of women's education lies not in attempting to iron out their differences from men, to reduce them to neuters, but to teach girls how to grow into women and to relearn the graces which so many have forgotten in the past thirty years.'[29]

Although therefore commentators argued that there was now greater equality in marriage, it was at best equality in the sense of an emotional partnership rather than equality of roles or income. At its most extreme, the roles of the sexes were so strictly separated as to produce a gulf that even marriage could not bridge. When Dennis and Henriques made a study of the coal-mining village of Featherstone, in the West Riding of Yorkshire, they discovered that the lives of men and women were rigidly segregated, a consequence of the fact that coal-mining was an all-male occupation with a premium on physical toughness, while there were few opportunities for the employment of women in a single-industry area. The sexes lived together like two tribes, with separate loyalties and customs, the women in a subordinate role which they accepted from habit and the lack of any realistic alternative. In spite of the authors' cool and objective tone, the reader can sense how shocked they were by the emotional poverty of their subjects' lives and the starkly contractual character of their marriages. A man's activities were almost all outside the house, a woman's inside. A husband expected that when he came home from work his wife would have a meal ready for him. One man, coming home to find that his wife had purchased fish and chips, threw them on the fire; his brother-in-law did the same with a meal which a friend of his wife's had prepared in order to free up her time for a shopping-trip.[30] At the end of the week a husband would hand over as much of the weekly wage packet to his wife as he judged necessary for housekeeping. A good husband would also agree to his wife's requests and pay for extras like a new carpet or a washing-machine, but he was always likely to be torn between the needs of his family and the pleasures of solidarity with his mates. With the exception of trips to the cinema, the leisure activities of husbands and wives were strictly segregated: husbands spending time with other men at the club, the pub, or watching Rugby League, while wives entertained friends or kin at home, or lost themselves in women's magazine tales of romance. 'As the years go by', wrote the authors of *Coal Is Our Life*, 'and any original sexual attraction fades, this rigid division between the activities of husband and wife cannot but make for an empty and uninspiring relationship.'[31] Marriages endured, but only because so little was expected of married life.

Love, Sex, and Marriage

Both during and after the war much concern was expressed over the stability of marriage and the family. The aphrodisiac effects of war are well known. Circumstances encouraged brief, intense relationships in which marriages were contracted in haste, then flung like confetti into the storm. Firmly established marriages experienced long periods of separation, a test of fidelity which many husbands and wives succeeded in passing, but others did not. The War Office was greatly alarmed by the effect on the morale of soldiers when they received from home a 'dear John' letter announcing that a wife or partner had broken off a relationship. A confidential War Office history compiled at the end of the war included a section entitled: 'Infidelity of Women':

> The effects [of prolonged absence from home] were most marked in those who had left a wife or 'girl' at home. Moreover, it was found that it was usually after from two to three years of separation that the woman's fidelity broke down. The number of wives and fiancees who were unfaithful to soldiers serving overseas almost defies belief…Nothing did more to lower the morale of troops serving overseas than news of female infidelity, or the suspicion of it.[32]

The infidelities of soldiers away from home, a familiar story, were evident in the rising figures of venereal disease in the Army and the extent of prostitution around military bases. But, whereas a wife's infidelity with a neighbour could well result in a long-term relationship that became public knowledge, a soldier's encounter with a prostitute in Cairo or Rome was a transient event of which no one at home need ever know. The wife's infidelity was no more reprehensible than the husband's, but it did pose a greater threat to the marriage.

Owing to the passage in 1937 of A. P. Herbert's Matrimonial Causes Act, which broadened the grounds for divorce in England to include cruelty and desertion, it is almost certain that the divorce rate would have increased even without the war. But between 1939 and 1945 the annual number of petitions for divorce increased from 8,517 to 24,857,[33] and common sense suggests that the war had much to do with this. From 1942 onwards legal aid was given to soldiers to enable them to pay for the cost of divorce proceedings, a move which inevitably multiplied the number of petitions. But the granting of legal aid was, of course, a *consequence* of the growing number of servicemen whose marriages were in difficulty. A second wave of divorce followed the demobilization of men from the armed forces, with petitions and decrees nisi reaching a peak in 1947, and a third wave following the extension of legal aid to all citizens in 1950. But after 1953 the incidence of divorce began to fall and the downward trend continued until about 1960:

Percentages of marriages terminated by divorce

Year	England and Wales	Scotland
1911	0.2	0.7
1922	0.8	1.5
1937	1.6	1.9
1950	7.1	5.1
1953	7.0	5.2
1954	6.7	4.9

Source: Report of the Royal Commission on Marriage and Divorce, Cmd 9678 (1956), p. 8 footnote 2.

Percentage of decrees granted per 1,000 married women aged 20–49 (England and Wales)

1953	4.11
1954	3.79
1955	3.62
1956	3.54
1957	3.19
1958	3.04
1959	3.25
1960	3.18

Source: Ronald Fletcher, *The Family and Marriage in Britain* (1977), p. 147.

Commenting in 1956 on the decline in the divorce rate *The People* was optimistic: 'The ten-year strain that came with the end of the war seems to have ended. In 1956 the prospects of a happy and settled marriage for young people are brighter than at any time since 1939.'[34]

The divorce rate would probably have been higher but for the thwarting of divorce law reform. In 1951 the Labour MP Mrs Eirene White introduced a Private Member's Bill proposing that a husband and wife who had lived apart for seven years, without a prospect of reconciliation, should be able to obtain a divorce. This would have introduced, for the first time, a type of divorce based on the breakdown of marriage instead of the guilt of the husband or wife. The Bill, however, was condemned by the Archbishops of Canterbury and York, Geoffrey Fisher and Cyril Garbett. 'Unless a resolute stand is taken against the new proposals of the Bill', wrote Garbett, 'within a few years marriage will be treated as a temporary contract which can be broken after a brief experiment.'[35] The Attlee government decided to kick the issue into touch by appointing in July 1951 a Royal Commission under Lord Morton of Henryton. True to the reputation of Royal Commissions, it proceeded at a stately pace and did not publish its Report until March 1956.

As the sociologist O. R. MacGregor pointed out, the Commission invited everyone to express their opinions, but signally failed to research or analyse the evidence. 'It is a matter of opinion', he wrote, 'whether the Morton Commission is intellectually the worst Royal Commission of the twentieth century, but there can be no dispute that its report is the most unreadable and confused.'[36] In attempting to explain the rising divorce rate, the Commission, while accepting that the war, and the introduction of legal aid, had played a part, also argued that greater equality between the sexes, and a general relaxation of moral standards, were significant factors:

> Women are no longer content to endure the treatment which in past times their inferior position obliged them to suffer. They expect of marriage that it shall be an equal partnership; and rightly so. But the working out of this ideal exposes new strains. Some husbands find it difficult to accept the changed position of women: some women do not appreciate that their new rights do not release them from the obligations arising out of marriage itself and, indeed, bring in their train certain new responsibilities.

Moreover, in the last thirty or forty years there have been rapid and far-reaching social changes—changes which, if not brought about, were certainly accelerated by the upheavals of two world wars. Old restraints, such as penalties on sexual relations outside marriage, have been weakened and new ideals to take their place are still in process of formation. It is perhaps inevitable that at such a time there should be a tendency to regard the assertion of one's own individuality as a right, and to pursue one's personal satisfaction, reckless of the consequences to others. The teaching of modern psychology has been widely interpreted as laying an emphasis on self-expression and the harmfulness of repression, with the consequent assumption that much that had previously held sexual licence in check could be jettisoned. The wider spread of knowledge of sex is of great value but may have produced in the popular mind an undue emphasis on the over-riding importance of a satisfactory sex relationship without a similar emphasis on the other stable and enduring factors of a lasting marriage.[37]

On the fundamental question of whether or not to extend the grounds of divorce by introducing the new principle of the breakdown of marriage, the Commission split, with nine members (including the chairman) against, and nine in favour. By the time the Report was published in 1956 the divorce rate was falling again and the Eden Government announced that no action would be taken. The outcome was an illuminating reflection of the state of public morality in the immediate postwar period—an era in which liberal pressures were usually overridden by conservative responses.

The Establishment view of divorce was restated in all its rigour early in the reign of Elizabeth II. During the winter of 1954–5 the press was full of speculation about the love affair between the Queen's younger sister Princess Margaret and Group Captain Peter Townsend, a handsome young courtier and Battle of Britain fighter pilot. Townsend, however, was divorced, and hence not entirely respectable by court standards: divorcees were not invited to royal garden parties or other social occasions at which the Queen was present. There was also a constitutional problem. As she was third in line to the throne Margaret might one day be Queen and as such Supreme Governor of the Church of England. The Church, however, refused to marry anyone who had been divorced and would not be able to recognize the marriage or any children of the marriage as legitimate. The editor of *The Times*, Sir

William Haley, argued that the problem lay in the symbolic role of the Queen as the head of the nation and the Commonwealth: 'The Princess will be entering into a union which vast numbers of her sister's people, all sincerely anxious for her lifelong happiness, cannot in conscience regard as marriage.' If therefore she did marry Townsend, she must renounce her right to the throne and withdraw entirely from public life. A few days later Margaret issued a statement in which, 'mindful of the Church's teaching that Christian marriage is indissoluble and conscious of my duty to the Commonwealth', she announced that the marriage would not take place.[38]

In retrospect it seems obvious that fears about the stability of marriage were greatly exaggerated *in the short term*. Neither the divorce law reform of 1937 nor the Second World War posed a serious threat. On the contrary, they were comparatively minor features of an era in which marriage was more popular and more enduring than it had been in the nineteenth century. Even at the height of the divorce wave the proportion of marriages ending in divorce was small by comparison with the figures for the later twentieth century. Over three-quarters of men and women got married, a higher proportion than in earlier decades, they married younger, and as life expectancy increased, couples stayed together for longer periods. Of all couples who married in the late 1930s, 79 per cent were married for at least twenty-five years. The importance attached by women to marriage was signalled by the nature of the wedding ceremony itself, an elaborate ritual solemnized by a male but organized largely by women with lengthy preparations in which the location of the wedding, the guest list, and the wedding presents were decided. A white wedding in church was the norm among all classes, and the custom of going away on honeymoon, already well established among the middle classes, was becoming more universal.[39] On a Whitsun rail journey from Hull, the poet Philip Larkin observed the wedding parties gathered on the station platforms to bid farewell to newly married couples as they boarded the train for London:

> The fathers with broad belts under their suits
> And seamy foreheads; mothers loud and fat;
> An uncle shouting smut; and then the perms,
> The nylon gloves and jewellery-substitutes
> The lemons, mauves, and olive-ochres that
> Marked off the girls unreally from the rest.[40]

One of the main reasons for the popularity of marriage was the fact that it was still, to a great extent, the only morally acceptable framework for sexual intercourse. A Mass-Observation 'street survey' of 2,000 people, completed in 1949, revealed a widespread though far from universal disapproval of extra-marital sex:

Percentage opposed to extra-marital relations

	%
Weekly church goers	73
Non-church goers	54
People leaving school up to the age of 15	64
People leaving school up to the age of 16.5	50
People in rural areas	68
Women	67
Men	57
Married people over 30	64
Single people over 30[41]	48

There was, in fact, still much ignorance and fear of sex, but there was also widespread recognition of the need for a satisfactory sex life *within marriage*. Helena Wright, a pioneer of birth control and sex education, claimed in 1947 that fifty per cent of wives 'still go through their years of married life without discovering that physical satisfaction can, and should, be as real and vivid for them as it is for their husbands'. If Chesser's findings were correct, this was too pessimistic a judgement, but many couples experienced serious problems which Wright herself sought to address in *The Sex Factor in Marriage* (1937) and *More About the Sex Factor in Marriage* (1947), the latter frequently reprinted in the 1950s and distributed though marriage guidance counsellors and birth control clinics.[42]

Birth control within marriage was by this time a generally accepted practice. A pioneering survey of more than 6,000 women carried out in 1954 by a group of researchers under the leadership of Dr Eustace Chesser reported that more than two-thirds of couples practised some form of birth control, with the husband taking the sole responsibility in the majority of cases.[43] The main contraceptive devices, the condom and the cap, were nevertheless difficult to obtain. Condoms were somewhat furtively supplied to men in barber's shops ('anything for the weekend, sir?') but were not on sale in high-street chemists. As Lesley Hall writes:

Vast areas of the country lacked birth control clinics (though provision was rapidly expanding) and medical education on the subject was sporadic. The subject was still considered distasteful and there were restrictions on advertising and promoting services. In 1956 the Family Planning Association received an accolade of respectability previously denied, with the well-publicized visit by the Minister of Health, Iain Macleod, for its Silver Jubilee: the media ban against mentioning its work lifted practically overnight.[44]

It is safe to assume that for many couples, interrupted sex was still the main form of contraception.

Anyone who supposes that family life was stable and harmonious before the 'permissive society' should read Lorna Sage's memoir of growing up in the 1940s and 1950s in the remote north Wales village of Hanmer. Her grandfather, the vicar of the parish, was an adulterer with a scar on his cheek 'which Grandma had done with a carving knife one of the many times he came home pissed and incapable'.[45] Common sense suggests that he was far from typical of anglican vicars, let alone of 'bourgeois morality', but the truth is that we will never know how many seriously dysfunctional marriages there were. Keeping up appearances in public was an integral part of marriage and this may have affected the responses of men and women to social surveys. Of the 3,777 married women who answered Eustace Chesser's questionnaire in 1954, 71 per cent declared that they were 'exceptionally happy' or 'very happy' with their marriage. 23 per cent were 'fairly happy', 6 per cent 'unhappy' or 'very unhappy'. The proportion declaring themselves to be 'exceptionally happy' declined during the first ten years of married life, but even after twenty years of marriage about two-thirds of wives still reported themselves to be very or exceptionally happy.[46] Predictably enough, almost all who described themselves as exceptionally or very happy declared that if they had their time over again they would marry the same man. Among those who were fairly happy one-third said they would marry the same man, and one-third that they would marry someone else, while the rest were undecided. 41 per cent of this group said that they would have separated from their husbands or divorced them if they had had no children.[47] According to Chesser and his colleagues the main factors likely to promote happiness in marriage for women were a happy childhood and positive attitude towards the enjoyment of sex. Social class was irrelevant except where husbands were on low incomes and wives felt obliged to go out to work 'when home circumstances, or our informants' own desires, would otherwise result in their remaining housewives'.[48]

By the 1950s the patterns established in the first half of the twentieth century had come to be thought of as traditional, but in historical time they were recent—and, as events were to prove, temporary: 'A popular myth about marriage is that the long, stable marriage was normal in "the past" in contrast to the instability and divorce of recent times. But this past golden age was short-lived, lasting only from the inter-war years to the 1960s, when divorce replaced death as the great disrupter of marriage.'[49]

The moral conservatism of the period did not formally approve of sex outside marriage, but in practice there was widespread tolerance of premarital sex between couples 'anticipating' marriage. An unpublished survey of the sex lives of 450 members of Mass-Observation's National Panel, completed in 1949, reported that 38 per cent of the single women and 49 per cent of the single men had had sex. Of the sample as a whole, one in five had experienced homosexual relations.[50] Predominantly middle-class and left-wing, the M-O Panel were untypical of the public in general, but Chesser and his colleagues reported that 38 per cent of married women and 27 per cent of single women had experienced premarital sex. This was enough to spark the hostility of some commentators to the very idea of investigating sexual behaviour. According to 'Dr Goodenough', a columnist in *The People*, the book which embodied Chesser's findings was 'drenched with sex' and 'succeeds only in insulting English womanhood'. It was more than likely, he argued, that 'most of the women who answered were sheer neurotics'.[51] Dr Goodenough would have been even more offended by the results of a questionnaire completed by 11,000 people at the request of the social anthropologist, Geoffrey Gorer. 40 per cent of the married admitted to a love affair—whether pre-marital or extra-marital—outside marriage.[52]

Teds and Delinquents

Conservative moralists had good reason to fear that the detachment of sex from marriage would undermine both marriage and the family. Their anxieties about the family, however, were focused mainly on the growth of petty crime among working-class youths. Between 1939 and 1945 the number of convictions for juvenile delinquency rose from 53,106 in 1939 to 73,620 in England and Wales, with an even greater increase in Scotland.[53] Contemporaries speculated that this was a result of the disruption of family life in wartime through evacuation, the absence of fathers in the services, and loss of control by parents over their children. As the Moderator of the Church of Scotland was reported telling a conference on delinquency in January 1944: 'It might turn out that the most serious damage which had been inflicted on this country by the circumstances of the present war was not the damage caused by battle and by bombing, and certainly not the financial strain, but the damage caused to our social organization by the breaking-up of family life.'[54]

The rise of juvenile delinquency was often attributed to the growing number of married women who were going out to work. The number of delinquents was small by comparison with the number of mothers in employment, and there was no reliable evidence to show that the two developments were in fact connected, but observers jumped to the conclusions they wished to find. 'When a child steals sugar', the psychoanalyst D. W. Winnicott wrote in 1946, 'he is looking for the good mother, his own, from whom he has a right to take what sweetness is there.'[55] The most influential British psychiatrist of the period is usually said to have been John Bowlby, whose *Childcare and the Growth of Love* (1953) was based on research into the behaviour of children separated from their parents and housed in institutions during the war. Bowlby argued that the separation of a baby from its mother on a regular daily basis was harmful to the baby's development. From this it was but a short step to the conclusion, which seems to have become an article of faith among government officials, magistrates, policemen, and social workers, that maternal deprivation was a prime cause of delinquency. The fact that most women with young children opted for part-time work, which enabled them to shoulder the 'double burden' of housework and paid employment, seems to have made no impression on the critics. The women's magazines of the period were ready to urge married women without children to go back to work, but committed to an idealized view of woman's domestic role. Putting a young child in a nursery, warned an 'expert' in *Picture Post* in 1956, 'may cause more lasting and irreparable damage to the child even than underfeeding it through poverty'.[56]

Anxieties about juvenile delinquency intensified in the 1950s and focused on the alarming figure of the 'Teddy Boy'. The 'Teds' were drawn from the poorer sections of the working class but made up for their lack of status by spending their money on a dandyish Edwardian style of dress. This derived from a look originally created by Savile Row tailors for upper-class young men of the late 1940s. Taken over by working-class boys from the East End, it was flaunted by gangs whose habitat was the dance hall, the café, and the street corner. Conspicuous consumers whose sense of style quite eclipsed that of their girl friends, they wore 'drape' suits in deep shades of pink, red, green, or blue. The jackets, which featured shoulder-pads and velveteen collars, were accompanied by bootlace ties, fancy waistcoats, drainpipe trousers, and a pair of 'beetle crusher' or 'brothel-creeper' shoes with thick crepe soles. Hair was worn long and heavily greased, with side-burns, a large quiff at the front, and a 'Duck's Arse' at the back. When Elvis Presley rose to fame, the 'Teds' put on blue suede shoes in his honour. They prefigured a working-class desire for something over and above social security: a share in the good life.

The sheer ostentation of the 'Teds' was enough to excite disapproval. The more serious charge was that they were mixed up in violence and gang warfare. In July 1953 a group of youths in Edwardian clothes were involved in a murder on Clapham Common. After this, the press began to refer to 'Edwardian' thugs and gangsters and in March 1954 the phrase 'Teddy Boy' first appeared in print. According to the verdict of two comparatively sympathetic authorities: 'It was undoubtedly true that the Teddy Boy was violent; that in the early 1950s he was becoming more violent; and that he did present a problem. Teddy Boys fought one another, they attacked solitary individuals, they slashed cinema seats. But their depravity was raised to a greater prominence through a distorting screen which upset its audience even more.' Among those caught up in street fights were national servicemen who dressed in Teddy Boys suits when they were off duty, a practice forbidden by Western Command.[57] In 1956 the Teds were prominent in the cinema riots which greeted the screening of *Rock Around The Clock*; in 1958 they played a violent and provocative role in the Notting Hill race riots.[58] Rebellious they might be, but they were also reactionaries, or as Jon Savage puts it: 'The Teds were as English as meat pies and racism.'[59]

The Teddy Boy phenomenon was sometimes blamed on the welfare state but aggressive gangs of 'hooligans' had roamed the streets at the end of the nineteenth century. The 'Teds' differed chiefly from earlier gangs in the amount of money they had to spend and the peacock style they spent it on. 'Youth' in general was law-abiding, the Boy Scouts or the Young Conservatives more typical of their generation. The media did not invent the Teddy Boy phenomenon but they exaggerated it and the problem was compounded by fashion. To dress like a Ted was not necessarily to behave like one. There were grammar school boys who put on the style at the weekend but re-appeared on Monday mornings, smartly turned out in school uniform with their homework ready to hand in. In any case the Teds grew up. 'When I got back from the Navy', one of them told the writer T. R. Fyvel, 'I found the top men married and settled down.'[60]

In the late 1950s a Home Office statistician, Leslie T. Wilkins, carried out an analysis of post-war crime rates which led him to the conclusion that males who passed through their fourth or fifth year during the Second World War were a 'delinquent generation', more prone to crime than previous cohorts. Estimating the number of delinquents at 1,320 for every 100,000 of the relevant age group, he attributed the phenomenon to the lack of parental authority in wartime. Parallel studies by researchers in Denmark, Poland, and New Zealand reached similar conclusions.[61] When juvenile delinquency continued to increase in the 1960s and 1970s it was of course no longer possible to blame the war. It could still, of course, be argued that lack of parental authority was to blame, but the claim was difficult to square with the very obvious fact that rebellious young men were reacting against that very authority.

'Inverts' and 'Queers'

'Homosexuality is far more prevalent in this country than is generally admitted', Lord Boothby told a meeting of the Hardwicke Society in February 1954. 'It is increasing steadily and it is by no means confined to the metropolis. There is, in fact, a homosexual "underground" in most of our large provincial cities of disturbing dimensions, which is a continuous menace to youth. We have reached a situation in which no man with any regard for his reputation will dare to enter a public urinal after dark; and in which the number of male prostitutes parading our streets is a by-word in every other country, and a disgrace to our own.'[62] As a bisexual adventurer himself, Boothby must have known what he was talking about, though he may have been exaggerating for effect. The fact remains that male homosexuality continued to flourish in a twilight zone where it was barely tolerated and frequently prosecuted as a criminal offence. Theobold Matthew, the Director of Public Prosecutions since 1944, and David Maxwell-Fyfe, Churchill's Home Secretary from 1951 to 1955, were particularly zealous in upholding the law. Among homosexual offences cases of indecent assault rose from 822 in 1938 to 3,305 in 1953.[63] Since lesbianism was not a criminal offence, and 'manly' women who might or might not be lesbians had long played a valuable part in voluntary activities and the women's armed forces, there was little prejudice against them and indeed little awareness that they existed. But identification as a homosexual remained a badge of shame and none of the homosexuals prominent in public life, such as the novelist E. M. Forster or the playwright Noel Coward, could ever admit to the fact beyond the company of close friends.

When Roy Harrod published his life of the great economist J. M. Keynes in 1951 he made no reference to the homosexual affairs of Keynes's youth. To have done so would have been to inflict serious damage on the reputation of a great economist and perhaps to undermine the 'Keynesian revolution' itself. 'Even in the 1950s', writes Noel Annan, 'none who wrote on Auden mentioned that the lines "Lay your sleeping head, my love, human on my faithless arm" were addressed to a homosexual.'[64] A politician convicted of a homosexual offence, like the Conservative MP Ian Harvey in 1958, had no hope of saving his career. More generally those in authority had to be above suspicion. Homosexuals were quietly tolerated in many walks of life, but strictly on condition that they stayed in the closet. In March 1952 Alan Turing, the Enigma codebreaker, was convicted on a charge of 'gross indecency'. As an alternative to a prison sentence he accepted a year's hormone therapy treatment, but his security clearance was withdrawn and he was kept under surveillance as a security risk. In what was almost certainly a case of suicide, he was found dead in June 1954 with a half-eaten apple laced with cyanide beside him. Always damaging, exposure was not always fatal. The actor Sir John Gielgud, knighted at the time of the Coronation, was convicted and fined in October 1953 for opportuning. A few months later he suffered a nervous breakdown, but soon returned to the stage and the applause of adoring audiences and critics.

In a notorious case in 1954 the prosecutors in their zeal overstepped the mark. Peter Wildeblood, the diplomatic correspondent of the *Daily Mail*, and Lord Montagu of Beaulieu were convicted of gross indecency and sent to prison on the evidence of men who had clearly been willing participants but subsequently turned Queen's evidence.[65] The case caused such unease that the Home Secretary, Sir David Maxwell-Fyfe, was compelled to set up an enquiry under the chairmanship of Sir John Wolfenden, who was also commissioned to make proposals on the subject of prostitution. Both Maxwell-Fyfe and Wolfenden himself regarded homosexuality as perverse and immoral, but Wolfenden's own son Jeremy was, as his father well knew, an active and indiscreet gay.

On the subject of prostitution the Wolfenden Report was far from permissive. Ever since the war years, when they thronged the approaches to Piccadilly in the black-out, prostitutes had been a blatant presence on the streets in red-light districts. Prosecution for street offences rose from an annual average of 2,000 a year in 1939 to over 10,000 in 1952 and almost 12,000 in 1955. The Wolfenden Report simply recommended that prostitutes should be driven off the streets through the introduction of harsher penalties for soliciting, a proposal subsequently embodied in the Street Offences Act of 1959. The effect, as Noel Annan writes, was 'to supplement the street walker by the call girl; and a wider public became aware of what services were on offer. In the late 1950s curiously worded notices appeared in newsagents' windows. Next to those which offered help with typing or removals were those which quoted phone numbers and promised French lessons or advertised a chest of drawers, or simply a black shiny mackintosh.'[66]

While not in any way endorsing or approving of homosexuality, Wolfenden proposed that homosexual acts between consenting adults in private should no longer be classified as a criminal offence. R. A. Butler, who had become Home Secretary in January 1957 was inclined to accept this and introduce the appropriate legislation, but his Under-Secretary, David Renton, refused on grounds of conscience to assist. As Butler soon discovered, the majority of Conservative MPs were also hostile to reform and he was compelled to drop the proposal.[67] The Church of England, meanwhile, was moving in a more liberal direction. The Archbishops of Canterbury and York expressed their approval of Wolfenden's proposal, and the National Assembly of the Church of England voted in favour of it by 155 to 138. The Church of Scotland, the Free Church of Scotland, the Salvation Army, and the Baptists all declared their opposition, while the Roman Catholic Church was reluctant to pronounce.[68] The Churches were still at one in regarding homosexual activity between consulting adults as a sin: they differed over whether or not it should be illegal.

'The law relating to homosexuality', wrote the Labour MP Roy Jenkins in 1959, 'remains in the brutal and unfair state in which the House of Commons almost accidentally placed it in 1885.' It was one of a number of restrictions on personal liberty, including the Lord Chamberlain's powers of censorship over the London theatre, the betting and licensing laws, and the divorce laws, that Jenkins wished to reform. 'A Labour majority', he wrote, 'would not automatically result in the achievement of all the reforms listed. A great deal would depend on the reforming zeal and liberal spirit of the man who became Home Secretary.'[69] Soon, of course, it was to be Jenkins himself.

4

When British Was Best

On 8 May 1945 the British celebrated victory in Europe. If anyone had paused at that moment to ask, 'who are the British?', a simple answer could have been given. They were the only European people who had waged war against Nazi Germany from the first day to the last. Of the Continental nations, some had been neutral, others fascist, and others again had suffered conquest and occupation. The British alone had fought without experiencing the suppression or destruction of their institutions. They had fought for freedom and decency and achieved a degree of social solidarity remarkable in spite of class divisions. The bonfires and street parties on VE-Day marked a deepening of that shared sense of a common past that marks off one people from another.

On closer inspection the identity of the British was more compli-cated. Churchill spoke of them as 'the island race', but, as he well knew the United Kingdom of Great Britain and Northern Ireland was a mul-tinational affair constructed over the centuries through the interactions of the English, the Scots, the Welsh, and the Irish. The Irish connection with the United Kingdom had always been problematical and the majority of the Irish had broken away from it in 1922 to form the Irish Free State. But the Protestants of northern Ireland—often referred to as 'Ulster'—had insisted on remaining a part of the United Kingdom and their Britishness was all the more fervent because of the presence within the province of a substantial Roman Catholic minority who were generally republican in sympathy.

Since the eighteenth century the English, the Scots, and the Welsh had been so tightly bound together that the British nation-state appeared to rest on unshakeable foundations. The popularity and prestige of the British monarchy had never been higher. It was British political parties for which people voted, the British Broadcasting Company which supplied them with news and entertainment, British trade unions to which employees belonged, the British Empire to which they could emigrate if they were frustrated by their prospects at home.

Despite all this the English, the Scots, and the Welsh retained their separate national identities. (All three, of course, were themselves of racially mixed origin, but to explore the point would take us much too far afield.) One of the consequences was a great deal of confusion over the meaning of 'Britain' and 'Britishness'. To most English people, the terms 'British' and 'English' were virtually interchangeable. They either forgot about the other nationalities or thought of them as 'the Celtic fringe', peoples of the periphery with outlandish accents and customs, who nevertheless shared many of the customs and virtues of the English, such as drinking tea or forming orderly queues.[1] As James Bryce wrote in 1887: 'An Englishman has but one patriotism because to him England and the United Kingdom are practically the same thing.'[2] When George Orwell wrote *The Lion and the Unicorn* (1941), his celebrated portrait of the British people, he referred mainly to the English while arguing that the Scots and the Welsh were not so very different when seen from the viewpoint of a foreigner. This Anglocentric habit of mind caused much irritation among the Scots and the Welsh, who complained to the BBC when broadcasters referred to Britain as England, or assumed that aspects of English life or history were representative of Britain as a whole.

The English had some excuse for Anglocentricity. The inhabitants of England made up over 80 per cent of the population of the United Kingdom:

Population of the United Kingdom

	1901	1931	1961
England	30,515	37,359	43,561
Wales	2,013	2,593	2,635
Scotland	4,472	4,043	5,184
Northern Ireland	1,237	1,243	1,427
United Kingdom	38,237	46,038	52,807

Source: Social Trends 30 (2000), p. 22.

Sheer weight of numbers gave the English economic and political predominance and the British state was really an English state with Welsh and Scottish additions. A Scot might think of 10 Downing

Street as the home of the British Prime Minister, and Westminster as the site of the British Parliament, but the political system was English and medieval in origin, predating the British state by centuries. Through English eyes, therefore, the House of Commons was as much a part of the English scene as Lord's cricket ground or the Henley Regatta. The Welsh and the Scots, meanwhile, knew that Britain never had been, and never could be, an extension of their own countries. For some purposes, mainly but not exclusively political, they were British: subjects of a British monarch, participants in a British political system, listeners to the BBC and fans of Arthur Askey or Tommy Handley. For other purposes, mainly cultural, they were profoundly Scottish or Welsh. The English had a dual nationality of which they were hardly aware, and one that caused them nothing more than a slight irritation from time to time. For the Scots and the Welsh dual nationality was more problematic. The Canadian Prime Minister Pierre Trudeau likened Canada's relations with the United States to the experience of 'sleeping with an elephant'. Likewise the Scots and the Welsh were in bed with an elephant, and although it was usually a friendly beast that kept to its side of the bed, there was always the risk, or at any rate the fear, that it would absent-mindedly roll over and crush them.[3]

In social and economic structure England, Scotland, and Wales were virtually a single nation with regional variations quite independent of the territorial divisions between the three countries. The industrial areas of south Wales, the north of England and the west of Scotland had more in common, from this point of view, than the north and south of England. It was mainly through institutions and culture that national differences were expressed. The Scots, with a long history of independent nationhood behind them, had the advantage over the Welsh of retaining some of the apparatus of a separate state. Under the 1707 Act of Union Scotland had lost its Parliament but retained its own Church, legal system, and local government, and a measure of administrative autonomy. North of the border the law courts and the police, health, education, industry, agriculture, and fishing were the responsibility of the Scottish Office, headed by a Secretary of State for Scotland with a permanent seat in the Cabinet. The established Church north of the border was the presbyterian Church of Scotland, which occupied a more prominent place in public life than its anglican counterpart. Its annual assembly debated the state of the nation as though it were a substitute Parliament. In Scotland the high street banks still enjoyed the right, which English banks had lost in the nineteenth century, to issue their own banknotes. The occasional refusal of English taxi-drivers, hoteliers, and others to accept payment in Scottish notes was a recurrent grievance, but they were technically within their rights. Only Bank of England notes were legal tender in the United Kingdom, and governments consistently refused to grant the same status to Scottish notes.

Linguistic distinctions were more subtle. At school Scots learned to read and write standard English, and in socially ambitious quarters to speak it with a standard BBC accent or 'received pronunciation'. Middle-class Scots, however, were often bilingual, with a 'posh' accent for formal occasions and a Glaswegian, Aberdonian, or other regional accent for friends and relations. 'Lallans', a dialect of English with a vocabulary so distinctive that it was almost a separate language, was widely spoken in the lowlands. But only three per cent of Scots, living mainly in the Outer Hebrides, still spoke Gaelic.[4]

Divided between Highlander and Lowlander, Protestant and Roman Catholic, a semi-anglicized elite and an impregnably Scottish working class, Scotland was a land of great diversity. There was no such thing as a typical Scot, and 'Scottishness' was a patchwork made up of the Calvinism of John Knox, the martial traditions of the Scottish soldier, the egalitarian spirit of Robert Burns, and the romantic Toryism of Walter Scott. It was all stitched together by a sense of difference from, or rivalry with, England. The unofficial national anthem was 'Scots Wha Hae', Burns's celebration of the defeat of the English at Bannockburn in 1314. A strong thread of militarism ran through Scottish history and the Scottish regiments, of which there were still a dozen in the late 1940s, were 'celebrated in music, story, painting and statue as the tartan clad icons of the Scottish nation'.[5] Scots also tended to see themselves as less class-ridden and more democratic than the English. Both the Church, with its presbyterian structure, and the educational system, with its ladder of opportunity for the bright working-class boy or 'lad o' pairts', nurtured the idea of a career open to the talents. Burns's poem, 'A Man's a Man for a' that', the equivalent in its day of John Lennon's 'Imagine', was a hymn to the virtues of the common man and a utopian future:

> For a' that, and a' that
> It's comin' yet for a' that
> That man to man, the world o'er
> Shall brithers be for a' that

These were noble sentiments but the Scots, like the English, were great imperialists, and the possession of a world-wide Empire was one of the major interests the two peoples had in common. The passionate desire of the Scots to defeat the English was expressed mainly through football. Alternating between Wembley and Hampden Park, the annual international served the Scots as a substitute for battle, with victory away from home the emotional equivalent of the invasion and conquest of England.[6]

Wales, a submerged and fragmented nation, had been governed since the sixteenth century as an integral part of England, yet in 1951 nearly one-third of the population were bilingual, speaking Welsh as well as English. Many of the English and Scots had a smattering or more of French, German, or Italian, but Welsh was as impenetrable to them as Finnish or Serbo-Croat. 'No Englishman can understand the Welsh', Megan Lloyd George told the House of Commons in 1944. 'However much he may try, and however sympathetic he may feel, he cannot get inside the skin and bones of a Welshman unless he be born again.'[7] Apart from such bodies as the University of Wales, the National Library of Wales, and the Welsh National Opera, national institutions were few and there was no Welsh Office or Secretary for Wales. It was also more difficult than it was in Scotland to establish a sense of common national identity. The English-speaking Welsh of the south, with their rugby clubs, male voice choirs, and local branches of the National Union of Mineworkers, were a familiar part of British life. The playwright Emlyn Williams, the poet Dylan Thomas, the actor Richard Burton, the comedian and singer Harry Secombe, personified an Anglo-Welsh identity that contrasted strongly with the identity of Welsh-speaking Wales, celebrated in poetry and song at the annual national *eisteddfod*. The strongest unifying thread in Welsh culture was an almost universal passion for rugby, which the Welsh had adopted, in preference to association football, as the people's game. 'Rugby', writes Richard Holt, 'became a new Welsh myth, a unifying belief, a strand in the national character that gained strength from being so tightly entwined with the idea of ancient liberties reborn, of a rich and independent culture.'[8]

In the 1940s and 1950s the differences between England, Scotland, and Wales were seldom political issues. All three countries were tightly bound into a two-party system based on distinctions of ideology and class that transcended issues of nationality. The Conservatives had long been the party of the Union and were known in Scotland as the Conservative and Unionist party. Labour, which in the past had displayed some interest in Home Rule for Scotland and Wales, was committed to a highly centralized model of state socialism. Beyond the creation of a Welsh Gas Board, and a Welsh Hospitals Board, there was no recognition of Wales as a separate entity in the nationalization programme. Where coal, electricity or transport were concerned, regional boundaries ignored national distinctions.[9] The cause of Home Rule lived on in the Liberal party, and still had the support of some Labour politicians in Scotland and Wales, but the big battalions were firmly opposed to devolution.

The Labour–Conservative duopoly was sustained in the 1940s and 1950s by the effectiveness of government from the centre and the benefits it conferred on both Scotland and Wales. Both nations had suffered greatly from the decline of staple industries between the wars, a predicament that gave rise to stirrings of nationalist resentment against rule from London. After the war, however, Whitehall and Westminster delivered the welfare state and appeared, at any rate, to be delivering full employment. In 1945 Labour captured 25 of the 36 Welsh seats, leaving the Liberals with seven and the Conservatives with four, the start of an era of Labour hegemony in Welsh politics. Scotland was more evenly balanced, with 29 Conservative seats, five Liberal and 37 Labour, and by the 1950s the pendulum was swinging back to the Conservatives. In the general election of 1955 they won 36 of the Scottish seats while Labour won 34 and the Liberals one.

The Nationalists

As long as the political system continued to work (or appear to work) in the interests of all parts of Britain there was little scope for Scottish and Welsh nationalism, but undercurrents of nationalism persisted. The Scottish National Party and Plaid Cymru, both founded between the wars, kept the cause of political independence alive, if only just. Their candidates won only a handful of votes in the seats they contested at general elections. More significant was the degree of sentiment in both countries in favour of a measure of self-government in home affairs. Scottish Convention, founded by John McCormick as a breakaway from the Scottish National Party in 1942, ran an effective non-party campaign for self-government in the late 1940s. In 1949 nearly two million people signed a Covenant in favour of Scottish Home Rule, but the numbers were more impressive than the momentum behind them. Compared with such issues as housing or the cost of living, constitutional reform was a comparatively minor issue, low down the list of voters' priorities. The Labour government ignored the Covenant while the Conservatives made sympathetic noises without any commitment to constitutional change.

McCormick now lent his assistance to an escapade more in tune with an older nationalist tradition of antiquarian romance. In the small hours of the morning of Christmas Day 1950 four young Scots, led by Ian Hamilton, a law student at the University of Glasgow, broke into Westminster Abbey and stole from beneath the Coronation throne the Stone of Destiny on which the early kings of Scotland had been crowned until its removal from Scone Abbey in 1296 by the marauding English monarch Edward I. As they took hold of it the Stone broke into two, but the conspirators managed to smuggle both parts north of the border, where it was reassembled by a stonemason and left to be rediscovered by the police in the ruins of Arbroath Abbey. Restored to Westminster Abbey, it took its place in the coronation of Elizabeth II in June 1953. Although the thieves were identified none of them was prosecuted, and there were no political repercussions beyond the fact that it fertilized once more the patriotic myth of the era of William Wallace and Robert the Bruce, when the Scots fought and won their independence from the English.[10]

In the general elections of 1950 and 1951 party politics resumed their sway and Scottish grievances were assuaged by full employment and the welfare state. 'Scotland', wrote *Time* magazine in December 1954,

> is enjoying a prosperity so bounteous that the canny Scots regard it almost with suspicion...Industrial production is at an all-time high, up 10 per cent in the past two years alone. From John o' Groats to the Mull of Galloway, unemployment is almost unknown. Glasgow, whose Clyde-side shipyards make it the world's biggest builders of ships, is booming. More important, through energetic promotion Scots have succeeded in diversifying their industry against a new time of trouble; in the past five years, 500 firms have established new factories or made major expansion in Scotland.[11]

In Wales nationalism took the predominantly cultural form of a campaign to preserve the Welsh language, whose speakers were fighting a rearguard battle in the rural west and north-west against a growing majority of English-speakers in the rest of the country. In October 1941 a petition signed by approximately 400,000 people, and appealing for the Welsh language to be placed on a footing of equality with English in the Welsh courts, was presented to Parliament. The demand was partly conceded by the Home Secretary, Herbert Morrison, in the Welsh Courts Act of 1942.[12] Apart from the language question there continued to be some sentiment in Welsh Labour circles in favour of the creation of a separate Welsh Office, or even an elected Welsh assembly. In the general election of 1945 Labour won 25 of the 36 Welsh constituencies, but Attlee and his colleagues were committed to centralized planning from Whitehall, and Bevan, the most powerful Welshman in the Cabinet, repeatedly opposed concessions to nationalism. Nor did they seem necessary at the time. Wales benefited more than any other region of Great Britain from the impact of war and regional policies on the economy. In 1951 the unemployment rate for the Principality stood at 2.7 per cent. In 1937 the figure had been 20.7 per cent.[13]

If nationalism was weak in Scotland and Wales, English nationalism—in the sense of a nationalism directed against the Scots and the Welsh—was either non-existent or very effectively concealed. Nor was it easy to define an English national identity. The North of England and the South were thought of as contrasting civilizations—hard and soft, industrial and pastoral, dissenting and anglican, radical and Tory. The trilogy of events which together constituted Britain's 'finest hour'—Dunkirk, the Battle of Britain, and the Blitz—were all set in the south of England and suffused in retrospect with the romantic imagery of Powell and Pressburger's great wartime film, *A Canterbury Tale*. The Humphrey Jennings documentary, *Diary for Timothy*, a record of events in the autumn and winter of 1944 compiled for the benefit of a fictional baby born on the fifth anniversary of the outbreak of war, features a Welsh miner, Goronwy, and a reference to the slums of Glasgow, but Timothy's home is in Henley-on-Thames, the script is by E. M. Forster and the narrator is Michael Redgrave. As so often, Britain was represented by England, and England by the Deep South.

Pride and Prejudice

In the mid-twentieth century the peoples of Europe were more distinctive in their customs and values than they are today. T. S. Eliot, writing in 1949, listed the characteristic interests of the English as 'Derby Day, Henley Regatta, Cowes, the twelfth of August, a cup final, the dog races, the pin table, the dart board, Wensleydale cheese, boiled cabbage cut into sections, beetroot in vinegar, nineteenth-century Gothic churches, and the music of Elgar.'[14]

If he made no mention of test matches, Colman's mustard, or afternoon tea, it was because there were scores of English peculiarities from which everyone was free to compile his or her own personal selection. That larger entity, Great Britain, stood out among the nation-states of Europe for its long unbroken record of parliamentary government, domestic peace, and social and economic progress. In the first half of the twentieth century two great wars had bound classes, regions, and nations together in a mighty collective effort. The First World War, however, was recalled with mixed emotions. The Second World War was fast becoming the British national myth.

Flattering descriptions of English/British national character were one of the growth industries of the war years, an inevitable consequence of the need to sustain morale by painting in black-and white terms the contrast between the civilized qualities of the British and the barbaric nature of the enemy. In his analysis of 'the myth of the blitz', Angus Calder sets out the conflict between British and German values as defined by the propagandists of the home front:[15]

England (Britain)	Germany
Freedom	Tyranny
Improvisation	Calculation
Volunteer spirit	Drilling
Friendliness	Brutality
Tolerance	Persecution
Timeless landscape	Mechanization
Patience	Aggression
Calm	Frenzy
A thousand years of peace	The 'Thousand-Year Reich' dedicated to war

It is almost impossible to overestimate the pride which the British took, between 1945 and the Suez debacle of 1956, in their contribution to the

Second World War. A generalization so broad must allow for some exceptions, but the war was enshrined in the collective memory of the British as an epic narrative in which they were engaged in an all-out struggle against evil. It was the story told in Churchill's war memoirs and the works of admirals, generals, air marshals, fighter pilots, and inmates of Colditz. It was recapitulated in television documentaries like the BBC's *War in the Air* (1954). Last but not least were the many feature films in which heroic episodes in the war were re-enacted by much loved actors like Jack Hawkins and John Mills. Hawkins appeared in *The Small Back Room* (1948), *Angels One Five* (1951), *The Cruel Sea* (1953), *The Malta Story* (1953), and *The Bridge on the River Kwai* (1957); Mills in *The Way to the Stars* (1945), *The Colditz Story* (1953), *Above Us the Waves* (1954), *I Was Monty's Double* (1958), and *Dunkirk* (1958). For more than a decade after 1945 the British fought the war all over again in the cinema. In 1953 'The Cruel Sea' was nominated, in response to a Gallup poll, as the best film people had seen that year; in 1955 it was 'The Dam Busters'.[16]

In British war movies the heroes were men who kept their emotions firmly under control and displayed a 'stiff upper lip' in times of crisis. There was much truth in the fiction. Men of all classes had been schooled in tough or at any rate stoical conceptions of manliness. The boarding schools to which the children of the upper classes were sent at an early age were for the most part institutions with chilly dormitories, harsh punishments, and an ethos of Darwinian competition. Emotional starvation was almost an essential precondition for anyone seeking to govern the country. In both the working and the middle classes it was still the norm (though not always the practice) for the husband to act as the breadwinner, sparing his wife from the necessity of going out to work and freeing her to manage the home. The welfare state had eased the burden a little, but most adult males of the 1940s and 1950s had been schooled in the harsher conditions of the inter-war years. The economy, meanwhile, still depended heavily on the muscular strength and physical endurance of the labourer or semi-skilled worker. War movies themselves were a constant reminder of the fact that men had an obligation to fight for their country. Women were expected to play a supporting role, to suffer and perhaps be killed, but never to enter the field of battle as combatants. The conscription of young men into the armed forces continued until 1961.

Geoffrey Gorer, a well-known contemporary commentator whose work was part journalism and part social anthropology, described the English—his research did not extend to Scotland or Wales—as 'among the most peaceful, gentle, courteous and orderly populations that the civilized world has ever seen'. The explanation lay, he argued, in the effectiveness with which they had repressed their more pugnacious instincts: 'The control of aggression, when it has gone to such remarkable lengths that you hardly ever see a fight in a bar (a not uncommon spectacle in most of the rest of Europe or in the USA), when football crowds are as orderly as church meetings, when all the frustrations and annoyances symbolized by queueing are met with orderliness and good humour modified, at most, by a few grumbles and high words, then this orderliness and gentleness...calls for an explanation if the dynamics of English character are to be effectively described.' Stripped to its essentials, Gorer's own explanation was that the orderly public behaviour of the English was due to their repression of their private emotions and sexual drives. Foreign observers were therefore close to the truth in describing the English as cold or puritanical.[17]

This widespread belief in English or British national character was accompanied by a sense of pride. The writer Doris Lessing, arriving in Britain from Rhodesia in 1949, was dismayed by the drabness of London but impressed by the self-belief of the inhabitants: 'Britain was still best: that was so deeply part of how citizens thought, it was taken for granted. Education, food, health, anything at all—best. The British Empire, then on its last legs—the best.'[18] She was certainly right about attitudes towards food. The first edition of the *Good Food Guide* in 1951 listed 484 restaurants, pubs, and hotels serving food outside London. Of these only eleven served mainly foreign food.[19]

Lessing, a Communist sympathizer, was reflecting on the patriotism of the Left, which took a special pride in the National Health Service and regarded the welfare state as a model of social progress and an example to the rest of the world. Aspects of this civic patriotism were on show in the 1951 Festival of Britain, which sought to show that the British had now recovered from the war and were now once more ready to lead the world in the arts of peace. By coincidence, the Festival was followed two years later by another great national celebration, the Coronation of Elizabeth II. If the Festival heralded a new social democratic

Britain, the Coronation was a quasi-religious celebration of the unity of the nation. Among those dropping in on the street parties of the East End were two sociologists: Michael Young, the Labour party research officer who had drafted the 1945 election manifesto, and Edward Shils, a visiting academic from Chicago. Riveted by the experience, they wrote an article in which they interpreted the Coronation as 'the ceremonial occasion for the affirmation of the moral values by which society lives. It was an act of national communion.' The depth of popular attachment to the monarchy, they argued, was a reflection of the role it had played in the creation of a set of common basic values: 'Over the past century British society, despite distinctions of nationality and social status, has achieved a degree of moral unity equalled by no other large national state. The assimilation of the working class into the moral consensus of British society, though certainly far from complete, has gone further in Britain than anywhere else...'[20]

The notion that Britain excelled in social harmony and civic pride was paralleled by the conviction that Britain still led the world in science and industry. There was much celebration of the 'boffins' who had pioneered radar, the jet engine, the 'bouncing bomb', and the Mulberry harbours. Whitehall officials were well aware of the long-term danger to British industry from German and Japanese competition. But the belief that British was best was deeply rooted and appeared for the moment to accord with the facts. 'More than half the world's merchant fleets are being built in this country', a Pathe News commentator told cinema audiences in September 1948. 'At Clydebank, the nerve-centre of the shipping industry and birthplace of the great Queen liners, one hundred and fifty-seven ships are being fitted out. Attention to detail, slim graceful lines, no mass produced ideas, that's what has given Scottish shipbuilders the greatest reputation around the world.'[21]

Two months later it was the turn of the car industry to receive the Pathe treatment. 'Britain's industrial skill is on parade. As the finest and latest British cars go on show at Earl's Court in the first motor exhibition for ten years, orders pour in from all over the world... The new cars are a great advance in looks and performance. By modernizing body styles home manufacturers have answered long-standing complaints that British design was too conservative. Low prices and low petrol consumption are likely to outstrip foreign competition.'[22] In reality the performance of the British motor industry was patchy. The 1948 motor show saw the launch of one of the most commercially successful of British cars, the Morris Minor. It was the work of Alec Issigonis, the son of a Greek father and a Bavarian mother displaced from Turkey by the Greco–Turkish war of 1920–2. An engineering graduate of Battersea Polytechnic who had repeatedly failed the maths element in the course, Issignonis had joined Morris Motors in 1936 and designed the car during the war. His employer, Lord Nuffield, disparaged it on the grounds that it looked like 'a poached egg', but it was easy to drive, inspired the affection of its owners, and continued in production with many variations until 1972, by which time 1.6 million Morris Minors had been sold. British cars in general, however, 'acquired a reputation for unreliability that would take years to live down'. Their success in overseas markets was mainly due to the temporary absence of competition from Volkswagen, Renault, and other European manufacturers. By 1956 the German car industry had overtaken the British in output and exports.[23]

If British car manufacturers were losing ground in Europe, there were still soft markets in the Commonwealth and Empire, and the home market was almost monopolized by domestic producers. In 1956 Britain imported 6,885 cars and exported 335,397. A Renault Deux-Chevaux or Volkswagen Beatle would have been an unusual sight in a British street. In aircraft, clothing, footwear, machine tools, even toys, the British exported more goods than they imported, and British brand names enjoyed international recognition. In the mid-1950s, 70 per cent of all the motorcycles in the world were made in Britain by Triumph, Norton Villiers, and BSA.[24]

Integral to this sense of national self-esteem was the conviction that the British way of life was exceptional and Anglo-Saxon destinies forever separate from those of any other European people.

Race and Immigration

The Irish, defined as all those born in Eire but resident in Britain, were by far the largest of the ethnic minorities in Britain. Although Eire had remained neutral during the Second World War, it was still technically in 1945 a Dominion within the British Commonwealth, thus entitling Irish citizens to live and work in Britain and enjoy the same rights as other British citizens. When in 1948 Ireland became a republic and left the Commonwealth, the Attlee government decided to allow the Irish the same rights as they had possessed before. This unique arrangement ensured a supply of largely unskilled labour for the British economy, while Irish migrants earned a higher wage, or found employment opportunities that were unobtainable at home.

According to the 1951 census residents of Britain born in Eire numbered 716,028, compared with the next largest group of 17,218 West Indians.[25] They were also the most rapidly growing of the immigrant communities. Between 1946 and 1956 about 320,000 people emigrated from Ireland. The vast majority were destined for Britain, though not necessarily as permanent residents: many took seasonal or temporary work after which they returned home. By 1961 the total born in Eire had risen to 950,978.[26]

Most Irish immigrants—like most immigrants from the Caribbean and the Indian subcontinent—were from rural backgrounds, and their first encounter with urban Britain was likely to be a shock. In his study of the Irish in post-war Britain, Enda Delaney cites the experience of Richard Power, who moved to England in the mid-1950s. Like many other Irish immigrants, he took the train from Holyhead to Euston:

> Euston Station, a foggy winter morning. Derelicts still sleeping under the pillars in the main hall, like the cold clay statues of the poor who built this Victorian temple. In a barber's shop, beneath the platform, a gang of Teddy boys waited for the barber, looking as though they hadn't had a wink of sleep the night before. Grafffiti on the walls of the toilet; swearwords, illicit appointments, obscene verses...[27]

The ugliness of so many urban areas, the factory-driven pace of life after the seasonal rhythms of the countryside, the vast crowds and the traffic rushing to and fro, were the most visible signs of a foreign country and an alien way of life. It was alien morally as well. Ireland was still dominated by Roman Catholicism and the teachings of clergy who preached that England/Britain was a pagan country, pagan and Protestant being more or less interchangeable terms. This must certainly have increased the attraction and excitement of Britain for migrants seeking to escape 'from the relentless social control that had such a suffocating influence on communities across small-town and rural Ireland'.[28] Many expected to return home after a year or two of earning good money, but most of them put down roots and stayed.

The men worked mainly in the building trades, though they were also beginning to break into the professions: in England and Wales one in every ten doctors was of Irish birth. The acute shortage of nurses in the newly created National Health Service made nursing a popular choice for women immigrants, along with domestic service and office work. Ever since the nineteenth century Irish immigrants had tended to settle in London, or in Glasgow, Liverpool and the surrounding regions. In the 1950s about one-third of the Irish-born population were inhabitants of Greater London, with new arrivals tending to settle in Hammersmith, Kensington, and Paddington.[29] But the booming industrial Midlands were also a magnet for Irish workers who settled mainly in the poorer districts of Birmingham where rents were low. In 1951 an Irish official working for the Young Christian Workers' Association visited the city to report on the conditions of Irish workers there. 'The results', writes Enda Delaney,

> were quite shocking: in one house he found 50 Irishmen living together with 15 people sleeping in one room.... The 'morals' of Irish migrants in Britain were also the source of particular anxiety. Unmarried mothers, married men whose wives were in Ireland and who were living with other women, and the inevitable drunk and disorderly behaviour of Irish males were noted. Apparently, on one Monday morning, of 75 people before the courts for drink-related charges, 48 were Irish.[30]

Circumstances like this had inspired a hostile reaction to immigrants in the past, but apart from occasional signs in a landlady's window—'No Irish', or 'No coloureds, no Irish'—there was little sign of friction. The explanation could be that after more than a century of Irish settlement in Britain, and the presence of so many volunteers from the twenty-six counties in the armed forces in two world wars, the Irish were on the brink of acceptance as virtually British. Unlike some other English-speaking immigrants, they also had the advantage of being white. 'Many of those Irish who have been in Britain since the 1940s and 1950s openly acknowledge that the arrival of New Commonwealth immigrants, and their subsequent racialization, were the best things to happen to the Irish, reducing the pressures of prejudice and intolerance.'[31] An interdepartmental working party on immigration, which estimated in August 1955 that 58,700 Irish people had joined the national insurance scheme between July 1954 and June 1955, concluded that although there had been complaints from local authorities about their claims to council housing, the problems arising from Irish immigration were relatively minor:

> …it cannot be held that the same difficulties arise in the case of the Irish as in the case of coloured people. For instance an Irishman looking for lodgings is, generally speaking, not likely to have any more difficulty than an Englishman, whereas the coloured man is often turned away. In fact, the outstanding difference is that the Irish are not—whether they like it or not—a different race from the ordinary inhabitants of Great Britain, and indeed one of the difficulties in any attempt to estimate the economic and social consequences of the influx from the Republic would be to define who is Irish.[32]

Although Irish immigrants were generally accepted as British, this was by no means true of all white immigrants. During the war 190,000 Polish servicemen had served alongside the British armed forces. Rather than return to a Poland in the grip of Stalinism large numbers preferred to remain in Britain and the Labour government was keen to ease key shortages of labour by employing them. But as George Orwell recorded in November 1946:

> Recently we have seen a tremendous outcry at the T.U.C. Conference against allowing Poles to work in the two places where labour is most urgently needed—in the mines and on the land. The fact is that there is strong popular feeling in this country against foreign immigrants. It arises from simple xenophobia, partly from fear of undercutting in wages, but above all from the out-of-date notion that Britain is over-populated and that more population means more unemployment.

Two months later Orwell overheard in a Scottish hotel a conversation between two businessmen who accused the Poles of causing the housing problem in Edinburgh, taking jobs in the medical profession away from Scots, and contributing to the spread of immorality.[33]

Under pressure from the government, which was desperate to recruit additional labour for the coal mines, the National Union of Mineworkers did agree to allow Polish workers into the mines but only on three strict conditions: (1) No Polish worker was be given a job without the agreement of the local NUM branch; (2) Polish workers must join the NUM; (3) in the event of redundancy the Polish workers must be first to go. As part of its drive to deal with the general shortage of manpower the Ministry of Labour was also recruiting 'European Voluntary Workers' from displaced persons' camps in Germany and Austria. Again the National Union of Mineworkers agreed in principle to accept them, but the opposition from local branches was so strong that only 8,500 were absorbed into employment in spite of the fact that the target was 30,000. The scheme had to be abandoned, as did a similar attempt in 1951–2 to employ Italians in the coal mines. Resistance from local NUM branches also thwarted the employment of all but a handful of Hungarian refugees recruited by the Coal Board after the Soviet suppression of the Hungarian revolt in 1956.[34]

Traditionally, all subjects of the British Crown were eligible to hold a British passport and legally entitled to live and work in Britain, but a problem arose in 1946 when Canada broke with precedent and created a separate Canadian citizenship. In response the Attlee government introduced the British Nationality Act of 1948, which established two categories of British citizenship: citizenship of the independent Commonwealth countries (which by this time included India and Pakistan), and citizenship of the United Kingdom and colonies. As both categories of citizen retained the right to a British passport, and the right to live and work in Britain, the effect was to retain the legal *status quo*. According to the statute book, some eight hundred million people had the right to settle in Britain.[35]

Among those who took advantage of Britain's open door were several thousand Chinese from Hong Kong, attracted by the growing demand for Chinese restaurants. The Chinese-born population of the United Kingdom rose from about 5,000 in 1951 to between 30,000 and 50,000 by the mid-1950s. Whereas other immigrant groups tended to concentrate in the metropolitan areas, the Chinese were to be found scattered across the country, wherever there was a restaurant to be run. For Greek and Turkish Cypriots, arriving from the mid-50s onwards, the main 'pull' factor was the demand for unskilled labour. Settling mainly in the greater London area, they tended to move into occupations from which other ethnic minorities, like Jews and Italians, were moving on.[36]

In practice, immigration was never left entirely to the laws of supply and demand. 'The British government', writes Ian Spencer, 'persisted in seeking—and succeeded in finding—a variety of ways to hinder the movement of British subjects from the Caribbean, the Indian sub-continent and Africa to the United Kingdom...'[37] The most common method was to obtain the co-operation of colonial or Commonwealth governments in creating administrative obstacles that made it more difficult for intending emigrants to obtain passports. When India and Pakistan achieved independence, the governments of both countries made the issue of passports for travel to the United Kingdom dependent on financial tests. The British High Commissions in India and Pakistan had the authority to issue British passports, but as a general rule only accepted applications from whites. Such apparent restrictions all rested on bluff and ignorance among potential immigrants of their rights: as Indians and Pakistanis began to discover, a British subject did not even require a valid passport to enter the United Kingdom. 'As the law stands', the Minister of State at the Colonial Office told the House of Commons in 1954, 'any British subject from the colonies is free to enter this country at any time as long as he can produce satisfactory evidence of his British status.'[38]

Among those who were eager to find work in the United Kingdom in the years immediately after the war were unemployed workers in Barbados, British Guiana, Trinidad, and Jamaica. Citing the precedent of the use of European labour, the Governors of Trinidad and Jamaica pressed the government in London to organize the recruitment of workers from the Caribbean but a Whitehall working party which explored the question concluded in 1948 that there was no need for colonial labour except in the health services. The attitudes expressed by officials were negative and much influenced by the likelihood of strong opposition to any government scheme from workers and trade unions.[39]

The government, therefore, made no attempt to recruit workers from the Caribbean, but it could not prevent them from arriving in Britain. Aware of the desperate poverty of the peoples under their rule, colonial governors refused to obstruct emigration and allowed private enterprise to take its course. As the map shows, immigrants from the West Indies were drawn from the far-flung archipelago of Caribbean islands as well as from two British colonies on the mainland, British Honduras and British Guyana. The descendants of African slaves, they were English-speakers who had been taught in school from English textbooks, attended a Christian church and 'learned as loyal subjects of the Crown to sing "Rule Britannia" and "God save the Queen" '. The majority of emigrants were skilled or semi-skilled.[40]

The beginning of large-scale West Indian immigration to Britain is usually dated to the arrival of the *Empire Windrush* at Tilbury dock on 22 June 1948. On the initiative of the shipping company which owned it, this former troopship had called in at Jamaica on its way from Australia to England, and picked up 492 passengers who paid £28.10s [=£649] each for the passage in the hope of finding work in the 'Mother Country'. They were mostly single men or married men who had left their wives at home—there were only five complete families on board—driven from Jamaica by unemployment and low wages. 'It was curiously touching', wrote the correspondent of *The Manchester Guardian,* 'to walk along the landing stage in the grey light of the early morning and see against the white walls of the ship row upon row of dark, pensive faces looking down upon England, mostly for the first time. Had they thought England a golden land in a golden age?'

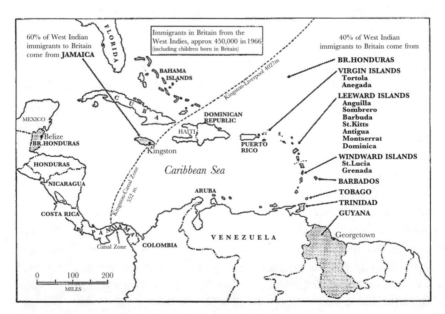

Map 4.1 Immigrants to Britain from the West Indies.

Source: Nicholas Deakin, *Colour, Citizenship and British Society* (1970), p. 31.

Whitehall, which had been apprehensive about the impending arrival of the Jamaicans, made some effort to assist them. A Colonial Office welfare official, Flight-Lieutenant Smythe from Sierra Leone, travelled with the party from Jamaica and gave them sobering advice about employment opportunities in Britain. They were met at Tilbury by more officials from the Colonial Office and the Ministry of Labour and 230 of them hastily accommodated in a disused air raid shelter in Clapham. As the nearest labour exchange was in Coldharbour Lane, Brixton, many of the newcomers settled there and founded one of the first West Indian communities in Britain.[41]

'Their arrival', the *Manchester Guardian* correspondent observed,

> has added to the worries of Mr Isaacs [the Minister of Labour] and the trade union leaders. But the more worldly-wise among them are conscious of the deeper problem posed. Britain has welcomed displaced persons and has given employment to Poles who cannot go home. 'This is right,' said one of the immigrants. 'Surely then, there is nothing against our coming, for we are British subjects. If there is—is it because we are coloured?'[42]

It was, of course. On the day the *Empire Windrush* arrived, eleven Labour MPs wrote as follows to the Prime Minister, Clement Attlee:

> The British people fortunately enjoy a profound unity without uniformity in their way of life, and are blest by the absence of a colour racial problem. An influx of coloured people domiciled here is likely to impair the harmony, strength and cohesion of our public and social life and to cause discord and unhappiness among all concerned.

They recommended legislative controls on immigration which 'would be almost universally approved by our people'.[43] Attlee decided that no action was necessary, but it would be wrong to conclude that the leaders of the party were necessarily liberal in their racial attitudes. When Attlee offered the post of Colonial Secretary to Hugh Dalton in 1950, the latter wrote in his diary: 'I had a horrid vision of pullulating, poverty stricken, diseased nigger communities, for whom one can do nothing in the short run and who, the more one tries to help them, are querulous and ungrateful...'[44]

Immigration from the Caribbean began slowly but accelerated during the 1950s:

West Indian Immigration: estimated annual totals

1951	1,500
1952	2,000
1953	2,000
1954	10,000
1955	24,000
1956	26,000
1957	22,000

Source: J. Wickenden, *Colour in Britain* (1958), reproduced in Spencer p. 90.

Labour councillors and trade unionists were among those who protested from an early stage against the immigration of coloured people. On 20 March 1950 the Labour Cabinet noted 'the difficulty of finding suitable employment for the coloured people who had come to this country in recent years from the West Indies and the view was expressed that serious difficulties would arise if this immigration of coloured people from British colonial possessions were to continue or increase'. A Cabinet Committee deliberated on the subject but warned that any action to restrict immigration would damage Britain's reputation with the colonies and the Commonwealth. This was a view endorsed by the Cabinet at a meeting on 12 February 1951, though the Home Secretary, James Chuter Ede, warned that any substantial inflow 'might produce a situation in the United Kingdom rendering legislation for its control essential'.[45]

From the mid-1950s onwards, the West Indians were joined by smaller numbers of Indians and Pakistanis:

Immigration from India and Pakistan

	Indians	Pakistanis
1955	5,800	1,850
1956	5,600	2,100
1957	6,000	5,200

Source: R.B. Davison, *Black British: Immigrants to England* (Oxford, 1966), p. 3, reproduced in Spencer p. 90.

There had of course been a scattering of immigrants from the Indian subcontinent before this, but they were mainly seamen living in the port towns. In 1949 there were fewer than 100 Indians in Birmingham.[46]

'By the early 1950s', wrote the social historian Harry Hopkins, 'Londoners had grown accustomed to the sight of loose-limbed Jamaicans strolling nonchalantly along in groups, strange hats perched on the backs of their heads, bright blue suits flapping about them, dazzle ties and black-and-white brogues bringing a touch of zaniness to the post-war scene. It was a gaiety, alas, which did not last.'[47] Of the Caribbean immigrants, more than half settled in such areas of London as Brixton, Stepney, and Notting Hill Gate, and the remainder mainly in Birmingham and the West Midlands. These same areas also attracted Indians and Pakistanis, but the pattern of Asian settlement was more widespread, extending into the Home Counties, the East Midlands, and West Yorkshire.[48]

In the case of both West Indians and South Asians, the first wave of immigrants consisted mainly of single males, who intended to work in Britain for a few years before returning to their homes and families. The West Indians were employed mostly as manual workers in the public sector, working for the Post Office, London Transport, the National Health Service, and municipal bus services, while the Asians, though very diverse, included many shopkeepers and white-collar workers. Once established, they were joined by networks of friends and relations, including wives-to-be, and the idea of returning home eventually faded. For the first generation of their children, born in the late 1950s and early 1960s, Britain was home.

Unlike the Turkish guest-workers in West Germany, coloured immigrants to Britain were entitled to the vote and were indeed in a position of legal equality with all other citizens. Unlike the black population of South Africa under apartheid, they were free to walk the same pavements, travel on the same bus, or enter the same café, as whites. For all that, the tolerance extended to New Commonwealth immigrants was limited. In formal legal terms there was no distinction between people on the basis of the colour of their skin. In social reality black people were usually treated either as second-class citizens, or as aliens with no right to be in Britain at all.

Since the first wave of post-war black immigrants consisted mainly of young men from the Caribbean it was they who attracted the most attention. At first, as Mike and Trevor Phillips write, newspaper stories about them were mainly friendly, if patronizing. 'Within a few months they had turned into stories which represented the migrants as a threat, often regurgitating urban myths about drugging and abducting young women.' The *South London Press* reported in November 1948: 'Many of the West Indians are skilled workers who quickly found jobs and homes, but others, reinforced by some who had come to this country earlier, are drifting into crime, vagrancy, and other anti-social activities.'[49] While some West Indians were involved in criminal activities, this had much to do with the fact that the areas in which they settled in London were already notorious for gambling, drinking, and prostitution. On a visit to London in 1955 the American 'sexologist', Dr Alfred Kinsey, said that he had never seen so much blatant sexual behaviour on the streets. He claimed to have counted a thousand prostitutes at work in the West End one Saturday night. Among those who recruited and organized them were a number of West Indian immigrants who made large sums of money out of 'the game'.[50] The fear that white women would become the victim of predatory black males was a recurrent factor in racial prejudice and a sample survey carried out by Michael Banton in 1956 showed that 30 per cent believed that coloured people had stronger sexual urges than white people. This was a fantasy: in the London underworld most of the customers were white, and white women were as likely as black men to reveal an appetite for inter-racial sex.[51]

In the phraseology of the time, a 'colour bar' was operated in many workplaces. But the main flashpoint in race relations was housing. Newly arrived immigrants could not obtain council housing, which was available only to those who had been residents of the United Kingdom for five years. Compelled to look elsewhere, coloured immigrants encountered many obstacles. Anthony Richmond described the situation in 1961: 'Whether he wishes to rent furnished rooms, with or without board, to take an unfurnished flat, to buy or lease a house or flat, or obtain temporary accommodation in a hotel, he is liable to find his colour a handicap to him. This is true irrespective of his social status. He may be a stowaway recently arrived from the colonies, a skilled worker or professional man, a student, politician, or member of the African nobility; it will make no difference.' Of landladies registering to offer accommodation to students in London, about 70 per cent were unwilling to accept coloured students, 'and as far as very dark Africans or West Indians were concerned the figure was nearer 85 per cent'. Landladies would display signs that read: 'Room for rent. No Irish. No Coloureds. No Children. No Dogs.'[52]

If landladies were of little help, there were always landlords with the capital to buy up whole houses, or even rows of houses, to let. Since most coloured immigrants were poor and could only afford a low rent, the key to profitability was overcrowding. Large houses which had been built for prosperous Victorians were subdivided and let out in rooms with two, three, or four people sharing a room, and many more sharing the basic facilities: a cooker, a toilet, a paraffin heater. Sometimes the house would also have a bath, sometimes not. Conditions like this could just about be tolerated as long as immigrants saw themselves as transients whose aim was to make a little money in Britain before returning home to Jamaica or Trinidad. But by the mid-1950s more and more women were coming to join the men and families with young children were becoming permanently settled in Britain. West Indian families began to buy their own properties and sub-let them, which of course did nothing to ease the anxieties of white residents who complained that expanding immigrant communities were turning respectable streets into slums and driving down the value of property.

In 1952 the Conservative MP for Louth, Cyril Osborne, began a lone campaign in the House of Commons for immigration controls. One of the very few Tory MPs from a working-class background, Osborne was the son of a Nottinghamshire coal-miner. Having left school at fourteen, and served in the ranks in the First World War, he obtained a qualification in economics and went on to become a successful businessman. A stern puritan who disapproved of all departures from high Victorian morality, Osborne feared that West Indian or Asian immigrants would undermine the moral and physical health of Britain. 'While insisting that he was not racially prejudiced', writes Robert Pearce, 'he called for restrictions on entry on several grounds: the sheer volume of actual or potential immigrants; the abuse of the welfare state ("the honey pot"); overcrowding; crime, especially drug trafficking and prostitution; unemployment; and health, especially tuberculosis and leprosy.'[53]

Though he gave no hint of his anxieties in public, Churchill too was apprehensive about the prospect of a 'magpie society'.[54] Both his own government (1951–5) and the government of his successor Anthony Eden (1955–7), secretly considered the question and debated the issue of controls. Some ministers spoke out in favour of legislation to restrict immigration. According to a Cabinet minute of 1955:

If immigration from the colonies and, for that matter, from India and Pakistan are allowed to continue unchecked, there is a real danger that over the years there would be a significant change in the racial character of the English people.

A Colonial Office minute declared that

a large coloured community as a noticeable feature of our social life would weaken that concept of England, or Britain, to which people of British stock throughout the Commonwealth are attached.[55]

Partly from fear of alienating 'liberal opinion' at home, and partly from the desire to maintain the 'Commonwealth ideal', the Cabinet procrastinated.

According to Anthony Richmond about one-third of the British were 'extremely prejudiced' against coloured people, one-third were tolerant and approved of their coming to Britain, and one-third were undecided.[56] But even the one-third who were tolerant, and quite innocent of conscious racism, had absorbed attitudes that would now be regarded as suspect.

This was also true to some extent of the pro-immigrant activities of the 1950s. 'Race relations in Britain', as Anna Coote and Mike Phillips put it,

began as a species of neo-colonial welfare, for which the precedents had been the colonial experience itself, and the experience of coping with foreign troops on British soil. As a result, the 1950s spawned a myriad of liaison committees, friendship councils, consultative committees, Anglo-Caribbean cricket matches and inter-racial tea parties.... Race relations in Britain were regarded as a local affair and were so 'non-political' that it was unacceptable even to use words like 'race' or 'colour'. Members of the pro-immigrant lobby had difficulty finding ways to describe black people and resorted to such euphemisms as 'overseas friends' and 'Commonwealth visitors.'[57]

The Last Days of Empire

The reality of imperial decline was camouflaged for a time by the growth of the 'British Commonwealth of Nations', the voluntary association of former British colonies that were now self-governing states. In 1945 the Commonwealth consisted of the white settler Dominions of

Canada, Australia, New Zealand, and South Africa, all of which accepted King George VI as their own head of state. In spite of the presence of a large French-speaking minority in Quebec, and the fact that Boers outnumbered Britons in South Africa, it was a fundamentally Anglo-Saxon association bound together by ties of kinship and sentiment, and a common allegiance to the Crown. Statesmen from the white Commonwealth, like Robert Menzies of Australia or Jan Christian Smuts of South Africa, were familiar figures in British public life. Smuts, as Bill Schwarz has pointed out, won a degree of popularity and respect in Britain that now seems rather mysterious. Speeches by him that now read like a string of platitudes were received at the time as great moral insights from the philosopher-king of the Empire. 'Like generations of Scots and Welsh before him', writes Schwarz, 'he was pulled into a field-force of English *ethnicity*, reviving it as no domestic could.' To put it another way, he expressed the idea of white supremacy in terms that were morally palatable to English audiences.

Meanwhile the colonial empire was recovering some of the importance it had once enjoyed under Joseph Chamberlain. As in his day, the Colonial Office was planning a great imperial project, the Central African Federation, to be constituted from Northern Rhodesia and Nyasaland, colonies with overwhelming black majorities, and Southern Rhodesia, which had a more substantial white minority and was intended to be the leading element in the Federation. The blueprint was inherited by the incoming Churchill government in 1951 and the Central African Federation finally established in 1953 under the leadership of Sir Roy Welensky. A new and promising chapter of imperial history had begun, with great opportunities for ambitious young Britons—or so it seemed at the time.

Up to a point, therefore, the withdrawal from India was counterbalanced by an imperial revival: for a decade or more the Commonwealth and Empire were of growing importance. Between 1946 and 1950 the proportion of British imports from the Sterling Area rose from 32.8 to 38 per cent, while the proportion of exports sold to the Sterling Area rose from 45.3 to 47.8 per cent. Though western Europe took a higher proportion of British exports than before the war it remained a less important market. By 1955 the Sterling Area was an even more important source of imports, accounting for 39.4 per cent; but where export markets were concerned the picture was changing fast: western Europe, which now took 36.4 per cent of British exports, had clearly overtaken the Sterling Area, which now accounted for only 27.4 per cent of exports. The British were in fact exploiting their colonies in order to keep down the costs of primary commodities like rubber, cocoa, and coffee, while at the same time relying on the Empire as a market for British manufactured goods. A resolution in favour of the maintenance of imperial preference was regularly passed with acclaim at the annual conference of the Conservative party.

Some historians argue that the Empire never had very much effect on British consciousness. If, as Sir John Seeley had once written, the British had acquired an Empire in a 'fit of absence of mind', they were no less absent-minded in the losing of it. Orwell thought this was true of the mass of the people. 'It is quite true that the English are hypocritical about their Empire', he wrote. 'In the working class this hypocrisy takes the form of not knowing that the Empire exists.' A survey conducted for the Colonial Office in 1948 discovered that three-quarters of those interviewed could not distinguish between a dominion and a colony, only half could name a single colony correctly, and only one-third could name a food or raw material and the colony it came from.[58] Ignorance of imperial facts, however, was perfectly compatible with a general belief in the superiority of whites over coloured peoples, a belief instilled into the British by the popular culture of imperialism which they encountered all around them. As one historian writes:

> A last generation of schoolchildren was raised on the certainties of imperial rule in the 1950s. The sentiments of the old school text books still prevailed; much children's literature continued to be pale, updated versions of the late nineteenth century children's classics; the cinema, both in feature films and in Saturday morning children's serials, continued to portray adventure in imperial settings, grappling with peoples at best quaint, at worst treacherous, and in both cases requiring a strong hand to lead them in paths designed for their own good. Youth organizations, Empire annuals, and a multitude of children's publications continued to carry an imperial message of missionary, administrative, and commercial endeavour that would lead to the betterment of all.[59]

It was the Suez fiasco of 1956, not the withdrawal from India in 1947, that dealt the final blow to British imperialism, and began to erode a sense of impregnable superiority based on memories of Wolfe at Quebec, Nelson at Trafalgar, Wellington at Waterloo, and victory in two world wars. Decolonisation posed little threat to the employment or living standards of most Britons, which may explain why the break-up of the Empire had so few domestic consequences. Perhaps, however, the knowledge that Britain had once possessed a world-wide empire, contributed over the next few years to the growth of a national inferiority complex.

The Legacy of War

This first section of the book is entitled 'the aftermath of war'. How then can we sum up its effects? Here I turn back to the photograph, referred to in the introduction, of my grammar school class of '57. Out of the war had come a Labour government, a welfare state, and an economy from which dole queues and hunger marches were banished, hopefully for all time. The threat of nuclear warfare hung over us but I doubt if many of us were seriously worried. Not only did we have our free secondary education, our free health service, and the virtual certainty of a job or university place on leaving school. We had television and Radio Luxemburg and, by the time we were in Sixth Form, *Lady Chatterley's Lover*. When the school held a mock general election—it must have been 1959—the Conservative candidate won, but Conservatives at that time saw themselves as the more modern and progressive of the two main parties. I feel sure that most of us were quite unconscious of the extent to which we were conservatives with a small 'c' and hence, by the standards of a future time, 'wrong' about many things. Wrong to believe in grammar schools. Wrong to believe that a woman's place was in the home. Wrong to think of homosexuals—though we hardly ever thought of them at all—as perverts. Wrong if we were Conservative, wrong if we were Labour, because the whole post-war consensus was misconceived. Wrong to believe, with Flanders and Swann, that the English were best (see below pp. 229–30).

In spite of full employment and the welfare state, the economic and social structure of Britain was much the same as it had been in the 1920s and 1930s and the same was true of moral and cultural attitudes. In his memoir of the Burma campaign, George MacDonald Fraser writes of the infantrymen with whom he served in the Border Regiment, and the votes they cast by postal ballot in the general election of 1945:

They wanted jobs, and security, and a better future for their children than they had had—and they got that, and were thankful for it. It was what they had fought for, over and beyond the pressing need of ensuring that Britain did not become a Nazi slave state.

Still, the Britain they see in their old age is hardly the 'land fit for heroes' that they envisaged—if that land existed in their imaginations, it was probably a place where the pre-war values co-existed with decent wages and housing. It was a reasonable, perfectly possible dream, and for a time it existed, more or less. And then it changed, in the name of progress and enlightenment, which meant the destruction of much that they had fought for and held dear, and the betrayal of familiar things that they had loved. Some of them, to superficial minds, will seem terribly trivial, even ludicrously so—things like county names, and shillings and pence, and the King James Version—and yards and feet and inches—yet they matter to a nation.

As he warms to his theme, MacDonald Fraser's lament turns into a bellow of rage against the assault of a liberal-progressive Establishment on traditional values.[60] The People's War, in other words, had resulted in a People's Peace. But the People, for the most part, had been moral and cultural conservatives, and as the historian Henry Pelling pointed out, the war had also deepened that conservatism by vindicating British institutions:

Parliament, the political parties, the press, the law, the trade unions— all emerged from the war with slightly different surface features, but basically unaltered. There had not been much of that 'inspection effect' which is supposed to be one of the by-products of war, or if there had been, it had found most institutions not unsatisfactory, and so served to reinforce the view which so many people in Britain still retained: that somehow or other, things in their own country were arranged much better than elsewhere in the world—even if, in limited directions only, there might be some room for improvements.[61]

PART II

The Quest for Modernity
1957–1974

5

Managing the New Britain

The Suez fiasco, followed by the creation of the European Common Market in 1957, and the subsequent discovery that Britain's rate of economic growth was falling behind that of France and Germany, were seized upon by the government's critics as proof that Britain was a nation in long-term decline. What, they demanded to know, was the explanation of Britain's relatively sluggish performance? From the public schools to the trade unions a number of scapegoats presented themselves and opinions varied about which was the most to blame, but all the critics assumed that in some way or other the problem lay in the ingrained conservatism of British elites and institutions. 'In surveying the more somnolent regions of industry and government', wrote Anthony Sampson in *Anatomy of Britain* (1962),

> or the procession of ancient families into the Government, I have had the feeling of observing, not a settled tradition, but a desperate rearguard action against a more professional and less complacent age. Among younger men in politics, banking, industrial management and trade unions, there is clearly a growing impatience with the class-bound attitude of their elders.[1]

In August 1953 the historian A. J. P. Taylor had coined the term 'the Establishment' to define the narrow circle of individuals who governed Britain, and the privileged social backgrounds from which they were drawn. Taken up by the journalist Henry Fairlie, the word 'Establishment' became a form of shorthand denoting most of the things that were wrong with the government of Britain. The critique extended to the higher civil service and the most powerful of the Whitehall departments, the Treasury, which, it was argued, were staffed almost exclusively by Oxbridge graduates whose education was too narrowly academic to equip them with the skills required in the handling of economic and industrial problems. But it was the governments of Harold Macmillan (January 1957 to October 1963) and Sir Alec Douglas-Home (October 1963 to October 1964) who bore the main brunt of an attack from which their reputations have never quite recovered. They were constantly under fire from academics and publicists who accused them, with the aid of numerous tables of statistics, of presiding complacently over a backward economy and a stagnant society. They were mocked on stage and television by the satirists of *Beyond the Fringe* and *That Was The Week That Was.* The critique and the caricatures were shallow but reflected a generational change: to the young and ambitious the old governing class had begun to look and sound preposterously out of date.

Both Macmillan and Douglas-Home seemed to epitomize the Establishment. Macmillan, a publisher by trade, had married a daughter of the duke of Devonshire and looked entirely at home shuffling over the grouse-moors in tweeds and plus fours. The prominence in his Cabinet of so many fellow Etonians, and the appointment to office of so many of his relations, gave rise to much unfriendly comment, but Macmillan turned a deaf ear to the critics. When ill health compelled him to retire in October 1963, he engineered the succession of the fourteenth earl of Home. Sir Alec Douglas-Home, as he became on disclaiming his title in order to stand for election to the House of Commons, was the owner of a great landed estate in the Scottish borders. A country gentleman whose favourite pastimes were shooting and fishing, he was a straightforward Tory with shrewd political instincts and the misfortune to look and sound like a character who had strayed out of the pages of P. G. Wodehouse. His premiership was a gift to propagandists who claimed that Britain was in the hands of aristocratic nincompoops, though the claim was superficial. As David Cannadine has pointed out: 'The driving force in the government came from the middle classes: Butler, Brooke, Marples, Lloyd in one generation, Heath, Maudling, Boyle, and Powell in another.'[2]

An aristocratic style prevailed at Number Ten, but the Macmillan/ Douglas-Home regime marked the beginning of a modernizing era with the state in a more ambitious role. The new *dirigisme* was evident in Harold Wilson's rhetoric about the 'white heat' of the technological revolution and Edward Heath's pledge to carry out a 'quiet revolution'. Though Wilson's governments leaned to the left, and Heath's government to the right, they shared in practice the goal of converting Britain into a flourishing social democracy on the West German or Swedish model, with expanding social services paid for by a high and sustained rate of economic growth, which in turn was to be achieved by expansionary government policies and the co-operation of 'both sides of industry' in raising productivity and damping down inflation. No government between 1957 and 1974 came close to achieving this and Heath, the boldest and most committed of the modernizers, ended up leading his government over the edge of a cliff.

If the quest for modernity had succeeded there would have been no need for the radical alternative of Thatcherism, but it failed. Economic growth was maintained at a modest pace; the great leap forward promised by the politicians never took place. The politicians soon discovered that a managed economy was far more problematical than they had imagined, and the trade unions were unwilling or unable to participate. Since living standards were sufficiently comfortable to generate an underlying sense of complacency, socialist and free market alternatives were ruled out as too extreme, and the outcome was an era of muddling through, tempered by occasional initiatives like the Buchanan report on road transport, the Beeching report on the railways, and the Robbins report on higher education. All three were commissioned by the Macmillan government.

Modernizing with Macmillan

Harold Macmillan was a politician of great style. Since he was also a great actor it was hard to be sure who the real Macmillan was. As an earnest young MP for Stockton in the 1930s he had occupied an isolated position on the left of the Conservative party, immersing himself in the statistics of poverty and unemployment and arguing in favour of Keynesian policies and industrial reorganization. Some residue of that radicalism was still to be seen in Macmillan the Prime Minister. In Cabinet debates over public spending he usually took the side of the expansionists against the Treasury. Together with his minister of defence, Duncan Sandys, he put through a radical programme of cuts in the defence budget and abolished conscription, which was phased out in stages between 1957 and 1963.[3] After some hesitation, he threw his support behind his Colonial Secretary, Iain Macleod, in accelerating the withdrawal of Britain from its African colonies. In a speech to the South African Parliament in Capetown in February 1960 he declared: 'The wind of change is blowing through this continent, and whether we like it or not, this growth of national consciousness is a political fact. We must all accept it as a fact and our national policies must take account of it.' In 1960–1 he led the Cabinet and the Conservative Party away from its imperial past and entered into negotiations over the entry of Britain into the Common Market. How far Macmillan was a radical by conviction, as distinct from an opportunist like Disraeli who 'caught the Whigs bathing and made off with their clothes', is one of those imponderable questions to which Macmillan himself may not have known the answer.

Between 1950 and 1964 the annual rate of economic growth was 2.9 per cent, higher than at any time since the mid-nineteenth century. By 1960, however, the critics were highlighting the fact that France and Germany were growing much faster. Britain was therefore in *relative* economic decline, though the qualifying adjective was sometimes omitted. There was talk of 'the British Disease' and the monthly magazine *Encounter* devoted a whole issue to the subject under the title 'Suicide of a Nation?' The remedy, the critics urged, was *modernization*. In economic affairs the modernizers insisted that Britain could only be rescued from decline by greater state intervention with the aim of ensuring a higher rate of economic growth. The overriding aim was to replace the 'stop-go' policies of the 1950s with policies to promote the continuous expansion of the economy and a higher rate of economic growth. It was assumed, or at any rate hoped, that governments could obtain the co-operation of 'both sides of industry', the employers and the trade unions, in measures to raise productivity and counteract inflation. The concept of 'economic planning', which had been out of fashion since 1951, was restored to favour.

Under Macmillan the government took one or two cautious steps in the direction of 'indicative planning'. The main objective was to prevent inflation by winning the consent of the trade unions to a voluntary incomes policy. A Council on Prices, Productivity and Incomes, also known as the 'Three Wise Men', had been set up in 1957. After a balance of payments crisis in July 1961 the Chancellor of the Exchequer, Selwyn Lloyd, was compelled to announce a pay pause in the public sector in order to obtain financial support from the International

Monetary Fund. This first Conservative experiment with incomes policy proved highly unpopular but was only ever intended as a temporary measure. Selwyn Lloyd, however, also announced an initiative to promote 'indicative planning' of the economy.

In the hope of escaping from the 'stop-go' cycle of economic management, the government invited representatives of the employers and the unions to join a new body, the National Economic Development Council (NEDC or 'Neddy'), charged with examining the nation's economic performance, identifying the obstacles to growth, and seeking agreement over methods of increasing the productivity and competitiveness of industry. Surprisingly, in view of the fact that the invitation came from a Conservative government, the General Council of the TUC agreed to participate. The first NEDC report, published in February 1963, presented the results of an enquiry into seventeen industries and concluded that it should be possible to achieve an average annual rate of growth of 4 per cent.[4] 'Neddy', of course, had no executive authority. It was an attempt to revive the tripartite system of consultation between employers, unions, and government departments which had been introduced during the war, perpetuated by the Attlee governments, and fallen into disuse after the return of the Conservatives to office in 1951.

Some historians are highly critical of Macmillan on the grounds that he talked of the need for modernization but did little about it. In fact his policy was to promote industrial consensus. If the supply-side problems of British industry were to be resolved, it seemed obvious at the time that the most rational method of achieving this was through direct discussions between workers and employers, with government holding the ring and trying to facilitate the outcome. The experiment, however, broke down early on due to the fact that the employers were incapable of co-operating with one another or indeed with the NEDC. Characteristically, the only thing they could agree on was the need for an incomes policy to control wages, an idea rejected by trade-union leaders who were hoping for a Labour government in the near future.[5]

There were already strong pressures in the Conservative Party in favour of measures to curb trade-union bargaining power. 'Throughout the 1950s and especially at the end of the decade', writes John Ramsden, 'the Party leaders had stifled or ignored the increasing demands of the rank and file for legislative action to curb the freedom of the trade unions.'[6] Macmillan too was alarmed by the power of the unions, and vulnerable to the charge of appeasing them, but he preferred to keep the door to industrial consensus open. In December 1962 Macmillan circulated to the Cabinet a memorandum entitled 'Modernization of Britain' in which he proposed 'to increase our productivity by bringing our productivity capacity into full use, by eliminating restrictive practices and by developing to the utmost the new methods which technology is bringing within our reach.' By 'bringing our productivity into full use' he meant finding work for the growing number of unemployed in the regions. Fundamentally this was an attempt to work with the trade unions, and conciliate the working classes. Addressing the Cabinet in May 1962, Macmillan argued that a consensus in favour of growth could only be achieved by the reduction of class distinctions:

> In my view the time has come to state definitely we can no longer accept the difference of status between the wage earner and the salary earner...That involves the abolition of the day contract or even in some cases the hour contract. It seems to me in a modern society a remnant of a mediaeval system and shameful to modern society. We should try to substitute if we can the monthly contract at any rate the weekly and gradually the monthly...I think we have also got to make better arrangements for redundancy, partly because it is fair and partly because it helps movement and mobility which is what we want. And we have got to get better methods for retraining. We must examine health and welfare arrangements and see in what degree there are still two nations— those of the manual day-to-day workers and those of the staffs. They have got to be brought up to a higher standard.[7]

Road and Rail

A minor episode set the tone of the modernizing era. In 1961 British Rail announced that its plans for the expansion of Euston Station would involve the destruction of the Euston Arch. A massive neo-classical structure featuring forty-four foot high Doric pillars, the Arch had been designed by the architect Philip Hardwick and served since 1838 as a grand ornamental entrance to the station. At a time when the word 'Victorian' had pejorative overtones of aggressively bad taste, the Arch was probably doomed, but the poet John Betjeman led a quixotic campaign to save it and a lively controversy ensued. The decision lay ultimately with Harold Macmillan, who after some agonizing came down on the side of British Rail. Without more ado, the Arch was demolished in the winter of 1961–2. 'Its grimy Grecian bulk', wrote an anonymous contributor in *The Economist*, 'seemed to emphasize everything that was pretentious and outmoded about England, way back in the coal-burning 1950s.'

It was ironic that the Euston Arch was destroyed in the interests of expanding a railway station. The railways themselves were a Victorian legacy under growing threat from the competition of the motor car. For many years plans for a network of motorways had been gathering dust in Whitehall. Under the Macmillan government work began and the first stretch of motorway, the eight-mile long Preston by-pass (a section of the future M6) was opened by the Prime Minister himself in 1958. The following year saw the completion of the first section of the M1. 'A hundred years ago', the *Guardian* complained, 'our Victorian ancestors could build 400 miles of railway in a year: in twelve years since the post-war plan for motorways was announced in 1947 we have contrived to build eighty miles of new motor road.'[8]

Although long delayed, motorway construction made steady progress over the coming years. By 1964, as the first of the maps shows, the M1 between London and Birmingham was close to completion and there were 277 miles of motorway in use; by 1970 there were 789 miles of motorway and by 1974, 1,265 miles.

One of the most spectacular feats of civil engineering in the construction of the motorway network was Junction 6 of the M6, in the northern suburbs of Birmingham, where 18 roads met in a sequence of looping viaducts mounted on 559 columns of up to 80 feet in height. Opened in 1972, and officially known as the Gravelly Hill Interchange, it was immortalized by Alan Eaglesfield, a sub-editor at the *Birmingham Evening Mail*, who dubbed it 'Spaghetti Junction'.

The irresistible rise of the motor car brought with it problems of congestion. In 1961 the Minister of Transport, Ernest Marples—a self-made businessman from a working-class background—invited the town planner Colin Buchanan to study the long-term development of traffic in the urban areas. Published in November 1963 under the title of *Traffic in Towns*, his report caused great alarm. Both supporters of public transport and conservationists, who were beginning to react against the redevelopment of city centres, interpreted it as a licence for the unbridled

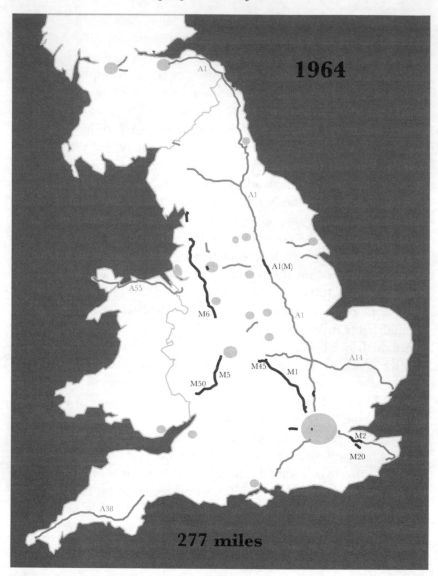

Map 5.1 Expanding the motorways 1964–74.

Source of maps: The Motorway Trust.

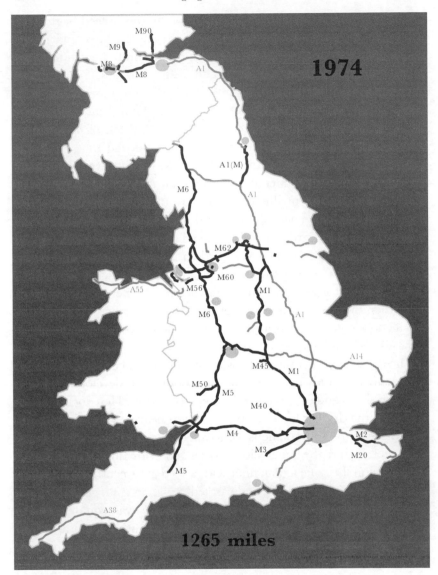

Map 5.1 Continued.

imperialism of the private motorist. Buchanan did indeed begin from the realistic assumption that the rise of the motor car could not be halted. But the aim of his report was to demonstrate how cities could absorb and manage the increase in road traffic, and he set out for urban authorities a range of options, some of which were more car-friendly than others. 'Its central premise', writes Peter Hall, 'was that certain environmental standards—maximum allowable levels of noise, pollution, etc.—must be imposed as fixed norms. Beyond that, economic trade-offs were possible and desirable. Thus, if a city was both financially able and willing, it could rebuild to admit more traffic. But if it was either unable or unwilling or both, it would have to restrain traffic, perhaps severely.' If a city wanted to admit traffic, it could build roads and car parks underground and overhead walkways to separate pedestrians from cars. If it wanted to exclude traffic it could restrict parking places or impose a congestion charge.[9] In the decades that followed *Traffic in Towns* became a manual for urban planners and it was not altogether Buchanan's fault if they tended to sacrifice eighteenth or nineteenth-century streets and squares in the interests of expressways, subways, and multi-storey car parks.

The construction of the motorway network was accompanied by the bulldozing of old town centres and the adoption of development plans in which shops and offices tended to replace homes. Here local government was the driving force. In Birmingham nearly everything around New Street station was demolished to make way for the Bull Ring shopping centre, and the inner city was ringed with dual carriageways. Birmingham 'became a doughnut with a void at its centre, cut off from the areas where people lived and worked'.[10]

The redevelopment of Newcastle upon Tyne was equally radical, driven by the local Labour Party boss T. Dan Smith, 'an abrasive and often ruthless town hall politician who had an intimidating physical presence and a booming voice which didn't brook argument'.[11] Smith accelerated Newcastle's housing programme, created a new civic centre, and won for himself in 1962 the accolade of 'planner of the year' from the *Architectural Review*. But he also engaged in extensive bribery of local government officials in order to win contracts for his company, a practice which may have been widespread in local government at the time. Though suspected of corruption he might never have been found out but for his greed in accepting bribes worth £156,000 [=£1,603,680] from an equally unscrupulous white-collar criminal, John Poulson, whose company, Open System, was one of the largest architectural practices in Britain. When Poulson went bankrupt in 1973 his dealings with Smith and other officials were exposed, and both men were sent to prison. The Conservative Home Secretary Reginald Maudling, who had chaired two of Poulson's companies, was compelled to resign, as was George Pottinger, a senior civil servant in the Scottish Office.[12]

The principal contribution of central government to urban development was the establishment of additional New Towns. Five more were approved under Macmillan and Douglas-Home: Redditch in Worcestershire, Skelmersdale in Lancashire, Runcorn in Cheshire, Washington in Tyne and Wear, and Livingston in the Scottish central belt. Seven more were designated under Harold Wilson: Northampton, Peterborough, Warrington in Cheshire, Telford in Shropshire, Milton Keynes in Buckinghamshire, Central Lancashire, and Irvine on the Ayrshire coast. By 1971 the total population of the New Towns of England and Wales was 1,432,219, and in every one of them the numbers were still growing.[13]

As the motor car advanced, question-marks gathered over the future of the rail network. 'The railways', wrote Anthony Sampson, 'are the most embarrassing of all Britain's Victorian leftovers. In the 150 years since they came into being, they have acquired a picturesque, feudal, and delightful way of life of their own, presided over by top-hatted stationmasters in cavernous halls.' Marples was again the stimulus for change. Resolved that the railways should be run as a business rather than a loss-making service to the public, he appointed the technical director of ICI, Dr Richard Beeching, the holder of a doctorate in electronics from Imperial College, London, as chairman of the British Transport Executive. His annual salary of £24,000 [=£367,200] a year, caused an outcry in the press.

Some gentle pruning of the rail network had already taken place. About 1,240 route miles were closed between the wars, leaving 19,414 miles for the nationalized industry to inherit in 1948. The British Transport Commission then formed a committee whose task was to identify little used branches like the Llangynog-Llanrhaeadr-ym-Mochnant line, whose annual income from ticket sales averaged less than a pound a day: it was closed in 1952. By the time of its abolition in 1962, the Commission had closed another 1,500 miles of railway, leaving British Railways with 17,500 miles of track and 6,800 stations.[14]

In his report of 1963, *The Reshaping of British Railways*, Beeching reported that half of the stations produced only 2 per cent of the income from passenger fares while half the routes carried only 4 per cent of the traffic. He recommended the closure of 250 routes totalling 5,000 miles of track, and 2,000 stations, a drastic scheme which the press dubbed the 'Beeching axe'. Critics of the report pointed out while the railways were being treated as a business to be judged by commercial criteria, the roads were treated as essential infrastructure paid for by the tax-payer and free of any direct charge to road-users. 'Of course', writes the rail historian and enthusiast Christian Wolmar, 'many of these branches and lines were not viable and were ripe to be axed, but the closure pro-gramme went too far, with little regard for the future needs of the railway once the roads filled up.' The rail unions and other opponents of the plan took heart from the declarations of the Labour opposition, which promised to halt the closures when the party came to power. In the event, the Wilson government accelerated the programme and announced additional closures. Between 1961 and 1969 the total length of the track was reduced from 18,124 miles to 12,098, and the number of stations from 7,025 to 3002.[15]

Mr Wilson and Mr Heath 1964–1974

Following the unexpected death of Hugh Gaitskell in January 1963, Harold Wilson was elected leader of the Labour Party. Wilson seized the opportunity of projecting Labour as the party of modernization which could break the stranglehold of the Old School Tie and restore the dynamism of the British economy. In place of the economics of stop-go—a touch on the accelerator one year, followed the year after by a slamming on of the brakes—he promised an economy planned to ensure continuous and rapid economic growth. In a famous speech at the annual Labour party conference at Scarborough in October 1963 he inspired his audience with a daring rhetorical gambit equating socialism with scientific progress:

> In all our plans for the future, we are re-defining and are restating our Socialism in terms of the scientific revolution. But that revolution can-not become a reality unless we are prepared to make far-reaching changes in economic and social attitudes which permeate our whole system of society.

The Britain that is going to be forged in the white heat of this revolution will be no place for restrictive practices or for outdated methods on either side of industry... In the Cabinet room and the board room alike those charged with the control of our affairs must be ready to think and to speak in the language of our scientific age.[16]

Here, then, was the Wilson doctrine. The remedy for Britain's malaise was state intervention to ensure economic planning and investment in science and technology. Sustained economic growth would provide the resources for an ambitious programme of social reform, and a new meritocratic Britain would take the place of the old class-divided society. In 1963–4 he almost certainly believed what he said. As a wartime civil servant, and President of the Board of Trade in the post-war Labour government, he had been a part of the regime of centralized economic planning which had delivered munitions in wartime, exports in peacetime, and 'fair shares for all'. What could be simpler than to apply similar techniques to Britain's current problems? Wilson himself, the ex-grammar schoolboy, economist, and northerner who still spoke with a Yorkshire accent, seemed to personify the values of the New Britain that Labour was planning to create.

In spite of all the currents of opinion in his favour, Wilson won the October 1964 general election by a very narrow margin with an overall majority of four seats. The high expectations he had aroused seemed at first to be borne out by Wilson's personal dynamism, the creation of a Ministry of Technology, and the remarkable achievement of George Brown, the head of the new Department of Economic Affairs, in persuading employers and unions to sign up to the 'National Plan'. Published with a great fanfare in September 1965, and claiming to cover all aspects of economic policy over the next five years, the Plan was intended to raise the annual rate of economic growth from 2 per cent to 4 per cent. The government promised to pursue a policy of expansion and the General Council of the TUC gave its blessing to a voluntary incomes policy, but the Plan was an exercise in optimism and wish-fulfilment. Economic policy remained firmly in the hands of the Treasury, which pursued a policy of moderate deflation intended to maintain the external value of the pound.

In a climate of optimism generated by the National Plan and Wilson's image as an economic wizard the Labour party won a second general election in March 1966 with a majority of 90, and political commentators speculated that Wilson had now fulfilled his ambition of making Labour into 'the natural party of government'. His reputation was punctured in July 1966, when a sterling crisis was precipitated by a seven-week long strike of merchant seamen, which had begun on 16 May. Rejecting the alternative option of a devaluation of the pound, Wilson and his Cabinet accepted a deflationary package that not only curbed social expenditure but to all intents and purposes wrecked the National Plan and the Department of Economic Affairs. The 'white heat of the scientific revolution' was no longer on the agenda, but the party's faith in public ownership was unshaken. Steel, which the Tories had privatized in the 1950s, was renationalized in 1967 when the fourteen largest companies, representing 90 per cent of production, were formed into British Steel with a merchant banker, Lord Melchett, as chairman.

In November 1967 the government was forced after all to devalue and in the end the balance of payments deficit was eliminated by the old stop-go technique of a touch on the brake followed by a touch on the accelerator. Over the six years of the Wilson governments the annual rate of economic growth was 2.6 per cent, compared with three per cent for the period 1950 to 1970 as a whole—hardly a disaster, but far from the economic miracle that had been promised.

The deflationary package of July 1966 was underpinned by a drastic new experiment in state intervention, a statutory prices and incomes policy which began with a six-month freeze on wages and salaries. Between July 1966 and the fall of the government in June 1970 there were five different phases of incomes policy in the course of which the ceiling for pay increases was gradually raised, though the policy remained statutory until January 1970:

Incomes Policies under Labour 1966–1970

July 1966–December 1966
Freeze on pay increases, exception being made for increases in pay resulting from increased output.

January 1967–June 1967
'Severe restraint': standstill continued but with exceptions for increases (a) on productivity and efficiency grounds; (b) for the lowest paid as defined by the National Board for Prices and Incomes; (c) to attract and retain manpower and (d) to eliminate anomalies in pay.

July 1967–March 1968
Prices and Incomes Acts 1967 came into effect giving the government statutory powers for a further period of seven months. Exceptions (a) to (c) of the previous policy were retained, and exception might also be made where pay for a particular group had fallen seriously out of line.

April 1968–December 1969
Statutory 3.5 per cent ceiling imposed on increases and special exceptions for pay increases (a) to attract and retain manpower; (b) low pay; (c) productivity exception bound by the rule that some benefits to the community should be felt in the form of lower prices.

January 1970–June 1970
Government guidelines with a norm of 2.5–4.5 per cent for most settlements. Exceptional increases permitted after study by the NPBI for the low paid, and for efficiency arrangements. Restructuring, extreme manpower needs and moves towards equal pay for women were also grounds for exceptional increase.

Source: Robert Taylor, *The Fifth Estate: Britain's Unions in the Modern World*, p. 241.

The honeymoon between the Labour government and the unions came to an end with the introduction of the freeze on incomes in July 1966. Frank Cousins resigned from the government and some of the largest unions elected left-wing leaders, among them Hugh Scanlon as President of the AEU (1967), Lawrence Daley as General Secretary of the National Union of Mineworkers (1969) and Jack Jones as General Secretary of the TGWU (1969).[17] The union leaders, however, were not in the position of military commanders giving orders to the rank-and-file. Negotiations with managers and employers were increasingly in the hands of shop stewards or 'workplace representatives' whose mandate was to resolve issues that arose at local level. If matters could not be resolved, shop stewards would often call an unofficial strike.

Against a background of growing industrial unrest, and political pressure from the Conservatives to act, Wilson decided in 1969 to address the issue of trade union reform. Under the Trade Disputes Act of 1906 industrial relations were largely unregulated by the law. Since bargains struck between employers and unions could not be enforced in the courts both sides were in practice free to break agreements, and there were no legal restrictions on the right to strike. In 1968 a Royal Commission under Lord Donovan acknowledged the case for the reform of industrial relations but argued that this could best be accomplished by voluntary action, without the intervention of the law. Not content with this, Wilson and his Secretary for Employment, Barbara Castle, published a White Paper, *In Place of Strife*, which included proposals hedging the right to strike around with preconditions such as strike ballots in major disputes, or compulsory pauses for conciliation. If they had understood where their own best interests lay, the trade unions would have welcomed the proposals but the TUC, which could cite the Donovan Report in its favour, rejected them. The parliamentary Labour Party followed suit, and Wilson and Castle were forced into a humiliating surrender.

Like the National Plan of 1965, trade union reform had come to nothing and Wilson had no more radical schemes to propose. But his government had taken one modernizing decision of lasting benefit to business and consumers, not to mention generations of schoolchildren to come. On 1 March 1966 the Chancellor of the Exchequer, James Callaghan, had announced that Britain would convert to a decimal currency in five years' time. Under the existing system the pound was divided into twenty shillings and the shilling into twelve pence. The pound itself was to be retained as the major unit of currency, but henceforth it would be split into a hundred new pennies. (The alternative would have been to adopt 10 shillings, or what is now 50p, as the basic unit, but this would have felt uncomfortably like a devaluation of the mighty pound.)

The existing currency was charming but anomalous. The bronze farthing, halfpenny, and penny, the twelve-sided brass threepenny bit, and the cupro-nickel sixpence (5p), shilling, florin (two shillings), and half-crown, each had their own size, weight, history, and character which made them a joy for numismatists. As a medium of exchange, however, they were a time-consuming nuisance. Twelve pence to the shillings and twenty shillings to the pound may sound like a simple formula, but the arithmetic was a trial for adults as well as for children learning their sums at school. If, for example you had £1.4s.6d in your pocket and spent 17s.9d, how much would you have left? If a customer were offered a discount of 10 per cent on an item priced at £2.9s.2d, what price would the customer have to pay? The decimal system would do away with long hours of learning by rote in primary school, and long hours of accountancy for banks and offices handling small change.

Cash-handling machines would be simpler and cheaper. South Africa, Australia, and New Zealand had either done away with pounds, shillings, and pence or were planning to do so: Britain was almost the last country in the world without a decimal currency. Industry and commerce were in favour, and according to the Gallup poll 56 per cent of the public approved of the idea.[18] For once, change was accomplished without a hitch or delay. A Decimal Currency Board was set up with instructions to carry out the necessary preparations over a five-year period. The changeover was implemented on schedule and the new currency was introduced when the banks opened for business on Monday 13 February 1971. It was exactly the kind of technocratic measure that most appealed to the new Prime Minister, Edward Heath.

Heath, who had succeeded Douglas-Home as the leader of the Conservative Party in July 1965, was the first of the party's leaders to be elected by MPs, instead of chosen by a cabal. Apart from the fact that he was a hard-working politician of great ability, he was chosen because he presented the modern face of Toryism to the world. The son of a carpenter and a maidservant from the Isle of Thanet, Heath had won a scholarship to his county grammar-school and a place at Balliol College, Oxford. It was hard work, not social connections, that had propelled Heath to the top but it was perhaps due to this long, arduous climb that he lacked social graces and the ability to express human warmth. Even his best friends could not describe him as a colourful character but he was a politician of high ambition, formidable efficiency, and strong convictions. Like Macmillan and Wilson, he accepted as axiomatic the post-war settlement of full employment and expanding social services, but 'the future which Heath believed would work lay in Europe'. According to his friend Madron Seligman, with whom he often travelled in post-war Europe, 'he was always struck by the speed at which Europe was modernizing and everywhere we went he pointed out the way in which Europe was investing in new transport, in new facilities and generally higher standards in many ways, and he felt Britain was falling behind'.[19]

As leader of the Opposition, Heath's great ambition was to lead Britain into the Common Market. In order to achieve this, however, he believed that the British economy must first of all be made more competitive by restoring the disciplines and incentives of the market. Although he had no experience of owning or managing a business, he was confident that he knew how to manage the economy. 'Heath', observed a sceptical John Biffen, 'is basically a super management consultant, brought in to improve the performance of Great Britain Ltd by that marginal 1 per cent that makes the difference between profit and loss... He is the technocrat in politics, and this applies as much to his political techniques as to his policies and priorities.'[20] Taxes and public expenditure must be reduced, and state subsidies to industry removed. A statutory incomes policy was explicitly ruled out, but the government proposed to impose strict restraints on the pay of its own employees.

When Heath unexpectedly won the general election of June 1970 he embarked on this programme with the enthusiastic support of some of the younger, more right-wing Tories who were now entering the House of Commons. The Conservatives were pledged by their manifesto not to introduce a statutory incomes policy, thus removing one potential source of conflict with the trade unions. But the flagship of the new administration was the Industrial Relations Bill, a comprehensive legal framework for industrial relations, drawn up without consulting the unions, which was bound to be opposed by the TUC. It was a bill with mixed motives, intended partly to promote a corporatist style of co-operation between government, unions, and employers, and partly to curb excessive wage demands by reducing the bargaining power of the unions.

The White Paper *In Place of Strife* had been short and intelligible. The Industrial Relations Bill was long and obscure. Its provisions were based on a distinction between unions which registered with the new Industrial Relations Court and those which did not. Unions which registered won the right of recognition from the employer and better protection against unfair dismissal. But agreements between unions and employers were to be legally binding and registered unions were liable to prosecution and fines for breaking them. In the case of registered unions, however, there were fixed limits to the fines. There were no limits to the fines payable by unregistered unions. When a major industrial dispute was in prospect, the Minister could appeal to the Industrial Relations Court to impose a secret ballot or a compulsory cooling off period of up to 60 days.[21]

Instead of co-operating with the government, the unions decided to challenge it. On the instructions of the TUC they decided to deregister from the Industrial Relations Court. In January 1972 the National Union of Mineworkers, whose members had voted in favour of strike action, went on strike in support of a demand for a 47 per cent increase in pay. Having in the past few years slipped down the league table of earnings, they hoped to restore their fortunes in one decisive stroke. The government, taken by surprise, discovered that there were only two months' coal stocks at the power stations. Acting in sympathy with the miners, the railwaymen and many of the road-haulage workers refused to move coal to the power stations. When 'blackleg' drivers were hired to deliver the coal they were met at the coal depots by flying pickets organized by the NUM.

The strike culminated in a quasi-revolutionary scene in the drab setting of the Saltley coal depot of the West Midlands Gas Board in Birmingham. Robert Taylor has described for us one of the most politically traumatic moments of post-war British history:

> An estimated 15,000 workers led by the Yorkshire miners under the Napoleonic style leadership of the young Arthur Scargill forced the police to close the gates and turn the coal lorries away. 'Here was living proof that the working class had only to flex its muscles and it could bring governments, employers, society to a complete standstill', declared Scargill at the time. The events at Saltley certainly caused a panic among ministers and their civil service advisers as they looked on helplessly at the exercise of brutal industrial force. Indeed the government was being forced to its knees. Its officials wondered excitedly whether the miners strike would provoke rioting on the streets, epidemics and a complete breakdown of civil order.'[22]

The government climbed down and agreed to a court of inquiry under Lord Wilberforce, who recommended a 20 per cent pay increase over 16 months. The miners rejected this and squeezed still more out of the government before calling off the strike. When a national rail strike threatened in April the government resorted to the Industrial Relations Act and the Industrial Relations Court ordered a 14-day cooling off period and a strike ballot. Over 80 per cent of the railwaymen voted in favour of the union's wage demands, compelling the government to give in and award a 13 per cent wage increase.

The subsequent fate of the Industrial Relations Act was a script which any satirist would have been proud to write. A private employer on Merseyside sought to prevent a group of dockers who belonged to the TGWU from picketing the new container terminals which were gradually displacing the docks. When the TGWU ignored a ruling on the subject from the Industrial Relations Court it was fined for contempt, but took the case to the Court of Appeal, which to the consternation of the government ruled that the union could not be held responsible for the actions of its members. If the union was not responsible, the only recourse for an aggrieved party was to prosecute individual workers, but if they refused to recognize the court they would be liable to imprisonment for contempt. Nothing was more certain to discredit a government than imprisoning workers for industrial action, but shortly afterwards five dockers were arrested for picketing and sent to Pentonville. A one-day general strike was called for 31 July 1972 but to the government's infinite relief the men were released when the House of Lords overruled the Court of Appeal and declared that unions were, after all, responsible for their members' actions. It was too late to rescue the act: it had expired among scenes of laughter and jubilation.[23]

The government, meanwhile, abandoned its initial policy of reducing public spending. In his leisure time Heath enjoyed sailing aboard his yacht, *Morning Cloud*. In a series of U-Turns beginning in 1971 he now changed tack and swung the tiller towards a course of government-led economic expansion. In spite of the apparently right-wing character of some of his early decisions, he had always belonged as firmly as Macmillan to the 'Never Again' school of Conservatives whose main priority was to avoid a repetition of the mass unemployment of the 1930s. The failure of the Industrial Relations Act, coupled with the announcement in January 1972 that unemployment had almost reached the then shocking total of almost a million, persuaded him to set a course of economic expansion. In Heath's mind this was simply a change of tactics in pursuit of a goal to which he had always been committed: in Thatcherite retrospect, an abandonment of ideological principle.

In the spring the government performed a U-Turn over Upper Clyde Shipbuilders, a company on the brink of bankruptcy which it had refused in the past to assist. A work-in at the shipyards, led and skilfully publicized by Jimmy Reid, a Communist shop steward, won public sympathy and awoke Heath's fears of rising unemployment. Extra capital was injected into the yards to keep them open. A more spectacular U-Turn, the 1972 Industry Act, conferred on the Department of Trade and Industry extensive powers to grant financial assistance to industries in difficulty. From the Labour front bench Tony Benn pointed out that it allowed four times as much spending at the discretion of ministers as Labour's Industrial Reorganization Corporation, which Heath had abolished on coming to power.[24]

In wrecking the government's Industrial Relations Act the trade unions had destroyed its main strategy for moderating wage claims. The brutal alternative, of allowing unemployment to rise to the point where union bargaining power was undermined by the fear of redundancy, had been rejected in favour of measures to boost employment. The Heath government now faced a situation which had been predicted by William Beveridge in his book *Full Employment in a Free Society* (1944):

> Particular wage demands which exceed what employers are prepared to pay with their existing prices and which force a raising of prices, may bring gains to the workers of the industry concerned, but they will do so at the expense of all other workers, whose real wages fall owing to the rise in prices. The other workers will naturally try to restore the position, by putting forward demands of their own. There is a real danger that sectional wage bargaining, pursued without regard to its effects upon prices, may lead to a vicious spiral of inflation, with money wages chasing prices and without any gain in real wages for the working class as a whole.[25]

The inflationary spiral was accelerated by the decision of the Chancellor of the Exchequer, Anthony Barber, who was acting under pressure from Heath, to embark on a 'dash for growth'. In the autumn of 1971 the government relaxed the restrictions on the size of the loans that banks could make to borrowers, unleashing a major credit expansion. Whereas loans had comprised 40 per cent of the banks' total assets in 1948–50, they made up nearly 80 per cent of assets by the end of 1974. Manufacturing industry was a major beneficiary, and consumers found it easier to take out loans, but much of the additional credit was channelled into a speculative boom in commercial property by 'secondary' or 'fringe' banks. When property values began to fall and the bubble burst, in December 1973, the Bank of England secretly organized a rescue operation by the main City banks, which collectively extended borrowing facilities of £1,000 million to prevent a financial collapse. The depressing effect on the value of shares was to linger on for two or three years as the remaining assets of the property companies were sold off.[26]

Last but not least, the entry of Britain into the Common Market on 1 January 1973 committed Britain to the support of the Common Agricultural Policy (CAP) a protectionist regime which kept up food prices in the interests of peasant farmers on the continent, and restricted the quantity of food Britain could buy from outside Europe. According to the economist and politician Douglas Jay, an opponent of British entry into Europe, the CAP played a major part in pushing up the price of foodstuffs in Britain and accelerating the inflationary spiral.[27]

Heath's response to inflation was to seek a new industrial consensus by summoning the unions and the employers to a series of meetings at Chequers in the autumn of 1972. When they failed to produce agreement, Heath announced a statutory prices and incomes policy which took effect in November with a statutory freeze on all incomes. It was followed by two further statutory phases, with complex provisions:

Incomes Policy under the Heath Government 1972–1974

November 1972–April 1973

Statutory stage one—freeze on all pay increases

April 1973 to November 1973

Statutory stage two with £1 [=£5.57] per week plus 4 per cent limit on increases in average pay bill per head, £250 [£1392] limit on individual rises. Increases to implement equal pay for women up to one third of the remaining differential allowable outside limit. Settlements prior to stage two allowed to be implemented in full.

November 1973 to July 1974

Statutory stage 3 with limits of £2.25 [=£12.53] per week or 7 per cent on increases in average pay bill per head. One per cent flexibility margin plus threshold payments. £350 [=£1949] a year limit on increases. Increases to implement equal pay for women up to one half remaining difference allowable outside limit. Exceptional increases allowable for new efficiency schemes, unsocial hours, London allowances, cases meeting Pay Board criteria for anomalies and in special cases receiving ministerial consent.

Source: Taylor, *The Fifth Estate*, pp. 241–2.

Stage 3, beginning in November 1973, was to be Heath's undoing. Following the Yom Kippur war in October the oil-producing Arab states decided to put economic pressure on the West by quadrupling the price of oil. The long post-war boom was over and a reduction in the standard of living was now inevitable, but the miners were in an exceptionally strong bargaining position. Having rejected an offer of about 13 per cent from the National Coal Board, they started an overtime ban on 12 November. In an attempt to square a settlement in the coal industry with stage 3 of the incomes policy, Heath entered into direct negotiations with the NUM executive. At their first meeting one of the miners spoke up from the back of the room: 'If you can pay the bloody Arabs, why can't you pay us? We're British.'[28] This was good advice, but Heath was too entangled in stage 3 to heed it.

In order to conserve coal stocks, the government declared a state of emergency and subsequently (13 December) a three-day working week. Heath still hoped for a settlement, but in the New Year party officials and backbench MPs began to call for an early general election, with 7 February as the most likely date. Heath hesitated until 4 February, when the National Union of Mineworkers voted to escalate the go-slow into a strike. Heath announced that polling day would be 28 February and launched an election campaign on the theme of 'who governs?' The outcome was a hung Parliament. The Conservatives won 297 seats and Labour 301, leaving the Liberals with 14 seats, and the Scottish and Welsh nationalists, to hold the balance. Over the following weekend Heath tried and failed to do a deal with the Liberal leader, Jeremy Thorpe. On the Monday he resigned and the Queen invited Harold Wilson to form a government.

Wilson had promised a 'New Britain', Edward Heath a 'quiet revolution'. With hindsight we can see that although the rhetoric implied radical change, the quest for modernity was bounded by the assumptions of the post-war political settlement. Both Labour and Conservative governments were still committed to a mixed economy, full employment, the tripartite system of co-operation between government, employers, and trade unions, and expanding social services: what David Marquand has termed 'Keynesian social democracy'. Perhaps it was because the political class were attempting to modernize Britain within the framework of the post-war settlement that modernization was, in the main, frustrated. Judged by the expectations they had aroused, both the Wilson and Heath governments had failed, leaving the middle ground of British politics vulnerable to the assaults of the Labour Left and the radical Right of the Conservative party. Nor were these the only developments that called the role of the state into question.

The Welfare State: Onwards and Upwards?

The attempts of successive governments to manage and modernize the economy were paralleled by innovations and experiments in social policy. The expansion of higher education, the 'comprehensive revolution' in the secondary schools, the building of high-rise housing estates, were all undertaken in a spirit of great optimism. Social policy was never free of controversy over questions of policy, or disputes over the allocation of resources, but the welfare state was firmly established and the prospects for the social services looked brighter than ever with the election in October 1964 of the Labour government. By 1974, however, the welfare state was in trouble on a number of fronts and the future overshadowed by a sharp downturn in the economy. Education and housing, in particular, became focal points of argument and protest.

After cutting back on the education budget in the early 1950s, the Conservatives changed tack and financed a sustained drive to fulfil the main objective of the 1944 Education Act: secondary education for all. As Rodney Lowe writes: 'There was a belated reduction of all-age schools between 1954 and 1963 from 3228 to 411 (catering for 93,000 as opposed to 636,000 pupils) and the building of over 2000 new schools, mainly secondary modern.'[29] This marked the beginning of an era of expansion in which successive governments invested heavily in education at all levels from primary school to university. Between 1955 and 1975 the proportion of GNP devoted to education more than doubled. Spending on consumer goods and services rose by 49.8 per cent between 1960 and 1970, but spending on education (including further and higher education) rose by 78.2 per cent. Nor was this largesse for the benefit of elite institutions only. The cost per pupil of secondary schooling up to the age of 15 rose (at constant 1960–1 prices) from £77.00 in 1960 to £97.00 in 1970. 'As a result', writes A. H. Halsey, 'the average worker received much more education, measured in terms of costs, than his father or grandfather.'[30] Expansion, however, was accompanied almost from the start by controversy.

In the late 1950s the Conservatives faced a growing dilemma over the role of the comprehensive school. Successive Conservative Ministers of Education declared their strong support for the grammar schools, and the existing system of selection by exam at the age of eleven—the 'eleven-plus'. But the lobby in favour of the comprehensive school was growing. It was championed by the Labour Party throughout its years in opposition (1951–64), and reinforced by the findings of educationalists, psychologists, and sociologists. They called into question the scientific basis of intelligence testing, argued that it was biased against working-class children, and highlighted the remarkably uneven distribution of grammar school places across the country. 'In Gateshead in the early 1950s', writes Nicholas Timmins, '8 per cent of children went to grammar school, while in Merioneth 64 per cent did so.'[31]

Local authorities had the right to make proposals for the reorganization of secondary education, and the Minister of Education the right to turn them down. By the late 1950s, however, a growing number of education authorities were pressing for comprehensive schools. Behind this movement lay the rapid expansion of the suburbs, which now had to be provided with new schools, the administrative convenience of building one large school rather than two smaller ones, and the aspirations of middle-class parents who could not afford a private education for children who were unable to get into a grammar school. The government, sensing that Conservatives at local level were sometimes in favour of comprehensive schooling, gradually softened its line. When the Labour-led London County Council proposed a new comprehensive school at Holland Park in west London, the Macmillan government gave its approval.

The opening of Holland Park in 1958 marked the beginning of an era in which the new comprehensive model carried almost all before it. The handful of comprehensive schools already in existence up to that time had been established mainly for reasons of administrative convenience in rural areas where the population was scattered and it was difficult to justify the existence of two different types of secondary school side by side. Holland Park, by contrast, was a flagship of progressive schooling intended to provide a high-quality education for a social mix of pupils drawn partly from middle-class South Kensington, and partly from working-class Shepherds Bush. Egalitarian in its social intake, the school was initially conservative in its educational methods. In the 1960s it was 'surprisingly strict, with streaming, caning and uniforms'.[32]

By 1962, when Macmillan appointed Sir Edward Boyle to the Ministry of Education, ninety of the 146 education authorities in England and Wales had either gone comprehensive or were planning to do so.[33] Boyle, a left-wing Tory, was the first Conservative Minister of Education to view the comprehensive school as equal in merit to the grammar school, but it was the victory of the Labour Party in the general election of October 1964, and the appointment the following January of Anthony Crosland as the Ministry of Education, that gave a decisive impetus to the 'comprehensive revolution'. Crosland, a suave, handsome ex-officer and Oxford don, with a drawling accent and the manners of a dandy, was a public-school rebel who loved to break the rules of polite society. He was also a formidable politician and political thinker who detested class distinctions. As Minister of Education he issued a circular, 10/65, requesting all local authorities to draw up plans for reorganizing secondary education on a comprehensive basis. This was the opening move in a complex tactical game in which Crosland deployed an array of carrots and sticks to cajole the local authorities into compliance. 'If it's the last thing I do', he confided to his wife, 'I'm going to destroy every fucking grammar school in England. And Wales. And Northern Ireland.'[34] By the time the Labour government fell in May 1970, the revolution was far from complete, but the proportion of pupils in comprehensive schools had risen from 10 per cent to 32 per cent and plans for more comprehensives were well advanced. Purpose-built comprehensive schools designed by modern architects were beginning to replace the old secondary modern and grammar schools, though sometimes existing buildings were amalgamated. (Northern Ireland opted out and retained the eleven-plus for another forty years, until 2008.)

The drive for comprehensive schooling produced intense controversy in the educational and political worlds. One of the foremost champions of the grammar schools and the eleven-plus was Walter James, the editor from 1952 to 1969 of *The Times Educational Supplement*. In the year that he retired from his editorial chair a new assault was launched by two lecturers in English literature, Anthony Dyson and Brian Cox, who edited and published the first of a series of 'Black Papers' in which dons, headmasters, and others denounced current educational policies and the trend towards egalitarianism. The main focus of the first Black

Paper was the student revolt of the late 1960s—of which more later. But the comprehensive school was a constant target of no less than five Black Papers published between 1969 and 1977. Dyson and Cox had both been Labour voters and supporters of the Campaign for Nuclear Disarmament. Dyson, a gay who lived with his lover, had founded the campaign for Homosexual Law Reform.

The effect of Labour's enthusiasm for comprehensive schooling was to alienate conservative educationalists who believed in the value of academic and educational elites, and the importance of maintaining standards at the expense, if necessary, of social inclusiveness. Their hopes were raised in May 1970 when a Conservative government was elected and the new Prime Minister, Edward Heath, appointed Margaret Thatcher, an ardent supporter of the grammar schools, as Secretary for Education. The sequel is well known. Whitehall lacked the power to override the wishes of a determined local authority. During Mrs Thatcher's spell at Education she approved all but 310 of the 3,420 schemes for comprehensivization submitted by local education authorities. The percentage of public sector pupils attending a comprehensive school rose from 34.4 per cent in 1970–1 to 68.8 per cent in 1975–6.[35]

The transition to comprehensive schooling converged with another educational trend, the spread of mixed-ability classes in place of the streaming of children by ability. Crosland had imagined the comprehensive school as socially inclusive but academically competitive. The teachers in the comprehensive schools were generally inclined to reject this approach as elitist, and the case for mixed ability classes was strengthened by the fact that they were also less costly. It was not only conservatives who worried about the consequences. The socialist Bernard Crick, defending his decision to send his sons to private schools, explained that he had done so because he was a scholar who wanted to give his sons a scholarly education:

> In some subjects the state sector is now almost doomed to inferiority. We may have got the worst of both worlds by leaving the private sector free but seeking to abolish the direct-grant grammar schools. I would hesitate long, however, in the name of liberty before abolishing the private sector in the name of equality until the public sector returns to the original ideal of the comprehensive school: that, under one roof pupils would be treated differently according to their different abilities in different

subjects or skills, but never all in the same class for everything, never treated *en masse*.[36]

While comprehensive schooling provoked some debate over standards in the classroom, it was socially a much less radical force than egalitarians had imagined. Comprehensive schools tended to reproduce the social and cultural character of the catchment areas from which their pupils were drawn. For parents who valued educational achievement, a 'good' comprehensive was therefore virtually the equivalent of a grammar school. In an analysis of comprehensive schooling in Birmingham in the 1970s, Roy Lowe writes:

> The gradations of society were reflected in gradations of attitude to school and school work. Those who had bought into the 'better' suburban areas did so in the secure knowledge that their children would be surrounded at school by pupils drawn from similar backgrounds, supportive of the school, willing to do homework, reliable in attendance, keen to participate in extra-curricular activities, able to afford the expense of school trips, and more likely to aspire to higher education. For the predominantly white working classes trapped in the outer suburbs, and for the black communities in the inner ring, the experience was otherwise...[37]

The expansion of higher education dated back to the second half of the 1950s. In part it was an inevitable response to the growing numbers of secondary school pupils, and pupils from grammar and independent schools with the appropriate qualifications for university entrance. There were also strong local pressures to establish new universities, which were not only objects of civic pride but sources of income and employment: more than twenty towns and cities were clamouring for the establishment of a university. Conservative politicians, meanwhile, had their own reasons for acting. They saw, of course, its vote-winning potential. But they also recognized that the expansion of higher education was one of the essential preconditions of economic growth, and it harmonized well with their broad social objective, which Roy Lowe has defined as 'focusing growth upon those upwardly mobile elements of society who were already to some degree advantaged'.[38] In 1956 the long-term target for the number of student places was 90,000; by 1959 it was 175,000.[39]

The Treasury loosened the purse-strings and the Macmillan/ Douglas-Home era saw the opening of several new universities: Sussex

(1961), York (1963), East Anglia (1963), Lancaster (1964), and Essex (1964). University expansion was already in the pipeline by 1960, when the Chancellor of the Exchequer, R. A. Butler, the Financial Secretary to the Treasury, Edward Boyle, and the Minister of Education, David Eccles, decided on a review to co-ordinate long-term planning. In 1961 a committee with a wide-ranging brief to investigate and report on all aspects of higher education was appointed under the chairmanship of Lionel Robbins, an eminent economist and former civil servant. A graduate of the same school of academic and Whitehall statecraft as Beveridge and Keynes, Robbins proved to be equally effective.

The Robbins Report, published in 1963, proposed that the total number of students in higher education of all kinds—teacher training colleges, polytechnics, universities, and colleges of further education—should be more than doubled by 1980 from 216,000 to 558,000. This fundamental recommendation was a frontal assault on the elitism of all those in the educational world who believed, as the novelist Kingsley Amis had put it in 1960, that 'more will mean worse'. The future of the university was the main issue at stake. Some, like the conservative philosopher Michael Oakeshott, believed that universities were set apart from other educational institutions by their dedication to the pursuit of learning for its own sake, and ought only to admit students with the inclination and ability to discuss scholarly topics. Others argued in pseudo-scientific fashion that 'the pool of ability' on which the universities drew had already been drained dry. Robbins and his committee accepted the findings of sociologists who argued that it was the class system as much as individual ability, that determined admission to university.[40]

Astonishingly, in view of the economic troubles of the 1970s, the target of 558,000 was almost met. The actual figure for 1980 was 524,000. University education was, however, more expensive than other types of education, which helps to explain why the number of students at university was 45,000 below Robbins' target of 346,000. Even larger was the gap that opened up between the numbers of science and technology students projected by Robbins, and the actual numbers for 1980, which represented a shortfall of 25 per cent. This was almost entirely due to the absence in science and technology courses of the women Robbins had planned for: they opted for the humanities instead.[41]

One of the few domestic acts during the brief premiership of Sir Alec Douglas-Home was his announcement of the government's decision to accept the main recommendation of the Robbins Report, that higher education should be expanded to provide places for all those capable of benefiting from it. The transition from elite to mass education now had the stamp of official approval and the Wilson governments of 1964–70 had no need to authorize the building of any more new universities: there were enough already open or near to completion. They did, however, ensure that the funds for expansion would be available. 'This it unflinchingly did', writes Ben Pimlott, 'despite the vagaries of the economy and of Treasury policy... Thus there began, under Labour, a brief golden age for high-performing school leavers; the new universities, the expanded old ones, and the new polytechnics, were funded with a generosity, and developed with an enthusiasm and a degree of imagination, which British higher education would never see again.'[42] University expansion, however, was mainly of benefit to the middle classes, and only readily accessible to teenagers with the appropriate qualifications. Wilson arrived in office with a pet project of his own for a University of the Air to be taught through radio and television programmes and correspondence courses. Jennie Lee was appointed as Minister of State at the Department of Education and Science with a mandate to implement the idea. Wilson was mainly interested in expanding technological education, but Lee converted this into a plan for a fully fledged Open University awarding degrees of a standard comparable with those of other universities. No formal education qualifications were required for admission. Wilson and Lee fought hard and successfully to overcome opposition and by 1970, when the government fell, the infrastructure of the university was in place, but no students had yet been admitted.[43]

The Conservatives in opposition had attacked the project on the grounds that other educational priorities were more important. When Mrs Thatcher became Secretary of Education she could probably have abolished the Open University if she had wished to but according to her memoirs she was genuinely attracted to the idea 'because I thought that it was an inexpensive way of giving wider access to higher education, because I thought that trainee teachers in particular would benefit from it, because I was alert to the opportunities offered by technology to bring the best teaching to schoolchildren and students, and above all because it gave people a second chance in life.'[44] With Mrs Thatcher's support, the 'OU' grew and flourished. By the 1980s it was awarding more degrees than Oxford and Cambridge combined.

As university education expanded, youth culture invaded the campus. At the start of the 1960s students looked and usually behaved like young adults. The women wore blouses and skirts, the men sports jackets and flannel trousers. Some worked hard while others did not, but there was very little to distinguish them culturally from their elders. In spite of the expansion in numbers, the social profile of students remained predominantly middle class. By the end of the decade, however, both male and female students were abandoning formal dress for casual wear of one kind or another: jeans were standard. The men, abandoning the 'short back and sides' of their fathers and grandfathers, grew their hair long and sometimes down to their shoulders. University students had invented their own version of youth culture, to the bafflement of the middle-aged who could be overheard whispering, when a student got on a bus, 'is it a boy or a girl?'

Many of the students who enjoyed the benefits of university expansion displayed little gratitude. What older generations regarded as a privilege they treated as a right. What the university authorities thought of as a duty to act *in loco parentis* they viewed as the repression of young adults. What the workaday world saw as the ivory towers of academic life were depicted by student radicals as pillars of a capitalist society. Trouble broke out at the London School of Economics in October 1966 when pamphlets were circulated attacking the appointment as Director of the School of Dr Walter Adams, previously head of the University College of Rhodesia, on the grounds that he was a racist. A student sit-in followed, the first of several demonstrations that disrupted the LSE over the next three years. Student protests then spread to other universities, affecting all 44 of them between 1968 and 1973, and also to polytechnics and art colleges. Sit-ins were the most common form of protest, but rent strikes, boycotts of classes, and break ins to university offices also occurred.

Student revolt was an international phenomenon which had begun at Berkeley in California in 1964 and spread like wildfire across the United States, mobilizing 'hippies, dropouts, anarchists, radicals, and revolutionaries, as well as *bona fide* students' on 700 campuses in protests against the draft, the war in Vietnam, racist admission policies, and so on.[45] Whatever the romantic delusions and excesses of the student movement in the United States, it was rooted in serious issues. This was equally true of the student riots in Paris in May 1968, but with the notable exception of the campaign for equality of civil rights organized by the students of Queen's College, Belfast, student protest in Britain was a relatively mild affair, the anger more histrionic. It was fuelled partly by disillusion on the Left with the foreign and domestic policies of the Wilson government and the consequent proliferation of small radical groups like the International Socialists and the International Marxists. The Vietnam war was condemned as an expression of the militarism and imperialism of the United States. There were also issues relating to the structure and government of universities themselves. The demand for student representation at all levels of the university was resisted at first, but eventually conceded almost everywhere in the knowledge that it would divert student protest and student politicians into safe channels. In the early 1970s the movement died down again but in the meantime the universities had suffered a blow to their public relations. As the outside world could see, radical students were relatively privileged young people, the universities, polytechnics, and art colleges uniquely tolerant institutions in which old-fashioned discipline was conspicuous by its absence. Instead of calling in the police, or expelling student radicals, the Principals and Vice-Chancellors negotiated with them.

On the new university campuses the welfare state was literally taking a concrete form. The same was true of many of the new housing estates where tower blocks constructed from prefabricated concrete slabs were built to rehouse the residents of slum properties condemned as unfit for habitation. The boom in high-rise housing was an unintended consequence of the Housing Subsidies Act of 1956, which gave housing authorities a larger subsidy the higher they built. 'It was hoped', write Paul Bridgen and Rodney Lowe, 'that the new subsidy structure would encourage mixed developments, with the use of a limited number of high-rise flats freeing space for a larger proportion of houses.'[46] The party-political competition to build the largest number of homes, the mistaken belief that systems-built housing would cost less than traditional building methods, the ascendancy of modernism among architects and planners, and the lobbying of local authorities by the big construction companies, all helped to set the ball rolling. Terraced homes that could have been rehabilitated were condemned as slums and demolished, and their inhabitants offered a council flat in one of the new blocks. Though he later repented, Sir Keith Joseph, the Conservative Minister of Housing and Local Government from 1962 to 1964, was a fervent believer in the policy. Tower blocks were regarded as prestigious civic achievements, inaugurated with great ceremony by Lord Mayors or other local dignitaries. Birmingham City Council alone commissioned 429 of them.[47]

Rarely were council tenants or the general public invited to express their own preferences. As they were being provided for the first time with facilities like fitted kitchens, indoor toilets, and central heating, there seemed no need to invite their views. 'For some', writes Nicholas Timmins, 'tower blocks and the massive slab flats proved a success: single people, the childless and even better off families can value them when they are built to a high standard and well maintained. The mighty towers of the Barbican development in the City of London remain popular.'[48] The Barbican estate, built between 1965 and 1976 on a 40-acre site, included three of the tallest tower blocks in London, all built in the New Brutalist style of modern architecture at its most extreme. The accommodation was high quality, high cost, and ideal for the politician who needed a base in London, or a young, single merchant banker. The social needs of rehoused families in the big cities were very different, but they were transferred by local housing authorities to high-rise blocks that looked impressive for a year or two, but soon revealed structural flaws caused by inferior materials and slapdash methods of construction. Populated by 'problem families' and people on low incomes whose morale was already low, they seem to have had a psychologically damaging effect, as though they were felt to be prisons or workhouses rather than homes. Ever since the 1940s survey after survey had shown that the majority of people preferred to live in an ordinary house with a garden. It was no wonder that they hated living in a concrete box far from the ground with the lift out of order and water seeping into the living room every time it rained.

The 1967 Housing Subsidies Act put an end to the government subsidies that had made high-rise housing (along with the occasional bribe from contractors) such an attractive option for local authorities. This marked the beginning of the decline of the tower block, but it was Ivy Hodge, a cake decorator living on the eighteenth floor of Ronan Point in Canning Town, who completed its downfall when she lit a match beneath her kettle at a quarter to six on the morning of 16 May 1968. Gas which had been gathering from a leak exploded, blowing a huge hole in one side of the building. Ivy Hodge survived but four people were killed.[49] This was by no means the end for the tower block as a system of mass housing. Although Ronan Point was evacuated it was then partly rebuilt, and reopened five years later. The initial response of the housing authorities was to reinforce seven hundred tower blocks, and the construction of 'slums in the sky' continued into the 1970s. By the end of the 1970s there were 4,500 of them, under a more stringent regime of regulation and inspection.[50] In the long run, however, the disaster proved fatal to high-rise housing. Ronan Point itself was demolished in 1986 and replaced by two-storey terraced homes.

The problems with high-rise housing converged with a second factor to produce a change of policy in Whitehall in 1968. The Wilson government took office in 1964 with ambitious plans to increase the annual output of houses in the public and private sectors combined to 500,000 a year. As the government's economic difficulties mounted it was decided to scale down the local authority housing programme and switch the emphasis to improvement grants for the renovation of existing properties, a strategy continued after 1970 by the Heath government. After 1968 the main difference between Labour and Conservative policy was Labour's commitment to subsidize council house rents. The Conservatives regarded a general subsidy as wasteful and replaced it with means-tested housing allowances, targeted on those most in need.

The National Health Service was from the beginning the most popular element in the welfare state. With approval ratings of around 80 per cent it was as firmly established as the monarchy and in one sense above party politics: no party dared to propose radical changes. The popularity of the NHS was, however, no guarantee that it was working as efficiently as it should be, or delivering services to the highest possible standard. Like the BBC in the days when it still retained a monopoly of broadcasting, there was nothing to compare it with.

When Enoch Powell was appointed Minister of Health in 1961 it was expected that his right-wing economic views would lead him to cut back on expenditure or put up charges or both. He did in fact double prescription charges and shift some of the cost of the NHS, at the expense of the low paid, from general taxation to national insurance. But in

January 1962 he announced the Hospital Plan, by far the largest programme of investment in the NHS to date. The centrepiece was to be the building of ninety new hospitals and the extension of 360 others, all centrally planned to ensure an even distribution of services across the country. 1,250 old hospitals were to be closed. In the event the Hospital Plan, repeatedly delayed by the cuts in public spending that accompanied the economic crises of the 1960s and 1970s, was only ever partially completed.

As the years passed it also became clear how difficult it was to organize and manage the NHS. The co-ordination of general practitioner and hospital services was a continuous problem, which the Ministry of Health sought to overcome through centralized planning, but an organization with nearly a million employees found it as difficult to change course as the proverbial oil-tanker. Changes had to be negotiated with the many professional and occupational groups in the NHS at a time when they were affected by the rising industrial militancy of the 1960s and 1970s. 'In the mid-1960s', writes Rodney Lowe,

> GPs threatened to withdraw from the service (only to be appeased by the granting of a 'G.Ps' Charter'); in 1966 junior hospital doctors formed their own association; following a pay freeze in 1962 nurses grew increasingly united and defied tradition to mount an aggressive campaign in 1969 to improve their conditions; and in 1973 ancillary workers (whose trade unions had only started to organize seriously in the late 1960s) held their first national strike.[51]

All in all, the social services had reached a point by the mid-1970s where they were in no danger of dissolution, but obviously ripe for reform. Over the very long term they were also threatened by a demographic factor, the growing number of young people in education and training, and the growing number of old people in retirement, who were economically inactive. The cost of maintaining them had to be borne by the shrinking proportion of the population in paid employment—unless, of course, they were out of work.

6

Great Expectations

On 20 July 1957 Harold Macmillan, who had succeeded Anthony Eden as Prime Minister on 10 January, addressed a crowd at Bedford football ground. 'Let's be frank about it', he declared, 'most of our people have never had it so good. Go around the country, go to the industrial towns, go to the farms, and you will see a state of prosperity such as we have never had in my lifetime—nor indeed ever in the history of this country. What is beginning to worry some of us is, "Is it too good to be true", or perhaps I should say, "Is it too good to last?"'[1] Intended to sound a warning note about the dangers of inflation, the speech was instantly interpreted as a boastful appeal to the materialism of the electorate. Nevertheless it captured in a phrase a particular historical moment. After the Slump and the long, stoical years of making do, prosperity was returning and with it the promise of abundance not just for the middle and upper classes, but for the working classes too.

Between 1950 and 1973 the British economy grew at an annual average rate of 3 per cent, and the purchasing power of average incomes doubled. Full employment, which Beveridge had defined in 1944 as a level of unemployment of 3 per cent or below, persisted all through the 1950s and 1960s. Only in 1971–2 did the annual average rise above the 3 per cent figure. Within this broad pattern of stability in the labour market many shifts were occurring in the social structure. Employment in manufacturing reached a peak in 1960 after which the numbers began slowly to fall. Meanwhile employment in services—a very diverse category including transport, retailing, transport, hotels and catering, education and health, local and central government—grew by more than two million between 1951 and 1971.[2] Local government added an average of 80,000 workers a year to the payroll between 1959 and 1973, with a more modest increase in central government. This expanding labour force ranged from part-time cleaners in schools and hospitals to secretarial and administrative staff, and professionals like nurses, teachers, and civil servants. In the private sector, employment in banking, finance, and insurance increased from 771,000 in 1964 to 1,154,100 in 1978.[3] As a proportion of the occupied population manual workers were in slow but steady decline, down from 64.2 per cent in 1951 to 59.3 per cent in 1961 and 55.7 per cent in 1971. The number of managers, professionals, and clerical workers was multiplying:

Occupational groups as a percentage of the total occupied population

	1951	1961	1971
Managers	5.5	5.4	9.8
Higher professionals	1.9	3.0	3.8
Lower professionals and technicians	4.7	6.0	7.7
Clerical and related	10.4	12.7	14.2
Totals	22.5	27.1	35.5

Beyond these figures we catch a glimpse an ever expanding vista of leafy suburbs with detached and semi-detached homes.

The once mighty Victorian industries and their labour forces were in decline. In 1957 the consumption of coal began to fall. By the late 1960s it was in free fall as the industry experienced the effects of competition from oil and gas in home and overseas markets. Between 1957 and 1974–5 more than six hundred pits were closed down, cutting employment in the coal industry from 704,000 to 246,000.[4] In shipbuilding Britain's total output was overtaken by Japan in 1956 and Germany in 1958. In 1963 ten shipyards closed and another twenty-eight were working on their last orders. Between 1958 and 1963 the labour force shrank from 215,000 to 160,000.[5] The Lancashire cotton trade, having already lost its export markets to foreign competition, now began to lose its domestic market as well. In an attempt to save the industry, the Macmillan government's Cotton Industry Act of 1959 proposed to close down one half of the industry and modernize the other half. When this failed to make the industry competitive, Courtaulds intervened, buying up in 1964 most of the companies still in business, and creating for the first time a structure in which spinning, weaving, finishing, and selling were integrated for the first time into a single firm. 'Within ten years', writes Richard Overy, 'the bold experiment and declaration of faith were over. Neither amalgamation, nor re-equipment, nor the three shift "continental" work pattern introduced to make use of the most expensive plant, were enough.'[6]

The long drawn-out convulsions of these industries contributed to the impression that Britain was a nation in relative economic decline. As yet, however, there was very little talk of 'de-industrialization'. This was partly because the decline of Victorian industries was counteracted, for the time being, by the expansion of more modern successors. In chemicals, mechanical and electrical engineering, motor cars, and aircraft, British companies were expanding output and creating employment. Hence it was axiomatic, throughout the era of the 'long boom', that manufacturing industry would continue to be the foundation of Britain's prosperity. This conviction was also grounded in the belief, common to the Conservative, Labour, and Liberal parties of the period, that economic decline could, and should be reversed by enlightened state intervention. The success of the 'sunrise' industries was, however, not always firmly based. Austin and Morris, amalgamated in 1952 as the British Motor Corporation (BMC) were outwardly prosperous with output and sales rising through the 1950s and 1960s. As late as 1970, 85 per cent of the cars sold on the home market were manufactured in Britain.[7] The structural problems of the company, including low productivity and a worsening record of industrial relations, were masked for the time being by the strength of home demand and the shelter of protective tariffs. A merger with British Leyland in 1968 produced a new conglomerate, the British Leyland Motor Corporation, but the percentage of cars imported into the British market began to rise ominously.

Bucknell's House

To an extent that it is now almost impossible to conceive, Britain was ruled from the late 1950s all the way through to the early 1970s by the assumption that the new was almost always better than the old. It was the heyday of modern architects working on commissions from the public sector for schools, housing estates, and universities. In a more homely fashion the spirit of the times was embodied on BBC television by the amiable figure of Barry Bucknell, a pioneer of do-it-yourself who soon became a household name. His accident-prone attempts in live broadcasts to demonstrate how to build shelves or put up wallpaper were entertaining as well as instructive. In 1962 the BBC bought a run-down house in Ealing and gave Bucknell the task of modernizing it in a series of *thirty-nine* programmes. As one of his obituarists wrote: 'During the transmission of "Bucknell's House", five and a half million watched as such unappealing features as Victorian fireplaces, panelled doors and cornices gave way to plywood, melamine, and head-ache inducing wallpapers.'[8] Bucknell took a pride in removing wooden shutters, replacing curtain rails with pelmets, boxing in fireplaces with hardboard, and covering kitchen work surfaces with formica or laminated plastic. The makeover was a great success: having bought the house for £2,250 [=£28,935] the BBC sold it for £7,000 [=£90,020].

Driven by consumerism, the routines of daily life were changing too. The number of cars and vans increased from 2,307,000 in 1950 to 5,650,000 in 1960 and 11,802,000 in 1970. As car ownership spread, the corner shop and the high street shop found themselves having to compete with supermarkets which combined under one roof the produce of several different retailers, and provided its customers with parking space.

The fortunes of the supermarkets were boosted when the government of Douglas-Home abolished resale price maintenance in 1964. Up until then the price of all branded products was determined by the producer, and a tin of baked beans cost the same no matter where it was purchased. With the abolition of resale price maintenance, the retailer was free to determine the price charged to the customer. Supermarkets, however, had more to offer than convenience or competitive prices. They opened up vistas of consumer *choice* that small shopkeepers could not rival. In 1960 Sainsbury's stocked 2,000 product-lines. By 1975 they stocked 5,000.[9]

The freedom and mobility conferred on millions of people by the ownership of a car was one of the great social advances of the second half of the twentieth century. By the 1960s, however, the brief age of innocence in which consumer goods were seen as fulfilling basic needs was over, and the costs of insatiable mass consumption were becoming apparent. As we have already seen, the Buchanan report was intended to find a middle way between the exclusion of the car from the city, and the destruction of the city by the car. But it was not only cities that were endangered. A growing proportion of holidaymakers—27 per cent in 1951, 70 per cent by 1972—were travelling to coastal resorts by car instead of by train or by coach. 'Everywhere', writes the historian of the British seaside, John Walton, 'the car was a damaging and disruptive influence, intruding into landscapes, clogging up central streets and promenades, colonizing vacant land, encouraging demolitions, siphoning demand away from established accommodation where parking was difficult, and bringing inner-city risks and fumes to holiday areas.'[10]

It was not the motor car, however, that brought about the decline of the British seaside holiday, but competition from more attractive alternatives. Blackpool, Bournemouth, Margate and other coastal resorts could offer all the familiar sights and rituals of the seaside holiday: the promenades, winter-gardens, and end-of-the-pier shows, the sticks of rock and saucy postcards, the donkey rides and crowded beaches where fully dressed men and women huddled together in family groups and the more intrepid mastered the art of struggling into a bathing costume while wrapped in a bath towel. What they could not offer was the guaranteed warmth and sunshine of the Mediterranean summer. The leading tour operators—Thomson, Clarkson, Horizon, and Cosmos—stepped in with attractively priced package deals combining flights and accommodation. In 1955 about two million British people took a holiday abroad. By 1972 the figure was 8.5 million, with Spain by far the most popular destination, Italy a modest second, Germany third, and Greece, which had yet to develop a mass market tourist industry, in fourth place.

As the numbers grew, and competition intensified, the expectations of holidaymakers rose. As one tour operator put it: 'Unless you offer private bathrooms and balconies for everyone, at least two swimming pools, a ladies' hairdressing salon, a boutique, several bars and a discotheque, you aren't even talking.' To most people a package holiday still meant a week or two at a hotel in Benidorm or Torremolinos, but the demand for alternatives was growing. In the late 1960s the travel trade successfully introduced winter packages to ski resorts or the ever warm and sunlit Canary Islands. Long-haul packages to the West Indies, the Seychelles, or Bangkok, were already on the market for those who could afford them.[11]

Sun-worship, however, was the main feature of the package holiday, and along with it came a growing market for sun-tan lotion, sunglasses, and new fashions in beachwear. Both men and women were also paying more attention to cleaning and grooming themselves. In 1957 about one-third of women between the ages of sixteen and sixty-four made some use of deodorants. By 1966 more than half were using deodorants every day. Men, who were already rubbing so much Brylcream into their hair that it glistened like the morning dew, were fearful of taking the next step and perfuming their bodies, lest they be thought effete or homosexual. 'The turning-point', James Obelkevich writes, 'came in 1957, when Old Spice entered the British market... Women liked after-shave and bought it for men because it made them smell nicer; men were less enthusiastic, but accepted it because it had a functional justifi-cation (that it was "good for the skin") and thus avoided the traditional male fragrance phobia. By 1969, after many Christmas presents and much prodding and encouragement from wives and girlfriends, after-shave was used regularly by over half the adult male population.'[12]

The material changes were also cultural changes that reflected the ever expanding range of choice available to consumers: a choice, in effect, of lifestyle. Writing in 1967, the authors of a social and economic history of modern Britain listed no fewer than twelve spheres in which the effects of improved living standards were to be seen:

(1) The booming demand in recent years for gramophones and records. (2) Increasing sporting opportunities and greater democratization over a number of sports, such as cricket, football, tennis, golf, sailing, fishing and so on. (3) The great expansion in private motoring at weekends. (4) The declining influence of exclusive clubs, yet the booming develop-ment of community clubs in the North over recent years. (5) The greater comfort of public houses and the spread of off-licences, 'pubs' being forced to diversify since families do not frequent them like they used to. (6) Falling church attendances. (7) Dancing, ten-pin bowling and bingo. (8) The popularity of public recreation grounds, swimming pools, lakes, judo, keep-fit exercises, fencing and mountaineering. (9) The popularity of gardening, photography, and do-it-yourself crafts. (10) The rising fig-ures for library loans, paperback books and magazines. (11) Declining attendance at horse-race meetings and greyhound tracks, but a tremen-dous boom in betting and betting shops. (12) The booming teenage market.

Critics of Consumerism

Consumer society always had its critics. For decades socialists had striven to raise the educational standards and the political conscious-ness of workers with the aim of turning them into active, emancipated citizens. Now it was obvious that commercial pressures were capturing the working classes, and turning them into home and family-centred consumers of fridges and quiz shows. As Lawrence Black writes: 'Socialists were hostile to hire-purchase, consumerism, commercial TV, and American mass culture, since their values were far from those on which they anticipated socialism might be built.'[13] He quotes a Labour youth pamphlet of 1956:

> The familiar round of pin-tables and cafes, the hours spent reading comics and half listening to the radio...the hypnotic glamour of the American movies; these are not life, they are a feeble substitute for it. This doesn't mean that socialists don't have their fun, don't go to movies and dances...but they keep things in proportion. They enjoy life at deeper levels and they enjoy it...more intensely because 'enjoyment' is not their main object.[14]

It was not uncommon in the 1950s for more earnest individuals to boast that they did not possess a television and had no intention of buying one.

Outright opposition to consumer society was sustained for a while by the hippies and drop-outs of the 1960s and 1970s but it was always a fringe phenomenon. More widespread, though still confined to minorities, was the rise of various forms of consumer activism. The Consumer's Association, founded in 1956, introduced the comparative testing of consumer goods and reported the findings in its monthly magazine, *Which?* From modest beginnings the circulation rose to nearly half a million ten years later, and summaries of its more newsworthy reports featured regularly in the media. Over the same period the scope of its investigations broadened out from basic household goods to contraceptives, motor cars, personal finance, do-it-yourself, and eating out: the Consumers' Association bought up Raymond Postgate's *Good Food Guide* in 1962.

Now that we take the critical assessment of products and brands for granted as a familiar feature of the market place, it is hard to appreciate what a radical innovation it was in its day. In the past the claims made by manufacturers for their products had gone largely uncontested. The Consumers' Association subjected them to critical scrutiny. An enquiry into slimming aids in 1958 demonstrated that they were completely useless. More daringly, a pioneering test of 800 samples of

27 brands of condom in 1963 revealed a failure rate of somewhere between three per cent and nineteen per cent. Motor manufacturers were driven to distraction by reports cataloguing the mechanical and design faults in British cars. In 1971 *Which?* revealed the results of a test of eleven makes of car of which seven were made by British and four by foreign companies. The four made overseas were the most reliable, a finding corroborated by a similar report by the Automobile Association.[15]

If Michael Young had not founded the Consumers' Association, someone else would have done sooner or later. Similar organizations were springing up in all the western democracies and consumer activism was a part of 'the spirit of the age'. Politicians of all parties were taking the issue of consumer protection seriously and incorporating it in numerous acts of Parliament.[16] With the entry of Britain into the European Economic Community in 1973, the rights of consumers became the subject of regulation from Brussels as well as Westminster. Consumerism, evidently, was a new and potent social force, but there was always a certain ambiguity about its aims.

Young himself was a social democrat who believed that in seeking to redress the social balance in favour of the 'small man', the Labour Party should champion the interests of consumers as well as employees. He also cherished a broader vision of consumerism as a social movement for great collective purposes. Speaking in 1970, he urged consumers to tackle such issues as deforestation, pesticides, recycling, and the plight of the poor.[17] It is unlikely that most subscribers to *Which?* looked beyond the immediate practical purpose of getting the best value for their money, but active consumerism did tend to question or challenge corporate interests.

During the 1960s a reaction was under way against the increasing use of pesticides and insecticides in the production of foodstuffs. Initially the concerns were environmental. 'There is a growing suspicion nowadays', wrote John Hillaby in the *Guardian* in November 1960, 'that the disappearance of considerable numbers of plants and animals on this island is due, either directly or indirectly, to the promiscuous use of chemicals on the land. If relatively sturdy foxes and pheasants are killed so easily by these chemicals, it may be wondered what vast numbers of insignificant organisms are being completely blotted out...'[18] The pressures in favour of restricting the use of chemicals on the land were intensified by the publication in 1963 of *Silent Spring*, a best-selling book by the American marine biologist Rachel Carson. In warning of the immediate dangers to wild life, and the more remote but alarming possibility of damage to human beings, she gave a powerful boost to conservationism, organic farming, and the nascent health food industry. 'Wholefood', the first shop of its kind, had already opened in Baker Street in 1961. Wheat germ, wholemeal bread, and muesli, organically produced fruit, vegetables, eggs, and cheese, free-range chickens, and home-made patés soon attracted an enthusiastic following of gourmets and conscientious objectors to 'agribusiness'.[19]

Consumer resistance to mass-produced food was matched by resistance to mass-produced beer. During the 1960s many small breweries were bought up by the six major brewing companies, and local ales phased out in favour of standardized, pasteurized, and carbonated beer. Since they also owned most of the pubs they also controlled the distribution of the various brands, the most famous or notorious of which was Watney's Red Barrel. In 1971 a group of disgruntled beer-drinkers in Salford initiated a 'Campaign for Revitalized Ale', later amended to the Campaign for Real Ale or CAMRA. By 1975, with the help of much press publicity, they had 30,000 members and sufficient clout to persuade the brewery companies to restore a selection of draught ales in the pubs.[20] It seemed obvious to members of CAMRA that a rich diversity of local ales was preferable to a homogenized product tasting the same at Land's End as it did at John O' Groats. But keg beer remained popular despite them, and the afficionados of real ale could be as irritatingly superior as wine snobs. As one publican pointed out keg beer had some advantages: 'It is far more hygienic than the traditional draught beer, it's far less liable to contamination, no ullage or spillage can be poured back into it, and the customer is guaranteed his pint of beer in first class condition.'[21]

The Affluent Worker

Amid all these trends, academics and the media were more obsessed than ever by the class structure. Riveted by the spectacle of working-class prosperity on a scale they had never seen before, they pored over the statistics and argued over the consequences. Between 1948 and 1958 one family in every six, most of them working class, moved to a newly built house or flat. Over that same period the average real earnings of industrial workers rose by more than 20 per cent. By 1959, among the more prosperous half of working-class families, 85 per cent possessed a television set, 44 per cent a washing-machine, and 32 per cent a car.[22] The luxuries of one period were becoming the necessities of the next, as the table indicates:

Percentage of households with certain consumer goods 1955–75

	1955	1965	1975
Vacuum cleaner	51	81	90
Washing machine	18	58	70
Refrigerator	8	46	85
Freezer	0	3	15
Television	35	85	96
Dishwasher	1	1.5	2
Telephone	19	35	52

Sources: *http://www.makingthemodernworld.org.uk* The Science Museum/Home/Stories Timeline/Design Diversity 1950–65/Home Comforts/Gas, Electricity and labour-saving devices; James Obelkevich, 'Consumption' in James Obelkevich and Peter Catterall (eds.), *Understanding Post-War British Society* (1994), p. 145.

The growth of working-class consumerism was encouraged by the spread of hire-purchase, which enabled people on low incomes to purchase goods on credit and pay off the remaining balance in weekly or monthly instalments. In the mid-1960s Barclays Bank converted a derelict boot and shoe factory in Northampton into the headquarters of Barclaycard. Launched as the first all-purpose credit card in June 1966 it encountered much resistance at first from retailers and consumers, and it was five years before it began to make a profit. By 1973 there were more than two million Barclaycard holders, and a group of high street banks had launched a rival card, Access. By 1977 there were 6.7 million card holders and the *Times* finance correspondent could venture a prophecy: 'Orwellian it may sound, but the time is coming when no one will be able to afford to be without some form of plastic card.'[23]

Contrary to what might be imagined, the rise in spending on consumer goods was accompanied by an increase in savings. 'In 1951', the Central Statistical Office recorded, 'individuals saved on average less than 2 per cent of their disposable incomes. By 1960 this proportion was 7 per cent, and by 1978 14 per cent, although there were fluctuations over the period.'[24] The lion's share of the growth in savings took the form of building society shares and deposits, which rose (at constant prices) from under £5,000m in 1952, to £24,000m in 1977. By the simple device of lending money at a higher rate of interest than they offered to savers, the building societies financed a large but prudent expansion of mortgages, which were only granted after strict criteria had been met.

By 1959, 35 per cent of manual workers were home-owners, but whether a home was owned or rented it acted as a powerful stimulus to consumer demand. In the words of Trevor Blackwell and Jeremy Seabrook:

> Who could not but rejoice at the throwing out of the fly-blown meat-safe on the wall when the fridge arrived; the home-coming from the first holiday abroad where working people had seen the wonder of oranges actually growing; the celebration of whole streets around the single TV set with its minuscule magic screen as the Archbishop raised the heavy crown over the young Queen's head; the appearance of the Ford Anglia with its bodywork, no longer black, but fawn or pale green, reflecting the inverted image of a row of terraced houses; the cold linoleum at the side of the bed transformed into soft yielding carpet?[25]

Another spectacle that transfixed contemporaries was the sight of working-class youths with money to spend in the shops. As usual the popular press highlighted exceptional cases as though they were typical:

> The *Sunday Graphic* in 1960 found a boy who could hang £127 [=£1,943] worth of suits in his parents' back yard to be photographed, another who earned £5 a week [=£76.50] and owned: five suits, two pairs of slacks, one pair of jeans, one casual jacket, five white and three coloured shirts, five pairs of shoes, twenty-five ties, and an overcoat. A sixteen-year-old typist owned six dresses, seven straight skirts and two pleated ones, one overcoat and a mac, one Italian suit, one pair of flat shoes, and three of high heels.[26]

On the face of it the word 'teenager', which had been invented in the United States in 1944, could only refer to young people between the ages of thirteen and nineteen, but Mark Abrams, the market researcher who published *The Teenage Consumer* (1959) reinterpreted it to include everyone who was unmarried in the age-group from fifteen (the school-leaving age) to twenty-five (by which time most of them were in fact married). Writing in 1961, he estimated that the average wages of 15–21 year-olds were more than 50 per cent higher in real terms than before the war. 'The teenage market' he explained, 'is almost exclusively working class. Its middle-class members are either still in school and college or else only just beginning on their careers: in either case they dispose of much smaller incomes than their working-class contemporaries and it is highly probable, therefore, that not far short of 90 per cent of all teenage spending is conditioned by working-class taste and values.'[27]

There was nothing new about youth cultures, but as Jon Savage contends, the rise of the teenager represented the victory of a specifically American version of youth culture, exported to western Europe in the aftermath of America's victory in the Second World War: 'This new type was the ultimate psychic match for the times: living in the now, pleasure-seeking, product hungry, embodying the new global society where social inclusion was to be granted through purchasing power.'[28] Apart from smart clothes for nights out, teenage demand focused on pop music. The emergence of skiffle was followed in the mid-1950s by the eruption of rock 'n' roll, an all-American import in which country music (white) was blended with rhythm and blues (black), with intoxicating effects on the young. In its first raw expression in the records of Elvis Presley or Little Richard, rock 'n' roll was so aggressively sexual and rebellious that it fuelled the anxieties of moralists in both Britain and the United States, proof that consumer goods have the power to subvert as well as to reinforce conformity. It did not take the music industry long to reduce rebellious rock to juvenile pap but there was always a danger that anarchic rock would break out again—as it repeatedly did.

In social history the emphasis usually falls on the new, and it is easy to forget that the new co-existed with the old. The young may have been heading for the Mediterranean, their bags packed with smart beachwear and accessories, but the middle aged and the old were still to be found in their old haunts. Revisiting the Lancashire resort of Morecambe in the summer of 1975, the journalist Richard West found it more or less unchanged since his last visit in 1962. The dance-hall had become a bingo club but Morecambe was 'totally, old-fashioned British' and the holiday-makers consisted overwhelmingly of working-class families from Clydeside, South Yorkshire, and South Lancashire:

Most of the men wear coats and ties, even in hot weather; most of the women look dumpy, for Morecambe is not a weight-watchers' town and thrives on chips, giant meat pies, cream teas, sweets, and especially rock that is sold in greater tonnage than ever before. Even this year, under sun almost as powerful as the Costa del Sol's, the Morecambe holiday-makers do not follow the middle-class cult of sun-bathing, a practice sold by the 'tourist industry' to northern people whose skins are more suited to wind and mist.[29]

The Mirage of a Classless Society

The 'traditional' working class was of much less interest to most observers than the 'affluent' worker. In May 1959, with a general election in the offing, *The Economist* urged the Conservative party to welcome and embrace working-class prosperity, which it saw as a social revolution in the making:

> The old-fashioned Conservative is one who looks out at the consumer comforts made achievable by rising incomes and the hire purchase revolution, and who feels vaguely that the workers are unfairly luckier than he was as a boy—that they are getting above their status. The modern Conservative should be one who looks up at the television aerials sprouting above the working-class homes of England, who looks down on the housewives' tight slacks on the back of the motor cycles and family side-cars on the summer road to Brighton, and who sees a great poetry in them. For this is what the deproletarianization of British society means; and the changes in social and industrial attitudes of mind which it could bring with it are immense.[30]

The Economist was not alone in expecting that the growing prosperity of manual workers would give them a stake in a capitalist society and break down the barriers separating them from the middle classes. The industrial editor of the *Financial Times*, Michael Shanks, wrote in 1961:

> The twentieth century is stretching its long unlovely tentacles into the remotest mining villages and into the grey tenements of dockland. Miners now take their families on Continental holidays and drive to the pit in their own cars. The tight cohesive working-class way of life is being eroded by commercial television and hire purchase, and the world of the pawnshop and the music hall is being lost forever. No longer is it a mark

of shame for a miner or a dockworker if his wife goes out to work or handles the family finances. And this social change, which has become quite marked in the last two or three years, is reflected in industrial attitudes. It has become noticeably more difficult to bring dockers out on strike on a large scale. The tinder has become damp, and the sparks fail to catch in the old way.

   The old working class, then, is dying—though like Charles II it is taking an unconscionable time about it. Its integration into the mainstream of society is proceeding apace, and while there is no doubt some element of sadness in its passing, from the national point of view it can hardly happen too soon.[31]

By the later 1950s many social commentators were convinced that the 'traditional' working class was in decline, while the younger and more modern sections of the working class were acquiring middle-class standards and mentalities. Ferdinand Zweig, a sociologist whose well researched studies of working-class life made him one of the leading authorities on the subject, concluded in his book *The Worker in an Affluent Society* (1961) that large sections of the working class were 'on the move towards middle-class values and middle-class existence'.[32]

   Nothing seemed to bear out this thesis of working-class 'embourgeoisement' thesis more than the result of the general election of October 1959. Under the leadership of Harold Macmillan, the Conservatives romped home to victory for a third time in a row, with a substantially increased majority of 100 seats. 'This election', Macmillan, declared, 'has shown that the class war is obsolete.' An editorial in the *Daily Telegraph* declared: 'This process of levelling up can be welcomed unreservedly. It is unquestionably the great vindication of the capitalist faith and the great rebuttal of the Marxist prophecy of ever-increasing proletarian impoverishment.'[33]

   The Conservatives were opposed to egalitarianism. When they spoke of ending the class war they were imagining a society in which workers were reconciled to capitalism and ready to co-operate with managers and employers. The Labour Party, of course, argued that as long as economic and social inequalities persisted, so did class distinctions and class consciousness. But Labour politicians were badly shaken by the outcome of the 1959 General Election. They began to fear that the class loyalties on which they had relied were beginning to crumble. They had always thought of manual workers as relatively poor people who owned little or nothing and were heavily dependent on the protection of the state. But suppose these same people were now becoming prosperous consumers with a home and a car and rising expectations?

The key mistake of the proponents of the embourgeoisement thesis was to imagine that consumerism was obliterating class distinctions that originated in the workplace. This was the main finding of a team of sociologists—Goldthorpe, Lockwood, Bechhofer, and Plant—who in 1963–4 conducted an exhaustive study of three groups of affluent male workers in Luton. They discovered that although the majority of affluent workers owned their own homes, they retained their class consciousness, trade-union membership, and a remarkably strong preference for the Labour Party. 83 per cent had voted Labour in 1955 as against 15 per cent for the Conservatives and 2 per cent for the Liberals. In 1959 80 per cent had voted Labour against 16 per cent for the Conservatives and 4 per cent for the Liberals.[34] The absence of women from the survey—characteristic of a period in which social scientists regarded class as all important, and women as adjuncts of their husband's or father's class position—raises a few question-marks, and the possibility that housewives were more likely than their husbands to see themselves as middle class, but as more and more women were taking on part-time manual work in the 1950s and 1960s it seems unlikely that they were a force for embourgeoisement, and right to conclude that it was simply a myth.

Goldthorpe and his collaborators nevertheless accepted that affluence *did* have important effects on working-class life. It resulted, they argued, in a shift away from membership of tightly knit working-class communities towards a way of life which revolved around the home, the family, and the ambition of achieving a higher standard of living. Hence a distinction could be drawn between the 'traditional' and the 'new' working class. The 'new' workers still regarded the trade unions and the Labour Party as organizations with a claim on their allegiance but, Goldthorpe and Lockwood warned, that attachment '*could* certainly become of an increasingly instrumental—and thus conditional—kind, and one devoid of all sense of participation in a class *movement* seeking structural changes in society or even pursuing more limited ends through concerted class action'. If the trade unions and the Labour Party failed to deliver, workers would look elsewhere.[35]

Were the British still class conscious? In a research project led by Gary Runciman in 1962 a representative sample of 1,415 people were asked: 'What social class would you say you belonged to?' Only one per cent of them, including the only titled lady in the sample, were unwilling to assign themselves to a class. When they were asked what sort of people they meant by 'middle class' or 'working class', the answers were often vague or ambiguous: had they been sitting a sociology exam many would have scored low marks. But although respondents differed over where the dividing line between middle and working class should be drawn, and how it should be described, they all believed that there *was* a dividing line, and it was most often equated with the distinction between manual and non-manual employment.

Did class consciousness necessarily result in class conflict? Runciman concluded that there was much less resentment of class distinctions in Britain than Marxists imagined. A sense of grievance was always relative, and arose when people compared their own situation unfavourably with that of others they regarded as more fortunate, but no more deserving. But in normal times their social horizons were limited: 'Most people's lives are governed more by the resentment of narrow inequalities, the cultivation of modest ambitions and the preservation of small differentials than by attitudes to public policy or the social structure as such.'[36] This was class consciousness of a distinctly moderate variety, compatible with the findings of Goldthorpe and his team in their survey of affluent workers in Luton. The majority of the workers they interviewed regarded 'money' as the most important determinant of class:

> Furthermore, virtually all those who held this idea were also alike in one respect: that is, in seeing as a major feature of present-day society a large 'central' class which embraced the bulk of wage and salary earners and to which they themselves felt that they belonged. In other words those of our affluent workers who regarded 'money' as the basis of class almost invariably discounted the manual–nonmanual distinction as a significant line of social cleavage.[37]

Affluent workers did recognize some conflict of economic interests between workers and employers. But the majority 'are disposed to define their relationship with their firm more as one of reciprocity and mutual accommodation rather than as one of coercion and exploitation'.[38]

Working-class life was changing, but as yet the connections between class and party remained. In a major survey of the British voter, published in 1963, David Butler and Donald Stokes showed that at one end of the social spectrum 86 per cent of higher managers voted Conservative while at the other 75 per cent of unskilled workers voted Labour.[39]

Although some areas were socially mixed, the frontiers between the working-class terrace or council estate on the one hand, and middle-class suburbia on the other, were clearly marked. In parts of London, however, the distinctions were highlighted as the middle classes expanded their territory. In 1964 the sociologist Ruth Glass invented a new term to describe the process:

> One by one, many of the working-class quarters of London have been invaded by the middle class—upper and lower—shabby modest mews and cottages...have been taken over when their leases expired, and have become elegant, expensive residences. Larger Victorian houses, downgraded in an earlier or recent period—which were used as lodging houses or were otherwise in multiple occupation—have been upgraded once again...Once this process of 'gentrification' starts in a district it goes on rapidly until all or most of the original working-class occupiers are displaced and the whole social character of the district is changed.[40]

Michael Thompson, a Ph.D. student in anthropology, observed gentrification at work in the streets of late 1960s Islington. They were becoming, he argued, the scene for a class struggle the middle classes were winning:

> In place of hardboard front doors studded with plastic bell pushes, the gentrifiers fitted pseudo-Georgian doors, restoring the fanlights, and adding brass knockers. A blue-and-white enamel number plate served as 'a little touch of provincial France proclaiming that the owner drinks Hirondelle vin ordinaire with his quiche lorraine for his dinner and not light ale with his ham-and-egg pie for his tea'.

Looking nosily through their windows, Thompson could see that the middle classes had knocked through their dividing walls to make their houses lighter and more spacious. Getting rid of interior walls was now a universal bourgeois signifier of good taste. So the gentrifiers were named the 'knockers-through', which flatteringly framed them as romantic renovators rather than hard-nosed property speculators.[41]

By 1974 the Conservative MP Hugh Rossi was explaining to the House of Commons that gentrification had now spread to parts of Camden, Lambeth, and Paddington.[42]

In the 1960s and 1970s the gentrifiers were often radical activists who saw themselves as allies of the working-class inhabitants, and were active in setting up tenants' associations and other community groups. But as owner-occupiers their interests diverged and the effect of their arrival on the scene was to create an alternative culture of wine bars, whole food shops, stripped pine furnishings, and investment in the re-development of homes that put up the price of housing in the area.

Class on the Brain

To most people class, however defined, was simply a fact of life. For academics and other social commentators it was a social and intellec-tual problem. The late 1950s and 1960s witnessed a remarkable out-pouring of investigations into the past, present, and future of the work-ing classes. First Richard Hoggart, then Raymond Williams, published classic studies of popular culture, grounded in their own life-histories and their experience as adult education tutors. Hoggart deplored the impact of mass communications on working-class life while Williams argued that mass communications could be democratized and con-verted to socialist purposes.[43] Michael Young and Peter Willmott pub-lished a study based on three years' field work in Bethnal Green and a new housing estate in Essex. *Family and Kinship in East London* (1957) was a warning to housing officials and town planners of the loss of family and kinship ties entailed—so they maintained—in the resettlement of long established communities. Sociologists were also reacting strongly against the assumptions, widespread in the 1950s, that the welfare state had abolished poverty and created equality of opportunity. In a landmark lecture at the University of Birmingham in 1955, Richard Titmuss persuasively argued that the welfare state as currently organ-ized tended to perpetuate or increase social inequality.[44] Peter Townsend and Brian Abel-Smith 'rediscovered' poverty by redefining it in relative terms as a measure of the gap between the lowest income groups and the average. By this test, poverty was actually getting worse.[45] Socio-logists of education, notably A. H. Halsey and Jean Floud, produced statistics to show that educational reform had failed to increase oppor-tunities for upward social mobility.[46] In the writing of British history, two great Marxist historians, Christopher Hill and Edward Thompson, reinterpreted the past in terms of the class struggle. In their hands the

seventeenth century was transformed into a century of social revolution, the era of industrialization into a narrative of political and industrial conflict that witnessed 'the making of the English working class'.

A similar shift of focus was taking place in the worlds of fiction, the
cinema, and the stage. John Braine's *Room at the Top* (1957), Alan Sillitoe's
Saturday Night and Sunday Morning, and David Storey's *This Sporting Life*
were all novels with provincial working-class settings, by authors from
working-class backgrounds. In the theatre John Osborne's *Look Back In
Anger* (1956) is rightly credited with taking drama beyond the upper-
middle-class conventions of the West End stage, though its ranting
misogynist hero, Jimmy Porter, was a suburban misfit on the fringes of
bohemia, much like Osborne himself before he achieved fame. Sheelagh
Delaney's *A Taste of Honey* (1958) and Arnold Wesker's *Chicken Soup With
Barley* (1958) did put working-class characters on the stage and by 1961
one critic could write: 'Today there are a dozen working-class dramas
as good as the standard fare of the West End playgoer.' Sensing a market trend, the film industry adapted many of the novels, and the plays
of Osborne and Delaney, for the screen. In the cinema, however, the
cycle of 'social realist' work was comparatively short-lived and virtually
all over by the time of Labour's victory in the general election of 1964.
The film industry moved on from gritty dramas in provincial settings
to the colourful hedonism and self-indulgence of swinging London and
the Bond movies. It was television that inherited the legacy of the 'new
wave'. Tony Warren, the originator of Granada Television's *Coronation
Street*, the first episode of which was broadcast on 9 December 1960,
explained: 'I am *not* having a joke at the expense of the people of the
North. What I have aimed at is a true picture of life there and the people's basic friendliness and essential humour.'[47] *Z-Cars* (1962–78), a BBC
police drama set in the fictional northern town of Newtown, was
another series that set out to blend entertainment with social realism.

On television the 'new wave' sometimes acquired a political edge
that it lacked in the cinema. The work of left-wing directors like Ken
Loach and Jim Allen, and left-wing writers like Jeremy Sandford and
Dennis Potter, featured among drama of many kinds in the BBC's
Wednesday Play series (1964–70). *Cathy Come Home*, a play about the
descent of a young couple into homelessness, and the separation of a
mother from her children by the workings of a heartless bureaucracy,
was an emotionally powerful assault by Loach and Sandford on the

inadequacies of the welfare state. First broadcast on 16 November 1966 it is sometimes said to have caused a storm of public outrage that led to changes in government policy, but the outrage was more apparent than the changes in policy. It did, however, coincide with the launching a fortnight later of Shelter, the charity which campaigned on behalf of the homeless, and gave it a flying start. The effects of the new docu-dramas of working class and provincial life were generally more indi-rect. By reminding the south of the problems of the north, and the middle classes of the problems of working-class life, they nourished a social consciousness that helped to underpin the political culture of Labour and the Left.

It was coupled in the late 1950s and early 1960s with a satirical view of the upper classes and 'the Establishment'. The pioneers were four electrifying young men, Peter Cook, Dudley Moore, Alan Bennett, and Jonathan Miller, whose review *Beyond The Fringe* opened at the Fortune Theatre in London in May 1961. Never politically correct, they did not hesitate to mock tyrannical black politicians, left-wing folk-song, or the music of Benjamin Britten, but the class system was a persistent target. In one of their sketches Peter Cook takes the audience into his confi-dence:

> It would be wise to point out to those of you who haven't noticed, though God knows it's been obvious enough, that Jonathan and I come from good families and have had the benefit of a public-school educa-tion, whereas the other two have worked their way up from working-class backgrounds. And yet Jonathan and I have worked together with them in the cast and treated them as equals. I'd like to say it's proved to be a most enjoyable, worthwhile, and stimulating experience for both of us.[48]

Between them the academics, novelists, playwrights, satirists, and tele-vision script-writers succeeded in making the class structure and the privileges of the elite hard to defend, and hardest of all when they were subverted by laughter. In a classic sketch from the BBC's *Frost Report* (1961) three men stand side by side in a row. The tallest, played by John Cleese, wears a bowler hat. Next to him is a man of medium height, played by Ronnie Barker, wearing a trilby. At the end of the row, wear-ing a working-man's flat cap and played by Ronnie Corbett, is the shortest of the three. Barker explains: 'I look up to him [Cleese] because he is upper class. I look down on him [Corbett] because he is lower class.' Corbett replies: 'I know my place.'

In emphasizing the continuing inequalities in British society the academics of the Left were pursuing an agenda. The goals were greater equality of opportunity and greater equality in the distribution of wealth and the problem, as they saw it, was how to explain the persistence of inequality in an era of mass democracy. From a historical perspective it was the wrong question. In spite of the contrasts between the rich and the poor, and the statistics demonstrating that in 1973 the top five per cent of the population owned 38.8 per cent of the wealth, society was *more* egalitarian between the 1940s and the 1970s than it had been before or was to be later. According to the figures presented in 1977 by the Royal Commission on the Distribution of Income and Wealth, the proportion of wealth owned by the bottom 80 per cent of the population rose from 23.8 per cent in 1960 to 33.4 per cent in 1973. The distribution of incomes was more stable, but with some flattening at the top (see Graph 6.1).

Strikers and Scapegoats

In Britain the economic 'golden age' was to culminate between 1968 and 1974 in a wave of industrial unrest greater than any that had occurred since the troubled aftermath of the First World War. The consumer boom, far from extinguishing the class war, had rekindled the flames. It came to be taken for granted that every year would bring with it an increase in the Gross Domestic Product and a rise in the purchasing power of real incomes. Meanwhile the number of strikes and stoppages multiplied as the expectation rose that they would succeed. 'Large-scale confrontations reflected a radical mood of dissatisfaction with the post-war consensus and saw the reassertion of the political strike, occupations and "work-ins", demands for greater control over the workplace and restructuring of the economy in the interests of the working classes.'[49]

The rise of shop-floor militancy was not peculiar to Britain but part of a more widespread phenomenon which the historian Henry Phelps-Brown dubbed 'The Hinge'. At the end of the 1960s, he argued, 'workers in much of the Western world began to display a deep-going change in their outlook—a heightening of expectations, an intensification of

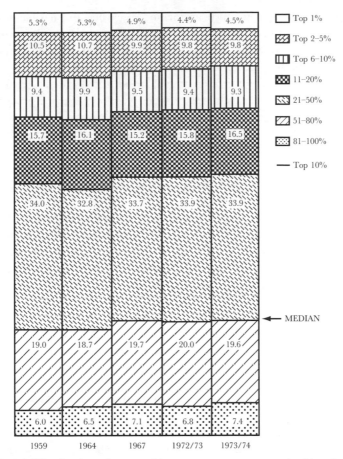

Graph 6.1 Distribution of personal income: percentages received by given quantile groups 1959–73/4.

Source: Royal Commission on the Distribution of Income and Wealth, *Report No 4: The Second Report on the Standing Reference*, PP 1975–6, Cmnd 6626, p. 92.

militancy, an increased capacity for independent action'. The origins of the shift, he argued, were not be found in changing economic circumstances—though they subsequently accelerated the trend—but in a generational change of attitudes, foreshadowed by the events of May 1968, when the students of Paris rose in revolt:

> In the first years of high employment and rising living standards after the Second World War, the attitudes of the majority of employees would

have remained as they had been formed in earlier and harder times: these employees would not have expected large advances, they would have rated security above militancy, and they would have been chary of acting without the support of their union. But the young people who are entering employment for the first time alongside them would be forming attitudes in settings of much greater security, and of alluring prospects within their reach: their experience would have taught them to expect more, and believe themselves capable of going for it and getting it. As their relative numbers grew, there came a time when, despite the hold that age and experience retain on leadership, the new attitudes must predominate. This time might well be reached at about the same number of years after the end of the War in each of several countries. A conspicuous example of spontaneous and independent action of the rank and file, such as the French students' revolt and the general strike that followed, portrayed by television, would serve as the precipitant. To many observers these events seemed the first flames from which a prairie fire of largely unofficial strikes swept across neighbouring countries in the following two years.[50]

Goldthorpe and his team, whose research into the affluent workers of union was carried out shortly before the 'wage explosion' of 1968–70, had already detected a sea-change of attitudes:

> Finally, on the question of aspirations for the future, we would think that there is at least one general characteristic of our affluent workers which will become increasingly common; namely, their awareness of themselves as carrying through some individual, or more probably family, project—their awareness of being engaged in a course of action aimed at effecting some basic change in their life situation and, perhaps, their social identity. As we noted earlier, such an outlook is in marked contrast to the fatalistic social philosophy which was frequently encountered among the inhabitants of the traditional working-class community. However, as the proportion of manual workers with personal experience of long-term economic insecurity diminishes, more optimistic attitudes towards the future may be expected to develop more widely.[51]

Trade unions had always been sectional organizations in the sense that each union was primarily devoted to the interests of its own members, and only secondarily to a wider trade union movement. But some of the major unions were also characterized by the growth of sectionalism within the union itself. The Donovan Commission on trade unions and employers' associations reported that Britain now had two systems of industrial relations, the formal and the informal. As Robert Taylor explains: 'On the one side were the official public institutions—the trade unions and the employers—bound together by substantive collectively bargained industry wide agreements. On the other side stood the reality of shop stewards and managers in individual companies bound together by custom and practice and a decentralized autonomy.' Wherever the dual system operated, the official union organization, with its head office and local branches, had become to some extent a façade, concluding national agreements with employers that were superseded by negotiations conducted in the workplace by committees that very often cut across union boundaries. Real earnings, as determined by workplace deals, were steadily diverging from the wage rates set out in industry-wide agreements. As Goldthorpe and his team found among the affluent workers of Luton, there was an 'almost complete divorce' between the unionism of the branch and the unionism of the workplace. The majority of workers belonged to a union, but few participated in the affairs of their local trade union branch. Conversely, there was a high level of participation in workplace unionism.[52] Trade unions were often said to be too powerful, but some of the major unions exercised only a fragile authority over large sections of their membership. The dual system was far from universal, applying to about one-third of the labour force and mainly to workers in private manufacturing industry. The other two-thirds consisted of workers whose pay was settled either by Wages Councils, or by genuine national agreements. Workplace bargaining was, nevertheless, so widespread as to place a large question mark over the viability of incomes policies.[53]

How far were the trade unions to blame for Britain's troubles? Sir Denis Barnes, who was Permanent Secretary at the Department of Employment from 1968 to 1972, argued that all governments since 1945 had been worried about the consequences of trade union power:

> They have regarded the wage increases produced by collective bargaining as impeding their attempts to maintain full employment, stable prices and a satisfactory balance of payments and to increase the rate of economic growth and generally manage the economy. They have been concerned also about industrial relations—the effect on the economy of strikes, restrictive practices, demarcation, and overmanning.[54]

Doubtless all these factors were discussed in Whitehall but it was strikes that repeatedly hit the headlines and aroused emotions, and strikes that more than anything else damaged the reputation of the unions. Coinciding with the spread of 'declinism', the belief that Britain was falling further and further behind other nations in the race for prosperity, strikes were singled out by the right-wing press as one of the major causes of Britain's economic troubles. Visible and newsworthy, a strike always gave the impression, whatever the cause of a dispute, that it was a challenge to authority led by shop stewards or other union officials. The very act of going on strike was disturbing to a Tory nation that still in its heart of hearts believed in the divine right of employers and managers, but pragmatists were also alarmed. They worried about the possible damage to British industry and its competitiveness in world markets.

The trade unions, however, had allies and friends in the academic world who argued that the significance of strikes was greatly exaggerated. The unions, they argued, were being made into scapegoats for economic difficulties that were as much or more the responsibility of management or government or (in the Marxist version) a consequence of the alienation of the labour force from the process of production. Besides, they pointed out, strikes were endemic in the western world and other nations were equally or more strike-prone. International comparisons had to be taken into account (see table below).

International trends since Donovan

	Stoppages per 100,000 employees		Striker-days per 1,000 employees	
	1965–9	1970–4	1965–9	1970–4
United Kingdom	9.5	12.0	156	585
Australia	31.4	45.2	217	581
Belgium	1.9	5.1	73	242
Canada	7.6	8.8	659	773
Denmark	1.2	4.1	30	360
Finland	4.2	44.7*	84	600*
France	9.6[†]	17.7	126[†]	166
German Fed. Rep.	(not available)		6	49
Ireland	10.2	15.4	543	434
Italy	16.3	25.6	817	1,070
Japan	3.0	6.2	68	115

(Cont.)

| | Stoppages per 100,000 employees | | Striker-days per 1,000 employees | |
	1965–9	1970–4	1965–9	1970–4
Norway	0.4	0.8	8	52
Sweden	0.5	1.9	25	56
United States	6.4	6.7	492	531

* Official criteria for recording strikes changed during this period.

† 1968 excluded from average.

Source: Arthur Marwick, *British Society since 1945* (1996 edition), p. 162.

On these figures the United Kingdom appeared to be muddling along in the centre lane between 1965 and 1969, but conspicuously more strike-prone than most other countries between 1970 and 1974. Even so Canada and Italy were more strike-prone during the turbulent years of the Heath government, with the United States not far behind.

It had to be admitted that the scale of strike action, and hence the number of working days lost, was increasing. Until 1968 or thereabouts, about 95 per cent of strikes were unofficial: short, sharp, localized actions that took place under the leadership of a shop steward without the sanction or approval of the union's national executive. But the seamen's strike of 1968 was a national dispute and it was followed by others in which unions mobilized all their members. 'The 1972 national coal strike', notes Robert Taylor, 'caused the loss of more working days than all 8,931 stoppages that took place during the four years of the Donovan era (1964–8).'[55] Between 1965 and 1967 the number of working days lost through strike action never exceeded three million. Between 1971 and 1973 it never fell below seven million.

If you were to judge by the headlines, you could only conclude that British industry was a battlefield over which two armies were battling for supremacy. But a Department of Employment survey of the years 1971–3 found that on average 98 per cent of establishments in manufacturing industry, covering 81 per cent of workers in the sector, were strike free. *Some* economic historians are also very sceptical of the idea that strikes inflicted serious damage on the economy. One calculation suggests that the impact of stoppages in 1972, the peak year for working days lost through strikes, amounted to only 0.25 per cent of output.[56]

Strike-prone British industries: annual averages, 1966–70

	Total strikes	Total striker-days ('000)	Strikes per 100,000 employees	Striker-days per 100 employees
Docks	195	398	140	286
Coal-mining	301	481	67	109
Motor vehicles	246	994	51	206
Shipbuilding	105	228	50	110
Iron and steel	184	383	31	65
Aircraft	62	152	25	60
General engineering	496	959	21	41
Construction	282	218	17	13
Bricks, pottery, glass, cement	45	116	12	32
Other transport and communications	170	510	11	34

Source: Richard Hyman, *Strikes* (1972), p. 30.

It was certainly true that strikes were heavily concentrated in a small number of industries, as the table above indicates, but when we look down the list we find that it includes several of the most important: not only coal, on which so much of the electricity supply depended, but leading export industries such as motor vehicles and shipbuilding, and industries facing fierce competition, like shipbuilding and the docks. It is hard to believe that interruptions of output in these industries were of little significance, especially when we also bear in mind the veto power of workers in maintaining restrictive practices and opposing changes in working conditions. The major flaw in the trade-union movement, however, was not the resistance of its members to change in the workplace, but the fragmentation of its structure, which prevented it from developing a collective strategy or purpose beyond resistance to managerial initiatives they disliked. The General Council of the TUC had no power to bind its member unions, and the union leaders had no power to bind the rank-and-file members on the shop floor. The trade-union 'movement' consisted in fact of thousands of separate and largely independent local bargaining units which were, in effect, competing with one another in a pay scramble fuelled by inflation. The 'power' of trade unions was at best the negative power to obstruct or prevent: they did not possess the power to reform themselves or the system of industrial relations.

The growth of militancy was due to a constellation of factors. The revival of consumerism, and the expectation of higher standards of living, was accompanied by full employment, which in turn strengthened the bargaining power of trades unions, and led to a 'pay scramble' in which unions struggled to maintain or increase pay differentials. The pay scramble, however, was locked into a vicious circle with rising inflation. Wage increases tended to push up prices and the cost of living, thereby provoking demands for more increases in pay. The threat of ever rising inflation, however, prompted governments to intervene in the sphere of industrial relations. Both Labour and Conservative governments attempted to impose incomes policies, and the Heath government legislated to curb the industrial power of the unions. The aspirations of governments to manage the economy were now in conflict with the determination of the unions to maintain their traditional freedom of action. Whatever the motive behind them, therefore, strikes took on a political character as a challenge to the authority of the politicians. It was no wonder that socialists detected in the workings of this vicious circle a crisis of capitalism.

7

The Liberal Hour

'We now have a permissive society', the Conservative MP Norman St John Stevas told the House of Commons on 1 December 1967. While admitting that some injustices had been removed, he warned that 'permissiveness has gone far enough and that we are in danger of destroying the moral consensus on which our society is based'.[1]

Just as the word 'austerity' came to be on everyone's lips in the 1940s, so the terms 'permissiveness' and 'permissive society' entered the vocabulary of the late 1960s. Sometimes employed in a very broad sense, to characterize a general decline in deference to authority in the home, the school, the workplace, and so on, they were most often associated with changes in attitudes towards sexual morality. Commentators wrote of the new 'permissive legislation' reforming the laws relating to homosexuality, abortion, and divorce. The changes, it was said, heralded the arrival of a new society in which repressive Victorian controls were replaced by more humane and civilized rules. Parallel shifts were to be seen in the relaxation of controls over the representation of sex in the arts and the media. From the publication of *Lady Chatterley's Lover* in 1960, to the first use of the word 'fuck' on television by Kenneth Tynan (13 November 1965) to the staging in 1970 of *Oh! Calcutta!*, with its full-frontal nudery and simulated sex scenes, one taboo after another was discarded.

That much did change is obvious: hence the backlash that ensued against the 'tide of permissiveness'. To measure the extent of the change is more difficult. It is easy, for example, to lose sight of the fact that the liberalism of government and Parliament operated within strict limits. Under the Criminal Justice Act of 1967 corporal punishment was finally abolished in prisons, and the birch and the cat-o'-nine-tails banished. So far, so liberal, but there was no question of abolishing corporal punishment in schools. The teaching profession clung tenaciously to the cane in England, and the tawse in Scotland, and even in the case of schools for the handicapped the government refused to rule out corporal punishment.[2] The Sexual Offences Act of 1967 decriminalized male homosexual acts between consenting adults but only if they were both over the age of twenty-one: the age of consent for heterosexuals was sixteen. Many homosexual activities remained criminal and the number of prosecutions actually *increased* after the act was passed.

Nor is it easy to fathom the extent to which popular attitudes and behaviour were changing. *Time* magazine wrote memorably in 1965 of 'swinging London', but greater London was a city of ten million people. The young might be swinging in Chelsea, but were they in Slough? And what of Grantham or Peterhead? The survey evidence does suggest that attitudes towards premarital sex were becoming more liberal, a change facilitated by the spread of the birth pill towards the end of the 1960s. Of women who married in the late 1950s, 35 per cent reported that they had had sexual relations with their husbands before marriage. For women who married in the early 1970s, the figure was 74 per cent.[3] But the institution of marriage, the cornerstone of conservative morals, was never more popular. Between 1966 and 1970 a higher proportion of men and women were married than at any other time in the twentieth century.[4] Marriage was not only compatible with the 'swinging sixties' but positively fashionable. In looking back on the 'liberal hour' we always have to keep our eyes open for the continuities and the cross-currents.

Conscience and Parliament

When Britain entered the 1950s the authorities were still vocal in defence of existing codes of morality.[5] By the late 1950s, however, there were signs that even a House of Commons with a Conservative majority was prepared to rethink issues of conscience. The Suicide Act of 1959 decriminalized a practice 'which had consistently (and almost universally) been condemned by Christian morality'. Legislation that same year enabled illegitimate children to be legitimized if their parents subsequently married. The Betting and Gambling Act of 1960 legalized both gambling clubs and betting shops.[6] According to the sociologist Christie Davies, who based his argument on a study of the relevant parliamentary debates, the reforms were a consequence of an underlying shift in the philosophy of the elite from 'moralism' to 'causalism':

> In the past the decision as to whether or not to forbid an activity and to punish those responsible for it, was taken on moralist grounds. Those in favour of forbidding it would argue that the activity was wrong, immoral, wicked, and that this was sufficient reason for preventing it and punishing people detected in it...Today the arguments for and against forbidding any activity are very different and are rooted in what I have termed causalist morality. Parliament argues today about the consequences of legalizing an activity compared with the consequences of not doing so. If it turns out that more harm is done by forbidding an activity than by allowing it, then Parliament will permit it, even if most of the members consider the activity to be wrong or immoral.[7]

In the 1940s, Davies argues, MPs still couched their arguments in moralist terms. By the 1960s both supporters and opponents of reform couched their arguments in moralist terms. Why the change? The main reason was 'that in other important sectors of society—in industry, in the economic ministries, in social welfare—men's thinking had come to be dominated by considerations of cause and effect, of technical rationality'. In place of socialism and free market economics both the Labour and Conservative Parties adopted a managerial philosophy in which the key question became, 'does it work?'[8]

Like other sociological theories this over-simplifies the past. There was, for example, no lack of managerial thinking before the 1960s, and the assumption that Victorian reforms were simply an expression of moralism is open to question. It seems more likely that from the nineteenth century onwards, moralism *and* causalism—in historical terms Evangelical Christianity and Utilitarianism—were rival philosophies which both played a part in the legislation governing sex, marriage, and the family.

In the politics of the Labour Party the cause of liberal reform was linked to a reaction against the party's nonconformist traditions. In his book *The Future of Socialism* (1956), an attempt to adapt socialism to changing times, Anthony Crosland sketched out a cultural agenda which included an assault on Puritanism. 'There come to mind at once', he wrote, 'the divorce laws, licensing laws, prehistoric (and flagrantly unfair) abortion laws, obsolete penalties for sexual abnormality, the illiterate censorship of books and plays, and remaining restrictions on the equal rights of women.'[9] Questions of sexual morality never became party political issues. In the House of Commons they were treated as matters of conscience on which every MP was free to vote according to his or her own convictions. Nevertheless the momentum for reform was provided mainly by Labour and Liberal politicians while Conservative MPs formed the bulk of the resistance.

The Labour and Liberal reformers, however, were reacting as much against the puritanical traditions of their own parties, as against the Conservatives. On the Conservative side, meanwhile, a progressive minority were strongly in favour of reform. It was clear that further reforms would have to await a Parliament with a Labour majority.

The Relaxation of Censorship

Under the Obscene Publications Act of 1857 a work could be banned if it was found to be obscene, and the test of obscenity, laid down by Chief Justice Cockburn in 1868, was 'whether the tendency of the matter charged is to deprave and corrupt those whose minds are open to such immoral influences and into whose hands a publication of this sort might fall'.[10] Publication of anything of a sexually explicit nature was therefore hazardous, and the work of eminent writers as likely to be prosecuted as routine pornography. The most celebrated case was that of D. H. Lawrence's novel *Lady Chatterley's Lover*, a mystical hymn to sexual intercourse which he had published privately in Florence in 1928. In Britain copies had been seized by the police and the book successfully prosecuted. Other works banned in Britain included Radclyffe Hall's novel about lesbianism, *The Well of Loneliness* (1928) and Henry Miller's Rabelaisian *Tropic of Cancer* (1934).

Working closely with the Society of Authors the Labour MP Roy Jenkins contrived in 1959 to secure the passage through Parliament of a new Obscene Publications Act. The Act made no change to the basic principle that pornography was a criminal offence. Indeed there were thirty-four prosecutions of pornographic material in the following twelve months.[11] But it did provide publishers with the potential defence of literary merit. The following year Penguin Books precipitated a test case by publishing *Lady Chatterley's Lover*, for which they were taken to court by the Director of Public Prosecutions. Penguin summoned a star cast of writers and critics to testify to the literary merit of the book while Mervyn Griffith-Jones, for the prosecution, asked the jury: 'Is it a book you would wish even your wife or your servants to read?' The jury acquitted Penguin, who sold two million copies of the book during the following year. The defence of literary merit was no doubt sincerely intended, but the book was not read by two million people for its literary merit. It was devoured for its 'adult content'.

After this, a number of books which could not previously have been published were put on the market, but there was no guarantee that the defence of literary merit would succeed. In 1963 the courts thwarted an attempt to publish an unexpurgated paperback edition of John Cleland's eighteenth-century work *Fanny Hill: Memoirs of a Woman of Pleasure*.[12] As was generally the case with the 'permissive' legislation of the period, the boundaries of the permitted were revised rather than abandoned.

While the law was the ultimate arbiter, it had long been the case in Britain that self-censorship was more important. In the case of the cinema the industry had set up its own regulatory body, the British Board of Film Censors, which in conjunction with the local licensing authorities had exercised strict control over what could be shown in cinemas between the wars. The appointment in 1958 of John Trevelyan as Secretary to the British Board of Film Censors marked the beginning of an era in which sex was more frankly presented in feature films. Though he described himself as 'a censor who did not believe in censorship' Trevelyan was an interventionist who paid close attention to both the visual content and the language of feature film, and frequently insisted on cuts or changes. He sought to achieve a compromise between the prudery of the past and the commercial exploitation of sex and violence. It was largely due to Trevelyan that the new wave films of the period, with their working class settings and adulterous sex, combined greater freedom of expression with some sensitivity to the bounds of traditional good taste. Among the more memorable films which he passed as censor were *Room at the Top* (1958), *Saturday Night and Sunday Morning* (1960), *The L-Shaped Room* (1962), and *A Kind of Loving* (1962).[13] Little by little the rules of censorship were relaxed. As John Sutherland remarks, Lindsay Anderson's *If*, put out on general release in 1968, included 'a tuft of female pubic hair visible to the 18-plus British population'.[14] Once the barriers were broken down by *auteurs* like Anderson, the way was open for the producers of bawdy British sex romps like *Confessions of a Driving Instructor* (1973) and *Confessions of a Window Cleaner* (1974).

Ever since its establishment as a public corporation in 1926, with Sir John Reith as its first Director-General, the BBC had sought to occupy the moral and educational high ground. Radio and television producers were expected to conform to standards of taste and decency which ruled out bad language, explicitly sexual topics, and the subversion of authority. Here again there was a notable shift during the reign as Director-General from 1960 to 1969 of Hugh Carleton Greene. An Establishment figure with an anti-Establishment streak, he encouraged programme-makers to experiment and break down taboos:

> Strong language in comedies, supposedly overexplicit portrayals of sexual activity in single plays, the undermining of authority figures in *Z Cars*, a long-running series about northern policemen, and ridicule directed at politicians and the church all stirred up intense controversies, short-lived in themselves, but contributing, despite the praise which the same programmes drew from other sections of the audience, to a persistent current of unease about the direction in which its director-general might be leading the BBC.[15]

In 1964 that unease came to a head with the formation of the Clean-Up TV campaign, renamed the following year as the National Viewers' and Listeners' Association (NVLA). The moving spirit behind the campaign was Mrs Mary Whitehouse, the first outraged wife and mother to storm on to the stage of national politics since Mrs Irene Lovelock in 1945. Mrs Whitehouse, who taught art and sex education at a girls' school, was galvanized into action by a BBC television programme of March 1964 in which premarital sex was discussed in a tolerant fashion. A fervent Christian and supporter of Moral Rearmament, she was deeply offended. Convinced that the BBC was fast becoming a source of moral pollution she organized a protest meeting at Birmingham Town Hall to launch her campaign.

Like Irene Lovelock before her, Mary Whitehouse saw herself as defending hearth and home against the Establishment: 'All the power of the permissive lobby in the 1960s was aimed—deliberately or otherwise—at the heart of the family, removing from parents responsibility and caring...'[16] And like the founder of the British Housewives' League she was an unsophisticated person who drew simple conclusions from complex realities and expressed them with absolute conviction. In this she was genuinely representative of a part of the viewing and listening public that was still wedded to Victorian ideals of morality and tone deaf to irony, scepticism, and irreverence. Nevertheless, she possessed courage and character, and hammered away at issues that the Establishment would have preferred to ignore. She was convinced that television influenced the behaviour of viewers and in particular of young viewers. Since companies bought advertising time on commercial television in order to persuade viewers to buy their products, and politicians hogged the camera in the hope of winning votes, common sense suggested that she was right: promiscuity or violence on television would encourage promiscuity or violence in the real world. When social scientists argued that there was no evidence to prove her correct, she told them they were wrong. Mrs Whitehouse, however, could never plausibly claim to represent the viewing public as a whole. The majority of viewers belonged to the saucy seaside postcard school of popular opinion. Though not anti-Christian, they no longer read the Bible or said their prayers. Secure in their own essential decency, they took a relaxed view of corrupt or evil characters in television drama, finding them more entertaining than alarming. They were surprised but not shocked when Kenneth Tynan uttered the word 'fuck', the word which more than any other had got the British through the more difficult stretches of the Second World War. The effect of television on the unstable and the insecure was the most important cause for concern.

On the stage, the Lord Chamberlain's powers of censorship were abolished by the Theatre Act of 1968. Taking advantage of the change in the law, Kenneth Tynan put together a revue in celebration of sexual liberation, four-letter words, and nudity on stage. When *Oh! Calcutta!* opened at the Round House Theatre in London in July 1970 a number of complaints were lodged with the Metropolitan Police and an officer from the obscene publications squad, Detective Inspector Frederick Luff, made an incognito visit to see the show. 'Sex', he reported to the Attorney-General, 'is not dealt with with respect, man is depicted as a performing dog, self-indulgently satisfying every whim and fancy thereby debasing every form of decency and attacking the very roots of the family unit.' Sir Peter Rawlinson, the Attorney-General in the newly elected Conservative government of Edward Heath, decided to make his own enquiries and sent his 'experts' to report: a professor of law, a vicar, and two distinguished headmistresses, Dame Mary Green and Dame Margaret Miles, champions both of comprehensive schooling. Resolutely tolerant and progressive, none of them could find anything to object to and Dame Mary Green wrote: 'The women in the play were lovely and seemed unspoilt, with a healthy freshness. I was neither shocked nor embarrassed.' The Bishop of Southwark, Mervyn Stockwood—a platonic homosexual—added that he found the show as 'boring as a boarding school bath night'. Spared from prosecution *Oh! Calcutta!* transferred to the West End where it ran for more than three years.[17] As with the record sales of *Lady Chatterley's Lover*, the commercial attractions of permissiveness were glaringly apparent.

The Liberal Reforms

The late 1960s were the liberal hour in British politics and the consequences were enduring. The campaigns waged by pressure-groups like the Abortion Law Reform Association, founded in 1936, and the Homosexual Law Reform Association, founded in 1958, had prepared the ground for change, but it was the fleeting conjunction of a liberalizing Home Secretary and a House of Commons receptive to change, that made the reforms possible. Neither the Labour Party nor the Labour government were formally committed on 'issues of conscience', which continued to be matters on which MPs were free to make up their minds as individuals. But since Labour MPs were generally more liberal than the Conservatives, the election in March 1966 of a new House of Commons with an overall Labour majority of 96 marked a tipping-point. Roy Jenkins, who was Home Secretary from December 1965 to November 1967, was one of the younger breed of Labour politicians who believed that full employment should be supplemented, provided it did no harm to others, by full enjoyment. Personally committed to reform, he used his powers to ensure that private members' bills of which he approved were granted sufficient parliamentary time to reach the statute book.

How important were the reforms themselves? All made significant differences to the lives of men and women who might otherwise have suffered from the consequences of previous legislation. As already mentioned, the Sexual Offences Act of 1967 decriminalized homosexual acts between consenting adults in private, thus removing a major cause of blackmail and public disgrace. This was a great liberation but in some ways a limited one. The new law did not apply in Scotland until 1980 or in Northern Ireland until 1981.[18] The age of consent was fixed at twenty-one, instead of sixteen as for heterosexuals, on the grounds that it was necessary to defend younger men from being 'corrupted' into homosexuality by older men. For buggery by a man with a consenting youth over the age of 16 the penalty was five years' imprisonment; where the offence was gross indecency the previous maximum penalty of two years' imprisonment was increased to five. While sex between two consenting adults in private was decriminalized, group sex remained illegal, and gays who went cruising for partners and were caught by the police were still liable to prosecution. The bill specifically excluded the armed forces and was amended in the course of its passage to exclude the merchant navy as well. Support for homosexual law reform did not necessarily imply approval of homosexuality. In 1965 Lord Arran had introduced a similar bill in the House of Lords. In a speech supporting the proposal Attlee said: 'I believe that homosexuality is an evil, and I do not think you will cure it. But I think that blackmail is a greater evil.' Field Marshall Lord Montgomery of Alamein was in the opposite camp: 'I regard the act of homosexuality in any form as the most abominable bestiality that any human can take part in and that reduces him almost to the state of an animal.' Montgomery, who was seventy-eight at the time, proposed to move an amendment raising the age of consent to eighty. 'Don't look so gloomy', Lord Boothby shouted out, 'you've only got two years to go.'[19]

Even as it stood the 1967 bill aroused much hostility within the Labour Party, as the leader of the House, Richard Crossman, reflected in his diary: 'It may well be twenty years ahead of public opinion; certainly working class people in the north jeer at their Members at the weekend and ask them why they're looking after the buggers at Westminster instead of looking after the unemployed at home. It has gone down very badly that the Labour Party should be associated with such a bill.'[20] Whether from tactical motives or genuine conviction, the supporters of the measure continued to refer to homosexuality as an unfortunate condition, akin to psychological illness, for which there was no medical remedy. Sympathy and compassion were the grounds on which they urged reform, and the stigma remained. It was underlined by vigorous action on the part of the police and the courts. 'Between 1967 and 1976', writes Jeffrey Weeks, 'the recorded incidence of indecency between males doubled, the number of prosecutions trebled, and the number of convictions quadrupled.'[21]

In the armed forces therefore homosexuals continued to inhabit an uncertain territory somewhere between a tacit policy of tolerance and outbreaks of homophobic zeal. In 1969 the Admiralty was greatly alarmed by the findings of an investigation carried out by Captain Donald MacIntyre of the naval historical branch into an alleged homosexual scandal. He reported that a large number of naval ratings were in the habit of visiting a male brothel in Bermuda, thereby exposing themselves to blackmail. Other reports were reaching the Admiralty of sailors lured into transvestite bars in Bugis Street, Singapore. During the 1960s about forty or fifty ratings were dismissed every year for being gay and a dozen officers were allowed to retire early. 'There is evidence', the Second Sea Lord noted, 'that some officers and senior ratings do not take a sufficiently stern attitude towards minor homosexual acts. The time has come to take a stricter and less permissive attitude in the fleet.'[22]

While homosexuals were still hedged around with prohibitions and penalties, the liberating effects of the 1967 Act should not be underestimated. The founding of the Gay Liberation Front in London in October 1970 marked the beginning of a more assertive gay culture, imported from the United States and based on the demand for rights. Gay clubs and societies began to spring up in London and also on university campuses. In April 1973 the National Union of Students committed itself to the support of the campaign for gay rights. By October of the same year societies for gay students had been established in sixty universities and colleges.[23]

The more conservative aspects of the 1960s were evident over the question of drugs. The 1960s were a period in which drug use, though impossible to measure with precision, was almost certainly growing among young people. The response of the authorities was to tighten up the restrictions. Under the Drugs (Prevention of Misuse) Act of 1964 the unauthorized possession of amphetamines was made a criminal offence. The Dangerous Drugs Act of 1964 made it an offence to cultivate cannabis. Both acts were introduced by the Conservative Home Secretary, Henry Brooke, a notably illiberal figure, but neither was repealed by the incoming Labour government. Possession of LSD was criminalized by a further Act in 1966. Between 1950 and 1970 the number of proscribed narcotics rose from 33 to 106.[24] The police raided the homes of rock stars in search of cannabis, possession of small quantities of which could lead to a prison sentence. In June 1967 Mick Jagger and Keith Richard of the Rolling Stones were convicted on a charge of possession and awarded prison sentences. They were reprieved on appeal but it would be wrong to imagine that popular opinion was equally liberal. 'In 1967', writes Peter Thompson, '88 per cent of the public thought that dealing in "soft" drugs should be a criminal offence. Some 77 per cent thought that taking them should be as well.'[25]

None of this, of course, prevented the spread of recreational drug-taking, but as John Davies writes, 'the British drug scene of the 1960s was overwhelmingly a London scene'.[26] Cannabis, which had first been introduced by West Indian immigrants in the 1950s, was the 'white drug of choice', increasingly popular in smart circles and apparently so mild in its effects that it came to be regarded as harmless. 'For the bourgeoisie nowadays', wrote the disapproving socialist David Widgery, 'cannabis can be bought by cheque and smoked with a smug impunity over the liqueurs.' At the same time far more dangerous alternatives were available in the form of heroin, injectable barbiturates, and LSD, all of which carried a risk of addiction, physical or mental collapse, or premature death. Commissioned to report on the subject, Baroness Wootton recommended a clear distinction between stringent penalties for the supply or possession of hard drugs, and mild penalties for the possession of small quantities of cannabis. James Callaghan, who by this time had succeeded Jenkins as Home Secretary, accepted her proposal for the reclassification of cannabis as a class B instead of a class A drug, but acting on the theory that the use of soft drugs was likely to lead on to the use of hard drugs, he insisted on a maximum penalty of five years in prison for the possession of cannabis. It was time, he said, to 'call a halt to the advancing tide of permissiveness'.[27] The provision was included in the government's Misuse of Drugs Bill which lapsed with the general election of 1970 but was then revived and put on the statute book by the Heath government in 1971. In practice—as Callaghan had expected—the maximum penalty was rarely enforced. Most first offenders for cannabis possession were let off with a fine: in 1973 the average penalty was £14 [=£78].

A survey by National Opinion Poll in 1965 recorded 72 per cent in favour of abortion law reform. Under the 1861 Offences Against the Persons Act an abortion could only legally be carried out if childbirth would put the pregnant woman's health severely at risk. 'An inquiry by the 1937 Birkett Committee estimated that out of 100,000 abortions that were carried out annually, 40 per cent were carried out illegally.'[28] Since wealthy women could obtain abortions from Harley Street specialists, while the poor had to rely on the ministrations of backstreet abortionists at whose hands about fifty women a year died, the social injustice of the situation was glaring. Given the shame that still attached to the unwanted pregnancies of single women, the sufferings they endured could be terrible.

The Abortion Act of 1967, which began as a private member's bill sponsored by the Liberal MP David Steel, allowed pregnancies to be terminated on social grounds, or because of a threat of abnormality in the foetus, up to twenty-eight weeks after conception. The Abortion Law Reform Association, a women's group of feminist outlook, had called initially for 'abortion on demand'—that is, for women to have the right to an abortion. Such a proposal would have been too radical for acceptance by the House of Commons. In order to lend more respectability to the process Steel agreed that the decision to terminate should be an exclusively medical one, for which the approval of two doctors would be required. One of the main arguments put forward by the supporters of the bill was that it would reduce the number of dangerous back-street abortions carried out by unqualified practitioners. There was strenuous opposition outside the House of Commons from the Roman Catholic Church, which was strictly opposed to abortion on doctrinal grounds. In the House of Commons, however, those who opposed the bill on moral or religious grounds recognized that such arguments would fail in a secular-minded assembly. They concentrated therefore on utilitarian arguments such as the persistence of illegal abortions in countries where legal abortion was permitted. The bill passed its second reading with 225 MPs in favour and thirty-one against,[29] but its opponents were irreconcilable. They set up a new pressure-group, the Society for the Protection of the Unborn Child, which campaigned for the repeal of the legislation.

In the event the 'safeguard' of medical control proved to be little more than a formality and abortion on demand was in effect conceded.

The number of recorded abortions rose from 35,000 per year in 1968 to 141,000 in 1975. 'In other words', as Jeffrey Weeks has written, 'many women were seizing the opportunity provided by the 1967 Act to deliberately control their own fertility.'[30] The figures encouraged the opponents of abortion to renew their efforts. Between 1969 and 1980 eight attempts were made to introduce legislation to restrict the scope for abortion.[31] (Owing to advances in medicine which made it possible to preserve the lives of babies born at 28 weeks or under, the time limit for abortions was reduced from 28 weeks to 24 weeks in 1991.)

Unlike the acts relating to homosexuality and abortion, the reform of the divorce laws arose out of the recommendations of the Law Commission, a body which the Wilson government had established in 1965 with a mandate to promote legal reform in general, and marriage and family law in particular. The three main grounds on which a divorce could be granted under the existing law were (1) adultery, (2) cruelty, and (3) desertion, which had to be proved in court by evidence produced by one party to demonstrate the guilt of the other. In practice divorce sometimes took place by mutual consent, but in order to satisfy the demands of the law one of the partners would agree to stage an offence. A husband, for example, would accept the role of 'guilty party' and agree to be discovered in a hotel room with another woman. But if a husband wanted to marry his mistress, and his wife refused to lodge a petition for divorce, there was nothing the husband could do to dissolve the marriage legally.

Soon after the establishment of the Law Commission the Church of England obligingly withdrew from the fray. *Putting Asunder* (1966), the report of the Archbishop of Canterbury's working party, 'acknowledged that the church should not interfere in the making of laws for a secular society or impose standards of behaviour expected of believers on those who were not'. Somewhat contradictorily, it also recommended that divorce should be granted where marriage had irretrievably broken down.[32]

The new divorce bill proposed 'no fault' procedures whereby a marriage could be terminated by mutual consent after separation for a period of at least two years, or if the partner petitioning for a divorce could prove that the marriage had irretrievably broken down. The standard matrimonial offences—adultery, cruelty and desertion—ceased to be offences but were retained as criteria for assessing the viability of the marriage. Denounced by Lady Summerskill as a 'Casanova's Charter' that would enable middle-aged men to abandon ageing wives in favour of younger women, the proposals were nevertheless incorporated in the Divorce Act of 1969, which came into effect in 1971.[33] A closely allied measure, the Matrimonial Property Act of 1970, aimed to ensure that in the event of a divorce, each partner received half the resources of the marriage, an arrangement intended mainly for the protection of wives.

A Permissive Society?

During the 1960s commentators were optimistic about the current state of marriage, convinced that husbands and wives were now much more likely to enjoy a more equal and a more rewarding relationship. Comparing the findings of the two surveys of sex and marriage which he had carried out in 1950 and 1969, Geoffrey Gorer observed that the segregation of roles within marriage was beginning to break down. In 1950 he wrote, 'it was considered to be a bad marriage if the husband did any housework which was not dependent on his greater physical strength and imputed mechanical skills (such as carrying coal or mending fuses)...and a woman who didn't spend all her time looking after her home and her children but went "gadding about" was a bad wife and a bad mother'. Such attitudes, reported Gorer, persisted among older people. But among the younger generation, and particularly among skilled manual workers, 'this traditional complementary ideal has been replaced by an ideal of equality, of husband and wife doing everything together, of minimal separation of interests and pursuits outside working hours, which I am here calling the ideal of symmetrical marriage.'[34] Yet Gorer also reported an interesting difference between the qualities wives looked for in husbands, and the qualities husbands looked for in wives. The wives stressed the value in a husband of understanding, love, and affection: the husbands put the main emphasis on a wife's skills as mother and housekeeper. Gorer interpreted this as evidence that husbands were now more interested in their homes and their children, but it is more likely to suggest to us that husbands expected their wives to play their traditional role efficiently.[35]

Needless to say sociologists reported that patterns of marriage and family life varied greatly. But as Jane Lewis writes: 'The general view from a range of such community studies was first, that companionate marriage was the modern form of marriage and inherently desirable; second, that it was filtering down from middle-class families to the working class; and third, that it was becoming more widespread as the years passed.'[36]

In March 1959 the British Medical Association published *Getting Married*, a book intended for a popular audience which included an article by Dr Eustace Chesser entitled: 'Is Chastity Outmoded? Outdated? Out?' The mere suggestion that it might be acceptable for couples to have premarital sex caused a furore. 'We are stunned at the suggestion that pre-marital sexual intercourse might not really be a bad thing', wrote *Woman's Mirror*. 'Subversive stuff' was the verdict of an editorial in the *Daily Mail*. The controversy did no harm to sales of the book but after 200,000 copies had been sold the BMA yielded to the critics and suspended publication.

It is easy to mock the conservative moralists of the period and to forget the case for premarital chastity as they saw it, namely that it provided women with a necessary protection from the sexual opportunism of men. The typical young man, in other words, wanted sex for its own sake and would, if allowed to, exploit a woman's need for love and security, and just as readily abandon her. Chesser, ironically, began from the same starting-point:

> The average woman demands to be loved, first; all else is incidental. She feels sure of being loved when she is persuaded that the relationship is more than the expression of passing desire. The best proof of its permanence is the promise of marriage.
>
> She may be deceived, she may even deceive herself. One thing is certain: her attitude is fundamentally different from that of the man. To the man the urge for a genital relationship is often more insistent than marriage. And it remains so until he develops greater maturity.
>
> Consequently it would be a mistake to conclude that once women had won their independence and were freed of the fear of pregnancy they would indulge in sexual promiscuity. Equality does not do away with basic differences between the sexes.
>
> Birth control aided the man in breaking down feminine resistance; there are however obstacles other than the fear of pregnancy. These are rooted in the maternal instinct, which demands a fuller relationship. Indeed it is my view that the woman in risking pregnancy before marriage unconsciously (at least) desires childbirth.[37]

1 Statues of Clement Attlee and Margaret Thatcher in the Members' Lobby of the House of Commons.

Week ending December 21 1946   Every Thursday Threepence

JOHN BULL

J. B. PRIESTLEY
on "The Spirit of Christmas"
SEE PAGE 7

2   Christmas 1946: the Family Reunited.

3 Beside the Seaside: Isle of Wight beach, July 1956.

Ronson's new Essex

Here's the world's most luxurious lighter... the gift so *new* it could never be given before! Twenty-four karat gold plate, designed with incredible elegance. For someone you don't mind impressing...no other gift can *touch* the Essex! 12.50* Also in Jewelers Bronze, 8.50.

New! Exclusive easy-fill swivel base, swings wide open for fast, spill-proof fuelings! *Look for the name* RONSON *world's greatest lighter.*

*PLUS TAX ©1954 RONSON CORPORATION

4 Sex and cigarettes: advertisement for Ronson, 1950s.

5 February 1950: council housing and steelworks, Corby, Northants.

6 Kenyan Asians arriving at London airport, February 1968.

7a NUPE workers picket Queen Mary's Hospital, Roehampton: (no date but probably late 1978 or early 1979).

7b Members of the Transport and General Workers Union protest against the Industrial Relations Bill, December 1970.

8 Sir Alec Issigonis and the Mini, which he designed for the British Motor Corporation.

9 Pro-life marchers walking past pro-abortion protestors, London, August 1974.

10 The collapse of Ronan Point, 16 May 1968.

11 Carnaby Street gets ready for Christmas, November 1967.

12 Mary Whitehouse.

13 'Breaking the Union grip' *Economist* 8–12 February 1982.

14 Grammar school boys 1957.

15 Barry Bucknell with tool-box.

16 Punks on the Kings Road, 1984.

17　The Young Urban Professional, 1980s.

18　England football supporters, 1996.

19 Sean Connery comes to the aid of the SNP, April 1999.

20 The burning of The Satanic Verses: Bradford, February 1989.

Chesser, therefore, was as firmly opposed to promiscuity as the advocates of premarital chastity. He simply argued that if a couple were emotionally committed to one another, they should be allowed to make their own decision.

Little by little 'opinion formers' chipped away at the doctrine of chastity. In the BBC Reith Lectures for 1962 G. M. Carstairs, the Professor of Psychiatry at the University of Edinburgh, suggested that charity was a more important moral value than chastity. Young people, he added, regarded sexual experience as a 'sensible preliminary' to marriage.[38] While he may have been right about the behaviour of young adults, the evidence suggests that most teenagers were still inhibited by moral concerns or the fear of pregnancy. In the early 1960s, Michael Schofield carried out a survey of the heterosexual behaviour and experience of 1,873 young people aged between fifteen and nineteen. He found that only 20 per cent of the boys and 12 per cent of the girls in the sample had had sexual intercourse. Attitudes to premarital sex among the young were also fairly conservative. 35 per cent of boys and 61 per cent girls agreed that sexual intercourse before marriage was wrong. 64 per cent of boys said that they would like to marry a virgin, and 85 per cent of girls said that they would like to be virgins when they married. 46 per cent of boys and 57 per cent of girls agreed that if a girl had sex before marriage she would get a bad reputation.[39] They may of course have been telling interviewers what they felt they ought to say, rather than what they actually thought, but even if this were the case, the results would still be an illuminating reflection of the norms as young people understood them. Confirmation that attitudes were indeed conservative is to be found in a survey of 949 men and 1,037 women published by Geoffrey Gorer in 1971. A quarter of the men and two-thirds of the women claimed to have been virgins when they married.[40] If so the poet Philip Larkin was exaggerating when he wrote that 'sexual intercourse began in 1963 / Between the end of the Chatterley ban and the Beatles' first LP'.

Potentially the most radical force for change in sexual behaviour was the introduction of the birth pill, which gave both single and married women control over their own fertility. In the past heterosexual sex had usually entailed the risk of pregnancy unless the man used a condom or practised interrupted sex. Owing to the efforts of the Consumer Association, which tested a variety of contraceptives and published the results in 1963, the condom was becoming more reliable: a British Standard was adopted in 1964.[41] By this time, too, condoms were generally available for male customers in barber's shops or dispensers installed in men's toilets. But contraceptive techniques that could be used by women independently—the cap and the spermicide—were difficult to obtain and sometimes unreliable. In the past women had often, and wisely, resisted male advances until they could be sure that a steady relationship with a promise of marriage was in view. The pill enabled them to enjoy sex without risk of pregnancy, a liberating prospect. 'This freedom', wrote the novelist Margaret Drabble, 'is evidently connected to that other major revolution of our society, emancipation for women. It is the clinching argument. Education, freedom to work, equal pay, and social equality did not mean much when they could be negated by the arrival of one small unintended baby. We ought to be entering on the golden age of free adult sexual equality and companionship that the feminists fought for.'[42] The use of the pill spread gradually at first, with family planning clinics unevenly distributed around the country, and advice restricted to married couples. Advice for the unmarried was pioneered by Helen Brook, whose voluntary work in family planning clinics had convinced her that the failure to provide it was a cause of many unwanted pregnancies and much needless suffering. The charity she founded established the first Brook Centres in London (1964), Birmingham (1966), Bristol, and Edinburgh (1968). The spread of the pill was also facilitated by the Family Planning Act of 1967, which enabled local authorities to provide contraceptive advice free of charge to all, married or unmarried, through the National Health Service. Only 9 per cent of unmarried women were 'on the pill' by 1970, but the trend was set.[43] Finally Sir Keith Joseph, the Secretary of State for Social Services in Edward Heath's Cabinet, introduced legislation in 1973 which incorporated 'family planning' services within the NHS. Barbara Castle, his successor in the incoming Labour administration, announced that contraceptives, as well as advice on contraception, would be supplied free of charge to all.

The idea that contraceptive advice should be restricted to married couples had quietly faded away. The 1960s and early 1970s witnessed a growing toleration and acceptance of premarital sex. In 1963 and again in 1970 a sample of grammar school sixth-formers were invited to express their views on the rights and wrongs of premarital sex. The results were as follows:

Premarital sex 'always wrong'

	Boys	Girls
1963	28.6 per cent	55.8 per cent
1970	10.3 per cent	14.6 per cent

Premarital sex 'never wrong'

	Boys	Girls
1963	10.2 per cent	2.4 per cent
1970	33.7 per cent	17.7 per cent

Source: Derek Wright, *The Psychology of Moral Behaviour* (1971), pp. 177–9.

The merging of grammar and modern schools into comprehensives may have contributed to the relaxation of attitudes. In 1964 two thirds of all grammar schools and more than one third of secondary moderns were single-sex schools, but the overwhelming majority of comprehensives were co-educational[44]: first love, and first sexual experience, were virtually a part of the curriculum.

Was behaviour changing as well as attitudes? The rise in the number of girls having sex before the age of sixteen gives some indication that it was (see Graph 7.1). 'Clearly', wrote Christie Davies in 1975, 'there has been a massive change in attitudes in a permissive direction and especially among the girls. The view that premarital sex is wrong is rapidly disappearing.'[45] This is not to imply that *promiscuity* was widespread or generally approved. Gorer's survey did produce an 18-year old schoolgirl who was on the pill and had already had a series of lovers. Asked how often she had intercourse she replied: 'Twice a week if I like the boy. It depends on exams!' Gorer estimated that about 11 per cent of the unmarried population, overwhelmingly male and young, could be described as promiscuous in 1969.[46] Of 376 men and women aged 25 questioned by Schofield in the early 1970s, only 17 per cent had had sex with more than one partner during the past twelve months.[47]

The divorce statistics suggest a similar pattern: a loosening of ties which as yet hardly affected the 'silent majority'. Between 1966 and 1970, before the Divorce Act came into effect, the average number of

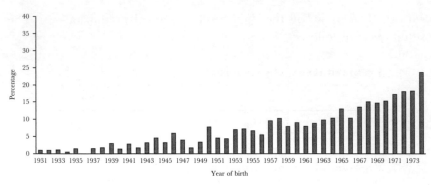

Year of birth

Graph 7.1 Girls having first intercourse before 16 years of age by year of birth, Great Britain.

Source: Population Trends Summer 2000, p. 37, Figure 10.

petitions per year for divorce in England and Wales was 57,089. Between 1971 and 1975 the figure more than doubled to 121,772, but divorce was still fairly uncommon. In 1961 one marriage in every thousand ended in divorce; by 1971 it was six in every thousand.[48] In the course of his Reith Lectures for 1967 the social anthropologist Edmund Leach, whose theme was the need to adjust to a scientific age, touched in a controversial passage on the state of the nuclear family. 'Far from being the basis of the good society', he said, 'the "family" with its narrow privacy and tawdry secrets, is the source of all our discontents.' The contemporary family, he argued, had become too isolated and its emotional fuse-box overloaded. 'The parents and children huddled together in their loneliness take too much out of each other. The parents fight; the children rebel. Children need to grow up in larger, more relaxed domestic groups centred on the community rather than on mother's kitchen; something like an Israeli kibbutz, perhaps, or a Chinese commune.'[49]

Leach, the Provost of King's College, Cambridge, was the first Provost to refuse to read the lessons in the College Chapel. An atheist and left-winger he was at once cast by his critics in the role of enemy of the family, but as Leach saw it he was merely analysing and describing the problems of the nuclear family. He was indeed prescient in drawing attention to the changing role of women as the key factor. The kingpin of the nuclear family, he observed, was the mother rather than the father. 'It really is too much', he wrote, 'to expect any one individual to be the social equal and cultural companion of her husband, career woman, and cook-housekeeper-nursemaid all at the same time . . . Considered as a domestic group the presumed role of the wife-mother is that of domestic serf, which is radically inconsistent with our other notion that there should be status equality between the sexes.'[50]

Youth Culture and Swinging London

At the beginning of the 1960s 'youth' still occupied a relatively humble place in the cultural order as an adolescent prelude to the adult world, or a phase of life associated with delinquency and anti-social behaviour. By the end of the decade the vanguard of youth culture had broken free of its origins in pop music, fashion, and teenage gangs, and exploded into a firework display of counter-cultural experiment and political protest. Much was ephemeral but sex, drugs, and rock 'n' roll, and the cult of youth itself —with its implicit devaluation of the old—had come to stay.

The 'cultural revolution' of the 1960s is always, and with good reason, associated with the Beatles. They were the Pied Pipers on the road from the skiffle groups and coffee bars of the 1950s to the swinging London of the 1960s. In July 1957 Paul McCartney heard a skiffle group called the Quarry Men, led by John Lennon, playing at a fete in the Liverpool suburb of Woolton. Soon McCartney was a member of the group and he and Lennon began to write songs together. Early the following year they were joined as lead guitarist by George Harrison but it was not until 1962 that the group, now known after a number of name changes as the Beatles, recruited Ringo Starr as drummer. By this time the Beatles were the most successful of a large number of bands which had sprung up on Merseyside, and had acquired a manager: Brian Epstein, the owner of a local record store. They began to achieve national recognition when EMI signed them to a contract and their first record, 'Love Me Do', entered the lower reaches of the pop charts. It was in 1963, when three of their records in a row reached number one, that 'Beatlemania' broke out.

Most pop groups enjoyed a year or two of success before breaking up or fading away. The Beatles went from strength to strength. They were the first British group to take the American market by storm. After their first American tour, in April 1964, Beatles records occupied the top five positions in the *Billboard* charts: even the 'King' himself, Elvis Presley, had been eclipsed. With the assistance of their EMI producer, George Martin, sometimes referred to as 'the fifth Beatle', they were writing and arranging much of their own material and getting better all the time, each of their albums marking a progression from the previous one. At the height of Beatlemania in 1963–4 the screams of their female fans drowned out the sound of their live performances and distracted attention from their abilities as musicians and composers. But they received recognition from the music critic of *The Times*, William Mann, who described them as the greatest songwriters since Schubert. In the manner of Bob Dylan their song lyrics became more poetic, and also more surreal as they experimented first with cannabis (to which Dylan had introduced them in 1964) and then with LSD. The prosecution of Mick Jagger and Keith Richard for possession of cannabis in June 1967 led to a 'legalize pot' campaign. On 24 July 1967 all four Beatles were among the signatories to a manifesto in *The Times* calling on the Home Secretary to decriminalize the smoking of cannabis on private premises, and abolish or reduce to a fine the penalty for possession. Citing medical evidence to the effect that it was harmless, the manifesto observed: 'Cannabis smoking is widespread in the universities and the custom has been taken up by writers, teachers, doctors, businessmen, musicians, scientists, and priests. Such persons do not fit the stereotype of the unemployed criminal dope fiend. Smoking the herb also forms a traditional part of the social and religious life of hundreds of thousands of immigrants to Britain.'[51]

As the Beatles grew in fame they made connections with others of their generation in the *avant-garde*. In 1964 they broke into film with *A Hard Day's Night*, directed by Richard Lester, and John Lennon published with Jonathan Cape a book of comic verses and sketches, *In His Own Write*. George Harrison taught himself the sitar and sat at the feet of the Indian musician Ravi Shankar. It was also Harrison who induced them to flirt with mysticism in the person of the Maharishi Mahesh Yogi, with whom they spent some time studying and meditating in India in 1968. Their use of drugs aligned them with the hippy 'counter-culture' of the late 1960s, and Harrison's mysticism with oriental religion.

In 1967 the 'Fab Four' signalled their new born-again, drug-inspired identity by dressing up in camp military uniform for the cover of their most famous album, *Sergeant Pepper's Lonelyhearts Club Band*, designed by the artist Peter Blake. They had evolved from a provincial band into the leaders of gilded youth in a metropolitan scene of high fashion and pop art. The moment of its emergence was captured forever, like a butterfly photographed on the wing, in a celebrated edition of *Time* magazine in April 1965. The cover bore a picture of London and the caption: 'London, the Swinging City.' The accompanying essay made some play with the idea that the traditional Establishment was giving way to a 'swinging meritocracy' which was said to include economists, professors, TV executives, admen, and the Prime Minister, Harold Wilson. This was not very convincing. Harold Wilson had awarded the OBE to all four Beatles but his interest in swinging London was nil, and much the same was true for everyone over the age of forty. Swinging London was a non-stop fancy-dress party in which the fashions were set by an aristocracy of youthful trend-setters: models, clothes designers, actors, photographers, rock stars, the promoters of boutiques and art galleries. John Stephen, Mary Quant, David Bailey, Jean Shrimpton, Michael Caine, Terence Stamp, Robert Fraser, Mick Jagger—and of course the Beatles—represented a new elite. A working-class or provincial background was, if anything, an advantage, but there was nothing to prevent the son or daughter of an earl from joining, provided they had some cultural or entrepreneurial flair. As *Time* pointed out, London was inventing and exporting 'its films, its fads, its styles, its people'.

Apart from discotheques and restaurants, *Time* observed, shops were the most important landmarks:

> Nine of the shops for boys on Carnaby Street are owned by Designer John Stephen, 29, who last week took his Tattersall shirts, Dutch boy caps, form-fitting pants, and vinyl vests to Manhattan to put the fear of God into parents there. As for the girls, the most in shop for gear is Biba's boutique in Kensington, which is a must scene for the switched-on dolly-bird at least twice a week. Designer Barbara Hulanicki, owner of Biba's, estimates that a typical secretary or shop girl, earning $31 a week, will spend at least $17 of it on clothing, which leaves her with a cup of coffee for lunch—but happy.

The 'cultural revolution' of the 1960s was highly entrepreneurial, with the Beatles forming themselves into a company, Apple Records, to market their work. Richard Branson began his career in the 1960s as the owner of a record shop out of which the Virgin label was to emerge. John Stephen and Mary Quant were among the pioneers of the new rag-trade who climbed to the top of the entrepreneurial tree.

In spite of all the references to with-it or switched-on people there was no mention in *Time* of recreational drugs. The spread of drug use, which the Beatles and their friends did so much to publicize, was to be the most important and enduring consequence of 1960s youth culture. In this respect the 'permissive society' was to extend far beyond the bounds envisaged by the liberal reformers of the 1960s who, as we have seen, were strongly opposed to the recreational use of drugs.

The Women's Movement and Gay Liberation

The women's movement in Britain was inspired partly by developments in the United States, where the publication of Betty Friedan's book *The Feminine Mystique* (1963) stimulated a rebellion of middle-class American women against the housewife role. They rebelled also against the role of sex object. At the Miss American pageant at Atlantic City in 1968 they staged a protest by dumping bras and girdles into a trash bucket, an event which an enterprising reporter elaborated into a story of bra-burning. In fact no bras were burned but the story was too good to abandon and almost universally believed.

The demand for women's rights sprang more directly from the student protest movements of the late 1960s and the experience of women in socialist, Marxist, or Trotskyite groups where male chauvinism was the norm, and the contradiction between the rhetoric of universal rights and the subordination of women was glaring. 'There was all this supposed liberation', recalled Ken Livingstone, 'but it was more a greater ease by which men got to go to bed with women.'[52] As Anna Coote and Beatrix Campbell write:

> Women who were participating in the struggles to liberate Blacks and Vietnamese began to realize that they themselves needed liberating—and they needed it now, not 'after the revolution'. Black leader Stokely Carmichael was heard to say that in the SNCC (Student Non-Violent Co-ordinating Committee) the only place for a woman was 'prone'. Here was the front-line hero of the radical left, who seemed to favour

not simply the *deferral* of liberation for women, but their continued subordination.[53]

No longer prepared to cook the supper and service the sexual needs of male gurus, they called for a socialism in which there was genuine equality between men and women in the home as well as the workplace.

A National Women's Liberation Conference—initiated by women historians reacting against the all-male focus of socialist historians— was held at Ruskin College, Oxford, in February 1970. Out of this emerged a National Women's Co-ordinating Committee, based on a network of autonomous local groups, which set out four basic demands: equal pay; equal education and job opportunities; free contraception and abortion on demand; and free 24-hour nurseries. (They were to be open all the time in order to provide child-care for women who worked unsocial hours.)[54]

Most feminists were on the radical left and under the age of thirty. This cut them off from the majority of middle or working-class women, and like the suffragettes before them they were caricatured by their opponents as man-haters, crackpots, and bluestockings. Their rejection of orthodox politics, their theoretical talk of gender and patriarchy, their love of demonstrations and street theatre, their shockingly frank discussions of the clitoris, the vagina, and the female orgasm, and the presence of a vocal lesbian element, were too much of a shock for mainstream society. In spite of the potential appeal to women of their more practical demands, the feminists remained a part of the counter-culture. Germaine Greer, whose book *The Female Eunuch* urged women to rebel against marriage and live in heterosexual communes, became a well-known media personality without sacrificing her feminism, but she was one of the very few exceptions that proved the rule: in popular culture feminism was generally treated as a bit of a joke.

Feminists looked back to their predecessors in the 'first women's movement' of the nineteenth and early twentieth centuries: Mary Wollstonecraft, Emily Davies, Josephine Butler, the Pankhursts, and the suffragettes. There was no comparable tradition of agitation for homosexual rights. The Gay Liberation Front, founded in London in October 1970, was inspired by the Gay Liberation Movement in the United States. As Jeffrey Weeks explains, there were three central principles: 'a sense of the absolute validity of homosexuality as a sexual orientation

("Gay is Good"); a belief in the vital importance of being open about one's homosexuality ("Coming Out"); and an emphasis on the importance of collective endeavour, self activity, and self help'.[55] Lesbians who sought to assert themselves in the same way faced a tactical dilemma. In a gay rights movement overwhelmingly dominated by men they were likely to be marginalized, but if they joined the women's movement they found themselves in alliance with heterosexual women from whom they differed on the subject of relations with men.[56] Most gays and lesbians, however, had no desire to come out or to parade through the streets. They preferred their private lives to be private.

The liberalism of the 1960s was mutating, nevertheless, into something different and more subversive. Permissive legislation was an expression of the tolerance of the Great and the Good and their readiness to extend the scope of personal liberty. But the movements for women's rights and gay rights had more radical goals. Like the civil rights movements in the United States and Northern Ireland, they were not content with improvements and concessions. They demanded equality of status and rights, a goal that could only be achieved if old ascendancies were challenged and swept away.

Liberty and Regulation

Once set in motion greater freedom in sexual behaviour, and greater freedom of expression on sexual matters, were to prove largely irreversible, but it would be misleading to see the 1960s as a one-way ticket to a more libertarian society. The moral regulation of society was relaxed in areas of sexual behaviour but intensified in new areas like health and safety. Between 1950 and 1966 the number of people killed in road accidents had increased from 5,012 in 1950 to 7,985 in 1966. Since the number of cars had more than quadrupled the increase was comparatively modest but more than enough to justify stricter controls over drivers and their vehicles. When the first motorways were opened they had no speed limits, but in 1966 Labour's Minister of Transport, Barbara Castle, introduced over loud protests a limit of 70 miles per hour. Castle also led a campaign for the introduction of seat-belts, which became compulsory in 1968, and it was she who first gave the police the power to breathalize motorists they suspected of driving under the influence of alcohol.[57] The government's attention was also beginning to turn to smokers. Since 1950, when Richard Doll and A. Bradford Hill had published a landmark paper on the subject, Whitehall had every reason to suspect that smoking was a major cause of lung cancer, but it was not until 1956 that the link was officially confirmed. The attitude of the government, which in 1950 derived 16 per cent of its revenue from the duty on tobacco, was inevitably ambivalent. 'Cabinet approved a statement to be made by the Minister of Health about tobacco and cancer of the lung', wrote Harold Macmillan, the Chancellor of the Exchequer, in his diary in May 1956. 'I only hope it won't stop people smoking!'[58] It did not. All through the 1960s and 1970s people puffed happily away in offices, pubs, restaurants, cinemas, and theatres. Professors chain-smoked in lectures and women in pregnancy, and governments were slow to intervene. In 1965 the commercial television companies were banned from advertising cigarettes. In April 1971 the government and the tobacco companies agreed that henceforth all cigarette packets in the United Kingdom should carry the words: 'Warning by HM Government: Smoking can damage your health.' By pursuing a policy that relied on voluntary agreement with the industry, and advice to the consumer, the government avoided compulsion and regulation, but the 'nanny state' has often preferred public information campaigns to statutory regulation. In 1971 a new anti-smoking pressure-group—ASH (Action on Smoking and Health)—was founded with the aim of persuading the public to give up cigarette smoking, and pressing the government to take stronger measures. Its activities were financed by the government itself.[59]

8

National Identities

In the late 1950s the idea that the British were a people bound together by a common history was so widely shared that there was hardly any need to articulate it. It had always been something of a myth, but a pervasive one, sustained by forces that were still powerful: the monarchy, the BBC, the party system, the collective memory of two great wars. By 1974 the consensus was beginning to fray at the edges as competing versions of national identity appeared. The growth of the black and Asian immigrant population opened up a gulf between those who believed that Britain should remain a homogenous white nation, and those who looked forward to the creation of a tolerant, multiracial society. The rise of nationalism in Scotland and Wales placed a question-mark over the future of the British nation state and raised baffling questions about the nature of Englishness. The possibility that Britain would break up altogether still seemed remote, but proposals for Scottish and Welsh home rule were on the agenda at Westminster for the first time since 1914. With hindsight we can see that the British were also faced with a third crucial issue of national identity, the question of whether they were ready to sacrifice some part of their national sovereignty as members of a federal Europe, or to hold on to it all at some risk of exclusion and isolation. Only in retrospect does the choice appear as clear as this. The British entered the European Community in a fog of ambiguity and confusion. As with the transition to a multiracial Britain, and a devolutionary Britain, the reshaping of national identity was determined mainly by the time-honoured practice of muddling through.

The issues were diverse and fought out in scattered engagements that cut across party politics. The only major politician who came close to combining the issues into a coherent doctrine was Enoch Powell, whose 'rivers of blood' speech of 1968 proved to be very effective in stirring up racial prejudice, but failed to achieve the ultimate objective of putting the clock back to an exclusively Anglo-Saxon nation. Few of those who rallied to his support over immigration shared his passionate hostility to British membership of the European Economic Community or indeed his profound mistrust of the United States. But if narrow nationalism had failed it was not yet clear what would succeed. The Britain of 1974 fell a long way short of the aspirations of campaigners for racial equality, self-government for Scotland and Wales, or a wholehearted commitment to Europe. Things were not what they used to be but what they would become was anyone's guess.

The Nationalist Challenge

While a multiracial Britain was in the making, there appeared on the horizon a challenge to the unity of Britain itself. In the Carmarthen by-election of July 1966 Gwynfor Evans won the seat from Labour for Plaid Cymru, the first time the party had ever won a parliamentary election. When the new bridge over the Tay at Dundee was opened the following month, the first car to cross after the official ceremony bore the flag of the Welsh dragon on its bonnet, a signal to the Scots that it was their turn next.[1] There was not long to wait. At the Hamilton by-election of November 1967 Mrs Winifred Ewing captured the seat for the Scottish National Party from Labour. Only once before, in the peculiar wartime circumstances of an electoral truce between the three main parties, had the SNP returned an MP to the House of Commons.

While Scottish and Welsh circumstances were different, it cannot be a coincidence that nationalist movements were undergoing a simultaneous revival in both countries, or that the campaign of the Roman Catholic minority for equality of civil rights in Northern Ireland took off at almost exactly the same time. There must therefore have been some general loosening of the ties that held the United Kingdom together but in trying to explain how and why this happened we are in the realm of imponderables and can only speculate. Some historians maintain that the rise of nationalism was a result of the break-up of the British Empire and the loss of all the material and psychological benefits associated with membership of that most exclusive of white men's clubs. Given the high level of public apathy towards the Empire and the comparatively small number of people whose fortunes were bound up with it, this seems too narrow an explanation. But it may well have been one element in a broader phenomenon, the declining status of Britain and the British state. By the late 1960s 'declinism'—the belief that Britain was a nation in decline—was commonplace. There was room at last for alternative patriotisms to flourish. Over and above that, authority of all kinds was under attack, and the authority of the British state, defied by striking workers and mocked by protesting students, was diminishing.

The most distinctive feature of the post-war state was the assumption by governments of the responsibility for the management of the economy. Politicians claimed that they could promote full employment, accelerate economic growth, revive a declining industry or ensure the prosperity of a region. But could they? At the beginning of the 1960s the prestige of the British state was still high. Whitehall was thought to have delivered an era of growing prosperity in which all parts of Britain shared. Already, however, the notion that Britain was in relative economic decline was taking a firm grip on the political class, academics and commentators, and the media. Labour in 1964 and the Conservatives in 1970 came to power pledged to reverse the decline and inaugurate an era of sustained economic growth. Both suffered severe setbacks, the Wilson government in the sterling crisis of July 1966, the Heath government as it descended into the debacle of the miners' strike and the three-day week in the winter of 1973–4. As voting was still mainly along class lines, disappointed voters found it difficult to switch from one of the two main parties to the other. But the situation created an opportunity for third parties—the Liberals in England, Plaid Cymru in Wales, and the SNP in Scotland—to act as vehicles of discontent.

Ironically, the emergence of nationalism was partly a consequence of the attempts of successive governments to appease sentiment in Scotland and Wales through the growth of administrative devolution. By the 1950s seventeen Whitehall departments had established administrative sub-divisions in Wales. In 1955 Cardiff was designated the capital city and in 1960 the Welsh flag was officially recognized by the British government. When Harold Wilson took office in 1964, he created a Welsh Office and appointed James Griffiths as the first Secretary of State for Wales. At the same time Scotland took its place as one of the regions in Wilson's grand if somewhat illusory scheme of economic planning. The Secretary of State, Willie Ross, a vehement opponent of Scottish nationalism, skilfully extracted large sums of money from Whitehall. The whole of Scotland was declared a development area,

£600 million of aid given to the Scottish Office, and a range of new projects set on foot: the Highlands and Islands Development Board (1965), the Dounreay nuclear reactor (1966), and a new smelting plant at Invergordon (1968).[2]

Administrative devolution was a far cry from self-government, and the powers of both the Scottish and Welsh Secretaries of State were limited by the need to conform to party policy and Cabinet decisions. But the existence of the Scottish and Welsh Offices was a recognition of nationhood, and the more that administrative functions were devolved, the more distinctive the political cultures of Scotland and Wales. One of the most striking examples was the degree of autonomy enjoyed by the Scottish Office, and the Scottish local authorities, in housing policy. From the mid-1950s onwards, as we have already seen, Conservative governments gave priority in housing policy to the private sector and the encouragement of a 'property-owning democracy'. From 1959 onwards the number of private sector completions usually exceeded the number in the public sector, though occasionally the public sector edged ahead. By 1975, 53 per cent of homes in Britain were owner-occupied.[3] In Scotland the picture was quite different. Until the late 1970s the building of local authority homes for rent to council tenants ran far ahead of building for sale to home owners:

New houses built in Scotland: the private and public sectors 1957–75

Year	Private	Public*
1957	3,513	28,924
1958	4,061	28,109
1959	4,232	23,061
1960	6,529	22,063
1961	7,147	20,083
1962	7,784	18,977
1963	6,622	21,595
1964	7,662	29,509
1965	7,553	27,563
1966	7,870	28,159
1967	7,498	33,960
1968	8,719	33,269
1969	8,327	34,302
1970	8,220	34,906
1971	11,614	29,169

(Cont.)

Year	Private	Public*
1972	11,835	20,157
1973	12,215	17,818
1974	11,239	17,097
1975	10,371	23,952

* Local authority and housing associations.

Source: Housing Statistics for Scotland, Housing and Regeneration *www.scotland.gov.uk/Topics/Statistics/Browse/Housing-Regeneration/HSfS* (2009).

When Mrs Thatcher came to power in 1979, 53 per cent of Scots households were in the public sector, compared with 28 per cent in England, and the rents paid by Scottish council tenants were on average 30 per cent below those of English tenants.[4] Under the impression that they were outmanoeuvring nationalists, governments were building up devolutionary platforms on which nationalists could stand. In constitutional logic it was only a short step from Scottish and Welsh administrative systems to elected Scottish and Welsh assemblies.

The issue that first set the nationalist pot boiling was the future of the Welsh language. Welsh was still the language of everyday life in the more westerly parts of the country, still widely taught in primary schools, and still the source of a flourishing literature. But it was rarely employed in government offices, post offices, or public libraries, and road-signs in Welsh were few and far between. Meanwhile the proportion of the population who could speak Welsh was declining from 28 per cent in 1951 to 25 per cent in 1961 and 20 per cent in 1971.[5]

Unless action were taken, the Welsh tongue, with all its cultural heritage, seemed doomed to extinction. It was almost out of desperation that the veteran nationalist Saunders Lewis, an authentic reactionary who longed to put the clock back, gave a broadcast talk in February 1962 demanding that Welsh be given parity of status with English for official purposes. He also urged the adoption of 'revolutionary methods' by which he meant mass demonstrations and tactics of civil disobedience. The outcome was the formation in 1962 of the Welsh Language Society. Consisting mainly of young people eager to put the advice of Saunders Lewis into practice, it was solely concerned with the language question, but as its membership overlapped with that of Plaid Cymru, it also gave a new impetus to the latter's demand for self-government. As Kenneth Morgan writes, its tactics were not always peaceful or non-violent and several of its members were prosecuted for sabotage or damage to property: 'They climbed up television masts, they defaced public buildings, they placarded and sometimes invaded the studios of the BBC and commercial television...Most familiar of all, they assaulted road signs with their paint brushes, white or tarred, to obliterate English names such as Newtown or Lampeter...'[6] On the lunatic fringes of nationalism a shadowy organization known as the Free Wales Army set off in 1968–9 a series of explosions, most of which were intended to disrupt the supply of water from Welsh reservoirs to English consumers.

Although it was the language issue that inspired the most militant tactics, it was not a demand for self-government and posed no direct challenge to the Union between England and Wales. Indeed the Welsh Language Act of 1967 demonstrated that the Westminster Parliament was ready to go some way—though not far enough in the view of the Welsh Language Society—to address linguistic grievances. But Plaid Cymru, which had been led ever since 1945 by the affable and moderate Gwynfor Evans, was no longer as it once had been a party devoted exclusively to the language question. It was now also committed to independence. It remained to be seen, however, whether the cause of independence would enjoy much electoral appeal. Gwynfor Evans's victory at Camarthen suggested that it would, but this was a predominantly Welsh-speaking community and it remained to be seen whether Plaid would have much impact in the urbanized and industrial south. At a by-election in Rhondda West in March 1967 Plaid came a close second, raising hopes that it could broaden its base. It failed to do so. In the general election of 1970 Labour recovered Caernarvon, and Plaid failed to win a seat. The party did not go away but their support was mainly confined to the six Welsh constituencies, out of thirty-six in all, that were largely Welsh-speaking. Although they went on to win three seats in the second general election of 1974, their share of the total Welsh vote was modest:

Electoral performance of Plaid Cymru

Election	Candidates	Seats	% of vote
1970	36	0	11.3
1974 Feb	36	2	10.7

Source: Vernon Bogdanor, *Devolution in the United Kingdom* (Oxford, 2001 edition), p. 156.

While nationalism stalled in Wales, the SNP advanced in Scotland. In October 1970 BP struck rich reserves of oil in the North Sea in what was later to be the Forties field. 'The SNP oil campaign', writes Tom Devine, 'began in 1971 and brilliantly exploited the contrasts between, on the one hand, the fabulous wealth found off Scotland's coasts and, on the other, the fact that by then the Scots had the worst unemployment rate in western Europe and were yoked to a British state that stumbled from crisis to crisis.'[7] This was the point at which the SNP, campaigning on the slogan 'It's Scotland's Oil', took over from Plaid Cymru as the pacemaker in the deconstruction of Britain.

The initial response of the Wilson government to the emergence of the SNP was to procrastinate. In order to gain time and postpone a decision, Wilson set up in 1968 a Royal Commission on the constitution under Lord Crowther, who was replaced after his death by Lord Kilbrandon. The task of the Commission, though never of course stated in so many words, was to checkmate the SNP by proposing some alternative formula for the government of Scotland. The Commissioners, however, were divided. The majority came out in favour of Home Rule: a devolved Parliament with a Scottish Cabinet and Prime Minister, funded by the Treasury. The minority produced a Unionist solution with a Scottish assembly confined to matters of administration. A third group of commissioners produced a memorandum of dissent calling for a federal United Kingdom. The Commission had failed to resolve the divisions within Whitehall over the Scottish question, and its findings were, in any case, completely overshadowed by the looming energy crisis and the impending clash between the government and the miners. Nor had it succeeded in halting the SNP bandwagon.

Whatever the short-term fluctuations in the popularity of the SNP, the two general elections of 1974 confirmed a pattern of long-term advance:

Electoral performance of the Scottish National Party

Election	Candidates	Seats	% of Scottish total
1959	5	0	0.5
1964	15	0	0.8
1966	23	0	2.4
1970	65	1	11.0
1974 Feb	70	7	22.0
1974 Oct	71	11	30.0

Source: Vernon Bogdanor, *Devolution in the United Kingdom* (Oxford, 2001 edition), p. 121.

If neither Scotland nor Wales responded wholeheartedly to the appeal of the nationalists, it was because class issues loomed much larger in an era of industrial strife than questions of national identity and constitutional reform. Besides, the Labour and Conservative parties in Scotland both presented themselves as champions of Scotland's interests within the Union. The choice for voters in Scotland was not between nationalists and puppets of English rule, as the SNP alleged, but between parties that were all sporting a kilt. The Scottish political scene, in Christopher Harvie's phrase, was 'a dance to the music of nationalism'.

The English Enigma

English attitudes towards the Irish, the Scots, and the Welsh were as varied as the English themselves, many of whom were married to, descended from, or in some other way related to these 'Celtic' folk. In popular culture an Irish Eamonn Andrews, a Welsh Harry Secombe, a Scottish Sean Connery, were embraced by English audiences without a moment's hesitation. But just as unflattering stereotypes of the English persisted among their neighbours, stereotypes of the Irishman, the Welshman, and the Scot (women being largely invisible in this context) persisted among the English. They were captured for posterity by Donald Swann and Michael Flanders, a duo whose comic songs in the manner of Noel Coward or Gilbert and Sullivan delighted audiences in the late 1950s and early 1960s.

Swann was of Russian parentage and Welsh birth, but like Flanders he had gone to Westminster, one of the most prestigious of English public schools, and thence to Oxford. In black tie and tails, with Swann at the grand piano and the wheelchair-bound Flanders acting as compere, they were the epitome of gentlemanly refinement and wit. Among the targets of their satirical barbs were General De Gaulle, the Beeching report, and the incompetence of tradesmen ('It all makes work for the working man to do'). Their 'Song of Patriotic Prejudice', from their 1963 review *At the Drop of Another Hat*, was at one level a humorous exercise in English self-mockery, at another an expression of deeply ingrained attitudes that well-bred Englishmen were normally too polite to express:

> The Scotsman is mean, as we're all well aware
> And bony and blotchy and covered with hair

He eats salty porridge, he works all the day
And he hasn't got bishops to show him the way!

The Welshman's dishonest and cheats when he can
And little and dark, more like monkey than man
He works underground with a lamp in his hat
And he sings far too loud, far too often, and flat!

And crossing the Channel, one cannot say much
Of French and the Spanish, the Danish or Dutch
The Germans are German, the Russians are red,
And the Greeks and Italians eat garlic in bed!
The English are moral, the English are good
And clever and modest and misunderstood.

And all the world over, each nation's the same
They've simply no notion of playing the game
They argue with umpires, they cheer when they've won
And they practice beforehand which ruins the fun!

The English, the English, the English are best
So up with the English and down with the rest.

Of all the forces that shaped post-war Britain, the nature of Englishness is one of the most unfathomable. This is partly because the English were so diverse, a confederation of tribes differing by region and class, and partly because of the perpetual confusion between 'England and Britain'. But it was also because there was no English nationalist movement or party. It is true that English patriotism expressed itself in sport. One of the greatest days in post-war English history was 30 July 1966, the day England beat West Germany 4-2 in the final of the World Cup. There was of course a nationalist edge to a contest with the Germans. There were elements of English nationalism, too, in the Conservative and Labour parties, and more peripherally in the National Front. But they were only bits and pieces that never formed a coherent pattern. Unlike Welshness or Scottishness, Englishness could not be translated into a nationalist party or programme. The English already governed their own country and one or two others as well. Their overmighty ally, the United States, inspired very mixed feelings but there was never a serious question of picking a fight with Uncle Sam. English nationalism was, therefore, a fugitive and subterranean phenomenon, but it would be a mistake to write it off altogether. The 1960s and 1970s posed a number of threats to traditional conceptions of England, and a backlash was only to be expected.

In April 1961, when he was Minister of Health, Enoch Powell gave an address to the Royal Society of St George in which he said: 'Herodotus relates how the Athenians, returning to their city after it had been sacked and burnt by Xerxes and the Persian army, were astonished to find, alive and flourishing in the midst of the blackened ruins, the sacred olive tree, the native symbol of their country. So we today at the heart of a vanished empire, amid the fragments of demolished glory, seem to find, like one of her own oak trees, standing and growing, the sap still rising from her ancient roots to meet the spring, England herself.' Imperialism, Powell argued, had been no more than a transient episode in the long history of an ancient state: 'The unbroken life of the English nation over a thousand years and more is a phenomenon unique in history, the product of a specific set of circumstances like those which in biology are supposed to start by chance a new line of evolution. Institutions which elsewhere are recent and artificial creations, appear in England almost as works of nature, spontaneous and unquestioned.'[8]

The early 1960s were perhaps the last point in time before the Falklands war of 1982 at which such things could be said without exciting widespread ridicule. If English patriotism had been a religion in the 1940s and 1950s, it was overwhelmed by agnosticism in the 1960s and 1970s. The aristocracy and the Establishment were mocked by satirists and denigrated by prophets of decline. Deference was on the wane along with respect for tradition and homage to the heroes of the past. After attending an annual dinner for veterans of the Battle of Britain in 1963, Noel Coward was full of melancholy reflections, not unconnected, one suspects, with the devaluation of his own work:

> I came away from that gentle, touching, tatty little party with a heavy and sad heart. The England those boys died for has disappeared...We are now beset by the 'clever ones', all the cheap frightened people who can see nothing but defeat and who have no pride, no knowledge of the past, no reverence for our lovely heritage. Perhaps, just perhaps—someone will rise up and say, 'That isn't good enough.' There is still the basic English character to hold on to. But *is* there?'[9]

Coward was right in thinking that patriotism of the kind he had always embraced was out of fashion with the young, or at any rate with the young and university-educated, but there were also other threats to the England of 'This Happy Breed' and 'In Which We Serve'. One was the prospect of entry into the European Economic Community, or Common Market as it was usually referred to at the time—a British as well as an English question. The other, the emergence of a multiracial society, affected England more deeply than Scotland or Wales.

In 1961, when Harold Macmillan first announced that Britain was entering into negotiations with the Common Market, public opinion was strongly in favour. Over the next few years the polls swung back and forth, but from 1967 to 1974 almost every poll showed a clear majority against entry. We cannot be sure of the explanation but it may not lie very deep if Hugo Young was right about the three main characteristics of public opinion on Europe: 'It was changeable, ignorant and half-hearted.'[10] Ratified by the House of Commons by the narrowest margins after fierce debates, the treaty of accession came into force on 1 January 1973, but without the 'full-hearted consent of the British people' that Heath had promised. As Powell saw it, the fundamental issue was one of nationalism versus internationalism. John Biffen, one of the small group of Powellite MPs, believed in the existence of 'a strong "almost primeval" nationalism' in Britain. Heath's brand of Conservatism, he believed, was unrepresentative of the country at large.[11] But it is far from clear that the public ever regarded membership of the Common Market as an issue of great importance: only ten per cent thought that it was in October 1974, and there is little evidence of popular nationalism. In any case the question of national sovereignty was consistently obscured by the tendency of both pro- and anti-marketeers to focus on the economic consequences of British membership. Labour, however, entered the general election of February 1974 pledged to hold a referendum, the first in British history, on whether or not Britain should remain a member of the European Community.

The Newcomers

In 1961 the largest of the immigrant communities in Britain, and the fastest-growing, were the Irish. According to the Census the Irish-born population of Britain totalled 950,978 and the population of Irish *descent* was of course much larger, though impossible to measure with accuracy. A change occurred in the 1960s as the growing prosperity of Ireland led to a decline in the numbers seeking work in Britain, and the return of others to their native land. The size of the Irish-born population stabilized, with slightly more than half settled in London and the South-East, and substantial concentrations in the North-West (Manchester and Merseyside) and the West Midlands (especially Birmingham). They were also beginning to clamber up the occupational ladder from unskilled and heavy labouring jobs to manufacturing, leaving a gap that was increasingly filled by immigrants from the West Indies and the Indian sub-continent.[12]

While the Irish-born population remained largely static, the flow of immigrants from the West Indies and the Indian subcontinent, together with a comparatively small number from east and west Africa, was steadily increasing the size of the black ethnic minorities. In 1953 there were 15,000 West Indians in London and 8,000 in Birmingham; by 1958 there were 40,000 in London and 30,000 in Birmingham. At first the number of immigrants from the Caribbean ran consistently ahead of the numbers from India and Pakistan:

Net immigration from colonies and the New Commonwealth 1956–62

	West Indies	India	Pakistan
1956	29,800	5,600	2,050
1957	23,000	6,600	5,200
1958	15,000	6,200	4,700
1959	16,400	2,950	850
1960	49,650	5,900	2,500
1961	66,300	23,570	25,100

Source: Arthur Marwick, *The Sixties* (Oxford, 1998), p. 231.

The rapid increase after 1960 was due, paradoxically enough, to the knowledge that the government was preparing to introduce restrictions on immigration. Owing to the nature of the controls introduced by the Commonwealth Immigrants Act of 1962 (of which more later), the pattern of immigration and settlement was greatly altered. Under the new system two categories of immigrant were admitted: those who were economically active and granted an employment voucher, and dependants

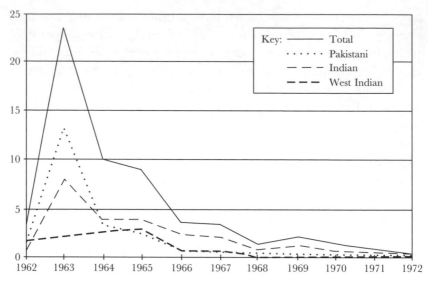

Graph 8.1 Voucher holders admitted (thousands).

Source: Ian R. G. Spencer, *British Immigration Policy since 1939*, p. 138.

of existing immigrants. One of the consequences of this was that, as Graph 8.1 shows, more vouchers were awarded to Indians and Pakistanis in total, than to West Indians.

Since the Act also gave dependants the right to join heads of household in Britain, the voucher system also worked in favour of the dependants of Indian and Pakistani immigrants, who were mainly women and children, but could also include elderly parents. The consequence was that by 1971 the number of people in Britain who had been born in India, Pakistan, or Bangladesh outnumbered those born in the West Indies by 462,125 to 302,970.[13]

As the map below shows, they came from very specific areas in the Indian subcontinent: Mirpur and the Punjab in West Pakistan, Gujarat in India, and parts of Bengal in East Pakistan, which was soon to declare its independence as Bangladesh. Although they included a substantial number of Sikhs from the Punjab, and some Hindus, the majority were Muslims.

The Home Office estimated in 1968 that the West Indian, African, and Asian populations of Britain added up to just over a million people, about two per cent of a total population of nearly 55 million.[14] They were mainly to be found in close-knit ethnic communities in the inner

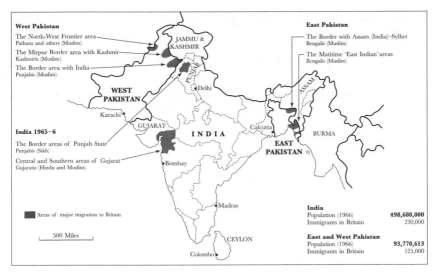

West Pakistan

The North-West Frontier area
Pathans and others (Muslim)

The Mirpur Border area with Kashmir
Kashmiris (Muslim)

The Border area with India
Punjabis (Muslim)

JAMMU &
KASHMIR

WEST
PAKISTAN

Karachi

India 1965–6

The Border areas of Punjab State
Punjabis (Sikh)

Central and Southern areas of Gujarat
Gujaratis (Hindu and Muslim)

GUJARAT

Delhi

I N D I A

Bombay

Madras

CEYLON

Colombo

East Pakistan

The Border with Assam (India)–Sylhet
Bengalis (Muslim)

The Matitime 'East Indian' areas
Bengalis (Muslim)

ASSAM

Calcutta

EAST
PAKISTAN

BURMA

Areas of major migration to Britain

500 Miles

India
Population (1966)   **498,680,000**
Immigrants in Britain   230,000

East and West Pakistan
Population (1966)   **93,770,613**
Immigrants in Britain   125,000

Map 8.1 Areas of major emigration from India and Pakistan.

Source: Nicholas Deakin, *Colour, Citizenship and British Society* (1970), p. 34.

cities and larger towns. Like the Irish before them, the majority of West Indians settled in the greater London area, as did about a third of migrants from India and a fifth of migrants from Pakistan. Both Indians and Pakistanis also settled in large numbers in the West Midlands and the North of England, with the mill towns of West Yorkshire becoming a Pakistani stronghold. Few settled in Scotland or Wales.

The majority of West Indian and Asian immigrants started near the bottom of the labour market in jobs that were semi-skilled or unskilled and also low paid. But this was by no means true of all of them. An interim census in 1966 showed that 39.4 per cent of West Indian males were in skilled manual employment compared with 23.6 per cent of Indians and 18.9 per cent of Pakistanis. 35.8 per cent of the Indian born were in non-manual work compared with 11.1 per cent of Pakistanis and 7.8 per cent of West Indians. With 30.6 per cent in unskilled employment the Pakistanis had the largest proportion of workers at the lower levels of the occupational ladder.[15]

No longer did West Indian or Asian immigrants consist mainly of young single men intending to live and work in Britain for a few years before returning home with their savings. Immigrant life was now family life, and more deeply involved in the workings of schools, hospitals, and the social services. The table below is a list of boroughs with a population of 50,000 or more where over ten per cent of all pupils in maintained schools were 'coloured' in January 1968.

Boroughs with a population of 50,000 or more where 'Immigrant' pupils exceed two per cent of all pupils in maintained primary and secondary schools

	(Figures in brackets are for January 1967) January 1968		
Borough	All Schools %	Primary Schools %	Secondary Schools %
Haringey	27.1 (22.6)	30.8	21.1
Brent	25.1 (21.8)	27.2	21.4
Hackney	23.6 (21.3)	26.2	19.6
Islington	23.4 (23.1)	20.0	23.4
Lambeth	19.9 (17.6)	22.0	16.4
Kensington and Chelsea	17.9 (16.3)	18.7	16.8
Camden	17.5 (17.1)	19.2	15.4
Westminster	17.0 (15.7)	20.6	12.4
Ealing	16.3 (13.6)	17.3	14.6
Hammersmith	16.2 (14.5)	18.7	12.5
Wandsworth	15.1 (12.7)	17.6	12.0
Southwark	12.7 (10.9)	13.7	11.3
Lewisham	12.3 (10.6)	14.8	8.5
Newham	11.9 (9.0)	13.1	10.0
Wolverhampton	11.8 (10.0)	13.2	9.7
Derby	10.0 (8.1)	11.4	8.2

Source: pp. 1968–9 (270), Report of the Race Relations Board for 1968–9, p. 57.

Reflecting on the comparisons and contrasts between these two broad groupings, the Commission for Race Relations observed in 1967:

The majority, whether West Indian, Indian, or Pakistani, come from poor, rural areas, and have moved into the industrial centres of the United Kingdom. The immigrants to this country have not only moved from one country to another, they have also had to adapt themselves to urban life in an advanced industrial environment. This is not to take into account the linguistic problems facing Indians and Pakistanis, or the difference in their cultural backgrounds and their religious beliefs. The West Indians have a different kind of adjustment to make on arrival in this country. Having been brought up to regard themselves as British, they are particularly shocked to find that here they are frequently not so regarded. The Indians and Pakistanis, on the other hand, are aware when they come here that they will be living in a different land with different language, customs, and religion.[16]

West Indians, finding themselves unwelcome or ill at ease in Anglican churches, began to form their own congregations which met at first in bedrooms or living rooms, and as the numbers grew moved out into hired halls. The black churches, which were often pentecostal in character, strengthened the sense of community among West Indian immigrants and demonstrated once more the limits of assimilation.[17] Muslim immigrants followed a parallel course. Initially religious observance took place mainly in rooms set aside for the purpose in private houses, but gradually halls were taken over and converted into mosques, and funds raised for the building of new mosques. Woking, the first mosque to be built in Britain, dated back to 1889, and the Nur al-Islam mosque in Cardiff to 1947. In 1963 there were only thirteen formally registered mosques in Britain, but a new phase of building began in the 1970s with financial assistance from oil-rich states in the Middle East. In 1975 alone eighteen new mosques were registered.[18]

Writing in 1970, Nicholas Deakin reflected on the cultural divide that was opening up between Pakistani communities and the society around them. Pakistani immigrants, he noted, tended to settle in kinship groups derived from the village they had come from. The young men were used to living in all-male houschold which ensured

> that the immigrant conforms to the norms of his community in respect of diet, thrift, recreation, language, avoidance of contacts outside the sub-group...Apart from visiting friends, leisure hours are spent in the house or in watching Indian and Pakistani films...These closely knit and self-segregated communities are served by their own shops and other services provided by fellow-countrymen: the growth of these services and the emergence of the Pakistani entrepreneur in the last few years is a measure of the growth of separate communities. In Bradford in 1967, there were fifty-one Pakistani grocers and butchers, compared with only two in 1959...The same kind of development has taken place around other Pakistani communities. For example, in Balsall Heath, whereas ten years earlier there were five Pakistani shops or cafes, in 1967 there were sixty.

A Pakistani man who brought his wife and children to live with him in Britain, Deakin observed, was thereby putting down roots in Britain, but in some ways the arrival of wives reinforced Muslim culture: 'They are kept in strict purdah and effectively isolated from the world around them. A Muslim woman who visited several Pakistani families in Bradford reported on the extreme loneliness of the wives and their dependence on their husbands.'[19]

During the winter of 1966–7 the Political and Economic Planning organization (PEP) undertook a survey of 1,000 immigrants in six English towns with above average proportions of residents of Caribbean, Indian, or Pakistani origin. In addition to questionnaires and interviews PEP conducted a practical experiment by sending test teams consisting of three individuals with the same level of qualifications but different ethnic backgrounds—a coloured immigrant, a white immigrant, and a white Englishman—to apply for a selection of jobs, houses, mortgages, insurance and so on. They also interviewed white British people who were in a position to practise discrimination: landlords, employers and so on.

There is no denying the fact that strong undercurrents of racism are still to be found in Britain, but the multiracial character of society and the presence of ethnic minorities have come to be regarded as normal. In the 1950s and 1960s, the evidence suggests, there were whole swathes of England (Scotland and Wales had comparatively few immigrants from the New Commonwealth) where black and Asian immigrants were viewed as profoundly alien, a source of anxiety and resentment. PEP, which recorded the opinions and experiences of people on both sides of the racial fence, quoted immigrants on the personal abuse they encountered in their daily lives:

'You see it every day. People say things "You should be sent back home on a banana boat." People's attitudes. Rude, unfriendly names like "black bastards", "niggers", and swearing.'

'Because I am black people say all sorts of things like "go back to the zoo". They don't believe we were born by human beings. They believe we spring from monkeys.'

'Motorists on the road swears at you with venom, "black bastards; why don't you go back to your jungle?"'

'On some parts of the street you can see written "Go home Blacks." On the buses you can hear them say the black niggers come and fill up all the bus.'

'Even in the buses they won't sit against you. They stand up or move away. They don't want to live near us and when we move in they move away. They don't speak to us.'

'You can't associate with whites even in church. This is not Christian.'

'When playing cricket, whites don't want to use the bath after you've used it.'[20]

Of the 1,000 immigrants 94 per cent were in regular employment, an unemployment rate of 6 per cent compared with the national average of about 2.5 per cent. Evidently racial prejudice was not so deep as to result in the large-scale exclusion of blacks or Asians from the labour market, but nearly a half of the West Indians, and a third of the Indians and Pakistanis, reported personal experience of acts of discrimination against them by employers. It was a common experience to apply for a job only to be told, 'sorry, no vacancies' or 'sorry, no coloureds'. PEP tested these claims by sending their test teams to apply for work in a sample of the firms named by their informants. 'The results of the tests', they concluded, 'showed that in nine out of every ten cases followed up, the claims of the coloured immigrants that they had been refused work because of race or colour were justified.'[21]

Employers accepted in principle that everyone should be treated equally, and in most cases they were unwilling to admit to practising discrimination. They did, however, argue that coloured immigrants were unsuitable for employment on other grounds, such as a lack of fluent English, or undesirable characteristics they associated with coloured people in general, or with particular groups:

'They're lazy. It's the tropical sun, it's in their blood. That makes them that way.'

'They are lazy, arrogant, shifty, difficult, and dirty. You can only get a day's work out of them if you stand over them.'

'A common reason is that they smell.'

'Cleanliness is another thing. Some can stink—I mean really stink. Workers object to being alongside them—it leads to all sorts of friction.'

'The only time they are sharp is when they are thinking up the latest dodge. Apart from that they're either asleep or looking for sex.'

'They're sex mad, you know. We're always having trouble with that. You find them at it all over the place. You get frightened to open a door.'

PEP also found that 'the paler people were, the more acceptable they became'. Asians, therefore, aroused less prejudice than West Indians, and were also seen as more educated, cultivated, and suitable for white-collar work:

'Indians fit better in offices. They look like us. They are just a bit darker. Quite often they just look like a dark European. But some of those blacks are quite different.'

'We only have Indians in clerical jobs. Although many of the Indians on the floor are not bright, a better-class Indian can be pretty good. They are gentle and have nice manners.'[22]

Racial discrimination was more widespread, and even more blatant, in housing. The great majority of advertisements for private lettings continued to specify that no coloureds need apply. PEP sent their test teams to discover what would happen when blacks or Asians sought accommodation in the minority of cases where no colour bar was specified. In thirty-eight out of sixty cases West Indians were told that the accommodation was taken, when white applicants were told that it was still vacant; on only fifteen occasions were West Indians offered accommodation on the same terms as a Hungarian and an English applicant.[23]

The only alternative to the private landlord was the local housing authority. Local government officials claimed to treat all applicants for council housing on equal terms, but council estates were virtually all white: less than one per cent of the tenants were blacks or Asians.[24] Discrimination on racial grounds would seem to be the obvious explanation but this was not in fact the case. In most of the areas surveyed by PEP the main explanation was lack of demand from immigrants themselves. When asked why they were not applying for council accommodation, 27 per cent replied that they were either buying their own home or would prefer to do so, another 16 per cent that they were content with the accommodation they had already. Another 29 per cent said that waiting lists were too long, or that they were not qualified.[25] As a general rule, council housing was only available to people who had lived in the area for a certain number of years: five was a common requirement. This was a long-established practice that predated the immigration of the 1950s and 1960s, and inevitably worked against newcomers of all kinds. PEP did however suspect that racial prejudice might be lurking in the personal assessments made by housing managers of the suitability of applicants, and the reluctance of local authorities to demolish slum areas inhabited mainly by blacks and Asians they would then have been obliged to rehouse.

However strong the evidence of racial prejudice, it would be wrong to pin the 'racist' label on the entire white population. In 1967 a detailed questionnaire completed by 500 white people in five boroughs, each with a high proportion of coloured residents, indicated that 35 per cent showed no overt prejudice, while 10 per cent at the other end of the spectrum exhibited intense prejudice. This left 55 per cent in between who were prejudiced in varying degrees.[26] Since people do not always own up to their real convictions it is always hard to know how far to rely on evidence of this kind, but it would be hypocritical to brand as *racist* everyone who objected to the transformation of a white neighbourhood into a West Indian one. Established communities are likely to react against any radical change in their social composition, no matter where the outsiders come from.

Like Helen Bannerman's *The Tale of Little Black Sambo*, a children's book first published in 1899, or the Golliwog which had first appeared on bottles of Robertson's jam in 1910, there were signs and symbols of racism so familiar that people were unconscious of their significance. On 14 June 1958 the BBC broadcast the first edition of a new light entertainment programme, *The Black and White Minstrel Show*, which featured the George Mitchell Singers and the BBC's troupe of high-kicking girl dancers, the Television Toppers. All the performers were white, but every week singers would black up as 'nigger minstrels' singing the ballads of Dixieland, a style of entertainment that dated back to the music halls of nineteenth-century America. The problem, of which no one seems to have been aware, was that blacks were being portrayed in line with white stereotypes of the negro in the Deep South of the United States. Doubtless the blacking-up of performers was viewed by the white audiences of the day as a show business convention as remote from reality as a red-nosed clown at a circus, or Dick Whittington's cat in a panto. Within a few years the show was attracting a regular audience of 16.5 million people. It gave great pleasure and probably never did anyone any harm, but for all its pleasing melodies and simple sentimentality it was too patronizing to survive in an era that aspired to racial equality. Perhaps in response to a long-running campaign against its racial implications, the black comedian Lenny Henry was recruited to the show, but pressure from friends and family eventually persuaded him that he had made a mistake, and he decided to quit.[27]

We do not have to look far to discover bodies of opinion in favour of racial tolerance and racial equality. The leaders of the Christian churches and their secular cousins, the liberal commentators in the broadsheet press, were consistent opponents of racism. The anti-apartheid movement, founded in London in 1959, demonstrated the readiness of white liberals, socialists, and churchmen to ally with the African National Congress in its bid to overthrow a white supremacist regime. The Anglican bishop Trevor Huddleston, the journalist Anthony Sampson, and the cricket commentator John Arlott—a lifelong Liberal whose childhood memories included tea with Lloyd George—were all ardent opponents of apartheid. The reflections cast on race in Britain were mixed. By comparison with South Africa, Britain's racial problems were comparatively mild. But the anti-apartheid movement kept the spotlight on racial issues and in particular the role of race in sport. The 1969 South African rugby tour of Britain was pursued around the country by anti-apartheid demonstrators and the South African cricket tour planned for 1970 had to be called off.

At street level there were numerous whites who enjoyed mixing socially with West Indians in clubs and pubs and found a multiracial milieu an enormous relief from suburban respectability. There were white women who defied popular disapproval by having affairs with black men and white men who had homosexual relations with black partners. There were white people of all ages who enjoyed the music of West Indian steel bands, and perhaps the occasional spliff. Infamous for the race riots of 1958, Notting Hill became in the 1960s the scene of an annual carnival in which for two days whites and West Indians thronged the streets and the bands played late into the night. As Mike and Trevor Phillips explain in their history of West Indians in Britain, the social character of the area was changing:

> Notting Dale and Ladbroke Grove had been filling up with social workers, workers from voluntary and religious groups, left-wing activists, housing campaigners, middle-class hippies, pop musicians and academic researchers of every kind. All of these embraced the new festival,

seeing in it a moment when, for once in a year, racial barriers could be surmounted and everyone could share the manna of West Indian *joie de vivre*.[28]

The Politics of Race and Immigration

In the immediate post-war years the racial tensions arising from New Commonwealth immigration were no secret but neither were they high on the social and political agenda. The issues were brushed under the carpet until the summer of 1958, when they were suddenly and violently exposed for all to see. On 23 August 1958 a crowd of whites attacked West Indians in Nottingham after the stabbing of six whites. A few hours later West Indians in Notting Hill were attacked with knives and iron bars in rioting that lasted for several days. No one was killed or seriously injured, but nine young men were sent to prison and the riots gave the question of race relations a higher profile than at any time since 1945. The Press for the most part blamed the attacks on 'Teddy Boys' and 'hooligans'. 'There in West London', wrote *The Economist*, 'is a stage they can strut upon; into the murky hinterland of the White City greyhound racing track, where there is a sizeable and rather conspicuous coloured minority, the youthful scum of even distant London is riding to battle on the evening tubes.'[29] Some observers also detected the influence in Notting Hill of Oswald Mosley and his fascist supporters in the British Union.

Although the riots were generally deplored, strong undercurrents of hostility to immigrants and immigration were revealed. West Indian men in Notting Hill were accused of organizing brothels and molesting white women. The Labour MP for North Kensington, George Rogers, declared that the government was at fault for failing to deal with the racial problem a long time ago. The government should take powers to detect criminal activities among coloured people, restrict them from entering the area, and deport undesirables.[30] Opinion polling in September 1958 indicated that 55 per cent of the British public favoured controls on black immigrants though this was not a clear-cut demonstration of prejudice on grounds of colour: 49 per cent favoured restrictions on white immigration as well. 77 per cent were against mixed marriages, a majority believed that coloured immigrants should not be on an equal footing with whites in the allocation of council housing, and one in three said they would consider moving if coloured people came to live next door. At the more tolerant end of the spectrum, a majority believed that coloured immigrants should be allowed to compete on equal terms for employment.[31]

By the end of the 1950s political pressure for the restriction of immigration was growing. In the West Midlands campaigners formed in October 1960 the Birmingham Immigration Control Association, and a number of Conservative MPs in the West Midlands rallied to the support of Cyril Osborne. Conservative ministers, however, were reluctant to exploit questions of race and immigration for electoral purposes. In 1961 the Cabinet decided to introduce immigration controls which in principle applied to all immigrants but were clearly intended to restrict the flow of immigrants from Asia and the West Indies. The Commonwealth Immigrants Act of 1962 put an end to unrestricted entry from the Commonwealth. Henceforth citizens of Commonwealth countries were only to be given permission to enter Britain if they had a job to come to, if they possessed skills that were in short supply, or if their numbers fell within an annual quota of workers, the size of which would be determined by the needs of the economy.[32] Anyone falling into one of these three categories would be issued with an employment voucher and the right to settle in Britain. Importantly the Act also gave the wives and children of existing or prospective immigrants the right to settle in Britain. Until 1962 the majority of Asians in Britain had been single males. The expansion of the Asian-born population of Britain, and the development of Asian family life, were to some extent unintended consequences of the Commonwealth Immigrants Act, and the prelude to its introduction.

While there was no overt reference to race in the legislation it introduced a distinction intended to restrict the number of coloured immigrants. Overseas holders of British passports issued on the authority of the British government—people who had been born in Britain and were mainly white—retained the right of unrestricted access to the UK. But although subjects of the colonial empire—including Afro-Caribbeans, Africans, and Asians—remained British citizens with the right to acquire a British passport, the possession of a passport issued by a colonial administration *no longer carried with it the automatic right to enter Britain*. Henceforth the holders of such passports were subject to immigration controls. The controls applied equally to white and coloured alike, but white applicants for entry were more likely to have a job to come to or an appropriate qualification or skill, and the numbers involved were small. It was coloured people, seeking to emigrate *en masse* from Third World economies, whose numbers would be curbed.

Ostensibly the policy of the Labour party was one of outright opposition to the Act, which had been passionately attacked by Hugh Gaitskell, the leader of the party, during its passage through the House of Commons. But Gaitskell's refusal to contemplate any controls over immigration was a source of anxiety to Labour MPs who understood the electoral sensitivity of the issue. When Harold Wilson succeeded Gaitskell as party leader, he announced a shift of position: a Labour government would initially retain the Act, but renegotiate the terms with other Commonwealth governments. Wilson also promised legislation to outlaw racial discrimination.

The shift was too subtle to persuade the voters of Smethwick, a West Midlands industrial town with a substantial minority of immigrants from the Caribbean, to vote Labour in the general election of October 1964. Normally a solid Labour constituency, it had been represented since 1945 by Patrick Gordon-Walker, Labour's shadow foreign secretary. He was defeated by the Conservative candidate, Peter Griffiths, a local primary school headmaster who campaigned against immigration. Griffith's supporters allegedly circulated leaflets with the message 'If you want a nigger for your neighbour, vote Labour.' Leading Conservative politicians kept their distance from Griffiths, and Wilson denounced him in the House of Commons as 'a parliamentary leper', but Griffiths himself maintained that it was his constituents who had raised the issue, not him. He received strong support from Enoch Powell, who since 1950 had been the MP for Wolverhampton, an industrial town which had attracted a substantial number of West Indian immigrants. For his constituents, Powell declared, immigration was issue number one.[33]

Labour ministers were well aware of the electoral importance of what Richard Crossman described in his diaries as 'the hottest potato in politics'. None of the Cabinet wished to repeal immigration controls and most were in favour of making them more restrictive. Labour's new Home Secretary, Sir Frank Soskice, spoke his mind in the privacy of a Home Office conference: 'If we do not have strict immigration rules our people will all soon be coffee coloured.' The Minister of Labour,

Ray Gunter, warned his colleagues of 'the increasing evidence of the reluctance in industry to work alongside coloured immigrants and the refusal to accept coloured people to supervisory positions'.[34]

Between the two general elections of October 1964 and March 1966 the Wilson government, with the assistance of the Conservative front bench, succeeded for the time being in defusing the immigration question. Ministers cobbled together a dual policy in which tighter controls on immigration were coupled with race relations legislation intended to promote racial harmony.

While practising a form of liberalism with a weak left hand, the government was tightening up, with a strong right hand, immigration controls based on racial discrimination. In August 1965 it was announced that the number of employment vouchers a year would be reduced to 8,500, of which 1,000 would be reserved for applicants from Malta. The rules governing the admission of other family members, which up to this point had often been relaxed, were also to be strictly applied, and documentary proof of identity produced at the port of entry. 'The systematic and effective control of Asian and black immigration', writes Ian Spencer, 'began in 1965 rather than 1962.'[35]

Labour and the Conservatives were at one in yielding to popular demands for the restriction of coloured immigration, but it was Labour that took the lead in the framing of race relations law. No true socialist could tolerate a society based on racial discrimination and the dissemination of racial hatred, nor were party managers likely to forget that much of Labour's electoral support in the inner cities was based on ethnic minorities. The Wilson government's White Paper of 1965 signalled a Labour government's acceptance of some degree of responsibility for sorting out the problems:

The United Kingdom is already a multiracial society and Commonwealth immigrants make a most valuable contribution to our economy. Most of them will stay and bring up their families here and there can be no question of allowing any of them to be regarded as second-class citizens. At the same time it must be recognized that the presence in this country of nearly one million immigrants from the Commonwealth with different social and cultural backgrounds raises a number of problems and creates social tensions in those areas where they have concentrated. If we are to avoid the evil of racial strife...these problems and tensions must be resolved and removed so that individual members of every racial group can mingle freely with all other citizens at school, at work and during their leisure time without any form of discrimination being exercised against them.[36]

The 1965 Race Relations Act was a very limited measure that outlawed racial discrimination in public places but not in housing or employment. Henceforth it was illegal 'to practise discrimination on the ground of colour, race, or ethnic or national origins' in hotels, restaurants, cafes and pubs, theatres, dance halls, sports grounds, and swimming pools, public transport, and 'any place of public resort maintained by a local authority or other public authority'.[37] Racial discrimination was classified as a civil rather than a criminal offence, a misdemeanour not a crime, and a Race Relations Board appointed to monitor grievances and attempt to resolve them through regional conciliation committees. If conciliation failed, legal action to prevent discrimination was available as a last resort. As the first chairman of the Board Jenkins appointed Mark Bonham-Carter, a prominent Liberal, and grandson of Asquith.[38]

In the general election of March 1966 the immigration question was conspicuous by its absence. Peter Griffiths was defeated in Smethwick by the Labour candidate, the actor Andrew Faulds, and front bench politicians on both sides of the House entertained the hope that the ticking bomb of racial conflict had been successfully defused. The Act, however, was far too limited a measure to satisfy the radical activists, inspired by the American civil rights movement, who were beginning to appear among the immigrant communities. Following a visit to Britain by Martin Luther King in December 1964 a new organization, the Campaign against Racial Discrimination, was set up with the aim of eliminating all racial discrimination against coloured people, including discrimination against immigrants. It was not taken very seriously by the authorities. In May 1967 the Campaign delivered a 'massive' petition to the BBC requesting that *The Black and White Minstrel Show* should be withdrawn because of its misrepresentation of black people. The programme remained on the air until July 1978.[39]

The immigration issue was reactivated by events in Kenya, which had obtained its independence from Britain in 1963 under the leadership of Jomo Kenyatta, the former leader of the Kikuyu rebellion. Among the majority African population was an ethnic minority of some 185,000 Asians. Under British rule they had flourished as a middle class of merchants, shopkeepers, clerks, and professional people, but as a comparatively wealthy community, and one which had displayed little enthusiasm for independence, they had aroused much jealousy and resentment among Africans. Under the terms of the settlement which granted Kenya its independence, the Kenyan Asians were given the choice of retaining their British citizenship or opting for Kenyan citizenship. About 20,000 of them opted to become citizens of Kenya while the great majority remained British citizens entitled to a British passport. But would they, as British passport holders, be entitled to enter the United Kingdom? Here the provisions of the 1962 Act introduced an unexpected twist in the plot. The Act had prescribed that the holders of passports issued by local colonial administrations would be subject to immigration controls. But once Kenya became independent no colonial administration existed. If therefore the Kenyan Asians were to exercise the right of opting for British citizenship, they could only do so by obtaining a passport directly from the British government, in which case they would be free of immigration controls. Could they then be denied a British passport? The issue was raised during the passage of the Kenyan Independence Bill by the Home Secretary, Henry Brooke, at a Cabinet committee attended by a number of ministers including the Colonial Secretary, Duncan Sandys. Brooke, a *bete noire* of liberal opinion and favourite target of the satirists of the day, came down firmly on the liberal side of the argument: 'It would be out of the question to withdraw their United Kingdom citizenship, so making them stateless; nor could the normal facilities for obtaining a passport be withheld from them as this would plainly be discrimination based on racial origin.'[40]

After independence the Kenyan government embarked on a policy of racial discrimination designed to exclude Asians from key areas of the economy and by degrees expel them from the country. Asians who had opted for Kenyan citizenship enjoyed some protection but all those who retained their British citizenship were defenceless against the march of 'Africanization'. By the beginning of 1967 they were arriving in Britain at a rate of approximately a thousand a month.[41] The 'flood' or 'influx' of new immigrants became a running story in the press and in television news bulletins which showed planeloads of Kenyan Asians arriving at Gatwick and Heathrow. Though it was a coincidence, and not a consequence of these events, February 1967 witnessed a revival of

British fascism with the formation of a new political party virulently opposed to black and Asian immigration: the National Front. Formed out of a merger between three small right-wing groups, A. K. Chesterton's League of Empire Loyalists, the British National Party, and the Racial Preservation Society, it also recruited many of the individual members of John Tyndall's Greater Britain movement.

In October 1967 Enoch Powell called for an urgent review of the immigration controls to prevent the migration of Kenyan Asians, which he attributed to the existence of a loophole in the law. He was supported by Duncan Sandys, who had conveniently forgotten the Cabinet committee ruling of 1963 to which he had been a party. Speaking in Walsall on 9 February 1968 Powell warned that unless new controls on immigration were introduced, another million coloured immigrants would arrive in Britain over the next twenty years, producing racial tensions as great as those which had recently erupted in the United States. Employment vouchers, and the unconditional right of dependants to enter Britain, should be terminated.[42]

The Labour Cabinet, running scared of public opinion, was in no mood to make a stand for principle. The new Home Secretary, James Callaghan, who shared the conservative outlook of many of the party's working class supporters on issues such as race and the 'permissive society', decided to act. After bulldozing his proposals through a largely supine Cabinet he announced on 22 February legislation to withdraw the right of the Kenyan Asians to enter Britain. By 1 March the new Commonwealth Immigrants Act was on the statute book. Asians arriving by plane were denied entry and returned to Africa or India as citizens of nowhere.

Ian Macleod, a former Conservative Colonial Secretary, alleged that the government had broken a solemn pledge to the Asians which had been made at the time of Kenyan independence. In terms of the letter of the law he was mistaken: no binding declaration had ever been made. But the moral commitment which Duncan Sandys and other Conservative ministers had accepted in 1963 had indeed been abandoned. The Labour Cabinet could reasonably claim that they were unaware of the decisions of their predecessors and were not, in any case, bound by them. But the contradiction between liberal principle on the one hand and the exclusion of the Kenyan Asians on the other was so glaring that no special pleading could obscure it.

In an effort to repair its battered liberal credentials the Labour government introduced in 1968 a new Race Relations Bill which grasped the nettle and outlawed racial discrimination in housing, employment, and the provisions of goods, facilities, and services by public authorities—a category from which the police were excluded. But as with the previous Act it was founded on the principle of conciliation through local committees, with legal enforcement as a last resort should conciliation fail. It was not really designed to prevent discrimination, but to educate and persuade, an unheroic course that was nevertheless more likely to succeed than confrontation or coercion.

The Conservative shadow cabinet, with Powell present, agreed to endorse the principle of equal treatment while declining to support the bill as a whole. Government and opposition thereby established a fragile consensus in which strict immigration control was accepted as the essential precondition for the reduction of racial tension, and the aim was to keep the temperature low. This was all too much of a compromise for Powell. While paying lip-service to the official Conservative line, he set out to stifle multiracial Britain in its cradle. But here we must pause to consider Powell himself and the nature of 'Powellism'.

The son of a Birmingham primary-school headmaster, Powell was a grammar-school boy who rose to the top through sheer brain-power and unremitting hard work. His intellect won him a scholarship to Trinity College, Cambridge, a double first in Greats, and an appointment at the age of twenty-five to the Chair of Greek at the University of Sydney in Australia. Returning home after the outbreak of war, he enlisted and became the only soldier in the wartime British Army to rise from the rank of private to Brigadier. Posted to Delhi, he fell passionately in love with the Raj and astonishingly it was with the ambition of one day becoming Viceroy of India that he entered politics after the war. By the mid-1950s he had written off the Empire as a lost cause and its successor, the British Commonwealth, as a sham. His patriotism was reserved for England.

He was no simple patriot, however, but a professional politician who took up the issue of immigration comparatively late in the day and it is fair to assume that personal ambition, fuelled by a deep Tory loathing of Edward Heath's managerial Conservatism, entered into the decision. When he rose to speak at the Midland Hotel in Birmingham, on

20 April 1968, it was with the intention of grabbing the headlines. 'What have you got coming up, Enoch?', asked his friend Clem Jones, the editor of the *Wolverhampton Express and Star*. Powell said: 'You know how a rocket goes up, breaks up in the air, and falls down, well, this speech I'm going to make is going to go up like a rocket, but when it gets up to the top, it's going to stay up.'[43]

Many of Powell's speeches on current political issues were academic and abstract in character but in Birmingham he deliberately adopted an apocalyptic and inflammatory tone. He was speaking against the background of the riots, looting, and arson triggered in scores of American cities by the assassination on 4 April of Martin Luther King.

'The supreme function of statesmanship', Powell declared, 'is to provide against preventable evils.' A week or two earlier, he explained, he had fallen into conversation with a constituent who told him that if he could afford to he would emigrate: ' "In this country in fifteen or twenty years' time the black man will have the whip hand over the white man." ' Here was the key to Powell's argument: in spite of the tightening of immigration controls the black and Asian populations of Britain were continuing to grow and destined to increase greatly in numbers. Citing an estimate by the Registrar-General, he predicted that by 1988, Britain would be home to 'three and a half million Commonwealth immigrants and their descendants'. No estimate was available for the year 2000 'but it must be in the region of five to seven million, approximately one-tenth of the whole population'. It would not be possible, Powell conceded, to prevent this development altogether, 'but the significance and consequences of an alien element introduced into a country or population are profoundly different according to whether that element is one per cent or ten per cent.' There were two answers to the problem, Powell argued: stopping, or virtually stopping, the inflow, and encouraging the maximum outflow through a generously assisted programme of voluntary repatriation. For good measure Powell also launched into a savage attack on the government's Race Relations Bill. Turning the logic of racial discrimination upside down, he argued that it gave ethnic minorities a privileged position under the law, and turned the native-born white population into second-class citizens.

Powell claimed that as a member of the shadow cabinet he was simply expounding official Conservative policy, but as John Campbell observes: 'As always with Powell there is a certain formal plausibility in his defence, but also a transparent disingenuousness.' The shadow cabinet had intended to lower the temperature of race relations but Powell's aim was to raise it to boiling point.[44] The Race Relations Bill, he predicted, would create 'vested interests in the preservation and sharpening of racial and religious differences'. Radical activists would take the opportunity of promoting strife between immigrant communities and their fellow citizens: 'As I look ahead, I am filled with foreboding; like the Roman, I seem to see "the River Tiber foaming with much blood".' But, while claiming to deplore the prospect of racial strife, Powell himself was inflaming race relations. He quoted at length from a correspondent who told a story of a white woman, a widow whose husband and two sons had been killed in the war, who ran a boarding house in Wolverhampton. When immigrants moved in all around her and she refused to accept them as lodgers she was reduced to penury and subjected to racial abuse:

> She is becoming afraid to go out. Windows are broken. She finds excreta pushed through her letter box. When she goes to the shops, she is followed by children, charming, wide-grinning piccaninnies. They cannot speak English but one word they know. 'Racialist' they chant. When the new Race Relations Bill is passed, this woman is convinced she will go to prison. And is she so wrong?

Anyone with an ear attuned to racist myth-making would have wondered about the veracity of this archetypal tale, and it was hardly surprising that all subsequent efforts by journalists to trace or identify the poor widow proved unsuccessful. The editor of the *Wolverhampton Express and Star*, a friend who was alienated by the speech, thought that Powell had been deceived on a previous occasion by one of the many anonymous letters fabricated by the National Front, which was very active in the area.[45] Whatever the case, he put the story into circulation as though it were a matter of fact.

Powell's speech caused him to be labelled a 'racist'. In his own mind, however, Powell was not a racist but a Tory who believed that English people had a right to conserve a national identity which had been created by a long and unique historical process, and which the great majority of them wished to preserve. To Powell 'race' was a cultural, not a biological, category. He did not believe that it was genetically determined or that one race was inherently superior to another. But a multiracial nation was for Powell a contradiction in terms and a prescription for conflict. As he argued in a later speech, an African or an Asian could become a British citizen, but that did not make him British. Powell, however, deliberately employed racist language and he must have known that in doing so he would win the support of racists and exacerbate race tensions. If he did not he must have been exceptionally naive.

Broadly speaking the political establishment—the front bench politicians, leader writers in the broadsheet press, and the ranks of 'the great and the good', condemned Powell. Heath dismissed him from the shadow cabinet on the grounds that his speech was calculated to inflame race relations. In an editorial headed 'An Evil Speech', *The Times* declared: 'The language, the innuendoes, the constant appeals to self-pity, the anecdotes, all combine to make a deliberate appeal to racial hatred.'[46] Liberals and socialists were not alone in accusing Powell of fascist tendencies. The Conservative MP, Humphrey Berkeley, likened him to Oswald Mosley in the 1930s, and when he arrived at the House of Commons a few days later he was shunned by most of the Conservative members.[47]

The speech also exposed a yawning gulf between the political elite and the general public. Four different opinion polls recorded very high levels of support for Powell: 67, 74, 79, and 82 per cent. Powell himself received a postbag of about 45,000 letters, the great majority of them favourable, while Heath was inundated with hate mail.[48] When Parliament assembled on 23 April, London dockers and Smithfield meat porters combined to march on Westminster under the slogan 'Enoch is Right' and there were several smaller demonstrations of support by factory workers in the West Midlands. 'It has been the real Labour core', reflected Richard Crossman,

> the illiterate industrial proletariat who have turned up in strength and revolted against the literate…It's the same problem we've had with the abolition of capital punishment, the repeal of laws against homosexuality, and all the other liberal causes where a minority of the well-informed public has leapt well ahead and dragged mass opinion resentfully behind it. Now we have the leaders of the Transport and General Workers and the AEU [Amalgamated Engineering Union] saying that these demonstrations are outrageous but it's their own mass rank and file…who are supporting Enoch Powell against the government's race relations policy.[49]

Powell had very few supporters in the House of Commons but he was idolized by many grassroots Conservatives and popular with the general public. 'There is no question', writes Heath's biographer John Campbell, 'that under pressure from Powell he toughened the party's stance on immigration. His principal proposal, unveiled in September 1968 in a speech at York, was to take away the remaining special privileges of Commonwealth citizens wishing to settle in Britain: henceforth they would be classified simply as aliens.'[50]

This was not sufficient to satisfy Powell, who raised the temperature again by calling, in a speech at Eastbourne in November, for the voluntary repatriation of coloured immigrants. 'The West Indian or Asian', he argued, 'does not, by being born in England, become an Englishman. In law he becomes a United Kingdom citizen by birth, in fact he is a West Indian or an Asian still.'[51]

Under the terms of the Heath government's Immigration Act of 1971, the only British passport holders entitled to enter Britain consisted of those 'who had at least one parent or grandparent born, adopted or naturalized in the UK, a blatant example of discrimination...'[52] In theory 'patrials', as the Act defined them, might include people of Asian or African descent but the provision was obviously designed to keep the door open for white kith and kin. Non-whites could only be admitted if they had a work permit from the Department of Employment, or could prove they were dependants, under the age of eighteen or over sixty-five, of relations already settled in Britain. 'For a generation', writes Phillip Whitehead, 'the number of black and brown patrials would be tiny. The number of white patrials ran into many millions.'[53] Ironically the Heath government's Immigration Act of 1971 was followed shortly afterwards by a crisis that led to the admission of thousands of Asian refugees fleeing from persecution at the hands of the Ugandan dictator, Idi Amin.

The Lights of Liberalism

The case against New Commonwealth immigration was based on the defence of an allegedly homogeneous white Britain, and the belief that non-whites posed a threat to national identity. In the 1950s and 1960s this was a commonplace view, by no means confined to a fringe of racist bigots. On the other side of the fence, the position of white liberals was more changeable. In the late 1950s and early 1960s, most were opposed on principle to restrictions on immigration, but they later came round to the conclusion that some restrictions were necessary in order to avoid racial tensions. Their views of race relations also shifted. The organizers of the Institute of Race Relations, founded in 1958 with the aim of improving race relations, tended at first to assume that the solution to racial tensions lay in the eventual *assimilation* of coloured immigrants into 'the British way of life'. In the words of Humayun Asari, assimilation can be defined as

> a process by which the language, customs and institutions of the adopted country become those of an immigrant or outsider group in a more thorough way than mere use implies. The group becomes indistinguishably integrated into the dominant host society. At the end of this process 'natives' accept them as their equals, in intimate social situations—as relatives by marriage or as friends. The immigrant feels at ease with the culture of the adopted land, and has internalized its values. The group has adapted to and identifies with the host society and been accepted by it so completely that it has merged into the whole and lost its separate identity.[54]

The aim must therefore be to assist in the process of transforming 'dark strangers' into brown or black Britons.[55] The key to this, it was assumed, was to be found in the educational system. The Commonwealth Immigrants Advisory Committee, which had been set up to advise the Home Office, defined the guiding principle in 1964: 'A national system of education must aim at producing citizens who can take their place in a society properly equipped to exercise rights and perform duties the same as those of other citizens. If their parents were brought up in another culture and another tradition, children should be encouraged to respect it, but *a national system cannot be expected to perpetuate the different values of immigrant groups*' [italics added].[56]

As English-speakers who had been raised in a Christian culture, immigrants from the Caribbean were thought of as likely candidates for assimilation, but there were two big obstacles in the way: their own sense of cultural difference, and the extent of white prejudice against them. The annual Notting Hill carnival, a celebration of Caribbean culture in which whites were welcome to join, was a landmark in the public recognition and acceptance of a distinctive West Indian identity, and hence in the shift towards what later became known as multiculturalism.[57] As the Home Secretary, Roy Jenkins, explained on the occasion of the launch of the Race Relations Board in May 1966, he thought of integration 'not as a flattening process of assimilation but as equal opportunity accompanied by cultural diversity, in an atmosphere of mutual tolerance'.[58]

In a House of Lords debate on the Heath government's Immigration Bill in June 1971 the Bishop of Coventry said: 'We must endeavour to take from people the purely negative attitude to immigration and to supplant it with a positive concept of a multi-cultural, multi-racial family, vibrant with life and rich with many-sided culture.'[59] This appears to have been the first occasion on which the concept of a *multicultural* society was employed in a parliamentary debate, and it was appropriate that it should have come from a bishop. Whether British society was fundamentally Christian, as some believed, or fundamentally secular as others maintained, it was simply not possible for Muslim, Hindu, Sikh, or other non-Christian religious communities to abandon their beliefs and blend imperceptibly into a secularized majority culture.

This was already becoming evident in the schools, where there were many potential sources of tension between the educational authorities and the Muslim population. By the early 1970s the comparatively poor performance of Muslim children in exams was a bone of contention, though it was debatable how far this was the fault of the schools themselves, and the gap was to persist into the 1990s. A number of cultural 'problem areas' had also been identified: school uniform, school meals, physical education, single-sex education, and extracurricular activities. Abandoning the assimilationist assumptions of the 1960s, the educational establishment switched in the 1970s to a multicultural approach. 'By exploring cultural differences, it was argued, understanding and acceptance of other cultures and faiths would be enhanced, ignorance and prejudice reduced, and the possibility of achieving social justice increased.'[60]

In terms of national identity the British had reached, by the mid-1970s, a half-way house. They were in Europe but not yet aware of the long-term implications of joining a federal union. The government was pledged to devolution for Scotland and Wales but only because the electoral and parliamentary arithmetic left them with little choice in the matter. Liberal opinion in all parties upheld the ideal of a tolerant, multiracial Britain but racial tensions in the streets showed that there was still a long way to go before it was achieved.

PART III

Transformations 1974–1997

9

Mrs Thatcher's Revolution

The downfall of the Heath government in 1974 was a debacle that left the Conservative party demoralized and divided. The Conservative front bench still consisted mainly of allies of Edward Heath who subscribed to his general approach to politics and could see no realistic alternative to it. Confronted by rampant inflation, industrial militancy, and the long-term decline of major industries, they adhered to the idea of a mixed and managed economy, consultation with 'both sides of industry', incomes policies and so on. Meanwhile there were rising undercurrents of right-wing radicalism. Intellectually the Right were inspired by the revival of free market doctrines, more viscerally by the backlash against trade union power and student protest, and a general sense that the social order was breaking up.

The depression of the 1930s had resulted in a shift towards collectivism and the Labour government of 1945. It was far from certain that the troubles of the 1970s would result in the political ascendancy of free market doctrines. Mrs Thatcher was known to sympathize with the Right: hence the invention, while she was still in opposition, of the term 'Thatcherism' to distinguish her outlook from the 'One Nation' Conservatism of Macmillan and Heath. But it was not inevitable that she would win the next general election, nor that she would succeed in imposing a more right-wing Conservatism on a Cabinet of Heathmen. Until the spring of 1982, when Argentina invaded the Falklands, her government was so unpopular that electoral defeat was staring her in the face and it looked as though 'Thatcherism' would be nipped in the bud.

Mrs Thatcher, of course, rode out the storm and led the Conservatives to decisive victories in two more general elections: June 1983, when they obtained an overall majority of 144 seats, and June 1987, when the majority fell to a scarcely less crushing 102. By the time she was forced from office in November 1990 she had carried through changes so far-reaching as to amount, by British standards, to a revolution. She had swept away the makeshift social democracy of *c.*1950 to 1979 and established a neo-liberal economy resting on three main pillars: the reduction of trade union power, the privatization of nationalized industry, and the deregulation of the City of London. There was, however, no economic miracle. During the eighteen years of Conservative rule from 1979 to 1997 the annual rate of growth was 2.1 per cent as compared with 2 per cent for France, 2.2 per cent for Germany, 2.4 per cent for the United States and 3.2 per cent for Japan.[1] In terms of income per head, the United Kingdom continued to lag behind most of the other countries in the OECD.

GDP per capita: UK ranking out of 25 OECD nations

1974	18
1979	18
1984	19
1989	18
1995	18

Source: House of Commons Research Paper 98/64 (1998), p. 12.

Mrs Thatcher was frequently accused of wrecking the social services and cutting social benefits to the bone, but as a percentage of GDP social expenditure stood at 22.9 per cent in 1979, the year she took office, and 22.2 per cent in 1990, the year in which she resigned. It then began to increase again under her successor, John Major. By 1995 the wheel had come full circle, and social expenditure was back to the level it had reached in 1975, in the free-spending days of a Labour government heading for the rocks. Founded by Labour as an integral part of a socialist Britain, a reformed and reorganized welfare state had become one of the pillars of a free market Britain.

Mrs Thatcher's governments were, however, more radical than Attlee's. In 1945 Labour ministers were working with the grain of a long established historical trend: the growth of a centralizing, interventionist state. Although they expanded the role of government, the changes they introduced owed an enormous amount to precedent and the accumulated experience of officials in peace and war. It did not occur to them to question the role of the civil service or the efficacy of state intervention. Mrs Thatcher, on the other hand, viewed the White-hall machine with deep suspicion. In rejecting the mixed and managed economy of the post-war years, she was breaking with an administrative and political tradition in which consultation and consensus were embedded in the *modus operandi* of government. No longer were senior civil servants expected to advise ministers on the pros and cons of a proposed course of action, or to listen patiently to the objections raised by lobbies and interest groups. Ministers laid down the policies: civil servants were expected to execute them. In 1945, however, the Labour Party was united in support of a clearly defined domestic agenda. In 1979 the Conservatives were divided, their policies in many ways tentative and ill-defined. The 'Thatcher revolution' was an exercise in radical opportunism, improvised while the party was in office.

The Experiment that Failed: The Social Contract 1974–1979

The immediate origins of that revolution can be traced back to 1973, when the British entered new and more troubled times. The 'Golden Age' of moderate inflation, high or full employment, and steady economic growth gave way to an era of rapid inflation, rising unemployment, and lower rates of growth, punctuated by periods of recession. In the 1930s lengthening dole queues had been associated with deflation. In the 1970s inflation and unemployment rose together:

	Average annual increase in retail prices	Average number of unemployed
Labour 1964–70	4.5	500,000
Conservative 1970–74	9.0	750,000
Labour 1974–79	15.0	1,250,000

Source: Dennis Kavanagh, *Thatcherism and British Politics: The End of Consensus?* (Oxford, 1987), p. 125.

'Stagflation' was the unlovely term coined to describe this new state of affairs.[2]

The most obvious cause of the downturn was the quadrupling by OPEC of the price of oil in the aftermath of the Yom Kippur War of October 1973, but economic historians point also to the collapse after 1971 of the Bretton Woods regime of fixed exchange rates.

First the dollar, then the currencies of western Europe, were 'floated'. In western Europe between 1971 and 1973 they floated downwards in response to the reflationary policies of governments and the activities of currency speculators over whom governments had no control. The cost of imports rose sharply, in the case of world food prices by 100 per cent. There was also a more deep-seated cause. 'By 1970', writes Tony Judt, 'the great European migration of surplus agricultural labour into productive urban industry was over: there was no more "slack" to be taken up and rates of productivity increase began inexorably to decline.'[3] The problems of manufacturing industry were exacerbated by the growth of competition from low-wage Asian economies like Taiwan and South Korea.

The root of the problem, according to Eric Hobsbawm, lay in a loss of control over the workings of capitalism by nation-states and international institutions alike: 'Nobody knew what to do about the vagaries of the world economy or possessed instruments to manage them.' In the 1970s, however, politicians, businessmen, and economists were slow to recognize the new reality: 'The policies of most governments in the 1970s, and the politics of most states, assumed that the troubles of the 1970s were only temporary. A year or two would bring a return to the old prosperity and the old growth. There was no need to change the policies that had served so well for a generation...As it happened, in most advanced capitalist countries social-democratic governments were in office in much of the 1970s, or returned to office after unsuccessful conservative interludes (as in Britain in 1974 and the USA in 1976). These were not likely to abandon the policies of the Golden Age.'[4]

When Harold Wilson returned to Downing Street as Prime Minister, he inherited a visible trade deficit of £800 million, a public sector borrowing requirement of more than £4 billion, inflation running at 13 per cent per annum, industry on a three-day week, and the miners on strike. The years 1974–5 were punctuated by two short but sharp periods of recession (see Graph 9.1a).

An incoming Labour government with the requisite political authority would have cut public spending, increased taxes, and introduced an incomes policy. But Harold Wilson was the head of a minority government, and the leader of a party more hostile than ever to the social democratic compromise with capitalism. The Cabinet lacked the authority to take a grip on inflation, public expenditure, or

(a)

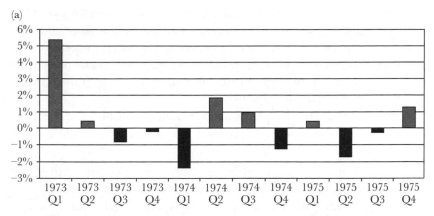

Graph 9.1a Mid-1970s recession: quarterly change in real GDP.

Source: Institute for Fiscal Studies, *Living Standards During Previous Recessions* (2009), p. 4.

wage demands. All they could do was play for time in the hope of winning another general election a few months later. But although the Cabinet was weak, it did possess the semblance of a strategy: the 'Social Contract'.

Traditionally the Labour Party had left industrial matters to the trade unions while the trade unions delegated political affairs to the Party. Under the Wilson governments of 1964 to 1970 the politicians had alienated the unions by intervening in the industrial sphere with incomes policies and proposals for trade union reform. During Labour's period in opposition from 1970 to 1974 the alliance between the party and the unions was restored, but this time on very different terms. A Labour Party/Trade Union Liaison Committee, which met regularly from January 1972 onwards, created a new policy-making forum in which the programme of a future Labour government was debated and agreed in advance. Beginning with proposals for measures which directly affected the role of the unions, the Committee branched out into economic and social policy and produced in January 1973 a radical policy statement reminiscent in many respects of the war economy of 1939–45. As Robert Taylor writes:

> The document called for a control of basic food prices and public trans-
> port fares through the introduction of subsidies, a 'large-scale' redistri-
> bution of wealth and income, the phasing out of social service charges
> and an 'immediate commitment' to raise old-age pensions to £16

[=£89] a week for a married couple and £10 [=£56] a week for a single person—a 25 per cent rise. The Liaison Committee statement added that it would be a new Labour government's first task to conclude 'a wide-ranging agreement' with the TUC 'on the policies to be pursued in all these aspects of our economic life and to discuss with them the order of priorities for their fulfilment'.[5]

Expectations that the next Labour government would 'soak the rich' were raised by the shadow Chancellor, Denis Healey, at the annual party conference in 1973. 'There are going to be howls of anguish', he predicted, 'from the eighty thousand people who are rich enough to pay over seventy-five per cent on the last slice of their income.'[6]

One of the most important areas on which the TUC and the Party found common ground was the extension of public ownership. The Labour Manifesto of February 1974 proposed to take into public ownership North Sea oil and gas, ship-building, ship-repairing and marine engineering, ports, the manufacture of airframes and aero-engines, and sections of pharmaceuticals, road haulage, construction, and machine tools. The Social Contract, was, therefore, very one-sided if it could be regarded as a contract at all. The leaders of the Labour party promised to carry through a semi-socialist programme. The leaders of the TUC made no specific promises at all. They refused to discuss a voluntary wages policy and were adamantly opposed to a statutory one.

Between March and October 1974, when Wilson called another general election, the government fulfilled its part of the social contract. Michael Foot, the Secretary for Employment, repealed the Industrial Relations Act and abolished the National Industrial Relations Court. The Chancellor of the Exchequer, Denis Healey, fulfilled the government's part of the Social Contract by increasing food subsidies, raising old age pensions by 25 per cent, and freezing council rents. When Heath's statutory pay policy expired on 1 July 1974 it was replaced by an understanding that in return for the 'social wage' of increased state benefits the general council of the TUC would take the lead in appealing for wage restraint. The Cabinet was, in fact, avoiding economic policy. The plan was to dispense enough soothing syrup to the voters to give Labour a workable parliamentary majority in an autumn general election: there would be time enough later for contentious or unpopular measures. The plan, however, did not quite succeed. When voters went to the polls on 10 October 1974 Labour made only twenty gains, enough to obtain an overall majority of three in the House of Commons.

The inflationary pot was now boiling merrily. Discounting the government's 'social wage', and ignoring the advice of the TUC to moderate wage claims, the unions pressed ahead with demands for increases well in excess of the rate of inflation, and likely to accelerate it. 'Union leaders', writes Robert Taylor, 'seemed powerless to contain the demands of their members for higher and higher money wages which led to pay settlement increases that averaged as much as 29 per cent in 1974.'[7] By the spring of 1975 union conferences were regularly passing resolutions in favour of a 30 or 40 per cent increase, and the miners obtained a 33 per cent pay settlement on top of the increase they had already won the previous year. The Chancellor, Denis Healey, pressed for the introduction of an incomes policy, but the idea was still taboo in the Labour Party and opposed by Wilson himself. In June the National Union of Railwaymen rejected an arbitration award of 27.5 per cent and its executive voted for strike action. The strike was called off when the Prime Minister found some extra cash and topped up the offer to 30 per cent.[8]

As the wages scramble reached fever pitch, a power struggle was in progress over the future of British industry. In February 1974 Wilson had appointed Tony Benn as Secretary of State for Industry. Benn, who had emerged since 1970 as the leader of the Labour Left, was determined to challenge the post-war settlement by implementing in full the radical industrial policy which the party had adopted in opposition. The Bennite programme was based on the assumption that British capitalists were either failing to invest in industry, or investing too little. The central feature was to be a National Enterprise Board with the power to enforce compulsory planning agreements on private industry, and a share in the ownership of all sectors of the economy. According to the plans which Benn and his advisers had drawn up in opposition, it would tower over the industrial scene like a kindly giant setting wrongs to right. As Phillip Whitehead writes: 'It was to attack unemployment through job creation, promote exports and assist import substitution, sustain investment and technological change, help the regions, combat the multinationals and aid the spread of industrial democracy. Where Heath was vainly exhorting the private sector to invest, the NEB would come in and do the job—with the private sector, if they were willing;

for them, if they were not.'[9] Economic planning, the dazzling mirage of 1945 and 1964, had reappeared as 'Bennism'.

Benn had few supporters in the Cabinet but the strength of his following in the party was a factor Wilson was compelled to take into account. Perhaps Wilson calculated that, once in office and exposed to the advice of the civil service, Benn would moderate his views, but if so he was mistaken. Such was Benn's obvious sincerity and zeal that he frightened the leaders of the Confederation of British Industry, who lobbied Wilson to curb his powers and dilute the programme. Wilson, for his part, kept a close watch on Benn's activities at the Department of Industry, and employed the powers of the Prime Minister to outmanoeuvre him. Harold Wilson's adviser Bernard Donoughue recalls: 'I'm sure that Tony Benn felt himself betrayed by his Prime Minister, because the moment the word got around, as it rapidly did in Whitehall—and the Cabinet Office made sure that it got around—that the Prime Minister was not giving support to Tony Benn, then the civil servants began to back off from their minister.'[10]

Benn pressed on, and with a visionary gleam in his eye announced a new scheme for government grants to assist workers in taking over and running failed businesses. The Norton Villiers motor bike factory at Meriden, the *Scottish Daily News*, a new venture intended to fill the gap left by the closure of the *Scottish Daily Express*, and KME at Kirby, a manufacturer of motor car components, were established as workers' co-operatives. While Benn's Cabinet colleagues humoured him by approving these initiatives, they were busy watering down his proposals for a National Enterprise Board. By the time legislation was announced, in February 1975, the Board had lost its powers of compulsory acquisition as well as its right to increase its stake in private companies to 51 per cent. The commitment to compulsory planning agreements with all major enterprises had been replaced by voluntary agreements, of which, in the end, only one was ever signed—an agreement with Chrysler UK by Harold Lever, ironically a minister highly critical of the idea of planning agreements.

In its revised form the NEB was unlikely to fulfil Benn's ambition of obtaining for the state a stake in the most profitable sectors of the economy. Industrial policy was already reverting to the post-war pattern of nationalizing or subsidizing declining enterprises.[11] British Leyland, Britain's largest volume producer of motor cars, was suffering heavily from the inroads of overseas competitors in the home market. In April 1975 the government took it into state ownership through the National Enterprise Board, which became the majority shareholder in the company. The shipyards, which had been badly affected by the end of the post-war boom, had already become dependent upon government subsidies. In fulfilment of a pledge in the Labour manifesto they were nationalized as British Shipbuilders in June 1977. The dependence of the aircraft industry upon state funds was the main justification for the creation that same year of British Aerospace, a state-owned company incorporating Hawker-Siddeley and the British Aircraft Corporation. Unlike the first wave of nationalization between 1945 and 1948, this second wave of nationalization turned the state into the owner and manager of key sectors of manufacturing.

The 1975 referendum on the Common Market gave Harold Wilson the opportunity of administering the final *coup de grace* to Benn's industrial policies. During Labour's spell in opposition Benn had persuaded the party to promise a referendum on British membership of the European Common Market. A passionate opponent of British entry into Europe, Benn no doubt assumed that the British public would vote for withdrawal. Under a curious arrangement which just about succeeded in holding the Labour Party together, members of the Cabinet were free to campaign for or against continued British membership, though the government urged the public to vote in favour. The outcome of the referendum was a resounding vote in favour of Britain remaining in Europe. With Benn on the losing side Wilson seized the opportunity of moving him sideways to the Department of Energy and replacing him with Eric Varley, a safe pair of hands who could be relied upon to adopt a consensual approach to industry.

The sidelining of Benn opened Wilson and his colleagues to the accusation of betraying socialism. This quasi-religious charge of heresy took no account of the fact that Benn's proposals were resisted mainly because they were naive and potentially disastrous. The Bennite model of centralized, top-down planning was probably too authoritarian to be acceptable in Britain in any circumstances short of total war: neither managers nor workers in the private sector would have put up with it. But even if it had been introduced it would surely have reproduced the failures of Soviet planning, which had proved effective in establishing heavy industries based on regimented labour, but almost incapable of

responding to consumer demand. The comprehensive control of investment and management decisions by politicians and officials who knew
little of industry or markets, but were eager to impose long lists of targets and conditions, would surely have been counter-productive. In
principle workers' co-operatives offered an alternative model, but it was
only applicable to small-scale concerns in urgent need of rescue. Nor
did any of the three co-operatives supported by Benn prove viable.

While Benn was trying to undermine the post-war settlement, Wilson and most of his ministers were struggling to prop it up. In May 1975
they received help from an unexpected quarter. Jack Jones, the general
secretary of the Transport and General Workers Union, announced his
support for a voluntary incomes policy and proposed a flat rate wage
increase for all employees. Although union leaders were in the habit of
denouncing incomes policies, they too had become alarmed by the hec-
tic pace of inflation, rising unemployment, and their minds were concentrated at the end of June 1975 by a sterling crisis, a demand from the
Treasury for a statutory incomes policy, and the possibility of a Cabinet
crisis leading to the fall of the government. A triumvirate of trade union
leaders consisting of Jones, Len Murray, the general secretary of the
TUC, and Hugh Scanlon of the Amalgamated Engineering Union,
negotiated a new agreement with ministers and won the support of the
TUC for a voluntary policy of limiting wage increases to £6 [=£33] a
week with no increases (except annual increments) for those earning
more than £8,500 [£47,345] a year.

Over the next twelve months the policy appeared to work well.
Between 1 July 1975 and 1 July 1976 the rate of earnings increases fell
from an average of 26.9 per cent to an average of 12.9 per cent.[12] The
deceleration in wages, and the accompanying reduction in the rate of
inflation, may have been due in part to the rising level of unemployment over the same period. Nonetheless the prospects were brightening.
'By the beginning of 1976', write Artis, Cobham, and Wickham-
Jones, 'inflation was already falling fast, the balance of payments was
improving, public expenditure was being brought under control, and
the leadership's authority within the party had been strengthened as a
result of the verdict on the revised terms for entry into the Common
Market. How far the control of inflation was due to the large rise in
unemployment and how far independently to the successful negotiation
of the incomes policy compact is not clear.'[13]

From the government's point of view, this was not the only cause for optimism. Like an evening star the prospect of economic salvation was slowly coming into view. On 18 June 1975, within a few days of his move to the Department of Energy, Tony Benn took part in a ceremony in which he turned on a tap to bring ashore the first gush of oil from the North Sea. Geologists in the 1950s had detected vast reserves of oil and gas beneath the ocean bed. On the eve of the 1964 general election the Conservatives had granted licences to oil companies to carry out explorations which resulted in the discovery of both gas (1965) and oil (1969) in the British sector of the North Sea.[14] The Conservatives under Heath had issued extraction licences in 1972. Texan oilmen with cowboy hats were seen in the streets of Aberdeen, which now became the headquarters of the North sea industry, and stupendous feats of engineering were accomplished as oil wells were sunk and oil platforms constructed hundreds of miles offshore.

The incoming Labour government took a 51 per cent share of future oil supplies, created a new nationalized concern, the British National Oil Corporation (also known as Britoil) to manage the state's interests, and introduced a petroleum tax on oil company profits. In the immediate future supplies of North Sea oil would be too little to make much difference to Britain's economic fortunes. But in the long term, as *The Economist* observed, oil might come to the rescue:

> Britain's post-war search for an economic miracle has been constantly thwarted by balance of payments problems. But if there are countless barrels of black gold at the end of the North sea rainbow then trade deficits will no longer constitute a significant constraint on the growth of the economy. Britain could then see through the 1980s with no balance of payments worries because of its extra £2-billion-a-year foreign exchange earnings from oil exports and a new source of government revenue worth over £3 billion a year.[15]

The Promised Land was in sight, but no one could tell whether it would be Labour or the Conservatives who would enter it. In March 1976 Harold Wilson took the political world completely by surprise by announcing his resignation as Prime Minister. He had in fact decided months before to retire at the age of sixty, a decision prompted by fears for his health. The following month Labour MPs elected James Callaghan as his successor. Like Wilson, Callaghan in his political formation was essentially a man of 1945, the year in which he had first been elected to Parliament, but in contrast with Wilson he had spent the war as an ordinary seaman in the Royal Navy and subsequently become a trade union official. Since his relations with trade union leaders were close, no one was better qualified to sustain the Social Contract, and with the possible exception of Healey, no one was more effective in communicating with the electorate. In his public persona Callaghan was very reminiscent of Dixon of Dock Green, the East End policeman played by Jack Warner in the long-running BBC television series written by Ted Willis. Dixon, who began every episode with the greeting 'Evening All!' and ended it with a few homely reflections on the moral of the story, was both a neighbourhood 'bobby' and the embodiment of a paternal state. Callaghan, whose avuncular manner concealed reserves of political brutality, had the art of calming and soothing his listeners with friendly words of common sense delivered in sonorous tones with an air of unflappable authority. Generous helpings of reassurance were about to be needed.

In March 1976 the Treasury and the Bank of England decided to bring about a 'gentle and controlled' depreciation in the value of the pound on world currency markets. The action was necessary, they believed, to counteract a problem caused by the attractiveness of Britain to investors in the oil-rich nations of OPEC, who were driving up the value of sterling by making investments in London. But the attempt to engineer a modest fall in the exchange rate was misread by the markets, which concluded that a big fall in the value of the pound was in the offing. Overseas investors began to sell sterling, a trend accelerated by the publication of Treasury estimates which greatly exaggerated the extent of public spending and the future size of the public sector borrowing requirement. In June 1976 Healey attempted to stave off a run on the pound with a stand-by loan of 5.3 billion dollars from the Group of Ten central banks, followed by an announcement of £1 billion in tax increases and £1 billion in public expenditure cuts. But the pound soon began to fall again and on 27 September 1976 Healey had to turn back from Heathrow airport, whence he was about to set off for a Commonwealth Finance Ministers' conference in Hong Kong, and return to London for emergency meetings at which it was decided to apply to the International Monetary Fund for a temporary loan. Weeks of strenuous negotiations with IMF representatives who demanded large cuts in public expenditure, and a series of fraught Cabinet meetings, concluded in December 1976 with an undertaking from the government to make additional cuts of £1 billion in 1977/8 and £1.5 billion in 1978/9, together with the sale of £0.5 billion of the government's shares in British Petroleum.

The leaders of the TUC supported the Callaghan government in the IMF crisis, and the Social Contract survived for the time being but in a weakened state. The two parties to the contract were being pulled in opposite directions. Long before the IMF crisis the government had been cutting back on public expenditure, in contradiction to the policy of higher spending implicit in the understanding with the TUC. But it was the IMF crisis that prompted Callaghan to spell out the government's position at the annual conference of the Labour Party in September 1976:

> We used to think you could spend your way out of a recession and increase employment by cutting taxes and boosting spending. I tell you in all candour that this option no longer exists and that in so far as it ever did exist it only worked by injecting a bigger dose of inflation into the system.[16]

This famous statement, written for him by the Prime Minister's son-in-law Peter Jay, has been over-interpreted as marking the conversion of the government from 'Keynesian social democracy' to monetarism, the doctrine that the rate of inflation was determined by the amount of money in circulation. Callaghan was no theorist and his Chancellor, Denis Healey, was sceptical of monetarism. The government was doing what the Labour governments of 1945 and 1964 had done before it: trying to reassure the markets by cutting public expenditure after an initial phase of over-expansion. Callaghan was right, however, to point out that there never had been a simple method of ensuring full employment, which had always depended upon the state of international trade and the competitiveness of British industry. To pump money into the economy when international trade was depressed and industries uncompetitive could only result in inflation.

Although the government had explicitly abandoned the goal of full employment it was still in practice trying to protect employment by subsidizing key industries that were operating at a loss—especially shipbuilding, steel, and motor cars. In February 1977 they set up a shipbuilding intervention fund with an initial capital of £65 million to assist three companies that were already partly state-owned: Cammell Laird, Harland and Wolff, and Govan Shipbuilders. The nationalization of shipbuilding followed in July of the same year when a new state corporation, British Shipbuilders, came into existence. The management of the new corporation recognized that employment in the shipyards would have to be reduced, but with a general election looming the government decided not to grasp the nettle.[17] British Leyland, too, was being kept afloat, but here the Callaghan government took a harder line. In November 1977 Michael Edwardes, a South African entrepreneur with strong right-wing convictions, was appointed as managing director. One of his first decisions was to close the Triumph plant at Speke, Liverpool, with the loss of 2,500 jobs in an area of high unemployment. Callaghan gave Edwardes his full backing.[18]

Unemployment was now above the million mark and in the aftermath of the IMF crisis spending on education, health, housing, and social security was reduced in real terms.[19] If the government now had less to offer the unions, the unions for their part had less to offer in return. They could no longer deliver effective wage restraint. The incomes policies of 1975–7 had cut the value of real wages and squeezed standards of living. Between 1952 and 1974 real disposable income per head increased every year with the exception of 1962. It fell in 1975, remained level in 1976, and fell again in 1977.[20] Pay policies had also narrowed the gap between the earnings of skilled and unskilled workers, prompting the skilled to demand a restoration of differentials. The prospects for a further round of pay policy were bleak.

Nor did the leaders of the TUC have the power to deliver wage restraint, even if they wished to. Over large parts of the private sector national agreements between unions and employers were no longer of much importance. In the case of two-thirds of manual workers, wage negotiations were now conducted within a single factory or plant by the shop stewards of the relevant union or unions. In the past managers had often had to conduct multilateral negotiations, leading to multilateral agreements, with a number of different unions. Now they could strike a single bargain with the shop stewards, an arrangement strongly supported by managers for whom it was administratively more convenient. It was partly due to the support of managers that the number of shop stewards quadrupled during the 1970s.[21]

In the circumstances it was remarkable that incomes policy worked as well as it did for the first two years. During the third year, from August 1977 to July 1978, it began to break down. This time there was no formally agreed limit on pay increases, and the government guideline of a 10 per cent maximum was frequently breached. Since earnings increased by 14.2 per cent, and prices by 7.9 per cent, it looked as though the inflationary spiral was starting up again. With the support of Healey, the Chancellor of the Exchequer, but without consulting the TUC, Callaghan decided in December 1977 that he would seek a fourth year of pay restraint, with a five per cent limit starting in August 1978. The new target never looked realistic. It was strongly opposed by trade union leaders and rejected by the annual conferences of the TUC and the Labour Party. 1978 was also the year in which Jack Jones and Hugh Scanlon retired, to be replaced by Moss Evans as general secretary of the TGWU and Terry Duffy as President of the AEU. Both were lesser figures than their predecessors, but even if Jones and Scanlon had stayed on they would have had to oppose the five per cent norm as unworkable.

It was generally expected that Callaghan would call a general election in October, during the early stages of the pay round. If he won he could then claim a popular mandate for the five per cent policy and supposedly strengthen his hands in carrying it out. By deciding not to call an election he unwittingly sealed the government's fate. In November 1978 a nine-week strike at the Ford Motor Company ended when the men obtained an average pay increase of 16.5 per cent. An attempt by the government to impose sanctions on the company was overturned by a vote in the House of Commons, and the Cabinet was left drifting and impotent as wave after wave of industrial action followed. When oil tanker drivers belonging to the TGWU threatened an all-out strike in support of their demand for a pay rise of 25 per cent they had to be bought off with 20 per cent.

On 3 January 1979 lorry drivers in Scotland, followed soon afterwards by drivers in England and Wales, went on strike in pursuit of another huge pay claim. They adopted the tactic of secondary picketing—seeking to block the movement of drivers who were not in dispute with their employers—and set up roadblocks at which local strike committees exercised the right to decide whether or not to permit the movement of essential goods like medical supplies for hospitals. Like the oil tanker drivers, the lorry drivers were members of the TGWU, whose general secretary Moss Evans was predictably reluctant to condemn what amounted to physical intimidation. The Prime Minister, meanwhile, flew off to the West Indian island of Guadeloupe for a conference of western leaders where he was photographed enjoying a swim in the tropical sunshine. When he returned to a shivering Britain on 10 January he was asked at Heathrow what he thought about the growing sense of chaos at home. 'I promise you', he replied, 'that if you look at it from the outside, and perhaps you're taking rather a parochial view at the moment, I don't think that other people in the world would share the view that there is mounting chaos.' The next day *The Sun* accurately captured the spirit of his reply in the headline: 'Crisis? What crisis?'[22]

After a three-week stoppage the lorry drivers were awarded a settlement worth around 21 per cent. Most damaging of all to the government was the strike by members of NUPE—the National Union of Public Employees—in support of a minimum wage of £60 [=£171] a week for low paid workers in local government and the health services. They had a good case. Why should the lowest paid workers be held to 5 per cent, a cut in their real wages, while other workers got away with 15 or 20 per cent increases? But their tactics consisted of seeking to inflict as much damage as possible on the welfare of other members of the public. The leader of the London ambulancemen said: 'If it means lives must be lost, that is how it must be.'[23] In the words of Robert Taylor: 'The resulting scenes—of refuse piling up in the streets, pickets turning away sick patients including children from hospitals, the dead left unburied and schools closed—inflicted incalculable moral damage on the Labour Movement... This was no heroic struggle of workers against their employers. The victims of the strikes were those who could least help themselves like the old, the sick, the bereaved, children, and the poor.'[24] Even when grave-diggers in Liverpool went on strike, and television pictures showed a funeral cortege turned away from the cemetery gates by pickets, Callaghan missed the opportunity of speaking out. As a bred-in-the-bone trade unionist, he was disorientated and demoralized. In February he announced a new 'concordat' with the trade unions that consisted mainly of platitudes and empty phrases. He gave way to NUPE, which obtained a 9 per cent increase plus an extra £1 on account of a study of pay comparability. But on 28 March the government was defeated in the House of Commons on a motion of no confidence, and a general election was announced for 3 May. One day during the election campaign Callaghan's adviser Bernard Donoughue remarked that the opinion polls were improving. 'You know', Callaghan replied, 'there are times, perhaps once every thirty years, when there is a sea change in politics. It then does not matter what you say or do. There is a shift in what the public wants and what it approves of. I suspect there is now such a sea-change—and it is for Mrs Thatcher.'[25]

Thatcherism on Trial 1979–1983

Until 1974 the main champion of free market economics in the Conservative party was Enoch Powell, but his 'rivers of blood' speech and opposition to British membership of the Common Market had relegated him to the margins. In August 1974 the cause was taken up by Sir Keith Joseph. Like Powell, Joseph was both an ambitious politician and an intellectual guided by the logic of his own conclusions, but unlike Powell he was a hypersensitive, self-questioning individual who wrestled with his conscience over the moral implications of political decisions. Like Mrs Thatcher, Joseph had been an outwardly loyal member of Edward Heath's Cabinet but with the fall of Heath he began to doubt whether he had ever been a true Conservative at all. With the permission of Edward Heath, who would not have granted it if he could have foreseen the outcome, Joseph established a new think tank, the Centre for Policy Studies (CPS), ostensibly with the aim of studying the success of social market economies like Germany and Japan. It was not the first free market think tank. The Institute of Economic Affairs (IEA) had been arguing the case for drastic reductions in the power of the state ever since its foundation in 1958 by Arthur Seldon and Ralph Harris. The IEA, however, was an independent organization, the CPS a party instrument.

It proved to be a Trojan Horse for the smuggling of free market ideas into the Conservative Party. The director was Alfred Sherman, an ex-Communist from the East End who had fought on the Republican side in the Spanish Civil War, and subsequently exchanged one inflexible dogma for another. In September 1974 Joseph announced his own conversion to the doctrine of monetarism in a speech interpreted as a bid for the leadership of the Conservative Party. He followed it up with a second speech in which he appeared to be arguing that the poor should be prevented from breeding, an ill-considered effort that led *Private Eye* to dub him 'Sir Sheath'. Most Conservatives were not looking for an ideologically driven leader, let alone one who was capable of dropping such a clanger. Reminded of his own limitations, Sir Keith took the wise decision not to stand for the leadership of the party, and the baton was picked up by his friend and ally Margaret Thatcher. She, however, was too shrewd a politician to lead a divisive ideological campaign against Heath. Although she was known to be in sympathy with Joseph, she had also been for many years a loyal front bench spokesman for the policies of Macmillan and Heath. 'Her election to the leadership in February 1975', writes John Vincent, 'is best defined by what it was not. It was not a victory for Thatcherism, for a body of doctrine, for no such thing existed. It was not a vote against the post-war consensus on economic and social policy, or for giving the party a new identity. It was a vote for getting rid of Ted Heath, and not much more. And it was a narrow vote, 130–119 on the first ballot.'[26]

Between 1975 and 1979 both Joseph and Sherman were important as mentors to Mrs Thatcher, as was Geoffrey Howe, another free marketeer whom she recruited as Shadow Chancellor. The key to the thinking of her right-wing advisers was the repudiation not only of Heath's policies, but of the post-war settlement as a whole. Here is Sir Keith, meditating in April 1975 on the Conservative party's mistakes:

> We made things worse when, after the war, we chose the path of consensus.... Against our better judgement, we competed with the Socialists in offering to perform what is in fact beyond the power of government. We undertook to ensure full employment in a sense of a job for everyone of the kind, location and reward he broadly considers right, regardless of wage-levels, productivity and the state of the economy and the world. In pursuit of this interpretation, we strained the economy to the point where jobs, living standards, and the savings of millions have been jeopardized.
>
> We undertook to ensure good housing for all, irrespective of their willingness to earn and save and their readiness to care for their home. The result of over-promising, reflected in decades of rent control and expensive council building, is more homelessness, costly new council slums, and a housing crisis in which dilapidation and decay of housing proceeds faster than new building.

In education we have co-operated in over-riding differences of talent, motivation and home background. The result has been a decline in levels of education and behaviour from which the least able and affluent have suffered most to the point where even educationalists are overcoming their reluctance to speak out.

In matters of behaviour we have gone along with what claimed to be progressive views. The result has been suffering for many. The increase in crime, which bears heaviest on ordinary men and women living in our large cities, and in violence, are not accidental, they are associated at least in part with our well-intentioned destruction of communities and the extended families they contained and with the educational fashions we have permitted.[27]

Given the divided character of the shadow cabinet, and the fact that Mrs Thatcher had yet to establish her authority as leader, she was cautious in opposition while tiptoeing to the Right. Incomes policy was quietly shelved and replaced by a dual strategy for curbing inflation through cuts in public expenditure and strict control of the money supply. On trade union reform the party was still scarred by the defeat of Heath's Industrial Relations Act and even Mrs Thatcher was content at first to postpone the day of reckoning with promises of a conciliatory approach to the unions. Her Shadow Minister for Employment, James Prior, a genial, rubicund protagonist of industrial consensus, had virtually ruled out legislative action to curb trade union power. But then came the 'winter of discontent'. Recognizing that popular opinion was turning against the unions, Mrs Thatcher seized the opportunity of toughening up the policy. The Conservatives now promised to make secondary picketing illegal, with a promise of more legislation to come if necessary.

Conservative politicians, Mrs Thatcher included, often spoke in measured, statesmanlike tones. They could rely on their allies in the right-wing press to amplify the message into a continuous drum-beat of emotive, hard-hitting propaganda in which economic and social anxieties were closely associated. In retrospect we think of strikes and inflation as the key issues of the 1970s but Conservatives were also reacting against a more widespread phenomenon: the collapse of deference. As they saw it, Britain was a land infested by scruffy student rebels, football hooligans, criminals mugging passers-by in the street, 'progressive' schoolteachers encouraging pupils to run riot in the classroom, and many other symptoms of social disintegration. To vote for Mrs Thatcher was to vote for the restoration of authority outside as well as inside the workplace.

The result of the general election, which produced the largest swing from one major party to another since 1945, bore out Callaghan's prediction of a political sea-change:

General Election of 3 May 1979

	Conservative	Labour	Liberal	Other
Seats	339	269	11	16
Votes % of total	43.9	36.9	13.8	5.4

Conservative overall majority 43.

'Margaret Thatcher may be a great historical figure', wrote the historian John Vincent in 1987. 'She may be a very limited woman. She may be both.'[28] It is hard to think of any British politician since 1945 with such a sharp cutting edge as Mrs Thatcher. She had an incisive mind that slashed its way through tangled problems, and a forceful and courageous personality to match. But if the blade was sharp it was also narrow. 'The only Prime Minister in British history whose formal education was devoted to the physical sciences',[29] she had read chemistry at Oxford and subsequently trained for the Bar. The humanities taught empathy with others and some respect for different points of view. So in rougher fashion did military service and the male camaraderie of the club and the pub. These were blank spots in Mrs Thatcher's education. When she chose to master a brief her intellect was formidable, but she was not a thinker. Given a choice between the findings of academic research and her own gut instincts, there was no doubt which she would trust. 'If she was aware of the complexities in general', Douglas Hurd remarked in 1987, 'she wouldn't be where she is today.'[30] Alfred Sherman wrote of her: 'In the eight years that we worked closely together I have never heard her express an original idea or even ask an insightful question.'[31]

A capacity for the rational analysis of problems can, of course, be a handicap in politics. 'He suffered', writes Richard Vinen of Sir Keith Joseph, 'from a catastrophic political weakness—a propensity to see the strength of his opponents' arguments.'[32] Mrs Thatcher had no such problems. She spoke the language of English middle-class individualism with absolute moral conviction. As she said in a radio interview in April 1983:

> I was brought up by a Victorian grandmother. We were taught to work jolly hard. We were taught to prove yourself; we were taught self-reliance; we were taught to live within our means.
>
> You were taught that cleanliness is next to godliness. You were taught self-respect. You were taught always to give a hand to your neighbour. You were taught tremendous pride in your country. All of these things are Victorian values. They are also perennial values.[33]

Such was the emphasis she placed on the moral responsibility of the individual that when riots and looting broke out in the inner cities in the spring and summer of 1981, she could not accept the simple truth that unemployment and social deprivation were among the causes. Anti-social behaviour, she concluded, was a consequence of the decline of authority. In this sense she really did believe, as she said in an interview with *Woman's Own*, that 'there is no such thing as society. There are individual men and women and there are families.'[34] When people she knew suffered personal misfortune there was no lack of warmth in her response, but her social sympathies were narrow, and it was this apparent lack of compassion for the underdog that opponents found so offensive. Though she never said so, she gave the impression of blaming the poor for their own fate.

In her first Cabinet Mrs Thatcher gave the key economic posts—the Treasury and the Department of Industry—to her free market allies Howe and Joseph. They formed an inner Cabinet while most of the other posts went to the 'wets', Mrs Thatcher's term for sentimental patricians and appeasers of the socialist enemy. James Prior, her Secretary for Employment, was eager to enlist the support of the TUC for a set of moderate reforms of picketing and the closed shop. She was unimpressed. 'Jim Prior', she wrote in her memoirs,

> was an example of a political type that had dominated, and in my view damaged, the post-war Tory Party. I call such figures the 'false squire'. They have all the outward show of a John Bull—ruddy face, white hair, bluff manner—but inwardly they are political calculators who see the task of Conservatives as one of retreating gracefully before the Left's inevitable advance ... In order to justify the series of

defeats that his philosophy entails, the false squire has to persuade rank-and-file Conservatives and indeed himself that advance is impossible. His whole political life would, after all, be a gigantic mistake if a policy of positive Tory reform turned out to be both practical and popular. Hence the passionate and obstinate resistance mounted by the 'wets' to the fiscal, economic and trade union reforms of the early 1980s.[35]

Convinced that anyone who disagreed with her was weak or opportunist, Mrs Thatcher pressed on with her free market agenda. In 1942 William Beveridge had spoken of the 'Five Giants' to be overcome on the road to reconstruction, but whereas his objective had been the elimination of poverty, hers was the elimination of 'socialism' and we can think of her as confronting five very different giants in her path: inflation, trades unionism, nationalized industry, the welfare state, and local government. Neither she nor her allies knew exactly how they could be dealt with, but they were determined to make a start with the conquest of inflation.

In June 1979 Geoffrey Howe introduced a budget in which spending was cut by £1.5 billion and the money supply tightened by raising the Bank of England base rate from 12 per cent to 14 per cent. These measures were accompanied by changes in fiscal policy intended to provide incentives to entrepreneurs and the middle classes. The top rate of income tax was cut from 83 to 60 per cent, the standard rate from 33p to 30p, and the revenue forfeited recovered by a swingeing increase in Value Added Tax (VAT) from 8 to 15 per cent. When the money supply failed to respond, more drastic medicine was administered: a 3 per cent rise in bank rate from 14 to 17 per cent in November 1979.

The consequences were severe. Already there was a wage explosion in progress due to the collapse of pay restraint in the 'winter of discontent' and a second hike in the price of oil. Howe's VAT increases exacerbated the problem by pushing up the cost of living. Meanwhile the value of sterling rose, boosted by the fact that Britain was now an oil producer, but also by the high interest rate increases required by the monetarist experiment. Imports became more expensive and exports less competitive. 'Between the second half of 1979 and the second half of 1980', writes Alec Cairncross, 'GDP fell by 4 per cent, a much bigger fall than in any other post-war year. Simultaneously the rate of exchange

(b)

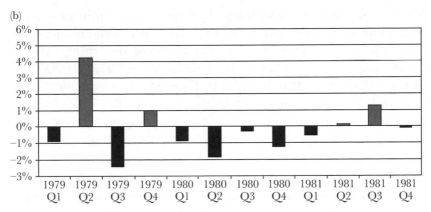

Graph 9.1b Early 1980s recession: quarterly change in real GDP.

Source: Institute for Fiscal Studies, *Living Standards During Previous Recessions* (2009), p. 6.

shot up over the next fifteen months by 15 per cent.'[36] With five successive quarters of negative growth this was the longest recession since the war (see Graph 9.1b).

During the general election campaign the Conservatives had featured a poster of a dole queue with the slogan: 'Labour isn't working'. No doubt they were under the impression that they would be able to bring the unemployment figures down. The theorists of monetarism assured them that after a short, sharp shock inflation would be overcome, and economic expansion resume. In the event the average number of men and women out of work rose during Mrs Thatcher's first term in office from 1,234,000 in 1979 to 2,984,000 in 1983. Unemployment was also rising in the other advanced economies over the same period, but it rose faster in Britain:

Unemployment rates in the UK and OECD

	UK	OECD	Difference
1978	6.3	5.2	1.1
1979	5.6	5.1	0.5
1980	6.9	5.8	1.1
1981	10.6	6.7	3.9
1982	12.3	8.2	4.1
1983	13.1	8.7	4.4

Source: Kavanagh, *Thatcherism and British Politics*, p. 233.

Mrs Thatcher responded with a steely display of determination not to repeat Edward Heath's U-Turn of 1971. 'You turn if you want to', she told the party conference in 1980. 'The lady's not for turning.' As with the Russian depiction of her as the 'Iron Lady', and less flattering epithets like 'Rhoda the Rhino' and 'The Great She-Elephant', this image of inflexibility needs some qualification. However resolute in pursuit of her goals, she was quite capable of tactical flexibility. When the National Union of Mineworkers threatened to go on strike in February 1981 over the closure of uneconomic pits, Mrs Thatcher decided to postpone a conflict with the union until the government was better prepared. She climbed down and the press declared another victory for the miners.

The attempt to measure and control the money supply had failed, but the Thatcherites pressed on. In March 1981, with businesses crashing all around, and unemployment at 2.75 million, Geoffrey Howe introduced a deflationary budget which cut government borrowing instead of the orthodox Keynesian response of increasing it. The Cabinet 'wets' were aghast and 364 economists wrote to *The Times* to protest. The 'wets', however, lived up to their name. Although they held the majority of Cabinet posts they hesitated to strike and remained in office awaiting their fate. In September 1981 they suffered a decisive defeat when Mrs Thatcher reshuffled the Cabinet, sacked three of the leading wets, sent Prior into exile as Secretary for Northern Ireland, and replaced him at Employment with the abrasive Norman Tebbit.

The government's defenders argued that although so many businesses were being destroyed, British industry would be leaner and fitter as a result: a Darwinian struggle would ensure the survival of the fittest. As Professor Geoffrey Maynard puts it:

> By refusing to accommodate rising costs and poor productivity with exchange rate depreciation, macro-policy imposed pressure on industry to raise productivity, lower costs, and generally move its product upmarket. Many firms whose managements were often vociferous in their criticism of government exchange rate policy subsequently achieved productivity improvements and product upgrading to an almost revolutionary degree.[37]

The opposite viewpoint was summed up by the Labour politician and economist, Douglas Jay:

> The outcome of this series of measures was that British industry found its labour costs raised by one-third in two years, its interest costs doubled,

its export earnings slashed, domestic demand cut, and import competition generously encouraged. From the point of view of the British economy as a whole the package was about as subtle in conception, and salutary in effect, as if one had driven a bulldozer into a symphony orchestra.[38]

During the winter of 1981–2 the opinion polls indicated that support for the Conservatives had slumped to below 30 per cent, as had the Prime Minister's approval ratings. None of the government's macro-economic goals had been achieved and the dragon of trade union power still roamed the land, breathing fire. There were, however, some glimmers of hope for the Conservatives.

By the time that Mrs Thatcher came to power, North Sea Oil had dramatically reduced Britain's dependence on oil imports, and created a healthy balance of payments surplus. The spectre of a balance of payments crisis, which had haunted governments ever since 1945, had vanished, and the British were free to import from abroad more and more of the manufactured goods that were no longer made at home. North Sea oil also yielded a second bonus. The Heath government had struck a deal with the oil companies under which they were to pay no taxes until they had recovered the cost of their initial investments. The critical moment at which the tax revenues began to flow into the Exchequer occurred between 1979 and 1981, at a time when oil prices had reached another peak (see Graph 9.2). In 1984–5 North Sea oil brought in £12 billion, enough to finance a substantial part of the total budget for Education (£27bn), or the National Health Service (£28bn). It was a spectacular stroke of luck, but too good to last. After 1986 tax revenue fell sharply as the price of oil fell and profits declined.

Political events, meanwhile, were playing into the government's hands. Since its defeat in 1979 the Labour Party had moved further to the left while descending into bitter faction fighting. It was now led by Michael Foot, a veteran orator and man of letters who was plainly not in charge of his party and looked as though he would be much happier pottering around the second-hand bookshops of Hampstead. In her memoirs Mrs Thatcher describes him as 'a highly principled and cultivated man, invariably courteous in our dealings. If I did not think it would offend him, I would say he was a gentleman. In debate and on the platform he has a kind of genius.'[39] Foot reluctantly took on the task of trying to unify his fractious party but given the circumstances it was an impossible

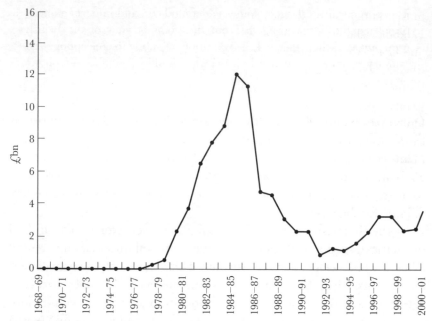

Graph 9.2 Government revenue from North Sea oil and gas.

Source: Scotland and Oil, Scottish Office Background Paper (2009), p. 3.

mission, and one for which a bookish romantic was particularly ill
suited. Foot was unable to prevent the secession from the party of thirteen Labour MPs, led by the 'Gang of Four'—Shirley Williams, David
Owen, William Rogers, and Roy Jenkins—to form the Social Democratic Party in March 1981. In September the SDP agreed an
electoral pact with the Liberals, thus creating the 'SDP–Liberal
Alliance'.

In the polarized politics of Thatcher's Britain, the SDP occupied the
middle ground of reconciliation and compromise. An attempt to revive
the post-war settlement in a more idealistic form, it was progressive in the
sense that it was pro-European, pro-incomes policy, and pro-welfare state,
but detached from trades unionism, and free of the Trotskyites and other
flat-earthers who made Michael Foot's life such a misery. In March 1982
the Gallup poll reported the Conservatives on 31 per cent, with Labour
and the Alliance both on 33 per cent. A hung Parliament appeared to be

in the offing, but on 2 April Argentine troops invaded and occupied the Falkland Islands. Given Mrs Thatcher's reputation as an ardent patriot and Cold Warrior, it is unlikely that she could have capitulated to Argentine aggression and accepted a South Atlantic version of Munich without losing her authority as Conservative leader. The Cabinet decided at once to take the extraordinary risk of sending a hastily prepared expeditionary force to the South Atlantic. Seventy-four days later, after a campaign of stomach-churning tension and tragedy that riveted the media and the public, British troops entered the capital, Port Stanley.

There has been some debate over the electoral effects of the war. According to the Gallup poll, Conservative support rose from 31 per cent in March to 46 per cent in July, and Mrs Thatcher's personal approval ratings from 34 to 52 per cent. After this they slipped back by a few points but remained well above the pre-war level all the way through to the general election of June 1983. This looks conclusive at first sight but it is hard to judge how far the generally higher level of Conservative support was due to the persistence of the 'Falklands factor' and how far to the economic recovery from the recession, which was well under way by the spring of 1983. Levels of unemployment were still creeping slowly upwards but as in the 1930s the unemployed were concentrated in the industrial belts of south Wales, the Scottish lowlands, and the north of England. In more fortunate regions employment was growing and consumer expenditure rising. By 1983 wage demands were far more moderate and the rate of inflation down to five per cent. Whether it was a consequence of the Falklands, of economic recovery, or of the competition between Labour and the Alliance for the anti-Tory vote, the outcome of the general election of 1983 was a thumping win for Mrs Thatcher:

General Election of 9 June 1983

	Conservative	Labour	Lib–SDP Alliance
Seats	397	209	23*
Votes % of total	42.4	27.6	25.4

Conservative overall majority 144.

* The disparity between Labour and the Alliance in terms of the number of seats won, by comparison with their broadly similar share of the vote, was a graphic demonstration of the distorting effects of the 'first past the post' system on the composition of the House of Commons.

The Defeat of the Unions

The general election of 1983 marked the point at which a risky experiment in government was transformed into a successful regime confident that the tides of history were in its favour and the Labour party
doomed to impotence. But if Labour had been defeated at the ballot-
box, the trade unions had yet to be defeated in the workplace, and a
serious threat to the government's authority was in the making. In
December 1981 the National Union of Mineworkers had elected Arthur
Scargill as President in place of Joe Gormley, a wily moderate who
had negotiated big pay increases for miners while allegedly keeping
MI5 well informed about the role of politically motivated militants in
the coalfields. Like Mrs Thatcher, Scargill abhorred compromise and
consensus. A Yorkshireman from a background of Primitive Method-
ism, he was a full-blooded socialist and class warrior who looked forward to the overthrow of the government and the capitalist system.
As President of the National Union of Mineworkers the first demand
he made of the National Coal Board (NCB), was a written guarantee
that no pit should ever be closed on the grounds that it was uneconomic. His plan for coal envisaged that instead of oil-fired or nuclear
power stations, the government should commission a new generation
of coal-fired power stations together with thirty or forty new pits to
keep them supplied. In return for working a four-day week miners
would receive high rates of pay with the option of retiring on a generous pension at the age of fifty-five. It was patently obvious that Scargill
and his Communist deputy Mick McGahey were putting forward
impossible demands with the aim of provoking a conflict in which the
miners would paralyse the economy and bring down the government
as they had in 1974. The miners, however, could not be relied upon to
support strike action, which they had rejected in three pithead ballots
between 1981 and 1983.[40]

In September 1983 Mrs Thatcher appointed Ian MacGregor, a Scot
who had made his reputation as a tough-minded business leader in the
United States, and more recently turned around the fortunes of British
Steel, as chairman of the National Coal Board (NCB). The coal industry was running at a loss and Macgregor announced in March 1984 a
plan to restore it to profitability by closing a number of pits, and getting
rid of 20,000 jobs. In response Scargill called an all-out strike from

4 March, but without the preliminary strike ballot required by the NUM constitution. His first mistake was to call a strike at a time of year when stocks of coal were high and the demand for coal falling. His second was to avoid a ballot, a tactic that split the union. The men of the Nottinghamshire coalfield, traditionally moderate, held their own ballot and voted to continue working. So did miners in several other pits: by mid-April forty-three pits out of 174 were still at work. Scargill retaliated by sending flying pickets all over the country in an attempt to prevent the movement of coal from ports or working pits. The government, however, was well prepared. Large coal stocks had been built up at the power stations and arrangements made to co-ordinate the actions of the police from a National Reporting Centre in New Scotland Yard.

On 29 May a pitched battle broke out at the Orgreave coke depot near Sheffield between 5,000 pickets and an even larger force of police, some of them mounted. This time there was no repeat of the Saltley affair of 1972, when the police were overwhelmed. The pickets failed to halt the movement of coal and after three weeks in which there was much violence on both sides, the pickets abandoned the struggle.[41] Scargill could have salvaged a compromise deal in July if he had been prepared to enter into genuine negotiations with MacGregor, who was ready to make some concessions. But as he would not admit that there was such a thing as an uneconomic pit, Scargill led his battle-weary troops on through the summer and autumn into a winter of demoralization and defeat. In March 1985 a conference of NUM delegates voted to go back to work.

Soon afterwards another long established bastion of trade union power came under attack. In 1983 a businessman called Eddie Shah, who owned half a dozen 'free' newspapers produced at a plant in Warrington, had thrown down the gauntlet to the print unions over restrictive practices. Braving the wrath of mass pickets he had fought and won his battle with the assistance of Mrs Thatcher's trade union reforms. The print unions in Fleet Street, long famed for their dogged defence of 'Spanish customs' that preserved overmanning, failed to read the writing on the wall. In January 1986 they broke off long-running negotiations with Rupert Murdoch's News International company, which owned *The Times*, *The Sunday Times*, the *News of the World* and the *Sun*, and went on strike. The government was not directly involved but the trade union reforms and the defeat of the miners had created the opportunity that Murdoch now exploited. He responded to the strike by transferring the printing of all his newspapers to a new plant at Wapping for which thorough preparations, partly veiled in secrecy, had been made over the previous months. Surrounded by razor wire with security guards on patrol, the new plant was fully equipped with computerized typesetting machines and technical staff recruited with the help of the maverick Electrical, Electronic, Telecommunications and Plumbing Union. By-passing the railways and the railwaymen, Murdoch had arranged nationwide distribution by road using his own company, TNT. Again the mass pickets assembled, shouting abuse at 'blacklegs' as they entered and left the plant, but after an epic twelve-month struggle punctuated by episodes of violence on the picket line, Murdoch prevailed. The cost of producing a newspaper was cut by half.[42]

Like the Wapping dispute, the miners' strike demonstrated that union militants were trapped in a time-warp. For Scargill and his followers it was 1974 all over again, but the outside world had moved on. 'In contrast to the 1974 dispute', writes Robert Wybrow in his survey of the data collected by Gallup, 'the public did not take the miners' side. In 1974, by a margin of two to one, the public had supported the miners, but in 1984 the public were on balance inclined to support the employers. Public disapproval of the miners' methods in the dispute, leading to violent clashes with the police, was also higher than it had been 10 years earlier.'[43] But if the striking miners were not very popular, neither was the Prime Minister. As John Campbell writes of the miners' strike: 'Mrs Thatcher reaped no political credit for having defeated them. On the contrary, she was felt to have been as inflexible and divisive a class warrior as Scargill himself.'[44] The popularity of the Conservative party was slipping again in the years 1984–5 as the number of people out of work continued above the three million mark, and there was precious little evidence of a mass conversion to Thatcherite values.

Be that as it may, industrial militancy *was* in decline. The bargaining power of the unions was weakened by large-scale unemployment, the steady decline in the number of trade unionists from 13,498,000 in 1979 to 9,947,000 in 1990, and the transfer of industries from the public to the private sector. Until the general election of 1983 the

TUC treated the Thatcher government as though it were only a bad dream from which Britain would soon awake. Afterwards the realization set in that there would be no more beer and sandwiches at 10 Downing Street for a long time to come, if ever. The government rammed home the lesson with Norman Tebbit's Trade Union Act of 1984, which compelled unions, on pain of loss of immunity from civil action in the courts, to hold a secret ballot before going on strike. Secret ballots were also introduced for the election of union executives, and for the purpose of deciding whether or not a union should maintain a political fund—i.e. contribute to the Labour Party. Three more 'Employment Acts' in 1988, 1989, and 1990, stripped the unions of all but the most basic right to strike. The 1988 Act gave trade unionists legal protection from disciplinary action by their union for refusing to go on strike or crossing a picket line in order to go to work. Trade unionists, the Department of Employment declared, were individuals, each of whom was free to make his or her own decision about whether or not to accept the collective decision of the union's members to go on strike.[45] This was another way of saying that trade unionists had no obligations to the other members of the voluntary association to which they belonged, a principle that would not have been acceptable to any club or society, anarchists always excepted. If applied to a local Conservative association, it would have entitled a member to give active support to the Labour Party without risk of expulsion or sanctions of any kind. Cumulatively the reforms to which the unions now had to submit were far more draconian than Edward Heath's Industrial Relations Act of 1971.

The trade unions had acted since the war as a countervailing factor to the play of market forces. They had not prevented the shrinking of some industries and the expansion of others but they had acted as a check on the authority of employers and managers. As the 1980s advanced they were steadily reduced to the role of minor players. Nor did the government confine itself to weakening the power of the unions. In their drive to 'free up' the labour market they even reversed some of the paternalistic measures of the nineteenth and early twentieth centuries. They removed the 1842 prohibition on women working underground in the coal industry, abandoned the Fair Wages Resolution introduced by the government of Lord Salisbury in 1891, and abolished the Wages Councils (originally known as Trade Boards) introduced by Winston Churchill in 1909.[46]

Privatizing Industry

One potent factor in the erosion of trade union power was privatization. As long as the government was the ultimate employer of a group of workers, it would always be subject to political pressures over pay and employment. Once an enterprise was in the private sector, it was much easier for the government to stand back and allow market forces to operate.

Between 1979 and 1990 about 60 per cent of the state-owned sector of industry was sold off to the private sector, and more than 600,000 employees were transferred along with the title-deeds. 'It constituted', wrote Mrs Thatcher in her memoirs, 'the greatest shift of ownership and power away from the state to individuals and their families in any country outside the former communist bloc. Indeed Britain set a world-wide trend in privatization in countries as different as Czechoslovakia and New Zealand.'[47]

With the exceptions of aerospace and shipbuilding there were few proposals for the privatization of industry in the Conservative manifesto of 1979. The initial plan was to ensure the more efficient management of state corporations by appointing powerful businessmen to run them, withdrawing government subsidies, and giving them greater freedom to behave as commercial enterprises. The plan was undermined almost from the start by the recession. With unemployment rising sharply the Cabinet was fearful of adding to the numbers and resorted, like other every post-war government, to rescue packages. Ironically it was Sir Keith Joseph, the stern prophet of free market economics, who as Secretary for Industry pumped the extra millions into British Shipbuilders, British Steel, and British Leyland. 'Look', one minister remarked of the nationalized industries in March 1982, 'we're bloody fed up with them. They make huge losses, they have bolshie unions, they are feather-bedded. It seems almost impossible to do anything with them: therefore, the view has grown, get rid of them.'[48]

There were in fact several motives behind privatization. There was the ideological case for the restoration of market forces, the need for cash to reduce the public sector borrowing requirement, and the desire to create a 'share-owning democracy', a popular stake in capitalism akin to the 'property-owning democracy' fostered by the sale of council housing. Between 1981 and the general election of June 1983 the government sold off the following:

Privatization 1981–1983

1980–1	Fairey (100%)
	Ferranti (50%)
	British Aerospace (49%)
1981–2	British Sugar Corporation (24%)
	Cable and Wireless (49%)
	Amersham International (100%)
	National Freight Corporation (100%)
	New Towns
1982–3	Britoil (first cash call)
	Associated British Ports (52%)
	Britoil (second cash call)

During Mrs Thatcher's second and third terms the sale of state assets broadened into a more ambitious programme in which key industries and public utilities were sold off:

Privatization 1983–1990

1983–4	British Petroleum (7%)
	Cable and Wireless (25%)
	Scott Lithgow shipyard
1984–5	British Ports (48%)
	Enterprise Oil
	British Telecom (first instalment)
	Forestry Commission land
1985–6	British Aerospace
	British Telecom (second instalment)
	Britoil
	Cable and Wireless
1986–7	British Telecom (third instalment)
	British Gas (first instalment)
	British Airways (first instalment)
	Wytch Farm
1987–8	Royal Ordnance
	Rolls-Royce
	British Gas (second instalment)

(Cont.)

	British Airports Authority
	British Airways (second instalment)
	British Petroleum (first instalment)
	Plant Breeding Institute
1988–9	Rover Group
	British Petroleum (second instalment)
	British Steel
	British Gas (third instalment)
	Short Brothers
	Harland and Wolff
	Water companies (first instalment)
1989–90	Water companies (second instalment)
	British Petroleum (third instalment)
	British Steel
	Short Brothers
	Harland and Wolff

Source: David Butler and Gareth Butler, *British Political Facts since 1979* (2006), pp. 205–6.

Lord Stockton, the former Harold Macmillan, complained that in privatizing state industries the government was 'selling the family silver'. A glance at the long list of assets disposed of is a reminder of the astonishing horde of enterprises the state had accumulated over the decades, and the huge revenues obtained by selling them off. In the financial year 1988–9 the government's revenue from all forms of taxation was £69,000 million. The revenue from privatization was £7,000 million, a sum equal to more than ten per cent of the total tax take.[49] By the end of Mrs Thatcher's premiership little remained of the family silver except for the Post Office, which had been a government agency since the reign of King Charles I, and a handful of the Attlee nationalizations: the Bank of England, the railways, the canals, and the few remaining coal mines. The corporations which had run the twenty English New Towns had been wound up and their assets transferred to local authorities or sold to developers.[50]

The flotation of British Telecom (BT) in 1984 marked the point at which the government turned privatization into a campaign for 'popular capitalism'. BT was itself a new entity, hived off from the General Post Office in 1981. A giant monopoly employing 241,000 people, it was not always responsive to the demands of consumers. The *Times* columnist Bernard Levin, a latter-day Orwell with more sense of humour, told farcical but true stories of his attempts to get the company to supply him with a new phone. Since BT urgently needed capital investment on a scale the government could not or would not afford, and the Treasury was hungry for cash, it was decided to sell the company as a monopoly rather than break it up into competing units, a process that might take many years. It was decided to sell off 51 per cent of the company with 39 per cent of the shares reserved for the British public and the rest on offer to financial institutions, overseas investors, and BT employees.

The privatization of BT was one of the most radical strokes of the Thatcher government. When the decision was first announced there was much scepticism in the City of London. At a dinner party attended by the Chancellor, Nigel Lawson, all but one of the industrialists and merchant bankers present declared that it would be impossible, as the sums involved were too large for the market to absorb. Doubts were also expressed about the feasibility of direct marketing to the public, which had never been attempted on anything like this scale before. In the event the offer, preceded by a barrage of press and TV advertising, was five times oversubscribed by the time it went on sale in November 1984.[51] A million people and 95 per cent of BT employees applied for shares, and since the initial price had been kept low for political reasons, investors were soon in possession of substantial profits. By the end of 1985, after the sale of two more instalments, the Treasury had raised nearly £4 billion and the share price was up from 130 pence to 192 pence.[52]

With BT guaranteed near-monopoly status for another seven years it was questionable whether customers were better off. The government had created a regulatory body, OFTEL (Office of Telecommunications) to protect the consumer from exploitation, but it was soon apparent that a monopoly culture in which the producer was king was not to be changed overnight. In the summer of 1987 *The Times* embarked on a campaign to highlight its failings, and shareholders at the annual general meeting accused senior management of 'arrogant disregard for legitimate customer complaints'. Other disputes followed:

> The Bank of England refused to pay its bill after it demonstrated it had been overcharged; the *Independent* took the opportunity to accuse BT of deriving 10 per cent per cent of its profits from faulty bills. The National Consumer Council issued a report which nominated BT as the most unpopular company in Britain and as a result BT was forced to freeze a price rise which they had anticipated for September 1987.[53]

Whatever the shortcomings of BT, privatization was a winning formula for cutting taxes, rewarding small investors, and enriching City institutions like Kleinwort Benson, the merchant bank that underwrote the sale, and Hoare Govett, the stockbrokers who marketed the shares. The government now pressed on with the privatization of British Gas, which was also sold off as a monopoly with a watchdog, OFGAS (the Office of Gas Supply) attached. The advertising campaign introduced the public to a character named 'Sid' and the catch-phrases 'Don't tell Sid', and (rather confusingly) 'Tell Sid'. Evidently there was no need to tell Charles or Nigel. When the first instalment of shares came to market in December 1986 they were oversubscribed twice, compared with five times for BT. No matter: the punters made a tidy profit and by the time both instalments had been sold the Treasury was richer by £5.4 billion.[54]

Under Neil Kinnock, who had been elected leader of the Labour party in succession to Michael Foot in October 1983, Labour was more united and also more professional in its public relations, but the Thatcher government was still riding high in the polls, unemployment was falling, the economy growing at a healthy rate, and the opposition still divided between Labour and the Liberal–SDP Alliance. The scene was set for Mrs Thatcher's third successive election victory:

General Election of 11 June 1987

	Conservative	Labour	Lib–SDP Alliance	Other
Seats	376	229	22	23
Votes % of total	42.2	30.8	22.6	4.4

Conservative overall majority 102.

The Conservatives had promised in their manifesto to privatize electricity, but Mrs Thatcher and Cecil Parkinson, the minister she entrusted with the privatization of electricity, were mindful of the criticisms levelled against BT and British Gas, and determined to introduce competition into the industry.

This was no simple task. The Central Electricity Generating Board (CEGB) operated the 297 power stations that generated electricity and the National Grid, which the Conservatives themselves had created between the wars. The distribution of electricity to customers was in the hands of twelve Area Electricity Boards. Under the solution devised by Parkinson and his advisers, the twelve Area Boards became regional companies with a monopoly over local distribution, and joint ownership of the National Grid, which was also converted into a company. But the CEGB was split into two companies, National Power and Powergen, which competed against one another to supply electricity at the lowest possible cost to the National Grid. In order to intensify the element of competition, external generators were also allowed to enter the market, and the distributing companies to generate some of their own electricity. After another massive sales campaign featuring many sweeteners and incentives, and the character 'Frank N. Stein', shares in the twelve regional companies were put on sale on 21 November 1990. The sale was three times oversubscribed with more than 50 per cent of shares purchased by the general public. Once more privatization proved to be a boon and a blessing for investors, who were soon showing a 20 per cent profit on their electricity shares. The launch was another triumph for Mrs Thatcher, but Frank N. Stein could not rescue her from the terminal political crisis of her premiership. She resigned on 28 November 1990.

When Mrs Thatcher first took office, about seven per cent of the population were share-owners. By the time she left, the figure was close to 25 per cent.[55] Despite the figures, popular capitalism was a fairly shallow phenomenon. 'The truth was', writes Andrew Marr, 'that the huge oversubscribing of shares reflected a general and accurate belief that something was being given away for nothing. Sid knew which side his bread was buttered on, but this did not necessarily make him a kitchen capitalist.'[56] The majority of individual shareholders only possessed shares in a single company: the idea of gradually building up a portfolio of savings and investments was incompatible with a far more characteristic activity of the Thatcher years—shopping with a credit card. Privatization did, however, bring the Thatcher government into closer contact with the City.

At the start of the Thatcher governments, politicians on all sides believed that Britain's relative economic decline was due to some deep-seated malaise in manufacturing industry. Mrs Thatcher and her allies proposed to subject it to a bracing douche of supply-side measures including macho management and the reduction of trade union power. The outcome, however, was a drastic contraction of the manufacturing base. The 1980s were the decade in which the British lost the habit of buying British. Imports of manufactured goods from Europe and Asia overtook exports and the balance of payments deficit was financed in part by North Sea oil. But it was financed also by the earnings of the City: the insurance companies, merchant banks, and investment trusts flourished as never before.

The changing terms of the relationship between Mrs Thatcher and the City have been perceptively analysed by Richard Vinen. Advocates of the free market had good reason to view the world of high finance with suspicion. Socially exclusive, it was a gentleman's club for graduates of Oxbridge and the more prestigious public schools, and conspicuous for its lack of competitive zeal. As eager to deregulate finance as to deregulate the labour market, Mrs Thatcher began with the abolition in October 1979 of exchange controls which had first been introduced forty years earlier by Neville Chamberlain. Capital could now flow freely into overseas markets. Later on restrictions on bank lending ('the corset') were lifted, and building societies allowed to provide the same services as high street banks.

When Mrs Thatcher first came to power, the Stock Exchange was at risk of prosecution from the Office of Fair Trading, but in 1983 the Secretary for Trade and Industry, Cecil Parkinson, obtained a pledge from the Stock Exchange to deregulate itself. The changes, which broke down the demarcation between jobbers and brokers, introduced on-screen technology, and opened up Stock Exchange trading to all comers including overseas companies, were all introduced on the day of the 'Big Bang', 27 October 1986. Though 'Big Bang' came to symbolize the transformation of the City into a world financial hub, this was a change that had largely taken place already. Between 1977 and 1987 the City's net foreign earnings rose from £1.5bn to £9.4bn. But one significant consequence of the 'Big Bang' was a rapid escalation in City salaries and bonuses, as institutions competed to hire the most talented traders. 'On the salaries in the City', Mrs Thatcher commented, 'I am the first to say this does cause me great concern. I understand the resentment...'[57]

The Survival of the Welfare State

It was no part of the free market project to let the poor starve. Even the high priests of *laissez-faire* accepted the need for some kind of state-provided safety net, but they were firmly opposed to the welfare state of 1945 to 1979, which they regarded as a socialist agency for the redistribution of wealth, a producers' monopoly for the exploitation of the taxpayer by trade unions and professional associations, and a political machine for the manipulation of the electorate by irresponsible politicians. The welfare state, it was argued, was a wasteful and costly Leviathan delivering benefits and services that most people could afford to provide for themselves through savings or private insurance, and could be more efficiently provided by the private sector or voluntary agencies than by government departments. By diverting resources from the private sector it was hindering the creation of wealth, and by depriving individuals of the responsibility for their own welfare, it was generating a morally debilitating 'dependency culture'.

'Opportunity means nothing unless it includes the right to be unequal', Mrs Thatcher declared in 1975. 'Let our children grow tall, and some grow taller than others if they have it in them to do so.'[58] Unlike the Tory wets, she and her allies were explicitly in favour of greater inequality and ready to bulldoze their way through the massed ranks of protesting churchmen, trade unionists, academics, liberal and socialist politicians, and left-of-centre voters who stood in the way. They did not believe that economic equality was a legitimate or desirable aim, nor did they subscribe to the left-wing definition of poverty as relative deprivation—a level of income substantially below the average. They liked to think that absolute poverty, as defined by Beveridge, had been abolished by the general rise in living standards. On the assumption that all were claiming the means-tested benefits to which they were entitled, they would have been right. At constant 1997 prices, the weekly rate of national assistance payable in 1948 was worth £23.92, compared with a weekly rate of £50.18 for supplementary benefit (which had replaced national assistance), in 1980.[59] Relatively poor you might be, but you still had more than twice the real income you would have had under Mr Attlee—if you could overcome the bureaucratic hurdles.

As in economic policy, the all-encompassing logic of free market principles generated radical proposals for change. The Centre for Policy Studies and the Social Affairs Unit (an offshoot of the Institute of Economic Affairs) issued pamphlets in favour of education vouchers, compulsory private health insurance and so on. The think-tankers hoped to catch the eye and win the support of a Prime Minister who was known to be with them in spirit. Mrs Thatcher was, of course, a fervent believer in self-help. As Kenneth Clarke, one of her ministers of health, recalls:

> She thought it was disgraceful that people who could afford it relied on the taxpayer to provide their health [care]...she was quite happy that the vulnerable, the poor, should have the taxpayer do it for them. But people like you and me should take responsibility for our own lives and should insure for these things. And anyway it was all part of her great campaign to roll back the frontiers of the state.[60]

The Thatcher revolution, however, stopped short at the ramparts of the welfare state and never stormed the citadel. Part of the explanation lay in the constraints imposed by social and political reality. An overwhelming majority of voters had a strong vested interest in a National Health Service free (except for prescription charges) at the point of treatment, and state schools for which there was no fee to pay. Then again there had to be safety nets for the old, the sick, and the poor. Inevitably there were strict limits to the cuts in spending or increased charges that were possible without a serious risk of defeat at the polls. Similarly all attempts at radical reorganization were likely to arouse the suspicions of voters who feared the dismantling of the welfare state. In the summer of 1982 the Cabinet's own think-tank, the Central Policy Review Staff (CPRS), produced a Treasury-inspired report setting out the options for deep cuts in social spending. They included further cuts in social security benefits, education vouchers, the abolition of state support for higher education, and a National Health Service based on compulsory private insurance. When the report came before the Cabinet on 9 September the majority of ministers rose in revolt and condemned it. 'My hair stood on end', recalled Lord Hailsham, the Lord Chancellor, 'and at my age that takes some doing.' Someone then leaked a copy of the report to *The Economist*, detonating a first-class political row in which the Opposition parties made hay with the damning allegation that the government was secretly planning to abolish the NHS. Appalled by the damage, Mrs Thatcher was compelled to shelve the report and issue a ringing declaration of support for the NHS at the annual conference of the Conservative Party.[61] The proportion of those who favoured an increase in taxes to pay for improved social services rose from 32 per cent in

1983 to 46 per cent in 1986, 54 per cent in 1990, and 63 per cent in 1993.[62]

'The National Health Service', wrote Nigel Lawson, 'is the closest thing the English have to a religion, with those who practice in it regarding themselves as a priesthood. This made it quite extraordinarily difficult to reform.'[63] In conjunction with the lobbying power of the doctors, the enduring popularity of the NHS made it the least vulnerable to attack of all the branches of the welfare state. During the first three years of Mrs Thatcher's premiership it enjoyed the unique protection of a promise the Conservative had made during the election campaign to maintain Labour's plans for spending increases over the next three years. An additional line of defence was provided by the report of a Royal Commission on the NHS, published in June 1979, which was critical of administrative waste and inefficiency, but otherwise opposed to fundamental change. The report also pointed out (with some reservations about the accuracy of the statistics) that Britain devoted a lower proportion of GDP to its health services than Australia, Canada, Finland, France, Italy, the Netherlands, Norway, Sweden, the United States, or West Germany.[64]

In the long run, however, a government devoted to the free market would never clasp a socialist institution to its bosom. The appointment of Norman Fowler as Secretary for Health and Social Services in September 1981 marked the beginning of a new phase dedicated to the containment of costs. New money was found for the expansion of general practice, but the budget for hospital and community services came virtually to a standstill for the rest of the 1980s. Given the ever-rising cost of drugs and hospital equipment, and the ever-increasing demand for hospital treatment from an ageing population, this was a perverse course of action, but ministers put their faith in the more efficient use of existing resources. This was to be achieved by putting in place a new tier of management recruited, wherever possible, from the private sector. Hence, for example, the appointment of Don Cruikshank, formerly of Times Newspapers and Richard Branson's Virgin Group, as chief executive of the NHS in Scotland. In the meantime some encouragement was given to the private sector by reversing Labour's policy of restricting the number of pay beds in NHS hospitals.

By the late 1980s the NHS was in a state of continuous financial crisis and the only way ministers could justify to themselves the inevitable decision to spend more on it was by undertaking a radical reorganization. The old-fashioned type of Conservative, who believed that reforms tended to make things worse, had long since disappeared. To expedite the change Mrs Thatcher decided in July 1988 to split the Department of Health and Social Security into its two component parts, with Kenneth Clarke as the new Minister of Health. Clarke was a pragmatic Tory who believed in a more generously funded NHS, but such was his barnstorming style and readiness to offend liberal opinion that he blended well enough into the Thatcherite scene. Relishing the prospect of a showdown with the doctors, he refused to consult them, and accused GPs of 'feeling nervously for their wallets every time I mention the word reform'.[65] Like Bevan before him, Clarke had to face down the clamorous opposition of the British Medical Association, which urged doctors not to co-operate with his proposals. The Labour Party warned that Clarke's proposals were a stepping-stone to wholesale privatization. The official historian of the NHS, writing in 1989, warned that it was 'on the verge of an experiment more dangerous than anything experienced in its forty-year history'.[66] Unlike Bevan, who could rely on the steadfast support of Attlee, Clarke was almost abandoned at the last minute by Mrs Thatcher, who lost her nerve and threatened to scrap the reforms. Clarke pressed on. The key element, embodied in the 1990 NHS and Community Care Act, was the creation of an internal market in which District Health Authorities acted as purchasers, and hospitals (both public and private) as providers competing for work from the purchasers. GPs were given the option of turning themselves into fundholders, and public sector hospitals the right to convert themselves into independent, self-governing trusts. Prophecies of disaster proved mistaken: the new system, which fell rapidly into place, worked as well or better than the old, and from 1990 onwards expenditure on the NHS began once more to increase as a proportion of GDP.[67] From the point of view of the general public the NHS continued to deliver GP and hospital services free at the point of treatment except for prescription charges and (since 1989) charges for eye tests. Dental charges, which had been rising fast, were another matter.

The headlines of the 1980s told of cuts, cuts, and more cuts. One of the primary targets was the social security budget, which had been rising rapidly in recent years. Owing to persistent and often exaggerated stories in the press of benefit fraud, it was also vulnerable to attack.

The Board of Inland Revenue estimated in 1979 that the black economy was worth 7.5 per cent of gross domestic product, and Mrs Thatcher believed that it cushioned the effects of unemployment.[68] Since the 1950s most cash benefits had been uprated in line with prices or average earnings, whichever was the higher. The idea was that recipients of social security should share in the growth of prosperity. The Thatcher governments abandoned this approach. Since earnings generally rose faster than prices, it was decided to link retirement pensions to prices, an economy that resulted in a long, slow decline in the value of pensions relative to earnings. Unemployment benefits were first of all cut then held below the rate of inflation, and the rules governing entitlement to benefit tightened up to restrict the number of claimants. The level of child benefit was frozen from 1981 to 1988. Maternity and funeral benefit were abolished for all except a handful of recipients. After a whole series of *ad hoc* measures the initiative was seized in 1984 by the Secretary for Health and Social Security, Norman Fowler, who announced what he claimed to be the biggest review of social security since Beveridge. The outcome was anti-climactic. The most significant change was the evisceration of SERPS, the state earnings related pension scheme which had been introduced by the Wilson government in 1975, with the support of the Conservatives.[69] Otherwise the review consisted of a rationalization of existing schemes and some tinkering with levels of benefit. In spite of many economies that would have commanded the admiration of a Victorian workhouse master, the social security budget rose from 12.7 per cent of GDP in 1980 to 13.1 per cent in 1990. This was partly due to the costs imposed by rising unemployment. The out of work were entitled to unemployment benefit for a period of twelve months, later cut to six, after which they could claim means-tested supplementary benefit. An increase of more than a million in the number of old-age pensioners—up from 8,918,000 in 1980 to 9,956,000 in 1990—gave an extra twist to the spiral.[70]

The Treasury also demanded, and got, substantial cuts in the education budget. Mrs Thatcher mistrusted the Department of Education, whose officials she blamed for making her complicit in the destruction of so many grammar schools during the Heath government. It was too late to reverse the comprehensive revolution but she attempted with little success to halt it, and preserve the remaining grammar schools, which had completely disappeared in Scotland and Wales, and were only to be found in England. (Northern Ireland, meanwhile, retained all its grammar schools.) In a revival of the Fleming experiment of the 1940s, an Assisted Places scheme was introduced to provide academically able children from low-income families with scholarships to independent schools. For state education, meanwhile, spending cuts were the order of the day. The 1981 White Paper on public expenditure announced a cut of seven per cent over the next three years, including a reduction of more than 30 per cent in capital expenditure. Relations between the teaching unions and the Minister, Mark Carlisle, were acrimonious, but worse was to follow when he was succeeded in September 1981 by Sir Keith Joseph, who imposed additional cuts, made speeches accusing the teachers of failing the nation, and radiated *angst* and pessimism. By 1985 the government and the National Union of Teachers were locked into 'the longest and most damaging confrontation between teachers and the state ever yet experienced…'[71]

Kenneth Baker, who replaced Joseph as Secretary for Education in May 1986, was a far more self-confident personality with an engaging manner, an air of beaming optimism, and a will of his own: he was not afraid to stand up to Mrs Thatcher. He settled the teachers' dispute with concessions on pay, but removed the negotiating rights of the teaching unions in the Teachers Pay and Conditions Act of 1987. His Education Bill, a far more sweeping measure than the Butler Act of 1944, was imposed from above on teachers and local authorities who fought hard against it but could not prevent its passage. There was barely a pretence of consultation: the comments of interested parties were invited but the 20,000 responses received were pigeonholed and ignored.[72] The Baker Act of 1988 introduced a national curriculum in England and Wales with ten compulsory core subjects and attainment targets on which children were to be tested at the ages of seven, eleven, fourteen, and sixteen. The results were to be published, creating a league table of schools intended to 'drive up standards' and facilitate parental choice. The local authority monopoly over state schooling was broken by giving secondary schools the right to opt for direct funding from the Department of Education, and the introduction of a new type of secondary school, the City Technology College, again funded directly by central government. The Act did not apply to Scotland, where a more loosely defined national curriculum was introduced by local education authorities under the guidance of the Scottish Education Department.

The Baker Act marked another stage in the progression from the producer-monopoly welfare state of the 1940s to the quasi-consumerist welfare state of the twenty-first century, but as there was very little scope in practice for choice or competition the main effect was to impose on the schools a bureaucratic system of targets, monitoring, and controls of the kind which the Attlee governments had attempted without much success to apply to industrial production. Banished from economic affairs, the ghost of Sir Stafford Cripps was prowling through the corridors of the welfare state. Controls over employers and managers in the private sector had been replaced by controls over doctors, teachers, and other public sector professionals. No wonder they filled the air with complaints, but they were right to sound the alarm. In centralized bureaucracies, one control tended to lead to another, multiplying the number of administrators needed to ensure compliance, and creating a new vested interest, a cadre of public sector managers more highly paid than the front-line staff they supervised and directed.

If school teachers could testify to this, so could academics. Mrs Thatcher was a graduate of Somerville College, Oxford, but there was no love lost between her and the universities. As Secretary for Education she had been mobbed and shouted down by protesting students whose attitudes and behaviour she abhorred. She had also been shocked to discover that most vice-chancellors and academics were too liberal in outlook to impose the kind of discipline and authority she expected to find on campus.[73] As she saw it, universities consumed a great deal of wealth but failed to promote entrepreneurial values or the merits of capitalism. With few exceptions academics in the humanities and social science—Marxist sociologists, Keynesian economists, labour historians, lecturers in social policy, town planning, and so on—were ideological opponents of the government, and university teachers of all kinds behaved as though the state owed them a living. 'Remembering her own student days of hard work and plain living', writes John Campbell, 'she regarded modern students and most of their lecturers as idle parasites who lived off the taxpayer while abusing the hand that fed them. But she blamed the students less than their tutors.'[74]

The Callaghan government had already begin to squeeze university budgets for purely economic reasons. From political as well as economic motives Mrs Thatcher squeezed them harder. The universities were a dissident estate whose pretensions had to be deflated. New spending restrictions were introduced, followed by the announcement in 1981 of a cut of 8.5 per cent over the next three years. The odium of distributing the cuts between the universities was born by the University Grants Committee (UGC) which decided to maintain quality and standards at the expense of student numbers. Paradoxically, given the priority attached by the government to the needs of industry, technological universities were some of the hardest hit: Salford was cut by 44 per cent, Bradford and Aston by a third.[75] Student numbers began to increase again in the late 1980s but at the time of Mrs Thatcher's resignation the number of full-time university students stood at 142,400, down slightly from 145,100 in 1980–1. It was the polytechnics and colleges of further education, under local authority control, who took advantage of the rising demand for higher education.

The majority of academics had loathed Mrs Thatcher before the cuts: afterwards they loathed her even more. Oxford had a tradition of awarding an honorary doctorate to prime ministers who were graduates of the university, but in January 1985 more than a thousand dons crowded into the Sheldonian and rejected by 738 votes to 319 a proposal to award the honour to Mrs Thatcher, whose government, they alleged, had done 'deep and systematic damage to the whole public education system in Britain'.[76] It was an understandable reaction to the *kulturkampf* the government was waging in the schools and universities, but also a reflection of the complacency and self-importance of academics. Mrs Thatcher was a democratically elected Prime Minister and had the right to pursue policies with which Oxford dons disagreed. The tolerant, open-minded liberalism they recommended to others had vanished the moment their own interests were at stake, and they had missed the opportunity of reminding the world that Oxford had produced Britain's first woman prime minister.

The political and administrative history of higher education in the Thatcher years is a long and complex tale but the main theme is unmistakable. The universities were increasingly subjected to strategic directives and financial controls dictated by central government, and administered within the universities by a new and expanding tier of managers. The UGC set the ball rolling by introducing its own regime for the assessment of the performance of universities in teaching and research. Kenneth Baker's Education Act took the trend towards top-down management a stage further by abolishing the UGC and replacing

it with a University Funding Council with the power to impose contractual obligations on the universities in return for grants. For good measure the Act also abolished academic tenure. The concept of universities
as self-governing, collegiate bodies dedicated to learning and operating
with the financial support of the state, was giving way to the concept of
university education as a nationalized industry with a labour force of
teachers and researchers whose efficiency was gauged by their success
in the fulfilment, under the direction and control of their line-manag-
ers, of production targets.

Mrs Thatcher's commitment to the free market never extended as far
as the market for housing, which she rigged and distorted without a hint
of self-irony. Ever since the 1950s the Conservatives had encouraged
home ownership and the creation of a 'property-owning democracy'.
The Heath government had given local authorities the right to sell
council houses to their tenants, but only a trickle of sales had resulted.
The Labour MP Frank Field was in favour of the right to buy and so
were Wilson and Callaghan. Mrs Thatcher, who regarded council
estates as socialist fiefdoms intended to keep tenants in a state of permanent dependency on the Labour Party, was determined to break them
up. A pledge to give council house tenants the right to buy their homes
at subsidized prices was included in the 1979 election manifesto, and
local authorities were compelled to comply by the Housing Act of 1980.
The right to buy proved to be very popular and by 1982, sales had
reached a peak of 200,000 a year. After this sales fluctuated at lower
levels but rising house prices pushed up cash receipts from £1,877 million in 1982–3 to £3,440 million in 1988–9. Local authorities received
the proceeds, but the gentleman in Whitehall forbade them to use most
of the money for new housing. It was to be used to pay off debts and cut
the cost of local government to the Exchequer. The revenues received
from the privatization of council housing were almost as great as the
combined proceeds of all the other privatizations of the Thatcher
years.[77]

Between 1981–2 and 1990–1 more than a million local authority or
New Town homes and flats were sold for owner-occupation. Strange to
say the four million homes remaining in the public sector represented
a larger share of the housing stock than the council houses of 1951, at
the end of six years of socialist rule. Rolling back the frontiers of the
welfare state was a long job and even then it was partly an affair of

smoke and mirrors. Under Mrs Thatcher public expenditure on housing fell steeply from £7.3 billion to £1.9 billion, a consequence of council house sales and a cut of about 50 per cent in the Exchequer subsidy to local housing authorities. But the figures are based on a very narrow definition of housing costs. The Thatcher governments put an end to the general subsidy for council house rents which the Wilson and Callaghan governments had provided as part of the social contract. The consequence was that real rents rose by about 40 per cent, but as the majority of tenants could not afford to pay them they became eligible for means-tested housing benefit, a part of the social security budget. Meanwhile, as home ownership increased and house prices rose, the cost to the Exchequer of tax relief on mortgage payments increased from £2,800 million in 1981/2 to £5,500 million in 1988/9.[78] Here again was a housing cost that did not appear in the housing budget. Arguably the same could be said of the exemption of owner-occupied homes from capital gains tax.

Town Hall and Whitehall

The break-up of council estates was only one episode in the government's campaign to reduce the powers and undermine the independence of local authorities. There was one simple reason why local government was high on Mrs Thatcher's list of obstructions to be removed on the road to a free market economy. In 1975 the total expenditure of central government (at 1997 prices) was £64,779 million. The total expenditure of local government was £44,233 million, but only about one-third of this was raised locally through the rates: the rest came from the Treasury. During the long post-war boom local and central government had expanded together and the number of jobs in local government had risen by 54 per cent between 1961 and 1974.[79] When public spending cuts were needed, as they were after the oil-shock of 1973, cuts in local government spending were inevitable. 'The party's over', Labour's Minister for the Environment, Anthony Crosland, told the local authorities in 1975. His Conservative successor, Michael Heseltine, tightened the screws by penalizing councils which spent beyond the limits laid down by the government. This drive to curb spending was intimately connected with the ideological objective of reversing socialism. Labour controlled councils still practised municipal socialism in such forms as Direct Labour departments with a monopoly over work for the council, municipally owned buses with subsidized fares, or generous budgets for education, libraries, and other social services. They were impediments, it was thought, to the revival of capitalist enterprise. Nor could decaying inner cities be revived by Labour councils hostile on principle to private investment.

Successive Conservative attempts to reduce local government spending gave left-wing Labour councillors the opportunity of casting themselves in the role of resistance leaders in the front line against Thatcherism. In the London borough of Lambeth the Trotskyite Ted Knight ('Red Ted' as the press inevitably called him) took up the cause of gays, lesbians, the IRA, and the Sandinista revolutionaries of Nicaragua, to whom he delivered in person a message of solidarity from the people of Lambeth. David Blunkett, the leader of the ruling Labour group on Sheffield city council, was a more traditional type of socialist. The son of a steelworker and blind from birth, he turned Sheffield into the flagship of the campaign by Labour local authorities to resist the 'Tory cuts'. When Labour won control of the Greater London Council in May 1981, the former Labour leader was ousted in a coup in favour of Ken Livingstone, a former hospital worker turned full-time politician. Although he described himself as a radical rather than a Marxist the policies of 'Red Ken' were closely aligned with those of 'Red Ted'. Then in May 1983 Labour won control of Liverpool city council, but the Labour group was itself controlled by the Militant Tendency, a Trotskyite party within a party, dedicated to class war and revolution. Though his official post was that of deputy leader of the council, the effective leader was Derek Hatton ('Degsy' to his admirers), who looked like a celebrity footballer, dressed in Armani suits, drove a Jaguar XJ6, and enthused mass demonstrations with incendiary speeches. His leadership of the council culminated in the decision to bankrupt the city and issue redundancy notices to all its employees.

In the end the resistance of the left-wing town halls was overcome, but with difficulty. The task of controlling local government expenditure was akin to wrestling with a giant octopus: no sooner was one tentacle pinned to the ground than another broke free. Gradually, through an accumulation of administrative and legislative sanctions, a measure of control was achieved. As we have already seen in the case of housing policy, one way of doing this was simply to strip local government of many of its powers and functions. Councils were compelled to introduce competitive tendering for work previously carried out by their own employees in Direct Labour departments. 'Bus wars' broke out as local bus services were deregulated, and municipally owned buses were exposed to competition from the private sector. Policy for the inner cities was based on the removal of planning powers from local authorities and their transfer to Urban Development Corporations and Enterprise Zones. 6,000 acres of London docklands and 900 acres of dockland in Liverpool were handed over in 1981 to Urban Development Corporations with comprehensive powers of development and financial support from Whitehall of up to 100 per cent. 'In all practical senses', wrote Michael Heseltine, the Minister of the Environment responsible for them, 'they were to be New Town corporations in old cities.'[80] In 1988 the scheme was extended to include several other declining industrial areas. In the Enterprise Zones, firms were granted automatic planning permission, exemption from local rates for up to ten years, and 100 per cent tax relief on all capital investment in buildings. Eleven Enterprise Zones were designated in 1980: by 1990 there were twenty-five.[81] 'Between 1979 and 1994', writes Andrew Marr, 'an astonishing 150 Acts of Parliament were passed removing powers from local authorities, and £24 billion a year, at 1994 prices, had been switched from them to unelected and mostly secretive gatherings.'[82]

The menace of 'Red Ken' was dealt with by more straightforward methods. The Greater London Council, which had been created by the Conservatives as a strategic authority for the capital in 1963, was simply abolished by the Local Government Act of 1985. So too were the six metropolitan county councils of Tyne and Wear, West Yorkshire, South Yorkshire, Greater Manchester, and the West Midlands, the offspring of a reorganization of local government under Edward Heath. Abolition was justified by the argument that a second tier of local government was wasteful and unnecessary, and tended to lead to bureaucratic empire-building. The subsequent experience of London suggested that it was not so much bureaucracy the Thatcher governments objected to, as bureaucracies under Labour control. Patrick Jenkin, the minister responsible for the Local Government Act, claimed that the powers of the GLC would be transferred, for the most part, to the London boroughs. 'This was untrue', writes Simon Jenkins, 'The powers of the GLC were almost all assumed not by the boroughs but by a government

Office for London in Whitehall. This operated alongside an astonishing array of fifty new quangos...They ran public transport, the
Thames, museums, the arts, sport, and even the South Bank Centre...By
1990 there were some 12,000 laymen and women running London on
an appointed basis against just 1,900 elected borough councils.'[83]

The most effective device for controlling local expenditure proved to
be rate-capping. The Rates Act of 1984 gave Whitehall the power to fix
the maximum rate that any or every local authority had the right to
impose. From his headquarters in the 'Republic of Sheffield' David
Blunkett put himself at the head of a campaign by hard-Left Labour
authorities to defy the law, but the dream of a great extra-parliamentary
protest movement faded and in the end even Lambeth and Liverpool
submitted to the inevitable and fixed a legal rate. The final blow against
'Degsy' Hatton and the Liverpool Militants was struck by the Labour
leader Neil Kinnock, who denounced them in a passionate speech at
the annual party conference in October 1985. A party enquiry into
their activities led to their expulsion from the party and their resignation from the council.

Mrs Thatcher had won. The giant of municipal socialism lay
prostrate at her feet like one of the trees that Mr Gladstone used to
chop down for recreation on his estate. Unfortunately for her, the
temptation to administer the *coup de grace* overrode her better judgement, and she was lured into the fatal trap of the community charge
or 'poll tax'.

In common with many other Conservatives she had always disliked
the rates, the taxes levied by local government on houses and businesses.
The problem was that of the 35 million people eligible to vote in local
government elections in England and Wales, ratepayers were in a
minority. Only householders, of whom there eighteen million, were
liable to pay, and of these six million on low incomes paid a reduced
rate or no rate at all.[84] Another seventeen million people were exempt.
Local councillors could therefore raise the domestic rate in the knowledge that the majority of electors would never have to pay it. As they
were also aware, the middle and upper classes would pay more than the
working classes. Rates were payable by householders whether or not
they owned their own home, but calculated on the basis of the notional
rental value of each property. The higher the valuation the larger the
bill for the ratepayer. The rates therefore gave Labour councils a means

of redistributing income from middle class and mainly Tory households to working class and mainly Labour households.[85] Local authorities also had the power to fix the business rate, which again gave Labour councils the opportunity of taxing a predominantly Tory interest group with little electoral clout.

In spite of all this Mrs Thatcher was reluctant at first to embroil the government in a complex and hazardous issue. She was persuaded to act when a steep revaluation of the rates in Scotland, announced in February 1985, caused an explosion of rage among Scottish Tories who demanded that something should be done. Coincidentally an enquiry into the rates led by two junior ministers, William Waldegrave and Kenneth Baker, came up with the idea that everyone who made use of council services should make a modest flat-rate contribution towards the cost, with rebates for the low paid and other special cases. Councils would be free to decide the level of the new 'community charge', the assumption being that Labour authorities would hesitate to increase it out of fear for the electoral consequences. They would also lose control of the business rate, which was to be standardized for the whole country at a level determined by central government. The Chancellor of the Exchequer, Nigel Lawson, warned that the community charge would be unworkable and a political catastrophe, and friendly voices expressed serious doubts, but Mrs Thatcher's initial caution had given way to ardent enthusiasm and the decision to introduce the community charge was announced in January 1986. After this there could be no going back for the Prime Minister in spite of mounting evidence of the political hazards and the administrative problems.

The fundamental flaw was the introduction of a tax that created many more losers than winners. To aggravate the problem, estimates of the level at which the charge would have to be set rose steadily and varied greatly from one local authority to another. Some ratepayers who had expected to gain found that they would actually be worse off. There were also problems of enforcement. A house could not run away but an individual could be hard to trace. Last but not least, and in spite of the rebate for people on low incomes, a flat charge that in most cases took no account of ability to pay was widely regarded as unfair and immoral. Not for the first time, Mrs Thatcher found her policies attacked as socially unjust by the leaders of the Christian churches.

In response to the clamour from Tories north of the border, the community charge was introduced in Scotland in April 1989, a year before its introduction in England and Wales. There followed, as described in the next chapter, an outbreak of popular protest reminiscent of the rebellion of the Scots against the introduction of the English prayer book in 1637. In England Mrs Thatcher pressed on regardless, facing down the vocal opposition of dissident Conservatives, the Opposition parties, and the hostile verdicts of the opinion polls. The government and its supporters tried to insist that the name of the tax was the 'community charge', but everyone else called it the 'poll tax', and the historically-minded pointed out that a previous attempt to introduce such a tax had resulted in the peasants' revolt of 1389. On 31 March 1990, the day before it was due to come into force in England, an anti-poll tax rally attended by about 200,000 people in Trafalgar Square degenerated into violence and several hours of fighting in the streets. 'Buildings were set on fire, police vehicles overturned, cars set ablaze, shops looted and scores of people injured', the *Observer* reported the following day. 'One crowd of about 2,000 demonstrators marched north up Regent Street across Oxford Circus and up Portland Place, looting as they went. Paving stones, rubbish bins, anything that came to hand was used to smash windows in some of London's most prestigious stores, Liberty, royal jewellers Garrards, Tower Records, Tie Rack, Acquascutum, Next, Dickens and Jones, fur shops and other jewellery shops were all raided...By 8pm much of London's West End looked like a sacked city. Streets were littered with clothes ripped from smashed windows and the air was full of the heady mixture of alcohol and perfume from looted shops.'[86]

Conservative attempts to blame the violence on the Labour Party had little effect. The opinion polls, which had begun to turn against the government in the summer of 1989, consistently showed a strong Labour lead from the beginning of 1990. The unpopularity of the poll tax was not the only factor at work. The economic recovery which had begun in 1983 had turned into the rip-roaring 'Lawson boom' of 1987–8, with investment and employment expanding, share prices rising, consumer expenditure soaring, and a massive bubble in house prices, which nearly doubled between 1985 and 1989. After much talk of an economic miracle, hubris followed. By the second half of 1990 output and employment were falling and house prices with them. Although there was no need of another general election before 1992, the Conservatives began to panic while the Cabinet split over Mrs Thatcher's increasingly strident tone over Britain's relations with the European Union. The resignation of the Foreign Secretary, Sir Geoffrey Howe, and the decision of Michael Heseltine to stand against Mrs Thatcher for the leadership of the party, led to the final, brutal scenes in which a political party turned against a leader who had won three general elections in a row, but succumbed to the myth of her own infallibility. She resigned on 28 November 1990. Ironically, her downfall occurred at a moment when her world-view was sweeping all before it. Many of the governments of western Europe were following the British example and privatizing state assets. The greatest triumph of all, the defeat of communism and the collapse of the Soviet Union, occurred with breathtaking speed in the revolutionary years 1989–91.

'Thatcher and Sons'[87]

John Major, who succeeded Margaret Thatcher as Prime Minister on 28 November 1990, personified the old-fashioned English ideal of a thoroughly nice man. Mild-mannered and quietly spoken, he addressed his fellow citizens as though they were equals. A child of the 1940s for whom England was still, in his more sentimental moments, a land of cricket on the village green and 'old maids biking to communion', he was more liberal socially than many Conservatives, but no less committed to free market economics than his predecessor.

In order to attract private investment into the public sector the Major government introduced the Private Finance Initiative whereby private companies bore the cost of constructing schools, hospitals, and other public buildings and leased them back to the government. They shut down half of what remained of the coal industry, putting 30,000 men out of work, and privatized the other half. They also outdid Mrs Thatcher, who was shrewd enough not to grasp this particular nettle, by privatizing the railways. It could have been done by selling off British Rail as a whole, or by breaking it up into regions, the option Major himself favoured, but the Treasury insisted on splitting the organization and management of the railways between Railtrack, which owned the lines and charged the operating companies for using them, the operating companies themselves, and another set of companies that owned and leased out the rolling stock. Superimposed on this fragmented structure were regulators whose decisions were subject to ministerial intervention. Tony Blair described it as 'replacing a comprehensive coordinated railway network with a hotchpotch of private companies linked together by a gigantic bureaucratic paperchase of contracts, overseen by a bunch of quangos'.[88]

The general election of May 1997 put an end to eighteen years of Conservative government, the longest period of single party rule since Lord Liverpool's administration of 1812–27. It felt more like the peaceful overthrow of an *ancien regime* than a simple change of government. Towards the end, John Major's government had petered out in sleaze, faction-fighting, and ridicule, but the banality of the ending cannot detract from the significance of the Thatcher–Major years. Major, it has to be said, put a friendlier face on the government's policies but his premiership was essentially a continuation of his predecessor's work. How then to sum up 'Mrs Thatcher's revolution'?

Mrs Thatcher was respected as a conviction politician by opponents who detested the convictions in question. She also gave strong and decisive leadership at a time when it was in very short supply. Beyond that opinion is divided and probably always will be. The case in favour of 'Thatcherism' is that by 1979 it offered the only escape from a vicious circle of inflation, industrial unrest, low investment, and long-term economic decline. State socialism would have had much the same consequences as it had in eastern Europe. The social democratic strategy of modernization through a mixed economy, industrial consensus, and progressive social policies had failed. There was, therefore, no realistic alternative to the revival of free market economics, however rough the process might be. Although therefore much dead wood had to be cut out, Thatcherite policies restored the profitability of industry through privatization, a tight rein on taxes and spending, the curbing of trade union power, the re-establishment of the right of managers to manage, and the revival of incentives to enterprise and risk-taking. The case against is that she and her governments unbalanced the economy by sacrificing so much of manufacturing industry on the altar of deflation between 1979 and 1982, created the illusion of an economic recovery out of a short-term boom in consumer spending, financial speculation, and property prices, starved the public sector of much needed investment in education and health, and promoted 'acquisitive individualism' at the expense of social justice. The issue at stake is not whether there were gains or losses, but how the balance should be struck. The political consequences of Mrs Thatcher are more certain: a transfer of power from the state to the market, from workers to managers and employers, from manufacturing to finance, from local to central government, and—much to her own regret—from Westminster to Brussels.

10

Haves and Have-Nots

By the beginning of the 1980s parts of Britain were all too visibly crumbling. Long established industries were contracting and making workers redundant, factories and warehouses falling derelict. There were riots in the inner cities where large numbers of young people were out of work with little hope of finding a job. No longer was it unusual to see a beggar in the street, or the homeless sleeping in shop doorways. At the other end of the social scale were young men who were making a fortune in the City, and splashing their money around like Loadsa-money, the loud-mouthed character invented by the comedian Harry Enfield.

The gulf between the haves and have-nots was more glaring than at any time since the hunger marches of the 1930s. The Churches and the Opposition parties put the blame on the Thatcher governments and accused them of neglecting the problems of poverty and social deprivation, but the longer Mrs Thatcher remained in power the more obvious it became that social change could not easily be reversed. By the end of the 1980s statistics confirmed that Britain was now a more unequal society but the issue of equality, which for decades had played such a prominent part in political debate, was beginning to fade from the radar screens of the politicians.

The Affluent Eighties

However unjust it was that three million people should be out of work in 1986, it was also true that nearly twenty million were in full-time employment, and another 6.7 m, mainly women, in part-time work. Buoyed up by North Sea Oil, the growth of the City of London, and a modest revival in manufacturing industry, the British economy was still delivering economic growth and a rising standard of living from which the majority of the population were benefiting. The state retirement pension was dwindling in value but more than one-third of women workers, and nearly two-thirds of male employees, were in occupational pension schemes. Between 1971 and 1990 the disposable income of the average household increased by nearly three-quarters.[1] Other indicators of health and well-being continued to demonstrate social advance on a broad front. Between 1980–2 and 1990–2 the average life expectancy of a man at birth increased from 71 to 73.4, the average life expectancy of a woman from 77 to 79.[2] Educational opportunities were expanding too. The number of students in full-time higher education rose from 534,900 in 1980/1 to 717,900 in 1990/1, and the proportion of women among them from 40 to 46 per cent.[3]

During Mrs Thatcher's premiership nearly one and a half million tenants of local authorities took advantage of the opportunity to buy their homes at stupendous discounts of up to 70 per cent of the value.[4] A mortal blow against council housing, the right-to-buy policy was one of her most radical initiatives, though as the graph below demonstrates she was working with the grain of social change. The effect of her policy was to accelerate a long-term trend towards home ownership that was already firmly established (see Graph 10.1).

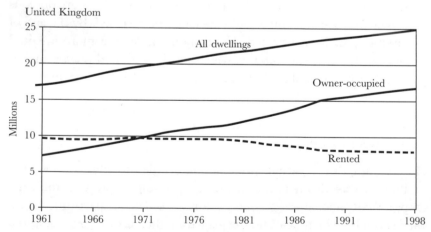

Graph 10.1 The expansion of home ownership 1961–98.

Source: *Social Trends 2000* (2000), p. 167, Table 10.4.

The expansion of housing was led by the private sector and the big construction companies like Wimpey and Barratt homes. Their new-build estates won few plaudits from architectural critics but proved to be extremely popular. At the same time landlords in the private sector were encouraged by local authority grants to provide their properties with basic amenities, and the remaining slums were cleared. The net effect was a general raising of standards. Between 1971 and 1986 the number of homes lacking a kitchen sink, bath or shower in a washroom, a wash handbasin and an indoor WC, fell by 80 per cent.[5]

The gentrification of working-class neighbourhoods in the inner city continued apace. One classic case was the Jericho district of Oxford, an urban village of narrow streets and two-up, two-down terraced homes, badly and hastily built for labourers and their families in the nineteenth century. A half-respectable, half-seedy area with a pub on every corner and a reputation as a haunt of prostitutes, Jericho began to attract ageing hippies, young professionals, and retired academics who moved in next door to long-established working-class residents and set about renovating their homes. The contrast between the old and the new was described in Peter Snow in a book on the changing Oxford scene published in 1991:

The houses of the old working-class residents had been full of *things*: a dense clutter of ornaments, and calendars (Oriental girl, sea scene, or sunset), horses' heads, toby jugs, colour photos of Royals, souvenirs from Torquay or Weston-super-Mare, encapsulated spires-in-snowstorms, and whole families of strange objects hammered out from livid orange copper. Everything was patterned and bold and floral. Every surface had its cover and most covers had a second cover...

As the gentrifiers moved in, out went all the clutter and in moved the toilets. Rooms were mercilessly knocked through, staircases gutted and rotated. In came the light, the white, and the gently patterned—the chill white walls, the stripped pine, the Berber carpets, the Japanese lampshades, and the Sanderson and Laura Ashley curtains. Later, in the 1980s, that harder decade of money values, there was something of a shift in taste. Interiors moved, as it were, to the right. Carpets became deeper and richer, walls became more ambiguous, full of hues, and hints, and stipples. Polished wood and brass suddenly surfaced, fitted kitchens and bathrooms became more expensive.[6]

The housing market was prone to bouts of inflationary excess. Between 1972 and 1974 house prices raced ahead of average earnings, but from 1974 to 1976 they fell much faster.[7] After this, house prices kept broadly in line with prices in general until the late-1980s when they suddenly leaped ahead again. In 1987 the average price of a new home was £49,692 [=£75,034]. By 1990 it was £75,037 [=£113,291].[8] The housing boom of the 1980s was facilitated by the deregulation of finance. Building societies were freed from restrictions on lending in 1979 and the high-street banks were allowed to enter the mortgage market in 1980. Between 1981 and 1990 the number of mortgages rose from 6,336,000 to 9,415,000, and the number who were more than six months in arrears with their repayments from 21,500 to 123,100. 'From mortgage queues', writes Peter York, 'we went in the space of two years to property queues. Instead of only lending on the solid stuff, the mainstream suburban stuff, building societies and banks were practically falling over themselves to lend on just about anything with windows and a door. Property of any kind became intensely desirable and it wasn't long before *gazumping* (etymology unknown) hit the streets and large numbers of people found themselves dazed and reeling after a robust encounter with an estate agent.'[9] Over and above the amount outstanding on loans for house purchase, the amount of outstanding debt, most of it accumulated on bank credit cards, more than doubled between 1981 and 1990.[10]

Bank cards overtook store cards in popularity but the expansion of credit was good news for retailers. In the course of the 1970s consumer expenditure on clothing and footwear, furniture, televisions and electrical appliances, and motor vehicles had all followed an upward curve. In the 1980s the curve continued upwards but at a faster rate. In both decades it was electrical goods that set the pace. Sales of microwave ovens rose from 45,000 in 1978 to 900,000 in 1984 and 50 per cent of homes had one by 1990. Ready-made meals, many of them suitable for microwaving, were taken upmarket by Marks & Spencer.[11] Videorecorders, first introduced in 1978, were to be found in 60 per cent of homes by 1990, but as yet only 19 per cent of homes had a computer and 16 per cent a CD player.[12] Dishwashers, on the other hand, were on the market by 1970, but only 4 per cent of homes possessed one in 1978. By 1990 the total had crept up to 13 per cent.[13]

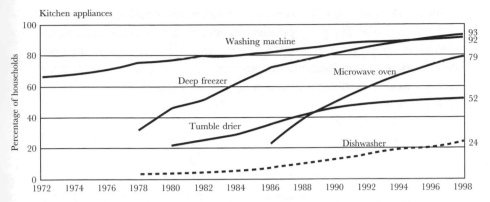

Graph 10.2 Percentage of households with kitchen appliances 1972–98.

The graphs track the steady accumulation of household consumer goods through the Thatcher/Major years. By the end of the period 90 per cent or more of homes were equipped with a landline telephone, colour television, deep freezer, washing machine, and central heating.

Hardly a year went by without the appearance of some electronic novelty. Pocket electronic calculators, pioneered by Japanese inventors in the early 1970s, were a liberation from the drudgery of sums worked out with pencil and paper. Clunky prototypes of the mobile phone began to appear

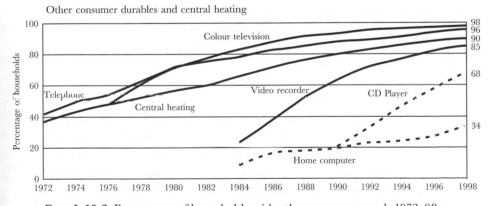

Graph 10.3 Percentages of households with other consumer goods 1972–98.

Source: Living in Britain: Results from the 1998 General Household Survey (1998), Figure 4D, p. 42.

in the 1980s. The first low cost home computer, the ZX80, was produced in 1980 by Clive Sinclair, a prolific inventor who was fascinated by the miniaturization of technology. The development by Alan Sugar of a low-cost word-processor, the Amstrad, marked the beginning of the end for the typewriter. Operations that had once been taken for granted, like the fitting of a new ribbon, the whiting out of errors, or the making of a carbon copy of a letter, were suddenly redundant.

Consumers were fascinated by new technologies but discriminating in their response. A number of Alan Sugar's products failed to catch on and the Amstrad word-processor itself, initially a runaway success, was superseded within a few years by rival brands. In January 1985 Sir Clive Sinclair, who had been knighted by Mrs Thatcher two years earlier, launched an electrically powered vehicle, the Sinclair C5, which looked like a giant shoe and carried a single passenger. The concept of a low-cost motor-vehicle which anyone could take on a public road (motorways excluded) without a driving licence was always problematic and it seems extraordinary that the C5 was designed partly with the needs of teenagers in mind. With a maximum speed of fifteen miles an hour, pedals that had to be used when it was going uphill, and an open top that exposed the driver to all weathers, the C5 excited much ridicule and proved to be a flop.[14]

Tastes in food were changing fast, with long-established favourites like beef and butter losing much of their popularity, and signs of a health-conscious move towards low-fat foods (see Graph 10.4).

The graphs, however, take no account of sweets, chocolates, and puddings consumed at home, or the appetite of children for burgers from MacDonald's. In food, as in clothing and interior design, the trend was towards greater choice and with it a greater consciousness of the lifestyles and fashions on display in advertising, or in magazines and newspaper colour supplements. The kaleidoscope of change, driven by creativity as well as commercial flair, was strictly for those who could afford it, and led by two vanguard groups: the Sloanes and the Yuppies. The Sloane Rangers, named after Sloane Square in their tribal hunting grounds of Chelsea, were young people with 'serious money' who modelled themselves on the aristocracy without quite belonging to it. Although the phrase 'Sloane Ranger' had entered the language in the 1970s, it was the *Official Sloane Ranger Handbook* (1982) by Ann Barr and Peter York that classified and anatomized them. 'It looked at first sight

Great Britain
Grams per person per week

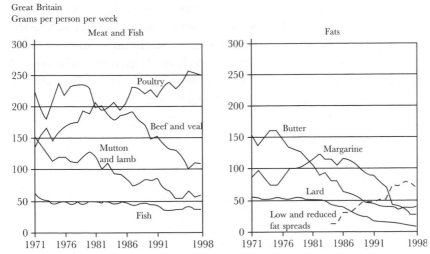

Graph 10.4 Changing patterns in the consumption of foods at home 1971–98.

Source: *Social Trends 2000* (2000), Table 7.16, p. 123.

like a Christmas spoof', York recalled. 'But it was really two books: the really funny bits were the pictures, which said it all by capturing the style exactly, and could be seen, by those who cared to, as in some way "revealing" or "satirical". And then there was the text. . . . It was an anthropologist's textbook (the hidden tribe, the society within a society) and, even more tellingly, it turned out to be an aspirant's guidebook.'[15] The *Handbook*, in effect, extended the purely linguistic distinctions between 'U' and 'non-U' of which Nancy Mitford had written, into the realm of lifestyle in all its dimensions.

What the hippies had been to the 1960s the 'yuppies'—young urban professionals—were to the 1980s. The word 'yuppie' was coined, or at any rate popularized, by Marissa Piesman and Marilee Hartley, the two American authors of *The Official Yuppie Handbook* (1983), which poked mildly satirical fun at its subject. As *Time* magazine explained: 'Yuppies are dedicated to the twin goals of making piles of money and achieving perfection through physical fitness and therapy.'[16]

'Yuppies' were the offspring of the market researchers' world-view in which social groups were more usefully defined by the way they spent their money rather than the way they earned it. By the spring of 1984 the word had arrived in Britain, with a British version of the *Handbook* anatomizing Yuppie tastes in everything from homes, food, wine, clothes, records, films, and leisure activities to the naming of babies. 'The classic Yuppiemobile', the authors noted, 'is, as always, a combination of good taste, style and functionalism. There are relatively few cars on the market that fulfil these demanding criteria. That's why all Yuppies end up with one of the following':

> Golden Eagle jeep
> BMW
> Volvo or Peugeot estate
> Citroen
> Volkswagen Golf Gti (black saloon or all-white convertible)
> Porsche
> Renault
> Range Rover (the only British vehicle in the list)
> Cherokee Chieftain
> Saab Turbo

Yuppies, they added, tended *not* to drive almost anything ending in 'a', as in Ford Anglia, Cortina, Fiesta, Granada or Sierra, or an Astra, Honda, Lada, Marina, Mazda, Nova, Panda, Samba, Simca, Skoda, Toyota or Viva.[17]

The infallible sign of a substantial yuppie presence was the wine-bar, a 1980s phenomenon that first appeared in London before spreading to other cities. The stereotypical patron, writes Joe Moran, 'was a flash yuppie stockbroker, conspicuously glugging Bollinger champagne ("Bolly") or Beaujolais Nouveau. But these bars were mainly successful because they appealed to professional women as calm, unthreatening places to meet after work.'[18]

While the majority of people continued to enjoy a rising standard of living in spite of the recessions of 1973–5 and 1980–1, there was no denying that some were more equal than others. That, of course, was an old story, but the late 1970s were marked by a shift towards greater inequality. The turning-point is visible in the rise of the Gini coefficient, a standard measure of the degree of inequality in the distribution of income.[19] The higher the coefficient, the greater the degree of inequality (see Graph 10.5).

The contrast between the 1960s and 1970s, when the Gini coefficient fluctuated within narrow limits, and the 1980s, during which it rose

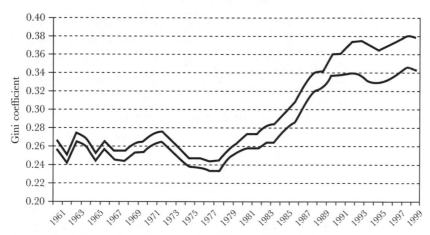

Graph 10.5 Inequality of income: the Gini coefficient 1961–91.

Source: Alissa Goodman, *Inequality and Living Standards in Great Britain: Some Facts*, Institute for Fiscal Studies Briefing Note No. 19 (2001), p. 11. The upper line is the Gini coefficient for income after housing costs; the lower line is the Gini coefficient for income before housing costs.

steeply and steadily, poses two important questions: what was happening, and why?

The Seventies

The frequency of strikes and industrial disputes in the 1970s suggested that a class struggle was in progress, but it was a ragged and confused one in which trade unions were competing against other unions at the same time as they were bargaining with employers. During the 'winter of discontent' the *Observer*'s labour correspondent, Robert Taylor, commented: 'Envy of the super-rich, or a revival of class warfare is not the inspiration behind the anger and frustration among tens of thousands of British workers which is boiling over in the form of big pay claims and industrial action... workers strive, through fragmented and localized bargaining, to hold their position relative to other workers in other work-places and other industries.' [20] In conjunction with the annual wage round, high levels of inflation created a pay scramble in which groups of workers jockeyed for position in the wages league table. Generally speaking they were successful in maintaining the differentials. In April 1975 the top ten most highly paid workers were as follows:

1. Electricity power engineer   £82.60 [=£461]
2. Miner (face)   £75.80
3. Miner (surface)   £65.30
4. Electrician (industry)   £64.90
5. Railway engine driver   £64.30
6. Policeman   £64.10
7. Clerical/executive (Post Office)   £63.40
8. Steel worker   £63.30
9. Water worker   £61.80
10. Gas worker   £61.70

Three years later, in April 1978, seven of these occupations were still in the top ten. Post Office and gas workers had slipped, but only to numbers 12 and 14 respectively. Water workers, at 21, had experienced the only sharp fall.

1. Electricity power engineer   £136.10 [=£388]
2. Miner (face)   £109.20
3. Electrician (industry)   £95.10
4. Draughtsman   £92.00
5. Steel worker   £91.70
6. Miner (surface)   £91.20
7. Policeman   £91.00
8. Car worker   £90.70
9. Toolmaker   £89.80
10. Train driver   £86.00

The same stability was evident among the ten lowest paid groups of workers. In April 1975 they were as follows:

1. Dustman   £49.50 [=£276]
2. Nurse (female)   £45.70
3. General clerk   £45.70
4. Caretaker   £43.80
5. Clerical officer (civil service)   £42.20
6. Catering worker   £41.80
7. Bank worker (woman)   £38.00
8. Farm worker   £37.40
9. Bespoke tailor (woman)   £28.80
10. Retail food worker (woman)   £27.40

By April 1978 the clerical officer had overtaken the caretaker, but categories were unchanged and the placings much as before:

1.	Dustman	£70.40 [=£201]
2.	Nurse	£68.20
3.	General clerk	£68.40
4.	Clerical officer (civil service)	£62.90
5.	Bank worker (woman)	£62.00
6.	Caretaker	£61.50
7.	Farm worker	£57.70
8.	Catering worker	£57.00
9.	Bespoke tailor	£43.00
10.	Retail food worker	£42.20

Source: Samuel H. Beer, *Britain Against Itself* (1982), pp. 58–9.

While workers in employment were able to maintain or improve their standard of living, unemployment was a growing problem. The 1970s were a period of slow but steady decline in manufacturing industry, which was losing ground in domestic as well as international markets. Meanwhile such traditional sources of manual work as the railways and the docks were shrinking. The scale of the problem was illustrated by the case of the London docks, where employment fell from 22,815 in 1967 to 4,100 in 1981. In the labour force as a whole the number of people out of work rose from 596,000, or 2.3 per cent in 1973, to 1,296,000, or 4.9 per cent in 1979.[21] By 1995 the combined turnover of the coal, steel, and shipbuilding industries was less than that of the 10,000 Indian restaurants in Britain.[22]

Unemployment was not the only factor threatening to increase the extent of poverty in Britain. In an exhaustive study of the problem, running to more than a thousand pages with 105 statistical tables in the Appendix, Peter Townsend also stressed the increase in the numbers of retired people and one-parent families. In spite of all this he concluded that the distribution of incomes during the 1970s had proved to be remarkably stable, due perhaps to the increasing participation of women in the labour market, the growth of white-collar employment, and improvements in some social security benefits.[23] The unemployment figures, it should be added, disguised the fact that the majority of people who were out of work were able to find another job within six

months. Poverty, which Townsend defined in terms of relative deprivation, was still in his view a serious flaw in British society, but it was not
getting worse.

In a White Paper of 1976 the government promised to make the
regeneration of the inner cities a priority and the following year parts of
Birmingham, Lambeth, Liverpool, Manchester, Salford, Newcastle,
and Gateshead were designated as focal points for action.[24] Officials
recognized that unemployment was slowly blighting parts of urban
Britain, and especially the inner cities, where there were higher concentrations of the unskilled and the unemployed. For the first time since
the 1930s, there were economic wastelands in which working-class
teenagers were growing up demoralized by lack of hope or incentive, a
predicament aggravated by family breakdown and extensive abuse of
drugs. Spearheaded by the Sex Pistols, the punk rock movement of the
late 1970s was a many-sided, incoherent rebellion of working-class
youths against an adult world of ageing, wealthy rockstars, and a political class whose rhetoric sounded meaningless. It was not a rebellion in
favour of anything but a negation of adult manners and values with a
topsy-turvy aesthetic dedicated to bog-standard musical skills, cheap,
casual clothes, and the celebration of ugliness and violence. 'Punk rock',
wrote the *Daily Mirror* in June 1977, 'is tailor-made for youngsters who
feel they only have a punk future. Is it any wonder they turn to anar-
chistic heroes like Johnny Rotten?'[25] The hippies who had once thronged
the King's Road in the most elegant and colourful of dress, breathing
optimism, and reeking of hash, had been replaced by shambling youths
whose costume (in Jon Savage's words) was 'theatricalized poverty':

> Everything was deliberately artificial and completely askew, from the
> dyed hair rubbed with KY or Vaseline, to the ripped and torn jackets.
> The leather jacket on the outside symbolized protection and aggression,
> while the T-shirts underneath were graffitied, like walls, with whatever
> came to mind. On the legs were the bondage trousers of claustrophobia
> and babyish incapacity.[26]

Another side-effect of the recession of 1973–5 was a renewed outbreak
of anxiety about the fate of the middle classes. All classes were experiencing a fall in their standard of living, wrote the economist Tim Cong-
don, but the middle classes were the biggest losers. With their salaries
restrained by incomes policies, but subject to high levels of taxation,

they were losing ground by comparison with manual workers. 'The Government', he wrote in May 1976, 'has shown little compassion for or understanding of what might be termed "the crisis of the middle classes."' Worst affected of all were the top managers and professionals. The decline in top incomes was confirmed by the Diamond Commission on the distribution of income and wealth, which reported:

> Real take-home pay, (i.e. after tax and adjustment for changes in the RPI), for jobs at most levels of management declined between July 1969 and July 1975. By July 1975, salaries after tax at constant prices had fallen by about 17 per cent at the £10,000 [=£55,700] a year level, and by about 25 per cent at the £20,000 [=£111,400] level from what they were in July 1969. Most of the decline occurred in the last two years of the period. On average the fall is unlikely to have been substantially offset by improvements in the provision of fringe benefits and superannuation for higher income earners.[27]

In 1977 the City Editor of the *Sunday Telegraph*, Patrick Hutber, published a tract for the times entitled *The Decline and Fall of the Middle Class and How it Can Fight Back*. Hutber, who defined the middle classes as consisting of all those whose ambition was to be independent of the state and responsible for their own welfare, argued that their standard of living was under attack from inflation, trade union power, and penal levels of taxation. Many of his readers agreed. 'It is my belief', wrote one correspondent, 'that the way things are going, the middle classes are doomed to a gradual extinction over the course of the next generation or two, and with that disappearance we shall have lost the last bulwark of society.' They should fight back, he argued, by defending grammar schools, paying as little tax as legally possible, and voting for Mrs Thatcher at the next general election.[28]

Traditionally the main body of the middle classes had formed the backbone of the market economy and upheld the rights of private property against the encroachments of the state. However as the public sector expanded, a growing number of professionals and white collar workers were employees of local or central government. 'In the name of socialism, egalitarianism and "irreversible change", wrote Roy Lewis in 1975, 'the middle classes are being bureaucratized. Not destroyed.'[29] The public sector was highly unionized and many professionals were turning to the unions to protect their living standards in the pay scramble of the 1960s and 1970s. Harold Perkin lists a number of professional unions which joined the TUC: the National Association of Local Government Officers in 1964, the Society of Civil Servants in 1973, the Association of University Teachers in 1976, the First Division Association of top civil servants in 1977. The Association of Scientific, Technical, and Managerial Staff, led by the irrepressible Clive Jenkins, began to recruit clergymen and airline pilots.[30]

Lewis, like Hutber, believed that *traditional* middle-class values were in decline. To put it another way, the middle classes were diverse and highly adaptable. We have already come across Michael Frayn's memorable classification of the middle classes into herbivores and carnivores. A middle-class schoolteacher in a duffle-coat, carrying a copy of the *Guardian*, was unlikely to share the views of a stockbroker in bowler hat and pinstripe suit, with a copy of the *Daily Telegraph* under his arm. Just as there had been members of the middle classes who joined the Communist or Labour parties in the 1930s, so there were dissenting minorities among the middle classes of the 1970s. Some were socialists who had been activists on university campuses in the 1960s but there were also campaigners for nuclear disarmament, feminists, gay rights activists, and conservationists.

The culture clash between the herbivores and carnivores of the 1970s was brilliantly captured by the scriptwriters John Esmonde and Bob Larbey in the thirty episodes of the BBC sitcom *The Good Life* (1975–8). Set in suburbia, it was a barbed social comedy in which two neighbouring couples, the Goods and the Leadbetters, pursue alternative lifestyles. Determined to opt out of the rat race, Tom Good and his wife Barbara, played by Richard Briars and Felicity Kendal, attempt to make themselves self-sufficient by turning their back-garden into a farm, raising pigs and chickens, and experimenting with alternative fuels and home-made technologies. Their neighbours, played by Paul Eddington and Penelope Keith, are Jerry and Margot Leadbetter, a successful businessman and his snobbish, social-climbing wife. Tom and Barbara's frugal existence and often farcical experiments meet with incomprehension on the part of the amiable Jerry and the derision of Margot (who bears an uncanny resemblance to Mrs Thatcher), though in the last resort they are all good neighbours, helping one another out in an emergency.

It would, however, be an oversimplification to suggest that the middle classes were divided into two rival camps with conflicting interests. Among married couples, one partner might work for a local authority as a teacher, the other as a sales manager for IBM. There was a further dimension to this partial collectivization of the middle classes. The welfare state had become such a central feature of post-war Britain that, whatever the social or political attitudes of the middle classes, they were to some extent dependent upon it. They might never need unemployment benefit. They might send their children to public schools. They probably belonged to an occupational pension scheme that freed them from dependence from the miserly state old age pension. But the majority of middle-class children were educated in state schools, university education was to a great extent a middle-class prerogative subsidized by the taxpayer, and the middle classes were still overwhelmingly reliant on the National Health Service. In the general election of 1979 the Conservatives won the support of 59 per cent of the 'salariat', Labour 22 per cent, and the Liberals 17 per cent.[31] 'Middle class' was by no means synonymous with 'Conservative'—nor 'Conservative' with 'Thatcherite'.

The Sea Change

After Mrs Thatcher's fall from office in 1990 the Institute of Fiscal Studies carried out, with the assistance of the Joseph Rowntree Foundation, a study of the changing living standards in the UK, based on a statistical analysis of the income of about 200,000 households. Reference has already been made to their findings for the Gini coefficient. They concluded: 'The increase in inequality during the 1980s dwarfed the fluctuations in inequality seen in previous decades...The share of the richest tenth rose from 22 per cent to 25 per cent over the three decades. Whilst real incomes (before housing costs) have grown by around 84 per cent on average over the last three decades, the incomes of the richest tenth have risen twice as fast (up 113 per cent) as those of the poorest tenth (57 per cent). Taking into account the effects of housing costs can greatly affect assessments of changes in real living standards. The real incomes of the poorest tenth ranked by income after housing costs actually fell sharply from a peak in 1979 of £73 [=£110] per week to just over £61 [=£92] per week in 1991 (both in 1991 prices).'[32]

The rise in inequality was therefore not a consequence of a restoration of the differentials between the middle and working classes, but a reflection of changes at the top and bottom ends of the income scale. The figures, admittedly, are frustratingly abstract, a triumph of statistical method over social reality. There is barely a reference in the IFS report to occupations or social classes. Individuals are ranked instead in percentiles in which each group represents one per cent of the population, or quintiles, each of which contains one-fifth of the population. Although they took many economic and social factors into account in seeking to explain the distribution of income, changes in the hierarchy of occupation and pay were excluded from the reckoning.

The IFS report gives us, nevertheless, a very good idea of why the gap between the top and the bottom was widening. Tempting though it is to attribute all the changes to the policies of Mrs Thatcher, it is noticeable that the sharp upward movement in high incomes began in 1977, two years before she came to power. But determined as she was to restore the incentives of top executives and managers, she deliberately accelerated the trend. In his first budget Sir Geoffrey Howe cut the top rate of income tax from 83 to 60 per cent, the first of a series of moves to 'restore incentives'. It was subsequently cut by Nigel Lawson to 40 per cent. Fiscal policy, however, was only one factor. Perhaps the Thatcherite ethos, which made it possible for the first time since the 1930s to extol the virtues of inequality, and to praise the rich as 'wealth creators', had the effect of removing inhibitions in the board-rooms, and legitimizing big increases in pay, accompanied by generous bonuses, the enhancement of pension schemes, and so on. The pace was set by the private sector and accelerated by privatization. In 1981, a permanent secretary in Whitehall earned 45 per cent of the average executive chairman's salary for one of the top hundred listed companies. By 1995, the permanent secretary was down to 19 per cent of his private sector counterpart.[33]

At the other end of the social scale, the main impoverishing factor was unemployment. 'Between 1978 and 1983', writes Bernard Alford, 'manufacturing output fell in real terms by 9.6 per cent and did not recover to the earlier level until 1987. Gross real fixed investment in manufacturing fell by a massive 31 per cent between 1979 and 1983, and it did not match the former level until 1988.' Taking the decade of the 1980s as a whole, two million jobs in manufacturing disappeared, with three-quarters of the fall occurring in the years 1979–82.[34] These were hammer blows, and although the economy began to climb out of recession in 1982, the unemployment total continued to climb relentlessly, reaching three million in 1984, and remaining above the three million mark until 1987. The effects were mitigated by the fact that so many women were going out to work but whether or not this was the case the hardest hit were couples with children and one-parent families. Surprisingly, perhaps, the IFS study concluded that by comparison with other social groups, old-age pensioners were rather better off under Mrs Thatcher than they had been in 1961.

There was a second reason for the stagnation of living standards among the relatively poor: a growing differential between the incomes of skilled and unskilled workers. The damage inflicted on Britain's manufacturing base by the recession of 1980–1 is very well known. Less familiar is the renaissance in manufacturing that followed. It is often argued that the recession was indiscriminate in its effects, killing off efficient enterprises along with failing concerns. This may well be true, but it was also a reflection of a shift away from traditional manufacturing industry that was occurring in all the advanced capitalist nations. Large-scale, labour intensive industries, like steel and shipbuilding, were contracting, and small-scale high-technology industries like electronic engineering, telecommunications, and pharmaceuticals, were expanding.

The large-scale did not disappear but were restructured with smaller and more productive labour forces. Sometimes the task was undertaken by overseas companies. The Nissan factory in Sunderland, built in 1985, became the most productive car plant in the world. The Govan shipyard was rescued from collapse in 1988 by the Norwegian conglomerate Kaverner and restored to profit. Meanwhile new high-technology firms, encouraged by a multitude of government schemes and incentives, were starting up: 19,000 of them between 1980 and 1986.

The new industries, however, could not replace many of the jobs that had been lost. The older industries had employed large numbers of semi-skilled or unskilled workers in the West Midlands, the North of England, and the industrial areas of Wales and Scotland. The new industries employed highly skilled and educated workers and preferred to locate in the South of England: East Anglia was the most favoured spot. Hence the re-emergence of a phenomenon familiar in the 1930s:

the 'North–South divide'. The phrase, however, is an anglocentric one that applies better to England than to Britain as a whole, where the divide was as much between a declining west and an expanding east. In the case of Scotland, for example, *The Economist* remarked in October 1973:

> In the east the arrival of oil has produced the country's biggest post-war boom. In the west there is still doubt, even depression...Although Glasgow is now only 40 minutes' drive from Edinburgh, the two cities belong to different worlds. Edinburgh has all the confidence of a prosperous capital city. It has a thriving middle class, a large number of home owners and a low unemployment rate, labour relations are passable and the two main political parties are equally strong. In Glasgow and the west the situation is quite the reverse. The middle class has been decimated; unemployment is massive; and the proportion of public housing is comparable to that in the Soviet Union. Labour relations are bitter.[35]

The recession of the early 1980s was concentrated in the west of Scotland, south Wales, and the north of England, and the recovery led by the City of London and the service or high-tech industries of the south-east. In the Northern Region of England in August 1980 there were 172 unskilled workers for every vacancy notified to the Labour Exchanges.[36] By the late 1980s such measures of the standard of living as disposable income, house prices, and unemployment indicated that the gap between 'North' and 'South' had widened during the decade. Map 10.1 gives a picture of the geographical distribution of unemployment in January 1989.

The contrast was also reflected in party politics. 'Labour is clearly the most popular party in Scotland, the North of England, and Wales', wrote John Curtice in 1988. 'The Conservatives dominate in the Midlands and the South. Only in London is there no clear advantage for either party. Politically, Britain appears to be divided along a line from the Humber to just south of the Mersey, and from there, along Offa's Dyke.'[37]

During the 1970s, incomes policies had tended to stabilize wage differentials or even to benefit the lower paid. In the 1980s the government allowed pay to be determined by the laws of supply and demand. Unskilled workers were in plentiful supply and low demand. They were also, perhaps, adversely affected by competition from workers on much

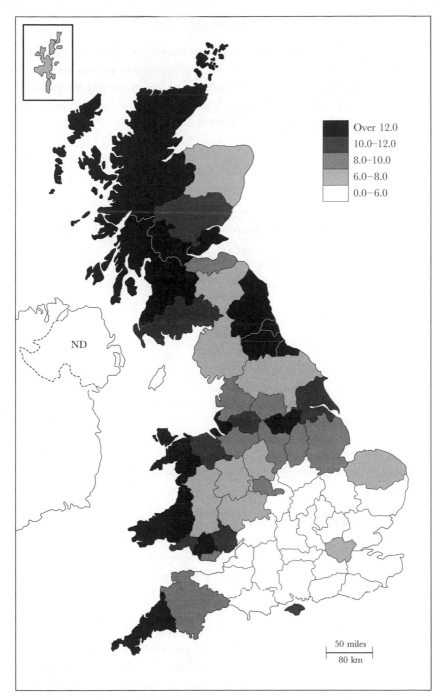

Map 10.1 The geography of unemployment.

Source: R. J. Johnston and Vince Gardner (eds.), *The Changing Geography of the United Kingdom* (1991), p. 480.

lower pay in the newly industrializing nations of Asia. Meanwhile government spending on economic aid for the regions was cut back. The plight of the unemployed was dramatized by the playwright Alan Bleasdale in *Boys from the Blackstuff*, a searing portrayal of the demoralization suffered by unskilled workers in Liverpool when they were made redundant. Screened on BBC TV in October and November 1982, its central character, Yosser Hughes, was a man whose self-confidence and self-respect were destroyed by circumstances beyond his control. Played by the actor Bernard Hill, his pathetic plea of 'Gizza job…I can do that', brought home to viewers the human cost of the unemployment figures.

At the other extreme were fortunes made by young men in the City of London, after the 'Big Bang' of 1986. Writing in the *Spectator* in March 1986, Nicholas Coleridge estimated that there were perhaps a couple of thousand commodity brokers earning £100,000 [=£201,000] a year. Most were between the ages of 26 and 34, and two years earlier they had been on £25,000 [=£50,250] a year:

> A couple of the Sunday colour magazines have written about newly mega-rich commodity brokers, but these have tended to give a misleading impression. They featured naïve young men posing with their sports cars in Totteridge, the inference being that the lucky winners are chirpy *nouveux riches*. This is erroneous because the majority of highly paid city boys are not *nouveaux riches* at all; they are traditional upper middle-class pinstripes who are banking the cheques as fast as they can while the going is good, and would never be so vulgar as to pose for a colour supplement.[38]

They were attracting resentment, Coleridge remarked, not so much from socialists, who had yet to grasp what was going on, as from the educated middle classes in jobs that were far more modestly paid.

The bonus culture, of which so much was to be heard in the banking crisis of 2008–9, was already flourishing. In February 1995 the activities of Nick Leeson, a rogue trader in Singapore, brought about the collapse of Barings, one of the most venerable of the City's merchant banks. As it happened, the bank collapsed on the day that bonuses were due to be paid to the staff for their performance in 1994. Fifty-eight employees were due to receive bonuses of between £250,000 and £499,000 each. Another five were to get between £500,000 and £749,000 each, and the top four more than £750,000 each. Within a few days Barings was sold to a Dutch merchant bank ING for the sum of £1, but as part of the deal ING agreed to pay the bonuses in full at a cost of £95 million, excluding only those directly implicated in the bank's collapse. 'The biggest crime I am guilty of', Leeson declared while awaiting trial, 'is trying to protect people and ensure that the bonuses they expected were paid, and it is this that led to the escalation of the problem.'[39]

The Big Bang in the City had spawned a new class of the Super-Rich whose abilities were so exceptional that it was vital to pay them internationally competitive rates for the job if they were not to be lured away by rival concerns. The logic was irrefutable. Without such high-flyers, banks like Barings would not have been able to compete successfully with banks like ING.

The shift towards greater inequality at both ends of the social scale was facilitated by the demoralization and defeat of the labour movement and the erosion of collectivist ideas. In March 1978 the historian Eric Hobsbawm delivered the annual Marx Memorial lecture under the title: 'The Forward March of Labour Halted?' In spite of the question-mark the main thrust of his argument was unambiguous, and extremely unwelcome to socialists. The forward march of labour—the Labour Party, the trade unions, and the British working class—had come to a halt some twenty-five or thirty years earlier. Manual occupations were in long-term decline and manual workers, who had once made up three-quarters of the population, now accounted for little over a half. Working-class solidarity had been weakened by the sectionalism of the trade unions, hostility to immigrant workers, the increasing employment of women, and the complacency with which well-paid workers in trade unions viewed the plight of the poor.[40]

The first reaction on the Left was to denounce Hobsbawm's analysis as a dangerous error. Socialists had always believed that whatever setbacks and defeats might befall them their day was sure to come:

> England arise, the long long night is over,
> Faint in the east, behold the dawn appear,
> Out of your evil dreams of toil and sorrow,
> Arise oh England for the day is here.

In the post-Stalinist era few socialists, Marxist or otherwise, professed uncritical admiration for the Soviet Union or Communist China. But the fact that so much of the world was under Communist rule seemed to prove that capitalism was still on trial, and the troubles afflicting the British economy suggested that it might collapse. 'The socialist argument is now relevant again', Michael Foot told a meeting of the Shadow Cabinet and Labour's National Executive in January 1973: 'Investment failure is a failure of the system and socialization of investment is the only answer. This drives us towards a more fundamental criticism of society and we are moving towards socialism...'[41] Nor was this all. The TUC had defeated Edward Heath's attempts to curb trade union power and the National Union of Mineworkers had, in effect, overthrown his government. The trade unions, it appeared, were not only fighting the class war but winning it.

It was a false dawn that distracted attention from the weaknesses in the labour movement which Hobsbawm had discerned with such prescience. The headlines told a story of industrial strife and socialist rhetoric that reached a climax in the year-long miners' strike of 1984–5, but the long-term trends were working in Mrs Thatcher's favour. The crushing defeat of the miners, followed the rapid run-down of the coal industry, revealed to all but the most purblind the truth that the social order had changed. The working classes never had been a united force. By the mid-1980s they were not only diminishing in numbers but more divided politically than at any time since the 1930s. In the general election of 1964, 70 per cent of manual workers voted Labour. In the general election of 1983, the figure was 49 per cent.[42] It was no longer possible to believe that miners, railwaymen, dockers, boilermakers, and other stalwarts of manual labour held the keys to the future.

The cause of socialism had always been associated with the drive for greater social and economic equality, but egalitarianism was out of fashion in Mrs Thatcher's Britain. It had little appeal for skilled workers who had always jealously guarded their status, and now had more advantages than ever. It had nothing to offer the roughnecks and roustabouts on the oil platforms at the height of the boom in the North Sea. Nor was there anything to be gained electorally by alienating the middle classes, who were now in the ascendancy. The growth of professional services in government, finance, health, and education, accompanied by the computerization of office work and the beginnings of a revolution in telecommunications, were creating more and more opportunities for graduates of universities and technical colleges. In 1971 there were 1,706,000 managers and administrators in Britain; by 1981

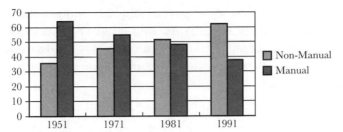

Graph 10.6 Percentage of manual workers in the employed population.

Source: A. H. Halsey and Josephine Webb (eds.), *Twentieth Century British Social Trends* (2000 edition), p. 288.

the figure was 2,305,000 and by 1991, 3,729,000. Over the same period the number in the lower professional bracket rose from 1,946,000 in 1971 to 2,736,000 in 1981 and 3,435,000 in 1991.[43]

The Censuses of 1981 and 1991 confirmed that manual workers were now, for the first time, in a minority (see Graph 10.6).

Although readers of the *Guardian* and the *Observer* were incandescent with rage against Mrs Thatcher, she worked wonders for the morale of the conservative middle classes. From the moment she took office the chorus of middle-class anxiety and complaint fell silent. 'Members of the bourgeoisie hold their heads high again', wrote Ian Bradley in February 1982, 'and no longer feel the need to be ashamed of being middle class. Perhaps more important, while the overall state of the British economy has continued to worsen since the mid-1970s, the relative position of the middle classes has actually improved.'[44] It would be a mistake to imagine that they were completely untouched by the recession, but middle-class unemployment was rare. The taming of the unions, the decline of industrial militancy, and the house price boom of the late 1980s, all seemed to tell the same story: the middle classes were taking possession of the promised land.

The emasculation of the unions, the collapse of the miners' strike, the demoralization of the Labour Party after three successive general election defeats (1979, 1983, and 1987), and the emergence of a new class structure all served to persuade the political nation that Hobsbawm had been right. The forward march of labour had come to a stop and the class war was over. In a conversation with Hugo Young in June 1985, the leader of the Labour Party, Neil Kinnock, 'explicitly condemned the idea that it [the party] should be a federation of the dispossessed and underprivileged, and said it must appeal to the afflu-ent or it is nothing...' In another conversation in May 1988 he explained that he recognized the problem of gross inequalities, but argued that there was no instant way of removing them:

> It is just not practical politics. It would affect too many people. He can-not make a cavalry charge and with some splendid dramatic move take back from people what has rendered inequality greater over the past eight years. Much as he might like to. He will not promise what he can-not deliver: i.e. won't promise a grand return to greater equality... There is no way in which millions of people are going to be persuaded to sur-render whole chunks of their improved standard of living.[45]

Did popular attitudes justify Kinnock's caution? When a representative sample of the electorate were asked in 1986 whether it should be the government's responsibility to reduce income differences between rich and poor, 72 per cent said that it definitely or probably should. But much depends on the precise wording of a question and it is a reason-able inference that most people, not seeing themselves as rich or poor, did not think their own incomes would be affected. When they were asked whether the government should redistribute income 'from the better off to those who are less well off', only 43 per cent agreed. As Peter Taylor-Gooby put it, in the annual report of the British Social Attitudes survey:

> While progressive taxation, the Robin Hood attack on the rich and the view that income gaps are too large are enthusiastically received, the prospect of a few more pence on one's own income tax to benefit a less fortunate neighbour receives only a lukewarm response. Similarly, while progressive taxation is supported in principle, a question about tax rates shows that just over two-thirds of all households think their own tax rate is too high and less than one per cent think it too low. Whatever you think about tax rates and income inequalities, redistribution has more charm when it enables you to put your hand in someone else's pocket.[46]

Egalitarianism was out of fashion and the Thatcher governments had little time for social scientists who defined poverty in relative terms, or dwelt on the theme of 'social deprivation'. In Whitehall, statisticians who had prided themselves on publishing accurate and independent data were under pressure to airbrush out politically inconvenient truths.

Muriel Nissel, a former civil servant who had been the first editor of *Social Trends* when the series began in 1970, described the course of events:

> *Social Trends* set out to give some answers to the questions people started asking in the 1960s about how far economic progress was being reflected in improvements in the quality of life. There was at that time very little such information, and so the development of *Social Trends* during its early years went hand in hand with a determined drive to improve social statistics. It was also thought to be part of the democratic tradition that the civil service should make widely available relevant facts about the economy and society.
>
> In 1979, after the Conservative victory in the General Election, there was a major change in ministerial attitudes. There were to be severe cuts in government expenditure and Sir Derek Rayner was asked to examine the Government Statistical Service. The review concluded that '... there is no more reason for government to act as universal provider in the statistical field than in any other'. Moreover the Rayner team could find little or no specific use within government for *Social Trends*.
>
> The publication survived, but with a revised editorial stressing the relevance of the material for government, and more closely arranged around departmental needs. The emphasis was more on Mr and Mrs Average and their families, rather than those who were vulnerable. There was less analysis by income group, region, social class or family type. Thus, the publication failed adequately to chart a fundamental trend of the decade: the growing inequality in incomes and the widening differences within the country.[47]

The stubborn facts of social class remained and fortunately the statisticians managed to smuggle some of them into *Social Trends*. The 1992 edition included the graph below, which records the remarkably close correlation between social and economic status and rates of infant mortality:

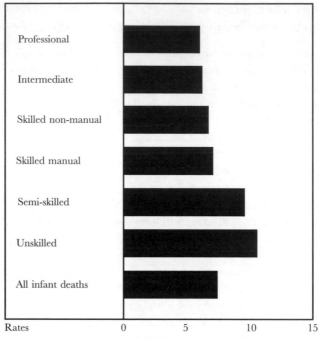

Rates   0   5   10   15

1 Deaths of infants under 1 year of age per thousand live births.
2 Data are for births within marriage only.

Graph 10.7 Infant mortality by social class of father 1989.

Source: *Social Trends 22* (1992), Table 7.2, p. 122.

11

The Permissive Age

The 'permissive society' is forever associated with the 1960s, or at any rate with the period from *c.*1958 to *c.*1973, which historians sometimes refer to as the 'long sixties'. These were the years in which the laws governing marriage and sexuality were reformed and the contraceptive pill was introduced. By the late 1960s no student party was complete without the reverential passing round of a joint. As Churchill might have said, however, this was not the end, nor the beginning of the end, but the end of the beginning. In the 1960s permissiveness was largely a counter-cultural affair in the hands of affluent, middle-class youth. It was during the 1970s and 1980s that widespread shifts in popular attitudes and behaviour marked the transition from a permissive minority to a permissive society. The traditional framework of marriage and family life did not collapse, but from a position of near hegemony in respectable society, it gradually lost ground to competing forces and was eventually reduced, by the turn of the century, to the status of one 'life-style' choice among others. Sexual morality and family relationships were undergoing a transformation analogous to that of the nationalized industries over the same period: privatization.

The British experience was far from unique. Movements in favour of easier divorce, women's liberation, homosexual rights, and the legalization of abortion were common to all the western democracies. As elsewhere, there was much opposition but in Britain it was poorly organized and seldom very effective. In predominantly Roman Catholic countries the Church fought a robust if ultimately unsuccessful rearguard action. In the United States the Republicans mobilized a formidable coalition of conservative Christians in a cultural assault on liberal values. In Britain, however, the Conservatives were divided between Christian fundamentalists and libertarians, while the established

Churches were towers of jelly, tolerant, deeply concerned, and wobbling tremulously in the breeze.

In the 1980s a nightmarish development looked for a time as though it might halt or even reverse the permissive trend. The appearance of acquired immuno-deficiency syndrome—AIDS—confronted the sexually active with the spectre of a disease that was both sexually transmitted and fatal. Most of its victims were homosexuals but it could and did kill heterosexuals too. In the event, however, the AIDS epidemic was never more than a brief setback for a sexual revolution that rolled on into the twenty-first century.

To describe what happened is much easier than to explain it. It is often thought of as a top-down process initiated by Parliament and it is clear that changes in the law did have important effects. The legalization of homosexual acts between consenting adults freed them from the fear of prosecution and made it more acceptable for openly gay clubs and societies to flourish. Divorce was itself a legal construct and the rise in the divorce rate that followed the 1969 Act must have been in due in part to the extended grounds for divorce which the law now provided. But if the relaxation of legal constraints made a more permissive society possible, it was the behaviour of millions of people, and the choices they made as individuals, that made it a reality. The dynamics of change came from within society: the continuing decline of organized religion, the rising aspirations of women, the commercialization of sex, the increasing emphasis, characteristic of a secure and prosperous society, on freedom of choice rather than social obligation.

Women and the Women's Movement

One of the great imponderables in the history of gender, love, and marriage is the extent to which attitudes were changed by the women's movement and the spread of feminist ideas. The attempt to maintain a single feminist movement collapsed when conflicts broke out between socialists, who were predominantly heterosexual, and radicals who were predominantly lesbian. After the bitter divisions exposed by the national conferences of 1977 and 1978, no more national conferences took place. At the local level women's groups remained active and continued to work together nationally in single-issue campaigns over abortion, equal pay, and the rights of single mothers. Radical feminists were prominent in 'Women Against Violence Against Women', a protest movement that organized 'reclaim the night' marches through the red-light disrticts of cities. Black feminists formed their own Black Women's Group. In August 1981 forty women, accompanied by four men and some children, marched from Cardiff to the RAF base at Greenham Common, to protest against the impending siting there of Cruise missiles. There they decided to establish a permanent peace camp, which grew into a community of some 2,000 women, many with babies and young children: men were excluded. 'They persistently blockaded and invaded the base', writes Sue Bruley, 'on one occasion with a four-and-a-half-mile serpent tail that had been sewn by 2000 women. They dressed as snakes, painted aeroplanes as peace symbols and wove a giant web to float over the base with helium balloons.'[1] Here was yet another strand of feminism, emphasizing the traditional role of women as mothers but transforming it into political activism: a British Housewives' League of the pacifist Left.

Feminists of all kinds insisted that women were still unequal to men and repressed by a patriarchal society, but the revival of feminism was itself proof that the role of women was beginning to change. However loosely organized and prone to faction it attracted scores of highly educated and creative women in the worlds of art, literature, and politics. The majority of women shied away from the 'feminist' label, which they associated with hostility to the male sex and acrimonious academic and political debate, but many who would never have called themselves feminists agreed with some of the major feminist objectives, like equal pay. This suggests that women might well have absorbed some part of the feminist message while still perceiving feminists themselves as man-hating extremists. If it achieved nothing else the women's movement of the 1970s and 1980s did succeed in propelling issues of sexual equality from the periphery to the centre of debate. How far the feminist movement was a cause of the changing role of women, and how far it was a consequence, is impossible to say. It was certainly connected with the 'Robbins revolution'. The number of full-time female students in higher education rose from 57,000 in 1970 to 96,200 in 1980, and 116,700 in 1990.[2] The ideological and intellectual character of the women's movement, and its middle-class, university-educated leadership, ensured that its core support would be found among young middle-class women.

A much more widespread factor in the lives of women was their increasing participation in the labour market. On the eve of the Second World War only ten per cent of married women were in paid work outside the home, and that was usually because of some special circumstance like an unemployed or disabled husband. By the 1990s the majority of married women were going out to work:

Women in the labour force, Great Britain, 1971–91

	1971	1981	1991
Women as a percentage of the total labour force	36.5	38.9	43.2
Percentage of married women going out to work	42.0	47.2	53.1
Part-timers as a percentage of all female employees	33.5	41.5	44.9

Source: Duncan Gallie, 'The Labour Force' in Halsey (ed.), *Twentieth Century British Social Trends*, pp. 292–3, 297.

There were signs of a breakthrough in the higher professions during the 1980s, the expansion of women's employment was largely accounted for by the growth of part-time employment in the service industries. The contraction of manufacturing industry greatly *reduced* the number of full-time jobs for women between 1971 and 1997.[3]

The Equal Pay Act of 1970, which applied to all employees the principle of equal pay for men and women for 'the same or similar work' came into force in 1975. The Sex Discrimination Act of that same year forbade discrimination in all aspects of employment, housing, education, recreational facilities, banking, insurance, and credit, and established an Equal Opportunities Commission to ensure compliance with both Acts. In the 1970s, boys regularly outperformed girls in school. By the 1990s the girls were outperforming the boys. The Sex Discrimination Act, which made it illegal for schools to distinguish between 'boys' subjects' and 'girls' subjects', may have had something to do with this.[4]

The principle of equal rights for women was now firmly embedded in law but as with much legislation, a sizeable gap remained between the law and the realities on the ground. Employers who wished to circumvent the law were able to find loopholes in both acts, and the Commission relied as far as possible upon persuasion rather than prosecution. Under the Equal Pay Act a woman had to prove that she was doing the same or similar work as a man and getting paid less for it. It was not difficult for an employer to argue that a man in the same line of work had more experience or qualifications and was therefore of greater worth. Alternatively it could be argued that the work was not 'the same or similar'. A woman cleaner who claimed that her pay should be the same as that of male cleaners in her company lost her case on the grounds that she worked in an office with a carpet, unlike the warehouse where the men were employed.[5] In 1983, however, the Thatcher government was compelled by the European Commission to amend the law to take into account 'work of comparable value'. This opened up a second front in the pay battle by enabling a woman to claim that she deserved the same pay as a man employed in very different kinds of work.[6] Equal pay legislation, therefore, led to a long-drawn out war of attrition argued out in front of industrial tribunals and sometimes the law courts. The outcome was uneven. There was no reduction of the pay gap between men and women in part-time work, but women in full-time work succeeded in raising their earnings from 74 per cent of the male level in 1977 to 80 per cent in 1996. 'It appears', writes Sue Bruley, 'that it is young, well-qualified women who have made the greatest gains.'[7]

Although women were not yet equal with men in earning power, the contrast between the second half of the twentieth century, with married women returning to work once the children were at school, and the Victorian pattern of seclusion within the home, was stark. Changes in attitudes towards work outside the home were reflected in surveys between 1965 and 1987 in which women of working age were asked whether they agreed with a series of propositions about three different categories of married women:

Married woman with no children	1965	1980	1987
Ought to work	13	33	27
Up to her	75	62	69
Only if she needs the money	9	4	3
Ought to stay at home	1	1	0

Married woman with children under school age			
Ought to work	0	0	0
Up to her	5	15	26
Only if she needs the money	15	25	29
Ought to stay at home	78	62	45

Married woman with children at school			
Ought to work	3	3	3
Up to her	35	50	61
Only if she needs the money	39	26	29
Ought to stay at home	20	11	7

Source: Sharon Witherspoon, 'Interim report: a woman's work' in Roger Jowell, Sharon Witherspoon and Lindsay Brook (eds.), *British Social Attitudes: the 5th report* (1988), p. 192.

As Sharon Witherspoon remarks, an enormous change had taken place since 1965 in beliefs about women with children.

Sex, Love, and Marriage

Writing of England between the wars, A. J. P. Taylor remarked on the difficulties of obtaining contraceptives, and the prevalence of interrupted sex as a means of birth control. 'The historian', he wrote, 'should bear in mind that between about 1880, when limitation started, and 1940 or so, when the use of the sheath at any rate became more general in all classes, he has on his hands a frustrated people.'[8] When we come to the 1970s and 1980s it would be truer to say that the historian has on his hands a sexually awakened people. Though there were still alarming levels of ignorance about sex and contraception among schoolchildren, it was as easy to buy a packet of condoms as a bar of chocolate or a tin of baked beans. Contraceptive advice was freely available on the NHS and so, from 1975, were contraceptives. The birth pill, which gave women control over their own fertility, was the most reliable method, and by the 1970s the most widespread form of contraception in use (see table).

With the deterrent of pregnancy removed, the attractions of sex (never to be underestimated in their own right) were exploited by the

Contraception[1]: by method used

Great Britain	Percentages			
	1976	1986	1995–6	1998–9
Non-surgical				
Pill	29	23	25	24
Male condom	14	13	18	18
IUD	6	7	4	5
Withdrawal	5	4	3	3
Injection	..	..	1	2
Cap	2	2	1	1
Safe period	1	1	1	1
Spermicides	..	1	-	-
Surgical				
Female sterilization	7	12	12	11
Male sterilization	6	11	11	12
At least one method	68	71	73	72

[1] By women aged 16 to 49, except for 1976 which is for women aged 18 to 44.

Source: Social Trends 2000, p. 45.

press, television, cinema, and the advertising industry. Popular culture was saturated with erotic imagery, the top shelves of newsagents stocked with soft porn, the plots of tired soap operas pepped up at regular intervals by adulterous love rats and pregnant teenage girls. Still celebrated by idealists as the ultimate expression of love within marriage, heterosexual sex was rebranded by entrepreneurs and marketed as an outrageously attractive leisure pursuit. There was nothing new, of course, about hedonistic sex, but it had never been easy to find. Now the gates of the pleasure gardens were flung open and experts were on hand to provide a guided tour to the wonders within: that, at any rate, was how it seemed at the time.

In the early 1970s the novelist, poet, and pacifist Alex Comfort was commissioned by his friend James Mitchell, of the publishers Mitchell Beasley, to write a sex manual. Written in two weeks, and published in 1972, *The Joy of Sex: A Gourmet Guide to Lovemaking*, sold twelve million copies world-wide. A manual that could be recommended with confidence to the physically fit, it was divided into sections entitled 'Ingredients', 'Appetizers', 'Main Courses', and 'Sauces', and accompanied by line drawings in which a bearded man vaguely reminiscent of D. H. Lawrence, and a dark-haired woman, showed readers how it should all be done. 'The unselfconscious text', writes the agony aunt Clare Rayner, 'showed a lively interest in all sorts of highways and byways of sexuality—like the role of the big toe in lovemaking, and the pleasures of a little light bondage—and made people feel comfortable . . . Comfort gave his readers permission to regard sex as a normal occupation and a perfectly respectable interest.'[9]

The boundaries of the acceptable were broadening but the law could still trap the unwary. In 1976 Mrs Mary Whitehouse sued *Gay News* for blasphemous libel over the publication in June 1976 of a poem by James Kirkup, 'The Love that Dares to Speak Its Name', in which a Roman centurion fantasizes about having sex with the body of a homosexual Christ. The Crown having taken over the prosecution, the case came to court at the Old Bailey in July 1977. John Mortimer appeared for the defence, with Bernard Levin and Margaret Drabble giving evidence in support of Kirkup, but the jury found him guilty and he was fined, along with the editor of *Gay News*, Denis Lemon, who received a suspended prison sentence of nine months. It would still have been illegal for a newspaper to publish the poem in 2009, the year of Kirkup's death.[10]

From the 1960s onwards the ties that had once bound sex, marriage, and child-rearing together were beginning to loosen. Among them was the teaching of the Christian churches, which had continued to inform ethical standards long after the majority of the public had ceased to be regular churchgoers. The liberal and secular onslaught on conservative morality exposed the vulnerability of the churches at a time when their membership, which had been fairly stable during the first half of the twentieth century, was dwindling rapidly. During the last quarter of the twentieth century, adherence to the Christian churches fell by about 45 per cent and churchgoing by about one-third. Church of England and nonconformist Sunday schools virtually died out. The numbers attending Roman Catholic mass in England declined by 42 per cent between 1965 and 1996, and the number of Roman Catholic-solemnized marriages by 63 per cent between 1960 and 1996. 'Overall', writes Callum Brown, 'Christian culture was progressively contracting, as society as a whole pushed its Christian heritage further and further from the rules of social behaviour and personal identity.'[11]

The majority of the white British public retained a vague belief in the existence of God, but the Christian code of conduct in family and private life was largely forgotten and little understood. What possible sense could teenagers make of the idea that chastity was a virtue? Why should teenage girls cherish their virginity? The average age at which women first had sex was falling steadily. Of the women born between 1926 and 1930, almost all were still virgins at the age of eighteen. Of those born between 1956 and 1959, about 40 per cent were sexually active by the time they reached the same age.[12]

There seem to be no comparable figures for men over the same timescale, but it is reasonable to assume that the trend towards earlier sex was common to both men and women. As the shift began long before women had access to the contraceptive pill there must have been other factors at work: earlier biological maturity, the greater social independence of young people, changes in the attitudes of young people towards sex. Up to about 1970 it was a trend associated with earlier marriage. Between 1910 and 1950 the average age of marriage for men fell from 27 to 24, for women from 25 to 22.[13] Whether earlier sex was a cause or a consequence—it could have been either depending on the character and circumstances of the couples involved—marriage and heterosexuality were still indissolubly connected. As we saw earlier, marriage was never more popular than in the 1960s.[14]

While age at which men and women first had sex continued to fall, the age at which they married was beginning to rise. 'In England and Wales', writes David Coleman, 'mean age at marriage has increased from 24.6 years for bachelors and 22.6 for spinsters in 1971 to 28.9 years and 26.9 years respectively in 1995.'[15] Instead of getting married more and more couples chose to live together. In the 'swinging sixties' cohabitation had been unusual. During the 1970s and 1980s it became widespread and although it was often a prelude to marriage it could also act as a substitute, with serial monogamy replacing lifetime commitment.

This new pattern of longer and more active sex lives before marriage also helps to explain the marked rise in the number of babies born outside wedlock. In 1982 the compilers of official statistics remarked that, whereas in 1970 the most frequent course of action for an unmarried woman who became pregnant was marriage, by 1980 she was more likely to have an abortion or give birth to an illegitimate child. Between 1980 and 1989 the percentage of births outside marriage in England and Wales rose from 12 to 27 per cent. In response to the change, the Family Law Reform Act of 1987 removed the remaining legal disadvantages attaching to illegitimacy.[16] Most of the births, however,

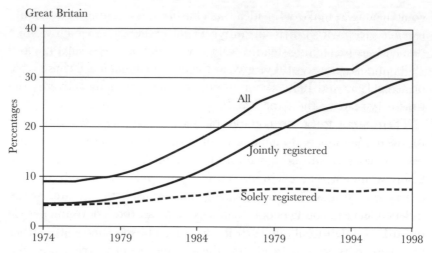

Great Britain

Graph 11.1 Births outside marriage as a percentage of all live births.
Source: Social Trends 2000, p. 43.

were jointly registered by the father and mother, a far cry from the days
when the mother of an illegitimate child was usually a lone parent (see
Graph 11.1).

As a *Times* editorial commented in May 1981, the social conventions
were shifting:

> Fewer single people are getting married and when they do it is later in life.
> None of this means the emotional security which a stable relationship can
> bring is valued any less highly. More and more young people especially are
> attempting to find that security outside what they see as the confines of mar-
> riage. The social stigma of bearing a child out of wedlock has diminished
> considerably, and more than one in ten births are now illegitimate. At the
> same time living together without marrying is gaining increasing accepta-
> bility, even among relatively conservative families and communities.[17]

The one-parent families of the 1980s (including a small minority in
which the parent in question was a man) consisted mainly of widows and
female divorcees. But the growing number of teenage mums was already
a talking-point in Parliament and the Press. How could a girl of fifteen
raise a child? How could an infant be provided with a loving and stable
home when the father was only a schoolboy or an older man who refused
to accept any responsibility? How could such pregnancies be prevented?

Since there was no realistic way of preventing sexual activity, and abortion was clearly a last resort, the common-sense answer was to encourage teenagers to make use of contraceptives. Boys, however, could not be relied upon to use a condom so the surest method was to make the birth pill available to girls. But what was to be done about the growing number of girls who were under the age of sixteen when they first had sex?

In December 1980 a circular from the Department of Health and Social Security advised local health authorities that they were entitled to give contraceptive advice to girls under sixteen at the discretion of a doctor and, if necessary, without the knowledge or consent of her parents. Although the British Medical Association endorsed the ruling, it was challenged by Mrs Victoria Gillick, a Roman Catholic with ten children, who claimed firstly that it was tantamount to assisting in the commission of an offence, and secondly that it overrode the rights of parents. Two thousand doctors signed a petition to the General Medical Council endorsing Mrs Gillick's views and 200 Conservative MPs, including Mrs Thatcher, signified their support. In July 1983 the High Court ruled against Mrs Gillick but the Appeal Court came down on her side in December 1984 and forbade doctors from prescribing the pill to girls under sixteen without their parents' consent. In a final swing of the pendulum in October 1985, the Law Lords decided by a majority of three to two that doctors had the right in 'exceptional cases' to prescribe the pill to girls under the age of 16 without parental knowledge or consent.[18] If it had so wished the government could have introduced legislation to override the Law Lords, but nothing of the kind was attempted and Mrs Gillick had to make do with expressions of sympathy from Conservatives.

The political correspondent of *The Times*, Ronald Butt, pointed to the underlying clash between liberal and conservative philosophies:

> What really lies behind this case is that children are proselytized in sex education, in and outside the classroom, to the belief that they are morally justified in indulging their sexual wishes provided they know the facts and take precautions against conception. If they do this, and provided their relationships are reasonably stable, they are told that they are being responsible.
>
> Of course the pressure groups who specialize in contraception for the young also offer them counselling, but it is usually of a pretty fatalistic kind. Whoever heard from them an unambiguous declaration that sexual activity at an early age is morally wrong?[19]

Like Mrs Gillick, Butt believed in the virtues of chastity and feared that a deliberate campaign was being waged to subvert the morals of the young. To this Mrs Gillick's opponents replied that nothing could stop young people from engaging in sexual activity: hence it was preferable to supply contraceptives that would prevent unwanted pregnancies, or the alternative of abortion.

Although the Abortion Act of 1967 had been followed by a sharp upward curve in the demand for abortions, a dip in the late 1970s had seemed for a year or two to show that the universal availability of contraception of the NHS was at last having an effect. But in the 1980s the numbers rose sharply again, with older and more sexually experienced women almost as much affected as teenagers. Between 1980 and 1990 the abortion rate in the age groups 16–19, 20–24, and 25–34 rose by 5 per cent or more.[20]

It is not easy to explain the figures, but it may be significant that only a minority of women made use of the pill, the most reliable form of contraception for women, and that the numbers using the pill fell during the early 1980s in response to fears about its effects on health. Whatever the explanation, one of the most notable features of the 1980s was the increase in the level of support for abortion expressed in public opinion surveys. By 1990 there were majorities in favour of abortion in a wide range of different circumstances.[21]

More and more marriages were ending in divorce. As Graph 11.2 shows, the number of first marriages began to fall after 1971, while the number of divorces began to rise from 1972, the year in which the new Divorce Act came into effect. By 1990 there were almost as many divorces every year as there were first marriages, and but for the popularity of remarriage the divorced would soon have been almost as numerous as the married. It was women who increasingly took the initiative in divorce petitions. Between 1961 and 1965, 42 per cent of petitions were from husbands, 58 per cent from wives. Between 1976 and 1980, 28 per cent of the petitions were from husbands, 72 per cent from wives.[22]

In one way or another, marriages that ended in divorce were exposed to public view. It was rarely a pretty sight. The mutual recriminations of embittered couples were imparted to friends and became a subject of gossip. Appalling tales of selfish, brutal, or dissolute behaviour were revealed in court, and reported in the press. The marriages of pop stars, footballers, media personalities, and members of the royal family fell apart under the pitiless gaze of the media. Of happy marriages,

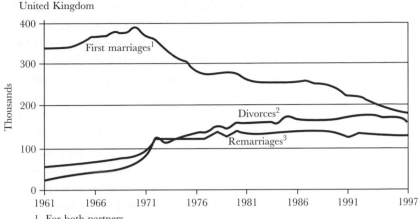

United Kingdom

1. For both partners.
2. Includes arrangements.
3. For one or both partners.

Graph 11.2 Marriages and divorces.
Source: Social Trends 2000, p. 37.

meanwhile, much less was said or written. A local newspaper might report the golden wedding of a Darby and Joan or publish in the 'personal announcements' columns the heartfelt tribute of a widow and children to her late husband, but happy marriages, like happy families, were very private affairs, their secret histories forever unrecorded.

The cause of the rising divorce rate of the 1970s appeared at first to be the broadening of the grounds on which a marriage might be annulled, but the rate continued to climb long after the new law had come into force. It could also be attributed to the fact that so many people were marrying at a younger age when they were not sufficiently mature to make the necessary commitment. But, from 1972 onwards, the mean age at marriage began slowly but steadily to rise, and the divorce rate rose with it. Here again it is worth remembering that the British experience was part of a European and North American pattern: between 1970 and 1983 divorce rates in Belgium, France, and the Netherlands tripled. In the United States the divorce rate more than doubled between 1965 and 1981, after which it fell back to a slightly lower level.[23] An almost universal factor was at work in the advanced western economies. To call it the emancipation of women is to overlook the fact that it also brought with it greater freedom for men, but it was the role of women that changed more radically.

In the past marriage had been sustained by two main pillars. The first was the almost complete economic dependence of wives on husbands. The second, following from it, was a clear-cut and generally accepted division of labour between husband and wife. Marriage, as contemporaries saw it, was in transition from a relationship based on different but complementary roles, to a relationship based on companionship and shared activities. One sign of this was the growing practice, encouraged by hospital maternity units, for husbands to be present when their wives gave birth. But there were aspects of marriage that changed slowly if at all. In 1986 a representative sample of the population were asked about the factors contributing to a happy marriage and asked to say which of thirteen features they considered the most important. Irrespective of age, sex, or class, respondents put faithfulness at the top of the list with a ranking of 86 per cent, ahead of mutual respect and appreciation (77%), or understanding and tolerance (69%). Less important, but more highly rated than factors such as adequate income (34%) and good housing (33%) was a happy sexual relationship (50%). The lower reaches of the scale featured shared chores (25%), tastes and interests in common (21%), and agreement on politics, which registered a tiny mouse-like squeak of three per cent.[24]

The importance of fidelity in marriage was not diminished by the fact that husbands and wives were sometimes unfaithful, or that marriages often survived adultery. Infidelity could sometimes be forgiven and the old idea that it was somehow more natural in a man than a woman lived on, perhaps because there was some truth in it. But potentially it was a stick of dynamite, a source of explosive rage and pain, an incitement to gross bodily harm, and the most commonly cited cause of divorce. Just as faithfulness was ranked as the most crucial factor in a successful marriage, so consistent unfaithfulness was regarded as the most important justification for divorce (94%), closely followed by violence (92%), and one partner's loss of love for the other (75%). An unsatisfactory sexual relationship was regarded as a comparatively weak justification for divorce (28%), a revealing measure of the distinction still drawn between love and sex. Surprisingly, perhaps, older people were more inclined than the young to cite unsatisfactory sex as grounds for divorce.[25]

If marriage was now egalitarian, and wives were going out to work, it would have been logical for husbands to take a larger share of the housework, a tendency Young and Willmott claimed to detect in their book

The Symmetrical Family (1973). The evidence was less than convincing. In the case of wives who did not go out to work 64 per cent of husbands reportedly gave some help with cooking, cleaning, looking after the children, and so on, *at least once a week*. For wives working part-time the figure was 68 per cent, for wives in full-time work 79 per cent.[26] With greater realism a Gallup poll enquiry for *Woman's Own* into the distribution of responsibilities for child care concluded in 1979:

> One in six husbands has never looked after his child on his own. One-quarter have never put their children to bed. One in three has never even read to their own children. Younger wives get slight help but, generally, wives are still left to shoulder the overwhelming majority of work involved in being a parent. Even in families where the mother works full time, three-quarters of fathers never take time off work if their children are ill, and never collect them from school.

The fact that many women found marriage an unattractive prospect, or a depressing experience, helps to explain the growing number who rebelled against it by never marrying in the first place, by divorcing a husband, by embracing a feminist agenda. 'Three political statements point the way to the liberation of housewives', wrote Ann Oakley in 1974. 'The housewife role must be abolished. The family must be abolished. Gender must be abolished.'[27] If most women had felt the same way, the institution of marriage would simply have become unworkable and collapsed. But well over half the adult population continued to get married, and often to re-marry after a divorce. Why was this? If we have to explain why marriage was in decline we also have to account for the fact that it survived as well as it did.

As ever women were the main obstacle in the path of the feminist revolution. 'Sociologists and economists', wrote Catherine Hakim in 1996, 'have overlooked the fact that most women, as well as men, still accept and even prefer differentiated sex roles.' Women, she argued, were diverse in their aspirations. Some were career women and others home-centred, but the career women were in the minority. A Gallup survey across five west European countries—Britain, Germany, France, Italy, and Spain—showed that between two-thirds and three-quarters of women regarded some combination of employment and family life as the ideal. Hence the fact that part-time employment was so popular with women. Nor did most of them think of housework as an intolerable imposition: 'The 1988 ISSP [International Social Survey Programme] shows that two-thirds of women as well as men in Britain and West Germany agree that being a housewife is just as fulfilling as working for pay.'[28]

Family Values and Gay Rights

Between 1975 and 1979, when the Conservatives were in opposition under the leadership of Margaret Thatcher, party spokesmen were critical of permissiveness and promised that the next Conservative government would seek to strengthen the family. At the annual party conference in October 1977 the spokesman on social services, Patrick Jenkin, lamented 'the rising tide of juvenile crime, the growth of truancy, the break-up of marriages, family violence, the loneliness of the aged, the growing dependence on the social services, the steadily mounting numbers of children in care'. All these problems, he argued, were connected with the fact that so many married women were now going out to work and it must be the aim of the Conservatives to restore 'parenthood' (i.e. motherhood) to a 'place of honour' in the home.[29] He was confident that it could be done. Shortly after his appointment as Secretary for Health and Social Services in 1979 he said on the radio: 'As the need for women's paid work outside the family evaporates...we may expect a gradual return to the education of women for domestic labour.'[30] Given the fact that Mrs Thatcher was herself a full-time career woman whose twins had been brought up with the aid of a nanny, there was always a glaring contradiction in the Conservative stance on motherhood.

Like Mary Whitehouse, of whom she was an admirer, the Prime Minister was determined to 'clean up' television. Hence the inclusion in the 1987 election manifesto of a pledge to curb the display of sex and violence on the small screen. Over lunch at the Garrick in October 1987 the Home Secretary, Douglas Hurd, the minister responsible for broadcasting, poured out his troubles to Hugo Young of the *Guardian*. Mrs Thatcher, he confided, was obsessed with television even though she only watched it on Sundays: 'Always ranting on about how shocking things are, and reminding DH that he has small children and how *could* he tolerate them seeing some of the dreadful stuff. "She's itching to get out the censor's scissors." ' The outcome was the setting up of a Broadcasting Standards Council to conduct research and adjudicate on complaints from the general public.[31] (Complaints that there was not enough sex and violence on television were, presumably, outside its terms of reference.) This was hardly more than a token gesture towards the 'moral majority'. Questions of sexual morality were never high on the list of the Cabinet's priorities, nor could the gospel of economic individualism be restricted to the male sex without alienating a large number of Tory women voters, and the party's own women's organization.[32] Attempts to restrict abortion came to nothing. A long-running controversy over sex education in schools resulted only in section 28 of the Local Government Act of 1988, which forbade local authorities from promoting homosexuality or from teaching it as 'a pretended family relationship'.

Conservative moralists never ceased to protest against the erosion of the traditional family, but the Thatcher governments dashed their hopes of a counter-revolution. The heterosexual majority—or at any rate a majority within that majority—had revised the rules to accommodate a wider range of behaviour both inside and outside marriage. It is easy to forget, however, that change was not always in a permissive direction. The greater candour with which sexual matters were now discussed enabled feminists to highlight the failure of the police and the magistrates to prosecute charges of rape or domestic violence with sufficient vigour. Another great evil exposed at about the same time was the sexual abuse of children. In November 1984 the National Society for the Prevention of Cruelty to Children claimed that 1,500 children a year were being sexually abused. 'Like child battering in the 1960s', wrote Clare Dyer in *The Times,* 'the scale of the problem of sexual molestation of children is surfacing into public consciousness. And the reality is less the man in the dirty mac lurking at the school gates than the familiar step on the stair which makes the blood run cold.' A MORI poll reported that one in ten of those questioned had been sexually abused as children.[33] In the sphere of sexual morality, the paedophile was fast becoming Public Enemy Number One.

Heterosexuals were deeply divided over their response to homosexuals. As we have seen, the Sexual Offences Act of 1967 was both liberating and repressive for male homosexuals. The effect of this tantalizing predicament was to stimulate a British Gay Rights movement which also drew much inspiration from the campaigns of gay activists in the United States. In the past, however, male homosexuals had in a sense benefited from an obscurity that concealed them from view: out of sight was out of mind. The arrival of a highly visible gay culture was bound to result in a backlash. Surveys of public opinion in Britain and the United States demonstrated that hostility to homosexuality was more widespread in the United States, but it was also deeply rooted in Britain. The first of the *British Social Attitudes* surveys reported that in 1983 50 per cent of the public regarded homosexual relationships as 'always wrong'. Another 12 per cent declared that they were 'mostly wrong'.[34] Nor was there an underlying trend towards more liberal attitudes: on the contrary, levels of disapproval increased.

The explanation lay in the shock and panic resulting from the appearance of a new global epidemic: Acquired Immunodeficiency Syndrome or AIDs. As we know now, the cause of AIDs was the Human Immunodeficiency Virus (HIV), which attacked and destroyed the immune system and in doing so passed sentence of death on its victims. Generally thought to have originated in Africa, it entered the bloodstream through the exchange of blood or body fluids in sexual intercourse, the use by drug addicts of infected needles, or the use of HIV-infected blood in blood transfusions. Most tragically of all, it could be transmitted to unborn infants in the womb.

The first reports of AIDs in the British press treated it as a mystery illness, the 'gay cancer', afflicting homosexuals in the United States. Only by degrees, between 1981 and 1984, was a clearer picture formed, the source of the disease identified, and the extent of the danger understood. At first the relatively small number of deaths among those infected suggested that the risk was low, but it was soon realized that this was because the virus could incubate for years before it struck. Although most of the victims were homosexuals, and the tabloid press called it 'the Gay Plague', heterosexuals had to be warned that they too were at risk of infection. As medical science could offer no cure, no one could be sure how many lives the epidemic would claim:

Known cases of death from AIDs in the United Kingdom

1983	22
1984	75
1985	149
1986	281
1987	597

Source: Simon Garfield, *The End of Innocence: Britain in the Time of AIDs* (1994), p. 360.

The slant put on the story in parts of the press has been summed up by Roy Greenslade, an assistant editor of the *Sun* from 1981 to 1986:

> The consensus that informed the debate, such as it was, was that all homosexuals are perverts. Flowing from that, AIDs appeared to be just desserts for being involved in deviant sexual behaviour. It was quickly realized that it came about due to anal sex, and heterosexual executives on the *Sun* thus fed in the fact that it was a Gay Plague.

The opportunity of engaging in queer-bashing was not to be missed. The Chief Constable of Greater Manchester, James Anderton, declared that 'homosexuals were swirling around in a cesspool of their own making'. Mrs Thatcher's adviser and confidant, Sir Alfred Sherman, wrote to *The Times* to say that AIDs was a problem of 'undesirable minorities...mainly sodomites and drug-abusers, together with numbers of women who voluntarily associate with the sexual underworld'.[35]

There may have been Cabinet ministers who privately harboured similar thoughts but, if so, they had the good sense not to express them in public. Whatever the moral construction placed on the AIDs epidemic it was a crisis in public health no government could ignore. After some hesitation the nettle was grasped and a Cabinet committee under the deputy Prime Minister, Willie Whitelaw, authorized a public information campaign featuring posters, press and television coverage. In January 1987 a leaflet entitled 'Avoiding AIDs' was delivered to every household in the country. The main message was the importance of safe sex. 'Stick to one partner', urged the Secretary for Health and Social Services, Norman Fowler, 'but if you do not, use a condom.' After all the emphasis Conservatives had placed on the need to strengthen the family, there was something bizarre in the spectacle of a Conservative government promoting packets of Durex. 'Everyone seemed to be putting condoms everywhere', writes Simon Garfield, 'on fingers, cucumbers, and especially bananas.' In order to familiarize younger viewers with the term, a number of celebrities were lined up to say one word to camera: 'condom'.[36]

In the short run the AIDs epidemic had the predictable effect of intensifying homophobia. According to the *British Social Attitudes* survey, disapproval of homosexual acts reached a peak in 1987—the year of the condom. By the early 1990s, however, apocalyptic predictions of a mass epidemic had been proved wrong and the death rate was stabilizing at around 1,500 a year. How much the change owed to the government's education campaign is difficult to judge, but homosexuals appear to have accepted the need to practice 'safe' sex.

Unlike some Conservatives, Mrs Thatcher's successor had no prejudice against homosexuality. At the annual Conservative party conference in October 1993, John Major defined the mission of his government in the phrase 'back to basics'. The Conservatives must lead the country back to basics in sound money, free trade, traditional teaching, the defeat of crime and 'respect for the family and the law'. The speech was widely misinterpreted as a plea for a restoration of traditional morality, but as Major writes in his memoirs: 'I wanted nothing to do with a moral crusade under the title "family policy". I had always been extremely wary about politicians trespassing into the field of sexual morality, and hostile to any campaign which appeared to demonize any group.'[37] He took the symbolic step of inviting the actor Ian McKellen, who had come out as gay and taken the lead in forming a pressure-group, Stonewall, to press for equal rights. Stonewall was pressing for the repeal of Section 28 and the reduction of the age of consent for homosexuals from twenty-one to sixteen, the age that applied to heterosexuals. Major did not agree with either demand but he gave his support in 1994 to the reduction by the House of Commons of the age of consent to sixteen. More radical changes had to await the coming of New Labour. The House of Commons voted to equalize the age of consent at sixteen in the year 2000. Section 28 was abolished by the Scottish Parliament in 1999 and the Westminster Parliament in 2003.

The Drug Culture

The permissive society still forbade the use, unless they were prescribed by a doctor, of a long list of drugs. Since it was a criminal offence to deal in a banned substance or be found in possession of it, reliable statistics are few and estimates of the extent of drug use are mainly guesswork. All that can be usefully said of the use of cannabis, for example, is that it was widespread. Whether 20 per cent of the young smoked pot, or 60 per cent, we simply do not know. As Arthur Marwick writes, however, we do know that in the course of the 1970s the law began to treat offenders more leniently. People convicted of possession were more likely to be fined than sent to prison, let alone gaoled for the maximum period of five years which the law prescribed.[38] The authorities were adamant in their refusal to legalize 'soft' drugs like cannabis, but there was growing anxiety about the extent of addiction to 'hard' drugs, especially heroin and cocaine. In 1973 a little over three kilograms of heroin were seized by customs officers and the police. In 1978 the figure was 60 kilograms and by 1983 it had risen to 247 kilograms.[39]

Under the Misuse of Drugs Act of 1973 doctors were obliged to notify the names of drug addicts to the Home Office. Since many addicts never sought treatment, while others were not reported by their doctors, the official register of drug addicts always underestimated the numbers involved. Research suggested that there might be five or even ten times as many addicts as were listed on the Home Office index.[40] But whatever their limitations the statistics showed that the number of new addicts notified each year was rising sharply.

New addicts notified, by type of drug

	1973	1981	1990
Heroin	508	1,660	5,819
Methadone	328	431	1,469
Cocaine	132	174	633

Source: *Social Trends 22* (1992), Table 7.20, p. 132.

Heroin was plainly the main source of drug addiction and helps to account for the numbers on methadone. Often prescribed by doctors as a less harmful substitute for heroin, it also led a double life as a commodity on the black market.

When the House of Commons Social Services Committee investigated the use of hard drugs in 1984, a number of witnesses referred to the 'moral panic' currently surrounding the use of heroin. The Committee's response was measured but firm:

> We accept that the dangers can be overstated. Not all heroin addicts die within 5 or 10 years: only a significant proportion. Of those who die, the cause of death is often a result of overdosing with a combination of opiates with other drugs and alcohol, or of complications arising from infected injections, rather than heroin itself...The danger of heroin is dependency, meaning that the drug takes priority over all other activities and radically impairs an individual's social functioning. The vast

majority of people cannot function properly when addicted to heroin: the exceptions are as misleading as the heavy smoker who lives to 100 or the baby who survives a 100-foot fall from a balcony. Heroin does not automatically induce criminal or anti-social behaviour. There is, for example, little evidence of crime actually being carried out while under the influence of heroin. Crime is however often committed by addicts to get money for drugs.[41]

Drug addiction, as the politicians were beginning to realize, was not only a problem in its own right, as the rotten apple that corrupted all the other apples in the barrel. Since heroin was often injected intravenously with dirty needles, heroin addiction became one of the means by which AIDs was spread. Since it was also a very expensive habit, it drove men to commit crime and women into prostitution in order to pay for it. The knock-on effects on parenthood were often disastrous, as the Social Services Committee reported:

> *We are particularly concerned at the number of young female addicts, some of whom are pregnant or have young children.* Drug-taking can have serious effects on the unborn baby, and the British Association of Social Workers (BASW) among others drew attention to the problem of 'drug-addicted babies', that is, babies born to addicted mothers presenting physical effects of addiction... There are also signs of growing concern over the effects on child care of addicted mothers. Drug abuse is not in itself a statutory ground for care, and indeed BASW suggested that authorities should make this fact more widely known. AIDA [Association of Independent Doctors in Addiction] deplored the tendency to remove babies and children from parents 'simply because they are addicts'. But the plain fact is that social services departments must sometimes remove babies and children from the care of addicts, and would be failing in their duty if they did not.[42]

Nowhere were such problems more acute than in the city of Edinburgh, one of the main distribution points for the heroin imported, by one devious route or another, from the poppy-fields of Afghanistan and the north-west frontier of Pakistan. In the Scottish capital, heroin addiction merged with housing estates in economic decay to generate a special kind of hell that was captured, with black humour, by the novelist Irvine Welsh in *Trainspotting* (1993). Horror stories of addiction and death abounded, but as the statistics go to show, moderate and occasional drug use was widespread, though not universal, among young people (see table).

Percentage of 16 to 24 year olds who have used drugs in the past year, 1998

England & Wales	Percentages		
	Males	Females	All
Cannabis	32	22	27
Amphetamines	12	8	10
Ecstasy	6	4	5
Magic mushrooms	5	2	4
LSD	5	2	3
Cocaine	4	3	3
Any drug	36	24	29

Source: Social Trends 2000, p. 126.

Towards the end of her time in office Mrs Thatcher turned her attention to one of the goals her government had failed to accomplish. 'By the time I left office', she wrote in her memoirs, 'my advisers and I were assembling a package of measures to strengthen the traditional family, whose disintegration was the common source of so much suffering. *We had not the slightest illusion that the effects of what could be done were more than marginal.*'[43] The most tangible outcome of these deliberations was the Child Support Agency, intended to compel all absconding fathers to pay a fair share of their income towards the cost of maintaining their children. The fact that such an agency was necessary was itself a demonstration of the extent to which the traditional family had already broken down, and it was realistic of Mrs Thatcher to acknowledge that it could not be restored by social engineering. Her governments had transformed the economy, but the permissive revolution had an unstoppable momentum accelerated by the very market forces in which she had put her trust. Only the British people could halt or reverse it, but as the years went by fewer and fewer wished to do so, and fewer and fewer could imagine a time when things had been different.

12

Uncharted Waters

The 1970s and 1980s were a period in which old conceptions of national identity were in decline, while new conceptions encountered strong resistance. Instead of moving in a straight line from an insular, imperial past to a cosmopolitan, multiracial future, British history entered a holding pattern or tried to double back on itself. In 1975, the British voted by a large majority in favour of remaining in the European Economic Community and the question of Britain's membership was settled once and for all, or so it appeared. By the end of the 1980s a rising tide of Euroscepticism was rocking the boat and destabilizing the Conservative party. Short of a revolution led by the National Front, Britain was irreversibly multiracial, but whether it was to be a Britain dominated by racial prejudice, with ethnic minorities permanently in the role of underdog, or a more tolerant, liberal nation from which racism was banished, was a problem yet to be resolved. In the mid-1970s Scottish nationalism was riding high and it seemed quite possible that the Scots would opt for independence with the Welsh following in their footsteps. In the event, the Scottish and Welsh referenda of 1979 proved to be setbacks from which nationalists were slow to recover.

All these aspects of national identity were the subject of almost continuous public debate. They were argued over by party politicians, discussed in the press, aired in television documentaries. But a comprehensive account of shifts in national identity has to take account of more subtle processes of change that operated slowly and quietly, as though by osmosis, and attracted little attention or controversy. In common with western Europe as a whole, Britain was partly Americanized during the post-war decades. The ever expanding consumer culture of the British was to a great extent imported from the United States, as were rock 'n' roll, commercial television, and a Hollywood culture of sex and violence. Although Mrs Thatcher's premiership preceded Ronald

Reagan's presidency, the doctrines of free market economics owed much to the American economist Milton Friedman and the American example of capitalism red in tooth and claw. American influence, however, also had its limits. There were features of the American way of life—the retention by many states of capital punishment, the gun laws, private health insurance, the religious Right—that were indigestible in Britain, and British institutions like the BBC and the NHS that were completely unacceptable in the United States. The British gave no sign of giving up cricket and soccer in favour of baseball and American football.

Important though it is, the political history of the United Kingdom's relations with the European Economic Community also tends to conceal the informal impact of western Europe on British culture. This was most obvious in the middle-class kitchen and the growing taste of consumers for croissants and baguettes, aubergines and olive oil, espressos and cappuccinos, in short continental dishes and delicacies of all kinds. Elizabeth David ruled. More imponderable is the extent of the cultural connection with western Europe at more ambitious levels in the worlds of business and the arts. Arguably, the British connection led to an appreciation of the economic, social, and political merits of, say, West Germany or Sweden, that balanced and counteracted American influence. This, however, is all very speculative and has to be weighed against that other well-known feature of British attitudes to Europe: xenophobia. Between 1974 and 2000 Britain became more American in some ways, more European in others, more multiracial and more multinational. The principal shock absorber of all these changes was England, which became as a result less distinctively English.

Multiracial Britain

Between 1971 and 1981, the black and Asian population of Britain increased in numbers from 1.2 million to 2.1 million.[1] Immigration from the Caribbean came virtually to a stop after 1971 as the general level of unemployment in Britain rose, with particularly severe effects on rates of unemployment among young West Indian males. More than one in four was out of work in 1981. Immigration from Africa from the 1950s onwards gave rise to a black African population of 109,000 by 1984.[2] Meanwhile the Asian minority, including east African Asians, rose from 546,000 in 1971 to 1,054,000 in 1981. This was partly due to the expulsion of Asians from east Africa, but mainly to the continuation of an earlier trend, the transition from a community of transitory male workers to a community of families, as wives, daughters, fiancees, and parents arrived in Britain. In every year from 1970 to 1982 upwards of 30,000 immigrants were accepted for settlement. According to the 1961 census there were only 81 Pakistani-born women in Bradford compared with 3,376 Asian-born men, most of whom were bachelors. By 1982 women accounted for 42 per cent of all Pakistanis in Britain; by 1991 for 48.5 per cent.[3] Caribbeans and Asians, who together made up about one per cent of the population in 1961, accounted for 4.1 per cent in 1981.[4] The momentum continued throughout the 1990s, during which the white population of Britain grew by about 600,000, the minority ethnic population by 1.6 million. Black Africans were the fastest growing group, with Bangladeshis and Pakistanis not far behind. By 2001, eight per cent of the population were non-white.[5]

The geographical pattern was much as before, with the Caribbean and black African population heavily concentrated in London while Indians, Pakistanis, and Bangladeshis were more widely distributed between London and the urban areas of the West Midlands, Lancashire, and Yorkshire. Few ventured as far as Scotland or Wales. Meanwhile generational change was tipping the numerical balance in favour of British-born blacks and Asians who did not belong wholly to the country their parents had come from or wholly to the country in which they were growing up. In formal terms they enjoyed the same legal and political rights as other Britons. In practice most were second-class citizens. *The Economist* was worried by low levels of educational attainment. 'In general, black and brown children (except perhaps Indians) are concentrated in the lower streams of schools and do less well even than deprived white children.' The alienation of growing numbers of black and Asian youths was partly due to the fact that white society discriminated against them, and partly to cultural differences that put them at a disadvantage. Of the Pakistanis of Bradford *The Economist* wrote in 1974:

> Walk down Lamb Lane, strung out with depressed looking Asian food and clothing shops. Barely a woman or girl is to be seen over the age of 12, except for one or two Indians and some lost-looking old English women. Almost all Moslem women are kept permanently indoors by their husbands, so that all they know of Britain, literally, are the four

walls of a slum house. Naturally, their younger children are almost equally confined; no pram outings for purdah babies.[6]

The growth of black and Asian communities was one of the reasons for continuing racial tensions. The Powellite refrain of the nation in danger, and the white working class under siege, was kept alive by Powell himself and by right-wing Conservative MPs like John Stokes. Speaking to the House of Commons in June 1976 he declared:

> The ordinary people of England were never asked to vote on this question. They did not want a multiracial society. They do not believe that integration will work. Incidentally, neither they nor the immigrants truly want integration. They never imagined 25 years ago that their lives would be turned upside down and their neighbourhoods utterly changed almost beyond recognition. If anyone had said a generation ago that one-third of the population of some of the big British cities would be black by the end of the century, he would have been considered a lunatic, but that is the prospect that faces us.
>
> I find it infinitely moving and pathetic—I am sure nearly all hon. Members must share my experience—when I get letters from working-class people, particularly older people not used to writing to Members of Parliament, who write slowly and carefully on lined paper to speak of the hard times they knew when there were few social benefits and to protest at the immediate cash handouts to these new peoples. I also hear from older people who served in the last war and who never realized that we in Great Britain had won that war only to hand over parts of our territory to alien races.[7]

Stokes, however, was living in the past. A great admirer of Franco's Spain, he was a character so reactionary that he was known as 'Parliament's last link with the Middle Ages'. The truth was that the multiracial character of Britain was by this date irreversible. Large-scale repatriation would have been impossible without coercive measures of a kind that could only have been introduced in a fascist Britain. But it would also have been very damaging to the British economy. Although blacks and Asians were more likely to be unemployed than white workers, the majority of them were in work and playing a crucial part in hotels and catering, retailing, transport, the National Health Service, the textile mills of Yorkshire, the metal trades of the West Midlands—and so on.

Mrs Thatcher, who knew all this well enough, was not to be deterred from exploiting the issue for electoral purposes. In an interview for

Granada Television's 'World In Action', broadcast on 30 January 1978, she struck an emotive note. Referring to an estimate that Britain would have a non-white population of four million by 2000 she continued:

> Now, that is an awful lot and I think it means that people are really rather afraid that this country might be rather swamped by people with a different culture and, you know, the British character has done so much for democracy, for law and done so much throughout the world that if there is any fear that it might be swamped people are going to react and be rather hostile to those coming in. So, if you want good race relations, you have got to allay people's fears on numbers.[8]

Her use of the word 'swamped' was much criticized as reminiscent of the language of the National Front, but served its purpose by boosting the party in the opinion polls while avoiding any new or detailed commitment.[9]

Here was a clash of cultures that could only be defused by long-term shifts in attitudes over the decades. In the short run the majority of white Britons were either indifferent to the welfare of blacks and Asians, or positively hostile. This was fertile soil for prejudice and intolerance. Immigrant communities became accustomed to verbal and physical abuse. Kenan Malik, who was born in India but moved to Britain as a small boy, recalls his own experience:

> When I arrived in Britain in the late 1960s, 'Paki-bashing' was becoming a national sport. My main memory of growing up in the 1970s was of being involved almost daily in fights with racists and of how normal it seemed to come home with a bloody nose or a black eye. Britain was a very different place then. I remember having to organize patrols on east London estates to protect Asian families from racist thugs.[10]

The Labour government made some attempt to improve matters. Roy Jenkins, who was now Home Secretary for the second time, was responsible for the Race Relations Act of 1976, which merged the Race Relations Board and the Community Relations Commission to form a new body, the Commission for Racial Equality. Its title was no guarantee that racial equality would ever be achieved, but words are important and the goal of equality was now inscribed as an official objective. The Act gave the Commission powers of formal investigation into cases of racial discrimination and the right to issue legally binding non-discrimination notices. It became unlawful for clubs or associations with more than twenty-five members to discriminate in the admission or treatment of members, and local authorities were placed under a statutory obligation to make sure that racial discrimination was avoided.

Under the chairmanship of David Lane, a former Conservative MP, the Commission set to work investigating individual cases of discrimination in employment, housing, health and social services, financial services, private clubs, public houses, restaurants, discos, dance halls. While urging governments of both parties to give a stronger lead on race relations, the Commission itself concentrated on case-work, research, and propaganda, but was criticized by race-relations campaigners as toothless and ineffective. It deserved more credit than it received for chipping away at racial discrimination in scores of unglamorous locations, far from the national headlines, but Lane found himself between the rock of Thatcherism, with which he was out of sympathy, and the hard place of black and Asian militancy.[11]

The higher unemployment levels of the 1970s were bad news for race relations, depressing still further the job prospects of black and Asian youths while making them convenient scapegoats for whites who were out of work. Wrong as it would be to brand all whites as racist, the verbal and physical abuse of 'niggers' and 'coons' was commonplace. Most parliamentary politicians tiptoed around the issue of immigration, but it was exploited with some success by the National Front, a racist organization which had been formed in 1967 by the amalgamation of the British National Party and the League of Empire Loyalists. Led by Martin Webster, the NF was a fringe party which contested parliamentary elections and sometimes chalked up a significant percentage of the vote at by-elections: 16 per cent at West Bromwich in 1973, 18.5 per cent in Leicester in 1976. 'More important to their strategy', writes Andrew Marr, 'were the street confrontations, engineered by marching with Union Jacks and anti-immigrant slogans through Bangladeshi or Pakistani areas in Leeds, Birmingham, and London.'[12] A second party of the far right, the British National Party, broke away from the NF under the leadership of John Kingsley Read who, after the murder of an Asian by white men in 1977, told a meeting: 'Last week in Southall one nigger stabbed another nigger. Very unfortunate. One down, a million to go.' Read was prosecuted on a charge of inciting racial hatred but at his trial Judge McKinnon summed up in his favour and he was acquitted by the jury. 'You have been rightly acquitted', the judge told him, 'but in these days and these times it would be well if you were careful to use moderate language.'[13]

In the borough of Newham, reported Francis Wheen in the *New Statesman*, a gang of white youths had taken to sitting on the rooftops and shooting with air rifles at black children in the playground. A nine-year old Asian boy who went home from school to have lunch with his grandmother was stopped outside his front gate by five white boys armed with a knife. 'Stab him now', said one. 'No, let's just take his eyes out', said another. They contented themselves with slashing him across the face. Few Asians now dared to go out after sunset as so many of them had been attacked in the streets. The police, Wheen concluded, were partly responsible for the problem: 'They have done little to prevent gangs of white youths roaming the streets in search of blood, while dealing harshly with any black people who attempt to defend themselves. If you are an Asian in Newham you spend each day in a state of siege.'[14] In its annual report for 1978 the Commission for Racial Equality noted 'deplorable outbursts of racial violence' incited by the National Front against Bengalis, West Indians, and Somalis in the East End of London. The media, the Commission reported, talked of immigrants 'as if they constituted some kind of plague or threat to the British way of life...'[15]

Racial stereotypes were still a prominent feature of popular culture, though not always with harmful intent. The comedian Bernard Manning, then at the height of his fame on television, was an authentic racist. His fellow comedian Benny Hill, a genius of schoolboy nonsense who could always get a laugh with the malapropisms of his Chinese character, Chow Mein, was not. In August 1976 the great blues guitarist Eric Clapton interrupted a performance at the Birmingham Odeon to declare that Enoch Powell had been right. 'We should send them all back', he continued, and 'keep Britain white.' He seemed to have forgotten that his own music was inspired by black performers. In the nihilistic realm of punk music things were complicated but it was fashionable to flirt with Nazi symbolism. Sid Vicious and Siouxsie Sioux adorned themselves with swastikas. David Bowie, who was photographed apparently giving a Nazi salute at Victoria Station, was reported as saying that he was a very strong believer in fascism. Yet this was the point at which a sustained and effective backlash against racial prejudice began.

Among those outraged by Clapton's remarks was Red Saunders, a rock photographer and left-wing activist. Along with other members of the Socialist Workers' Party he conceived the idea of Rock Against Racism (RAR), a movement to mobilize young people's love of punk, reggae, and pop in an anti-racist, anti-fascist cause. RAR began to organize concerts with a multiracial line-up of artists. 'The appeal of Rock Against Racism for music fans', writes Sarfraz Mansoor, 'was that it had recruited the biggest names in the emerging punk culture. By 1977 RAR could claim the support of most of the innovative bands of the time—Stiff Little Fingers, Sham 69, the Tom Robinson Band, Steel Pulse, Misty in Roots and the Clash.'[16] Following the success of RAR, its founders went on to establish, in November 1977, the Anti-Nazi League, which again demonstrated the flair of the SWP for attracting support from beyond its own ranks. The League was launched with the support of Brian Clough, the manager of Nottingham Forest, the playwright Arnold Wesker, the novelist Keith Waterhouse, and the actor Warren Mitchell, famous for his portrayal of the bigoted Alf Garnett.[17]

In April 1979, during the general election campaign, demonstrators against a National Front meeting in Southall clashed with the police of the Special Patrol Group and one of the demonstrators, Blair Peach, a schoolteacher from New Zealand, was killed, and there were numerous arrests, prosecutions, and convictions. Increasingly the flashpoint was the relationship between the police and young blacks and Asians whom they frequently stopped and searched under the 'sus' law originally passed in 1824 as a measure for the control of vagrants. This particular grievance was removed when the Thatcher government repealed the 'sus' law. But ethnic minorities were now severely affected by the recession. 'There was new evidence', the Commission for Racial Equality concluded in their report for 1980, 'that discrimination in employment, so far from being eliminated, was actually increasing in some areas, and it is clear that many whites still do not accept blacks, who were born here, as members of the community in the same way as themselves.'

On 2 April 1980 police raided the Black and White café in the St Paul's area of Bristol in search of cannabis and evidence of the illegal consumption of alcohol. They arrested the owner, questioned and searched the customers, who were mainly young and black, and began to put the drink in a van. At this point bricks began to fly and the police found themselves besieged in the café by up to 2,000 youths, some of them white. Police reinforcements eventually arrived and restored order but a second riot broke out in Brixton on 10 April when police tried to take a black youth wounded in a knife attack to hospital and a skirmish took place between forty police and about a hundred youths. Tensions were already running high in the area because the police had chosen Brixton as the site of an intensive stop-and-search exercise, Operation Swamp, in the course of which a thousand people had been stopped and questioned. The following day, a Saturday, an attempt by a plain clothes policeman to search a minicab driver led to another confrontation which triggered two days of rioting and looting. 149 policemen were injured and 224 rioters arrested. The government appointed a judge, Lord Scarman, to conduct an inquiry into the causes of the trouble, which was followed in July by riots in Toxteth (Liverpool), Moss Side (Manchester), Handsworth (Birmingham), and many other places in the London area, the Midlands, and the North.[18]

'What took place in St Paul's', the Commission for Racial Equality observed, 'could be described as a reaction to a number of factors not unfamiliar to many inner city areas starved of decent leisure and recreational facilities, faced by high unemployment, surrounded by urban decay, embittered by bad relations between black youth and the police, and trapped by the seeming hopelessness and despair of it all.'[19] Scarman, whose report was published in November 1981, concurred. Rather than confine himself to events in Brixton, he visited most of the troublespots and came up with recommendations about social policy as well as policing. While he specifically rejected the charge of 'institutional racism' against the police, he urged the compulsory training of officers in community relations, the recruitment of police from ethnic minorities, and measures to detect and prevent the recruitment of the racially prejudiced. Discriminatory behaviour was to become a specific offence under the police disciplinary code.

On the broader social issues Scarman concluded:

The attack on racial disadvantage must be more direct than it has been. It must be co-ordinated by central government, who with local authorities must ensure that the funds made available are directed to specific areas of racial disadvantage. I have in mind particularly education and employment. A policy of direct co-ordinated attack on racial disadvantage inevitably means that the ethnic minorities will enjoy for a time a positive discrimination in their favour. But it is a price worth paying if it accelerates the elimination of the unsettling factor of racial disadvantage from the social fabric of the United Kingdom. I believe this task to be even more urgent than the task of establishing on a permanent basis good relations between the ethnic minorities and the police. Good policing will be of no avail, unless we also tackle and eliminate the basic flaws in our society.[20]

The Scarman report was a liberal template for the solution of problems that were to prove highly intractable. To reform the attitudes and behaviour of the police was difficult enough. To discriminate in favour of ethnic minorities in employment and social policy was to invite a racist backlash. Tensions remained high in the inner cities and the Broadwater Farm estate in Tottenham exploded in 1985 into the worst riots of the period. A policeman, PC Keith Blakelock, was murdered by the crowd and attempts were apparently made to behead him.[21] The alienation of the young was, perhaps, rooted in factors beyond the power of economic and social policy to remedy: the breakdown of families, the absence of parental authority, the anomie suffered by black teenagers who did not fully belong to the country of their ancestors or to the country in which they were living. These were ills for which the welfare state could supply first aid but no cure.

The tensions between the police and ethnic minorities were exposed again after the murder in April 1993 of Stephen Lawrence, a black teenager who was waiting for a bus in Eltham, south London, when he was surrounded by five white youths and stabbed to death. Initial enquiries led the police to identify a number of prime suspects but they were unable to find sufficient evidence for a court case. A private prosecution, brought against three of the suspects, failed when they were acquitted by the jury. Two remarkable developments followed. First the *Daily Mail*, the newspaper most closely identified with Middle England, devoted the whole of the front page on 14 February 1997 to the accusation that five men, whose names and photographs they published, were guilty of Stephen's murder. The *Mail* challenged the five to sue the paper for libel but there was no response. Secondly, criticisms of the police for alleged shortcomings in handling the case led the incoming Labour Home Secretary, Jack Straw, to order a public enquiry under

Sir William Macpherson, a retired high court judge. Macpherson concluded that the police investigation had been flawed by incompetence and 'institutional racism', a controversial term which he defined as 'the collective failure of an organization to provide an appropriate and professional service to people because of their colour, culture, or ethnic origin. It can be seen or detected in processes, attitudes and behaviour which amount to discrimination through unwitting prejudice, ignorance, thoughtlessness and racist stereotyping which disadvantage minority ethnic people.'[22]

One of the consequences was an amendment to the Race Relations Act which brought the police and all other public bodies within the full force of the law and bound them actively to promote racial equality. A second consequence was that many other organizations took up Macpherson's suggestion that they should carry out internal reviews and audits of their own record on race. 'Never in British race relations history', wrote one commentator, 'has there been so much interest in exposing and combating racism.'[23] The problems, however, were deep-seated and unlikely to be resolved without the recruitment of substantial numbers of black and Asian policemen. In March 2001 less than three per cent of police officers in England and Wales were drawn from the ethnic minorities, and none of the 46 Police Constables.[24]

Islam in a Secular Society

Asian communities, threatened by the disintegrating influences of the secular western society all around them, relied increasingly upon the binding force of religious observance to hold them together. Pakistanis, Bangladeshis, Somalis, and other ethnic minorities in Britain were responding to a world-wide revival of Islam in which the faithful were expected to adhere ever more strictly to the teachings of their imams and the commands of the Koran. Whereas white society continued to think of immigrants of Asian descent as ethnic minorities with secular interests, the mosque was becoming more and more important as the organizational centre of their lives, and large numbers of mosques were being built. In 1963 there were thirteen buildings formally registered as mosques in Britain. By 1985 there were 338, by 1997 more than a thousand.[25]

Over and above the basic division between the Sunnis and the Shi'as in the Muslim world, there were many other sects and tendencies. Hence there was never a single body capable of representing all Muslims in Britain, nor a single body of Muslim opinion, but at the local level Muslims were becoming more organized and more vocal, engaging in the politics of local government and contesting any slight on their race or religion. Arguing that the state already gave financial support to Anglican and Roman Catholic schools, they began to demand state funding for Muslim schools, or permission to establish all-Muslim schools on a voluntary basis. Their demands were rejected. In 1984 Muslims in Bradford compelled the resignation of Ray Honeyford, the headmaster of the Drummond Middle School, on the grounds that he was a racist. The pupils were mainly Pakistanis and Honeyford was accused of denigrating Pakistan as a backward nation with a corrupt and tyrannical regime. Following his dismissal Honeyford joined forces with the Tory philosopher Roger Scruton in a campaign against multiculturalism in education, which they condemned as undermining the national identity of the indigenous English population.[26]

Ironically it was Muslim communities that retained, to a much greater extent than the English, the family and religious values extolled by Tory traditionalists. 'Throughout the 1970s', writes Humayun Ansari, 'many Muslim parents had serious misgivings about other aspects of schooling that they saw as un-Islamic—sex education, religious education, coeducation, dress, diet, assemblies and fund-raising activities such as raffles that involve gambling.'[27]

On 26 September 1988 Penguin Books published *The Satanic Verses*, a novel by Salman Rushdie in which he satirized Moslem clerics. 'Despite what is often said', writes Andrew Anthony, 'the book does not take direct aim at Islam or its prophet. Those sections which have caused the greatest controversy are contained within the dreams or nightmares of a character who is in the grip of psychosis.'[28] No matter: the book was attacked as blasphemous and banned in India. In Britain Saudi-financed organizations campaigned to suppress it. In January, Moslems staged a protest march in Bradford which ended with a burning of the book, but worse was to come. In February, the Iranian leader, Ayatollah Ruhhola Khomeini pronounced a fatwa calling for Rushdie's execution. When Rushdie issued an apology regretting the distress he had caused, the Ayatollah replied that even if Rushdie repented and became the most pious man in the world, the faithful were still under an obligation to kill him. Rushdie went into hiding under the protection of a Special Branch protection team.

The book burning, ominously reminiscent of the burning of the books by the Nazis, raised a fundamental question. In Bradford the council had pursued a conscientiously multicultural policy with the aim of improving race relations. It had dispensed substantial grants to local community organizations including the Bradford Council of Mosques, which it helped to set up. Every section of society, the Council declared, had 'an equal right to maintain its own identity, culture, language, religion and customs'. But how far could multiculturalism go before it amounted to an abdication of liberal values such as freedom of speech and expression? The effect of the Rushdie affair on Muslims themselves was summed up, twenty years later, by Inayat Bunglawala of the Muslim Council of Britain: 'It was a seminal moment in British Muslim history.... Before that they had been identified as ethnic communities but *The Satanic Verses* brought them together and helped develop a British Muslim identity, which I'm sure infuriated Salman Rushdie.'[29]

The Growth of Racial Tolerance

The follies and excesses of the world of rock and pop are all too familiar a topic. The narcissism and self-indulgence of so many of its leading performers, locked in a lucrative embrace with legions of adolescents who adored them, seemed to disqualify them from any significant role in social or political affairs. On issues of race, however, they found a cause authentically rooted in the nature of the business they were in. Rock and pop were as much the creation of black as of white musicians. In the United States the popularity of black artists with white teenagers had played a part in breaking down racial segregation. In Britain, as we have already seen, white artists took the lead in founding 'Rock against Racism', an explicitly political campaign against racism. Pop stars were not the role models many parents would have chosen for their children, but role models they were and the liberalism that came naturally to them where drugs or sex were concerned extended also to race.

In October 1984 the BBC screened a profoundly shocking documentary by Michael Buerk on the famine in Ethiopia. Bob Geldof, the lead singer of the Irish pop group the Boomtown Rats, conceived the idea of making a record to raise money for famine relief. With Midge Ure of

Ultravox he wrote the song 'Don't They Know it's Christmas' and persuaded an array of pop stars to give their services free of charge, under the name 'Band Aid', to a hastily arranged recording session. Released on 7 December 1984, the record proved to be the biggest-selling British single of all time and raised £8 million for Ethiopia. Out of this grew an even more ambitious project, masterminded by Geldof in conjunction with Midge Ure and the music promoter Harvey Goldsmith. This time the aim was to purchase a fleet of vehicles that would enable the Band Aid Trust to facilitate the distribution of food and other supplies to Ethiopia. The Live Aid event of 13 July 1985, the biggest rock concert ever staged, featured more than fifty acts performing at Wembley Stadium in London and the JFK Stadium in Philadelphia. Almost everyone who was anyone in rock music took part, including David Bowie and Eric Clapton in acts of repentance for the racist postures they had adopted in the 1970s. Televised around the world it was a combination of show business at its most egotistical and a universally comprehensible good cause. All the acts involved performed free of charge and the colossal sum of £110 million was raised. In spite of all these efforts more than a million people died in the Ethiopian famine. How many more would have died, but for Band Aid and Live Aid, we can only guess.[30]

The aim was to relieve poverty in Africa, not to combat racism at home, but in pursuing the first, Live Aid was facilitating the second. As a highly competitive branch of the economy the British music industry was a shining example of Thatcherism, but it also helped to move Britain on by imbuing the young with a sense of the normality of a multiracial society. Nor was it the only cultural force working in the same direction. The same was true of sport: 'First athletics, then boxing, football, and cricket saw the arrival of black and brown stars. The young Daley Thompson, the most comprehensively gifted of all British athletes, presented a very different picture of that "coffee-coloured nation" mulled over in the neurotic fantasies of the National Front.'[31] Most blacks in British sport were Afro-Caribbean: Asian footballers were rare and so too at this stage were Asian cricketers in spite of the passion for the game in India and Pakistan. Racial prejudice still reared its head when black footballers were pelted with banana skins and verbal abuse, but the direction of change was clear. By the mid-1980s about one-quarter of all English football league professionals were

Afro-Caribbeans.[32] Together with the pop industry and sport, television acted as a third factor in the normalization of multiracialism. Black reporters and presenters and black characters in soap operas ceased to stand out as exceptional and became a familiar part of the nation's mental furniture. There remained within the white working class an irreconcilable core who could not come to terms with the idea of a black or brown Briton, but the white working class was declining while immigrant communities were expanding and, in many cases, prospering.

In focusing on the plight of ethnic minorities afflicted by poverty and alienated by racial discrimination, it is easy to lose sight of the fact that so many blacks and Asians were adapting successfully to British society. There is no denying that specific ethnic groups, notably Afro-Caribbeans, were relatively deprived. But in 1991 the proportion of managers and proprietors among Pakistanis was higher than it was among whites, due no doubt to the fact that so many were shopkeepers. If 9.6 per cent of white males were professionals, so were 7.8 per cent of Pakistanis, 13.5 per cent of Indians, and 17.1 per cent of Africans. The proportion of home owners among Indians and Pakistanis was well above that for the white population of Britain.[33] Here were the green shoots of a more harmonious multiracial Britain.

The Break-up of Britain?

During the second half of the 1970s there was much talk of the possible 'break-up of Britain'. Prompted by the rise of Scottish and Welsh nationalism and the Labour government's proposals for devolved assemblies in Edinburgh and Cardiff, it came to nothing. Britain did not break up and in spite of the subsequent creation of a Scottish parliament and a Welsh assembly, it has still not happened at the time of writing (2009). But if Britain was not breaking up, Britishness was undergoing a transformation.

One way of putting this is to say that Britain was being redefined as a nation of multiple identities: multinational, multicultural, European, and cosmopolitan as well as British. This, however, implies a harmonious blending of different identities into a new ideal of Britishness that was generally understood and accepted. This would be too panglossian a reading of a transition that was fraught with tensions and conflicts, but the general trend of events was unmistakable, and almost certainly irreversible. The scarlet uniform of imperial Britain was discarded in favour of a patchwork coat of many colours.

In his book *The Break-up of Britain*, published in 1977, Tom Nairn predicted the collapse of 'the London state'. Like others on the Marxist left at the time, he believed that Britain was in the throes of a terminal economic decline that would lead inexorably to the destruction of the old regime. In the past, however, Marxists had expected the revolt against it to be led by the working classes, Nairn argued that the revolution would take a different form: the break-up of the United Kingdom. It might be a long and slow process, but the British state would break up under the combined assault of nationalist movements in Scotland and Wales and the IRA's campaign of bombing and terror in Northern Ireland.

In the circumstances of the mid-1970s this was a plausible scenario. In Scotland the SNP appeared at first to be a dynamic force on the brink of sweeping the country. In the general election of October 1974 they won 30.4 per cent of the vote in Scotland and eleven seats and came second to Labour in 35 of the 71 Scottish constituencies. They triumphed again in the local elections of 1976–7, but the SNP vote was deceptive in giving an exaggerated impression of the extent of support for independence. In February 1977, at a moment when the SNP was still riding high at 31 per cent in the opinion polls, support for independence stood at 18 per cent. In the general election of 1979, when the SNP won 17.3 per cent of the Scottish vote, support for independence stood at only 7 per cent. Evidently SNP voters had mixed motives.[34] The nationalist cause was also embarrassed by the activities of tiny extremist groups like the 'Workers Party of Scotland', which combined Marxism with armed robbery, and the 'Army of the Provisional Government', also known as the 'Tartan Army', which attacked oil pipelines and electricity pylons. No blood was shed, but three trials of militant nationalist groups in 1972, 1975, and 1976 led to convictions for terrorism.[35]

Such were the circumstances in which the juggernaut of devolution was set in motion. When Harold Wilson returned to office as Prime Minister in March 1974, he did so at the head of a government without a parliamentary majority and clinging to office by its fingernails. For reasons of pure, unalloyed expediency he decided that the best way to shore up the Labour vote in Scotland was to come out in favour of home rule. Some of his Cabinet colleagues were sceptical, and events might have taken a different course if his Scottish Secretary Willie Ross, a staunch Unionist at heart, had rebelled, but he too accepted that something had to be done. All that remained was for the Labour Party in Scotland to fall into line behind the Prime Minister at a meeting of the Scottish executive arranged for 22 June 1974 at the Glasgow Co-operative Hall in Dalintober Street. Unfortunately for Wilson, Scotland was playing Yugoslavia that evening in the final stages of the World Cup. Eighteen of the twenty-nine members of the executive stayed at home to watch the match (which ended in a 1-1 draw and the elimination of Scotland from the contest) leaving six of the eleven who did attend to pass a resolution opposing devolution. In order to clear the decks for the approaching general election, a special conference of the Scottish Labour Party had to be summoned in August 1974 for the purpose of reversing the executive's decision and ratifying the Downing Street line.[36] Just as the Church of England owes its origins to Henry VIII's need of a divorce, so the Scottish Parliament was initially conceived as a tactic for ensuring a Labour majority at Westminster.

Cabinet ministers, civil servants, and MPs were never likely to surrender their own powers without a fight, and the very idea of devolving policy decisions to Cardiff or Edinburgh ran against the grain of decades of centralization. Inevitably the proposals that emerged, after much wrangling, were strictly limited. The Scotland and Wales Bill, which the government put before the House of Commons in November 1976, proposed a Scottish Assembly with legislative powers over a carefully defined range of issues, but virtually no tax-raising powers, financed by a block grant to be determined by the Treasury. The Welsh Assembly was to exercise administrative authority only over devolved areas, with a budget again determined by the Treasury. As a further concession to the critics of devolution, the government promised to hold consultative referenda in both countries but the attempt to combine the proposals for Scotland and Wales in a single bill failed. In February 1977 it was voted down by the House of Commons, an act that might have signalled the end of devolution but for the government's slender majority and continuing fear of the electoral threat from the SNP. Separate bills for Scotland and Wales were introduced the following November. Although the government forced them through the House with the aid of the party machine and the support of the Liberals and the nationalist parties, the debates were notable for the vigorous dissent of such Welsh and Scottish Labour MPs as Neil Kinnock, Norman Buchan, and Tam Dalyell. Another obstacle to devolution was put in place by the Labour MP George Cunningham, a Scot who sat for the London constituency of Islington. He moved a successful amendment requiring the repeal of the Scotland Act if less than 40 per cent of all those entitled to vote were in favour of devolution. The same principle was then incorporated in the Wales Act. Both bills received the royal assent in July 1978, but the Cunningham amendment had raised the bar.

No matter what happened in the referenda, the devolution proposals had already fulfilled their primary purpose of derailing the SNP band-waggon. They exposed a split within the SNP between whole-hoggers who rejected devolution on the grounds that nothing but independence would do, and compromisers who supported devolution on the grounds that half a loaf was better than no bread. Meanwhile the government's commitment to a Scottish Parliament took some of the heat out of the national question and indeed turned into a tedious debate about constitutional machinery: the word 'devolution' was an anti-climax in itself. This was not the rousing cry of freedom for which blood had been shed in song and story. At a deeper level, Scotland was divided: a shifting morass of sentiment and opinion in which nationalists, home rulers, and unionists expressed their Scottishness in different ways.

Nationalists dreamed of a Scotland in which everyone shared the same kind of national consciousness as they did, but nationalism was a divisive creed. The one great passion capable of uniting all Scots (or at any rate nine out of ten Scottish males) in a spirit of fervent nationalism was football. 'To the Scots', wrote the sports reporter Hugh McIlvanney, 'a cosy, domesticated sense of identity, a national persona in carpet slippers, would never be enough. They want constantly to be making aggressive declarations about themselves to the rest of humanity. For many decades now, the nearest thing to a gunboat they could send out into the world has been a football team.'[37] By the 1970s Scottish supporters at international matches were booing the British national anthem, 'God Save the Queen' and singing 'The Flower of Scotland', a mournful ballad commemorating the Scots who fell at Bannockburn. Written by Roy Williamson of the Corries in 1968 it had already become an unofficial national anthem, chanted at rugby as well as football internationals.

In 1977 Scotland beat England at Wembley and the pitch was invaded by jubilant Scotland supporters who dug up pieces of the turf. When Scotland again qualified for the final stages of the World Cup in Argentina, the Scotland manager, Ally Macleod, began to talk of the prospect of a great historic victory. Third place, he predicted, was the worst outcome to be expected. 'In the run-up to the competition', wrote McIlvanney, 'he behaved with no more caution, subtlety or concern for planning than a man getting ready to lead a bayonet charge. The fans echoed his war cries, never bothering to wonder if the other contenders for the world title would be willing to stand still and be stabbed.' An artist in Perthshire painted an updated version of Leonardo's 'Last Supper' in which the disciples were replaced by players with their manager at the head of the table. Only five hundred tickets were allocated to 'Ally's Tartan Army', the Scotland supporters who travelled to Argentina to support the team. Other Scots made desperate efforts to reach Argentina in the hope of getting tickets on the spot. Rumours of an attempt to hire a submarine were too good to be true, but dozens flew to New York and set off on a greyhound bus for the Mexican border 'after which', *The Times* reported, 'their travel plans are, to say the least, vague'.[38]

In their first match against Peru Scotland were beaten 3-1. Reeling from the shock they could only manage a 1-1 draw with Iran, one of the weakest teams in the contest, but staged a last-minute recovery to beat Holland 3-2. It was not enough to prevent their elimination from the competition. The situation was well summed up by the headline in the *Scottish Daily Express*: END OF THE WORLD. The collapse of Scottish morale was palpable and Ally Macleod returned home in disgrace. Was this, perhaps, the moment at which the nationalist bubble burst? Alas this tempting theory is not borne out by the opinion polls. Support for the SNP, which had been hovering around the 30 per cent mark since 1974, began to slide in the spring of 1978, before the World Cup, and there was no significant dip after the debacle. Evidently the SNP had failed to strike deep roots and its popularity was more transient than commentators had appreciated. The party's performance in local government had been disappointing and it was riven by internal disputes. Possibly the reputation of the SNP was also damaged by the activities of 'tartan terrorists' whose amateurish attempts to imitate the terrorism of the IRA landed a number of them in gaol.

If support for the SNP was in decline, support for devolution had never been fervent and was now diminished by the vocal opposition of some sections of the Scottish Labour party and the disaster of the 'winter of discontent', which played into the hands of the Conservatives both north and south of the border. On referendum day, 1 March 1979, 63.8 per cent of the Scottish electorate turned out to vote. A bare majority voted in favour of devolution, but as they represented only 32.9 per cent of the electorate, they failed to clear the 40 per cent hurdle and the Scotland Act was doomed.

On the eve of the referendum in Wales the veteran nationalist Saunders Lewis, now eighty-six, gave his fellow countrymen a warning. 'May I', he wrote in a letter to the *Western Mail*, 'point out the probable consequences of a No majority. There will follow a general election. There may be a change of government. The first task of the Westminster Parliament will be to reduce and master inflation. In Wales there are coalmines that work at a loss; there are steelworks that are judged to be superfluous; there are valleys convenient for submersion. And there will be no Welsh defence.' These prescient words fell on the stoniest of ground. An opinion poll published in May 1978 showed opinion in Wales evenly divided over devolution, with 42.8 per cent in favour and 42.8 per cent against. But when the referendum came more than 40 per cent of the electorate failed to vote at all. Of those who did, 11.9 per cent voted in favour of a Welsh Assembly and 46.9 per cent against. All eight Welsh counties were strongly opposed. Even in Gwynedd, which was mainly Welsh-speaking, only 21.8 per cent voted in favour of an assembly.

The contrast with the outcome of the Scottish referendum was striking. The Scots were plainly divided, but their nationality did translate to some extent into nationalism, albeit of a moderate variety. Not so the Welsh. 'However powerful their sense of cultural and historical identity', writes Kenneth Morgan, 'the Welsh were, in political and economic terms, strictly unionist. Welsh devolution was promptly wiped off the political agenda.'[39]

That a strong sense of Welsh national identity did exist was not in doubt. As in the past it found expression in a collective passion for rugby:

Rugby belonged to all of Wales: to the elite schools that founded the early teams and the liberal professions that still loved it; to the miners of the South Wales valleys who took up the game and made it their own; to the policemen and the steelworkers who were so often at the heart of the team; and to those who became teachers instead of following their fathers to the pit.[40]

Between 1968–9 and 1979–80 Wales won the Five Nations Champion-ship no fewer than six times.

When it came to politics, however, Wales was a divided nation. In an article published in 1985 the political scientist Denis Balsom distin-guished, on the basis of data from the general election of 1979, three main socio-linguistic groups in Wales: a Welsh-identifying; Welsh-speaking group; a Welsh-identifying, non-Welsh speaking group; and a British-identifying, non-Welsh speaking group.[41] Each predominated in a different area or areas which he defined as Welsh-speaking Wales ('Y Fro Gymraeg'), Welsh Wales, and British Wales.

The overwhelming rejection of devolution in 1979 must have owed something to the unpopularity of the Callaghan government at the time, and something to the failings of the pro-devolution campaign in Wales, but the most likely explanation is that most of the Welsh pre-ferred to be governed from London rather than governed by a rival Welsh tribe.

The stronghold of the nationalist movement was Welsh-speaking Wales but only 22 per cent of Welsh speakers voted for Plaid Cymru in the general election of 1979: the majority voted Labour. The political agenda of Welsh-speaking Wales was cultural rather then consti-tutional and focused in the late 1970s on the creation of a Welsh-speaking television channel, a demand the Callaghan government readily conceded in return for the continued support of three Plaid Cymru MPs in the House of Commons. In Welsh Wales Labour was the dominant party. But, although Labour in Wales was officially in favour of devolution, much of the party adhered firmly to the socialism of the late Aneurin Bevan and shared his suspicion of nationalism as a movement likely to split the labour movement. In British Wales (which included a significant minority of English people) the Conservatives were the majority party and Unionism the dominant force. Although the powers of the proposed Welsh assembly were very limited, it was bound to awaken fears of the domination of one part of Wales by another.

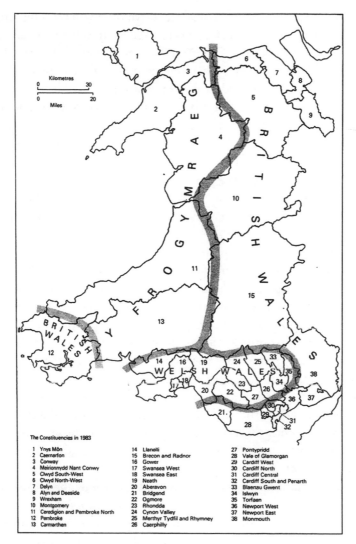

Map 12.1 The three-Wales model.

Source: Denis Balsom, 'The Three-Wales Model' in John Osmond (ed.), *The National Question Again: Welsh Political Identity in the 1980s* (Llandysul, 1985), p. 5.

The Impact of Mrs Thatcher

Mrs Thatcher was a firm believer in the Union and strongly opposed to devolution. But she was also profoundly Anglocentric and a centralizer whose radical right-wing policies alienated majority opinion in Scotland

and Wales. The effect of her governments was to give a renewed impetus to devolution in both countries, though Wales moved more slowly and reluctantly than Scotland. Contrary to their hopes and expectations, neither the SNP nor Plaid Cymru reaped much of the benefit. The role of defender of Scotland and Wales against the onslaught of Thatcherism fell to Labour, acting in alliance with cross-party movements in both countries. Devolution was no longer what it had been in 1979, a tactic necessitated by the needs of a Labour government at Westminster, but a shield for the protection of local elites inside Scotland and Wales from the overweening power of central government. The consequences only came to fruition seven years after Mrs Thatcher's departure from office but, much against her will, she was to become a Mother of Parliaments.

In the general election of 1979 the SNP won only two seats, and 17.3 per cent of the vote, compared with eleven seats and 30 per cent of the vote in October 1974. It was a decisive setback from which the party never fully recovered during the eighteen years of Conservative rule that followed. In Wales, Plaid Cymru were more successful in holding their ground in 1979, but it was very narrow ground: two seats and 8.1 per cent of the vote as against three seats and 10.8 per cent of the vote in the previous general election. After the anticlimax of the Scottish and Welsh referenda it looked as though devolution was dead in the water. The Thatcher governments rapidly repealed the Scotland and Wales Acts and the issues were swept under the carpet. In 1981 a Campaign for a Scottish Assembly was founded by Jack Brand, a politics professor at the University of Strathclyde, but it appeared to be in every sense of the word an academic exercise.

As the recession of 1979–81 tightened its grip and the Thatcher governments sank in the opinion polls the devolution issue was once more eclipsed by the politics of mass unemployment and the British version of the class war. It was marginalized again by the Argentine invasion of the Falklands on 2 April 1983, the despatch of the British Task Force to the South Atlantic, and the brief and bloody war which ended with 236 British dead and the surrender of the Argentine garrison on 15 June. For three months the Falklands war drove all other news stories out of the headlines. Astonishing as a military victory achieved against the odds at a distance of 8,000 miles from Britain, the Falklands war was no less remarkable as a revelation of a popular patriotism uncannily reminiscent of 1940 and Britain's 'finest hour'.

In 1980 the Falkland Islands had a tiny population of 1,849, twenty miles of surfaced road, and a gravel path from the capital, Port Stanley, to Bluff Cove. At a time when they were virtually defenceless they had been attacked and occupied by a force of 10,000 Argentinian troops, an act of aggression by a military dictatorship notorious for its abuse of civil liberties. Unlike the British of 1940, who were the rulers of a world-wide Empire, the Falkland Islanders were the subjects of a colonial administration, but historical distinctions of this kind were swept aside by the collective memory of the British as a peaceful island people standing alone against a brutal, militaristic aggressor. The tabloid press switched overnight from bingo to jingo. Vera Lynn and even 'Bomber' Harris could be heard again on the radio—or should that be the wireless? Winston Churchill junior repeated his grandfather's warnings against appeasement. Enoch Powell proclaimed the rebirth of national solidarity:

> All of a sudden thoughts and emotions which for years have been scouted or ridiculed are alive and unashamed. In both universities, where, until recently, anyone who mentioned 'sovereignty' or 'the nation' or 'the British people' would have been lucky not to be rabbled, students discuss with respect and approval arguments and propositions which presuppose these very things...As for the people at large, in the streets, the trains, the shops, of course there are exceptions and divergent strains—there always have been and always will be—but overwhelmingly a quiet, matter-of-fact unanimity of purpose has painted out, in a way irresistibly reminiscent of 1939 and 1940, differences of class, education, prejudice and party.[42]

The opinion polls suggest that Powell was broadly right about popular opinion. From the start of the crisis 83 per cent said that they cared personally that Britain should recover the Falklands, though 32 per cent cared 'only a little'. These percentages remained fairly constant. More than 80 per cent of those polled approved of the sending of the Task Force, though opinions on the military options varied. 52 per cent supported the bombing of Argentine ships, 67 per cent the landing of troops in the islands. When the fighting was over, 76 per cent expressed the view that the recapture of the Falklands had been worth the loss of lives involved.[43]

Powell also detected in the British response to the war the seeds of the kind of nationalist revival—anti-European, anti-American, anti-immigration—of which he was not only the main protagonist, but virtually the only one outside the ranks of the National Front. But if the war was an intense experience for the British public it was also a brief one, and unlike the home front of 1939 to 1945 it was an armchair war. No participation, no risk, no sacrifice, was required of anyone except the combatants, their families, and their friends.

In conjunction with the economic revival that began at about the same time, the 'Falklands factor' was important in rescuing Mrs Thatcher from the prospect of electoral defeat, and ensuring the continuation of the 'Thatcher revolution'. It also drew a line under 'declininism', the thesis that the British were forever sliding downhill and would never achieve anything of significance again. But it could not prevent the slow but continuous transformation of Britain into a more diverse and more loosely integrated nation.

The 'Falklands factor' seems to have been weaker in Scotland than in England: the tabloid *Daily Record* less jingoistic in Scotland than the *Sun* in England, the Church of Scotland decidedly cool. If we take an average of the monthly opinion polls for a period of six months before and after the war, and compare the figures for Scotland with the figures for the United Kingdom (heavily weighted towards England), we find an interesting contrast. For the UK the six-monthly average of support for the Conservative party was fourteen points higher after the war than it was before, for Scotland only five points higher. Without comparable figures it is harder to estimate the effect of the war in Wales.

Between 1945 and 1959 the Scots and the English voted in roughly similar proportions for the two main parties. In 1955, for example, the Conservatives won 50.1 per cent of the vote in Scotland and 50.3 per cent of the vote in England. From 1964 onwards, however, electoral patterns north and south of the border began to diverge. This was partly due to the fact that regions of declining industry and employment, like Scotland and the north of England, turned increasingly to Labour to protect them, but were outweighed in the electoral scales by the prosperous south of England. Thatcherite Conservatism accelerated the trend. In the general election of 1983 the Conservatives won 146 of the 162 seats in the south of England outside London, while the Labour party won 13, and the Liberals 3. Of the 71 Scottish seats, Labour won 41, the Conservatives 21, the Liberals 8, and the SNP 2.

Though similar to the economic problems of the north of England, the economic problems of Scotland came dressed in a kilt and marched to the sound of a different drum. It was not sufficient for opponents to say that Mrs Thatcher was destroying industries. It had to be said that she was destroying *Scotland's* industries. From 1983 onwards they also began to argue that she had no mandate to govern Scotland. By 1987 they were forecasting a 'Doomsday Scenario', a Conservative general election victory accompanied by a collapse of support in Scotland. Doomsday was postponed, but only just, when the number of Conservative MPs in Scotland was reduced from twenty-one to ten. The Conservatives for their part insisted that the United Kingdom was indivisible and that no part could opt out, but this was unconvincing: Northern Ireland was a part of the United Kingdom but elected its own Parliament from 1921 to 1972. Conservatives in Scotland also claimed that the Union represented Scotland's best interests, but to no avail. As the only mainstream party in Scotland opposed to a measure of self-government they stood out like a sore thumb. Nor could it be denied that the Scots were being governed against their own will.

As Mrs Thatcher admitted in her memoirs, she was baffled and frustrated by Scotland: 'There was no Tartan Thatcherite revolution.' She attributes this to the fact that in Scotland the Left were the establishment: 'The Labour and the trade unions had a powerful grip on office and influence at every level—from the local authorities, through quangos, right into the Scottish Office. In practice, the Left, not the Right, had held on to the levers of patronage. It had its arguments voiced by both Catholic and Protestant churches in Scotland and parrotted in the media—hardly any Scottish newspapers supported us and the electronic media were largely hostile.'[44] Some Thatcherite policies, like the sale of council houses and the capping of local government spending, were introduced in Scotland. The 'right to buy' proved popular and in 1988, for the first time since 1945, the number of owner-occupied homes in the housing stock exceeded the number of homes in the public sector.[45] Other attempts at radical reform of the public sector were thwarted or emasculated by an alliance of the Labour party, the unions, the Scottish Office, and the old guard of the Scottish Conservative Party. The Scottish Development agency, a corporatist body subsidizing urban and industrial development, was reorganized under the new title of Scottish Enterprise. The Highlands and Islands Development board was reborn as Highlands and Islands Enterprise. But in 1988, one in three Scots was still employed in the public sector, while Scots in general continued to benefit from levels of public expenditure per head higher than the rest of the United Kingdom.[46] Although Thatcherite policies were blunted in Scotland, they still posed a deadly threat to the power and influence of the Scottish labour movement, which responded by closing ranks and uniting beneath the banner of devolution. Unionists of the old school fell silent except for Tam Dalyell, the MP for West Lothian, who continued to warn that devolution was 'a motorway to independence with no exit'.

The party struggle between Labour and the Conservatives, and the clash of cultures between collectivism and individualism, were intensified in Scotland by the conflict between a kind of Englishness and a kind of Scottishness that had one thing at least in common: a moralizing mission. Each tried to preach to the other. Mrs Thatcher could not help it if she sounded like a Home Counties lady rebuking the servants for ignorance and fecklessness. In reply, her critics in Scotland extolled the virtues of a Scottish civic culture allegedly imbued with egalitarianism and communal spirit. Mutual incomprehension reached a climax in May 1988 when Mrs Thatcher, in effect at her own invitation, addressed the annual assembly of the Church of Scotland on the Mound in Edinburgh. It was a carefully argued speech in which she pointed out that the good Samaritan would not have been able to help the man who had fallen among thieves if he had not been a rich man. If she had been speaking to businessmen in Surrey this might have gone down well, but it was ill calculated to appeal to ministers of the Kirk who believed that there should be no division between rich and poor in the first place. Though she was politely received on the occasion itself, leading figures in the Kirk were quick to register their disagreement, political opponents denounced her, and the 'Sermon on the Mound' passed into political folklore as a misconceived attack on Scotland and its values.[47]

By the time Mrs Thatcher spoke to the General Assembly the temperature was already rising in the definitive controversy of her troubled relations with the Scots. The origins of the decision to replace local authority rates with a poll tax have already been described in an earlier chapter. Under pressure from the Tory party in Scotland, which had set the ball rolling in the first place, the Cabinet agreed to introduce the new tax a year earlier in Scotland than in England. First of all, however, the necessary legislation had to be passed, and after that a register compiled of everyone who was liable to pay. The tax duly came into force in April 1989.

'I may be the last person in Scotland—or certainly the last non-Tory', writes the former Labour MP Brian Wilson, 'who does not believe in the conspiracy theory that the Poll Tax was a pre-meditated experiment visited upon the people of Scotland by a malevolent political witch.'[48] The belief that the Scots had been used as guinea-pigs for the benefit of the English was a myth on a par with other tales of victimhood, but it helped to justify the SNP and the Militant Tendency in organizing a non-payment campaign. The Labour Party, which ran most of the local authorities, needed the revenue, and subscribed to the rule of law, urged the Scots to comply. It looked at first as if they would. Malcolm Rifkind, the Secretary for Scotland, announced in November 1988 that more than 99 per cent of adults in Scotland were on the poll tax registers. This was probably an overestimate: untold numbers had 'disappeared' rather than pay the tax, and it remained to be seen how many of those who had registered would refuse to pay up. When the poll tax charges were announced it was revealed that the government had got its sums wrong and underestimated them, on average, by 16 per cent. The poll tax for Edinburgh, for example, was £392 instead of £313 forecast by ministers.

This was the point at which the heather began to catch fire. A Scottish petition against the poll tax with 300,000 signatures was delivered to Mrs Thatcher in February 1989. When the tax came into force a substantial minority—16 per cent of the population according to a survey by *The Sunday Times*—dug in their heels and refused to pay it. Lothian Region, which was not untypical, had to ask sheriff's officers to send out 76,756 summary warrants threatening non-payers with 'poinding', the seizure of their property to the value of the missing payment. When the bailiffs arrived at a home to seize the television or the three-piece suite they found themselves mobbed by protesters from the Anti-Poll Tax Federation. Its leader Tommy Sheridan was an economics graduate from the University of Stirling who had recently been expelled from the Labour Party because of his membership of the Militant Tendency. A tireless agitator and organizer in the mould of Derek Hatton or Ken Livingstone, Sheridan was a charismatic speaker who could rouse an audience to anger as readily as he could make them laugh.[49]

The anti-poll tax campaign was organized by the romantic insurrectionists of Scottish politics, the Militant Tendency and the SNP. The popular support they attracted helped to discredit the poll tax, but the most important consequence of the tax was the creation of a cross-party alliance of local elites in support of a new constitutional settlement. Out of the Campaign for a Scottish Assembly there developed a new body, the Scottish Constitutional Convention, formed in March 1989 and comprising representatives of the local authorities, the Churches, the Scottish TUC, the Labour Party, and the Liberal Democrats. The Conservatives and the SNP declined to join. The chairman was Canon Kenyon Wright, an episcopalian and Liberal Democrat, with Campbell Christie, the general secretary of the TUC, in a supporting role as 'choirmaster'. They published their blueprint for a Scottish Parliament on St Andrew's Day 1990—two days, as it happened, after Mrs Thatcher's resignation. Another seven years were to elapse before devolution was enacted, but she was, in the words of Kenyon Wright, its 'unwitting and unwilling midwife'.[50]

After the referendum of 1979, and a general election in which Plaid Cymru won only eight per cent of the vote, Wales seemed firmly bound to the Union. Yet all the time an embryonic Welsh state was in the making with the active assistance of the Thatcher governments. The Welsh Office, which had begun with 225 civil servants in 1964, had 2,206 by 1984. From 1981–2 onwards it was given the right to negotiate a global sum for Wales each year and to determine its own spending priorities. Peter Walker, who was Welsh Secretary from 1987 to 1990, was an unrepentant one nation Tory who pumped public money into industry through the Welsh Development Agency. Meanwhile the quangos multiplied and flourished. There were eighty of them, employing 57,311 people, by 1993.[51] Administrative devolution was a strategy for killing home rule with kindness, but the more that decisions were devolved to Cardiff, the stronger the case in logic for a Welsh assembly.

In November 1979 the Conservative Home Secretary, William Whitelaw, announced that the government had decided not to go ahead with a separate Welsh language television channel. Plaid Cymru responded with a pledge by 2,000 of its members to go to prison rather than pay their TV licence and the leader of the party, Gwynfor Evans, announced that he would fast to the death if the channel were not established. The government gave in and Channel S4C was launched on 1 November 1982, but the audience for its most popular programmes was only about 150,000, a reminder if it were needed of the narrow base of linguistic nationalism. The development of a more broadly based movement in favour of devolution was a response, as in Scotland, to the contraction of heavy industry, the Thatcherite offensive against local government, and the poll tax, but the shift occurred more slowly in Wales, and ran into stiffer opposition. Neil Kinnock, the leader of the Labour party from 1983 to 1992, had strongly opposed the Callaghan government over devolution and probably never changed his views on the subject. The Labour manifesto of 1987 reiterated the party's commitment to an elected Scottish assembly, but as in 1983 there was no such pledge for Wales. By 1992, however, the Labour party in Wales had swung round in favour of devolution, and the manifesto promised an elected assembly.

The Babel Express

In the case of Scotland and Wales, the question was whether a sense of national identity that already existed would be translated into political action and constitutional change. In the case of Britain's relations with the European Community, the question was whether or not a European identity could be superimposed on the member states. So far as the British were concerned the answer was yes, but it was an identity imposed mechanistically from above, with the slenderest of roots in British society.

In 1975 the Wilson government fulfilled its promise to hold a referendum on the future of Britain's relations with Europe. The electorate were asked: 'Do you think that the United Kingdom should stay in the European Community (the Common Market)?' The outcome was a resounding victory for the pro-Marketeers. On a turnout of 65 per cent, 67.2 per cent of the electorate voted 'yes' and 32.8 per cent 'no'. Of the

68 British counties, all but two—Shetland and the Western Isles—voted 'yes'. In the course of the referendum campaign the Post Office delivered three leaflets to every household: one from the government, one from the pro-Marketeers, and one from the anti-Marketeers. The message from the anti-Marketeers placed a strong emphasis on the question of sovereignty:

> The fundamental question is whether or not we remain free to rule ourselves in our own way. For the British people, membership of the Common Market has already been a bad bargain. What is worse, it sets out by stages to merge Britain with France, Germany, Italy and other countries into a single nation. This will take away from us the right to rule ourselves which we have enjoyed for centuries. The Common Market increasingly does this by making our laws and deciding our policies on food, prices, trade, and employment—all matters which affect the lives of us all. Already, under the Treaty of Rome, policies are being decided, rules made, laws enacted, and taxes raised, not by our own Parliament elected by the British people, but by the Common Market—often by the unelected Commissioners in Brussels. As this system tightens—as it will—our right, by our votes, to change policies and laws in Britain will steadily dwindle. Unlike British laws, those of the Common Market—which will take precedence over our own laws—can only be changed if all the other members of the Common Market agree. This is wholly contrary to the wishes of ordinary people who everywhere want more, not less, control over their own lives.[52]

Although the anti-Marketeers were putting a negative gloss on the issue, they were right in claiming that British membership of the Community involved some loss of sovereignty in the short run with every prospect of more to follow. Under the Treaty of Rome, member states committed themselves to work for 'ever closer union among the peoples of Europe'. The Council of Ministers in Brussels, a kind of EuroCabinet composed of representatives of the various governments, had the power to issue directives, regulations, and decisions that were legally binding on all member states, provided they were all in agreement: on all the more important issues every member retained the right of veto. Much of the real power lay behind the scenes with the European Commission, the body of permanent officials which advised the Council, ran the administrative machinery, and stood guard over the sacred flame of European unity.

The law courts were quick to register the effects of British entry. In a famous pronouncement in the case of Bulmer versus Bollinger in 1974 Lord Denning explained that Community law did not touch matters concerned solely with England and its people. 'But on matters with a European element the Treaty was like an incoming tide. It flowed into the estuaries and up the rivers...In future, in transactions which crossed the frontiers, we must no longer speak or think of English law as something on its own. We must speak and think of Community law rights and obligations, and give effect to them.'[53]

The anti-Marketeers never succeeded in making the question of sovereignty central to the referendum campaign. This was partly because the cards were stacked against them. The campaign took the form of a contest between two cross-party organizations, with the government intervening to make its own recommendation. The pro-Marketeers could rely on the active support of the Confederation of British Industry, the whole of the national press, the Churches, the Liberals, the overwhelming majority of Conservatives, including the party leader Margaret Thatcher, and the pro-Market wing of the Labour party and the TUC.

They represented all the respectable faces and middle-of-the-road forces of British politics. The anti-Marketeers, on the other hand, were the awkward squad: Communists, Labour and trade union activists, maverick Tories, Ulster Unionists, Welsh and Scottish nationalists. The pro-Marketeers spent £1,481,583 on their campaign, the anti-Marketeers £133,630. Just in case the issue should be in doubt, the government in the person of Harold Wilson came down strongly in favour of a 'yes' vote.

The European Community, we have to remember, was largely the creation of Christian Democrats who stood for capitalism with a human face. It was regarded by the British Left as an expression of the interests of big business and a potential threat to the realization of socialism in Britain. Socialists, therefore, had much more reason to fear the loss of sovereignty than Conservatives, most of whom were relaxed to the point of complacency about the European Union. For decades British politics had been mainly concerned with bread-and-butter issues. Now Britain was in the throes of an economic crisis, and the headlines were dominated by stories of strikes, redundancies, wages, and prices. The Common Market fell neatly into place as another of the economic issues of the day. The Community itself was generally thought of in Britain as a trading arrangement, and talk of political union seen as a rhetorical flourish like the froth on a cappuccino. If Britain were to withdraw, the pro-Marketeers warned, 'the immediate effect on trade, on industrial confidence, on investment prospects, and hence on jobs, could well be disastrous'.[54] Even the Antis came reluctantly to the conclusion that they should give priority in their campaign to economic issues.

True, the issue of sovereignty was given an airing, but the pro-Marketeers were skilful in defusing it. They could argue that very little sovereignty would in practice be lost, since Britain would retain the right of veto over all decisions of importance, and Parliament could always repeal the Act which had taken Britain into the Market. There was therefore no threat to national identity: 'The Community does not mean dull uniformity. It hasn't made the French eat German food or the Dutch drink Italian beer. Nor will it damage our British traditions and way of life.' The real measure of sovereignty, the pro-Marketeers added, was not the amount of independence a nation possessed in legal theory, but the extent of its influence in the real world. If Britain were to withdraw from Europe 'we would be clinging to the shadow of British sovereignty while its substance flies out of the window'.[55]

The pro-Marketeers had the advantage of defending the status quo: it was the anti-Marketeers who were calling for an upheaval. But even if the referendum *had* been all about the independence of Britain it is possible that the vote would still have been in favour of staying in. One opinion poll during the campaign asked the question: 'The ultimate aim of the Common Market is to merge the member countries into a single state. Do you think this is a good idea or a bad idea?' 43 per cent said it was a good idea, 37 per cent a bad idea, an indication that the majority of British people were not losing any sleep over a transfer of power from Westminster to Brussels. 58 per cent of voters were worried about the cost of living, only nine per cent about sovereignty or national independence.[56]

'The referendum result', wrote *The Sunday Times*, 'is the most exhilarating event in British politics since the war. By a clear majority, uncomplicated by a bad electoral system, the British people have declared themselves to be Europeans...'[57] This was an exaggeration. What the result reflected was the tendency of voters—this time with the added complication of splits within the Labour Party—to support the politicians they would normally have voted for in a general election. But if they did not embrace Europe, Europe began slowly to embrace them. From the Council in Brussels there issued a steady stream of Directions, Regulations, and Decisions which became a part of United Kingdom law. In 1980 they sent out 51 directives, 312 regulations, and 136 decisions to member states; in 1981 another 45 directives, 414 regulations, and 150 decisions; in 1982 42 directives, 393 regulations, and 128 decisions. So it continued. Member states were often given an extended deadline for the implementation of policies, and as it was also for national governments to decide how the EEC's instructions should be interpreted, there was scope for 'wriggle-room' amounting at times to non-compliance. But the Commission in Brussels also had the right to prosecute defaulting governments in the European Court of Justice, and the British usually complied in the end.

Many of the EC's decisions were enshrined in UK law through primary legislation, the customary procedure whereby bills were debated and passed by both Houses of Parliament, or through delegated legislation in the form of Statutory Instruments, issued by ministers under powers already granted to them by Act of Parliament. In 1970 the EEC had issued a directive regulating the noise level and the exhaust systems of motor vehicles. No fewer than twenty-one Statutory Instruments were required in order to implement the directive in the UK. There seems to be no reliable estimate, for the period of Mrs Thatcher's premiership, of the extent to which UK legislation derived from the EEC. The President of the European Commission, Jacques Delors, caused an uproar in 1988 when he predicted that in ten years time 80 per cent of Europe's economic decisions would be taken in Brussels. This was an exaggeration but no fantasy. In 2006 a government minister gave an estimate of 50 per cent for the proportion of recent legislation affecting the interests of business and the voluntary sector.[58]

Long before Euroscepticism reached gale force in the 1990s, there were many straws in the wind to show that the Council and the Commission intended to extend their remit beyond strictly economic affairs. The emergence in the 1970s of Green parties in western Europe was the most visible sign of the growing importance of environmental issues. The Community was in the forefront of the movement with initiatives like the Bathing Water Directive of 1976, which was intended to ensure that lakes and bathing beaches were safe—free, that is, of raw sewage in the water. The 1985 Directive on the Quality of Water for Human Consumption laid down maximum levels for concentrations of nitrate in drinking water, a side-effect of the use of fertilizers in agriculture. Wild birds were protected by a Directive of 1979, extended in 1992 to include flora and fauna and their habitats. Interventions of this kind, however enlightened the thinking behind them, were not always welcome in Whitehall since they inevitably involved additional expenditure. The Department of the Environment managed to evade the spirit, if not the letter, of the Bathing Water Directive by reducing the number of beaches to be monitored from 600 to 27 by the simple device of defining a bathing beach as a place where more than 500 people were to be found bathing at the same time. If there were only three or four hundred of them they would have to take their chances.[59]

The main thrust of Community law was directed towards the objective of converting what were now nine separate national markets into a single European market, with economic and monetary union as the ultimate objective. The prospect of a Community-wide market in which there were no barriers to the movement of goods, labour, or capital, and competition was enforced by the creation of a 'level playingfield', held a great appeal for a Prime Minister who saw it as a means of exporting Thatcherite economics. During the first half of the 1980s progress was slow and Mrs Thatcher preoccupied with a long-running dispute over the size of the British contribution to the Community budget, but the appointment in January 1985 of a new President of the Commission marked the opening of a new phase. Jacques Delors, a former French minister of finance, was a Catholic, a socialist, and a federalist. Philosophically he was poles apart from Mrs Thatcher but she respected him as a practical man of business and welcomed his decision to make the completion of the single market his first priority. She also arranged for the appointment of a loyal supporter, the businessman-cum-politician Lord Cockfield, as Vice-President of the Commission. Cockfield proceeded to draw up a list of 292 imperfections in the existing market, together with a timetable for their elimination by 1992.

Wary of entrapment in the legal machinery of the Community, Mrs Thatcher hoped to implement the single market informally, through a 'gentleman's agreement' among the member states. She was outmanoeuvred. The Council of Ministers opted for the Single European Act, a revision of the Treaty of Rome which laid down that it was to be implemented by Qualified Majority Voting. Recognizing that no progress would be made if every state retained the right of veto, Mrs Thatcher signed the Act and proclaimed it a great step forward. By agreeing to Qualified Majority Voting, however, she had signed away British sovereignty over all areas covered by the Act.

For Mrs Thatcher, the Single European Act was a terminus. For Jacques Delors and the leading politicians of the Community it was a point of departure for an accelerated programme of European integration, 'the Babel Express' as Mrs Thatcher called it in her memoirs. Delors pressed ahead with plans for economic and monetary union and the introduction of a 'social dimension' into the Community. Some of his more provocative declarations, like the speech to the TUC (7 September 1988) in which he promised that a federal Europe would protect workers' rights, were direct challenges to 'Thatcherism'. Meanwhile the Commission was extending its powers by a variety of machiavellian techniques. 'Most seriously of all', she wrote in her memoirs, 'it consistently misemployed treaty articles requiring only a qualified majority to issue directives which it could not pass under articles which required unanimity.' The dice, she concluded, had been loaded against the British:

> The more I considered all this, the greater my frustration and the deeper my anger became. Were British democratic, parliamentary sovereignty, the common law, our traditional sense of fairness, our ability to run our own affairs in our own way to be subordinated to the demands of a remote European bureaucracy, resting on very different traditions?

A fortnight after Delors's appearance at the TUC she took the opportunity of a speech in Bruges (20 September 1988) to pick up the gauntlet and fling it back at him:

> We have not successfully rolled back the frontiers of the state in Britain only to see them reimposed at a European level, with a European super-state exercising a new dominance from Brussels.[60]

Since there was no halting the 'Babel Express', Mrs Thatcher's only option was to get off at the next stop. In 1989 all the member states except Britain signed the 'Social Charter' or 'Charter of Fundamental Social Rights of Workers' which gave the Commission the right to take action in a range of areas including sexual equality, health and safety, social security, collective bargaining rights, and worker participation in the direction of companies. It was no wonder that delegates to the TUC had serenaded Jacques Delors with a chorus of 'Frère Jacques'. The Social Charter would have given the Commission a mandate to modify or interfere with many of the Thatcher government's labour market and social policy reforms.

Conservatives in general were firmly opposed to the Charter which they saw as a Franco-German conspiracy to push up the social costs of other member states. When it was incorporated in the Maastricht Treaty of 1992, John Major's government secured a British opt-out. The Labour opposition was committed to the Social Charter and the Commission was as ingenious as ever in bending the rules. Under the pretext that it fell within the scope of the Single Market Act, the Commission adopted by qualified majority vote in 1993 the Working Time Directive, which laid down a maximum 48-hour week and minimum holiday entitlements for all employees. The British government appealed against it on the grounds that the Commission were exceeding their authority but the European Court of Justice ruled against Britain in 1996 and the Directive duly came into force in Britain in 1998, by which time the incoming government of Tony Blair had also signed up to the Social Charter.

Mrs Thatcher's fall from office in November 1990 was due to a combination of factors. Britain was again in recession, the poll tax deeply unpopular, and Labour a few points ahead in the polls. The 'Iron Lady' had gone on too long, made too many enemies, and begun to lose touch with political reality. But 'Europe' was also a part of the fatal mix. It was not so much her policies as the belligerence of her tone that prompted the resignation of Nigel Lawson as Chancellor in October 1989 and Geoffrey Howe as deputy Prime Minister in November 1990. But the European issue arose again in the person of Michael Heseltine, a passionate Europhile who deplored her combative approach. It was his decision to stand against her for the leadership of the party that dealt the fatal blow to her premiership. As Boris Johnson remarked, Mrs Thatcher might well have said: 'I fought Delors and Delors won.'

From 1988 onwards applicants for a British passport received a new burgundy-coloured document in place of the old navy blue one. As before, the royal coat of arms appeared on the front cover and below it the words 'United Kingdom of Great Britain and Northern Ireland'.

Above it appeared the words 'European Community' (later to be replaced, in 1997, by 'European Union'), but it remained a national passport in a standardized European format. This was one of the few signs in everyday life of the existence of 'Europe', which remained for most people a remote and obscure affair. In the first two direct elections to the European Parliament in 1979 and 1984, fewer than a third of the electorate voted. In 1989 and 1994 the turnout rose to just over a third. In the dying days of Mrs Thatcher's premiership the *Sun* newspaper attempted to whip up popular feeling against the 'bureaucrats of Brussels'. Under the front page headline UP YOURS DELORS the paper explained that it was calling on all its readers 'to tell the feelthy French to FROG off. They INSULT us, BURN our lambs, FLOOD our country with dodgy food and PLOT to abolish the dear old pound. Now it is your turn to kick them in the Gauls.'[61] The right-wing press was entering a phase of Europhobia that was intimately bound up with the struggle for power inside the Conservative party, and intensified by fears of a reunited Germany. Not that the *Sun* needed coaching in hoary British stereotypes of Germany. When the German ambassador visited the paper's offices in 1990 the story ran under the headline '*The Sun* meets the Hun'.

Seven weeks before she resigned, Mrs Thatcher reluctantly agreed to British membership of the Exchange Rate Mechanism, the means by which the other member states of the Community arranged to stabilize exchange rates. She was, however, determined that Britain should descend no further down the slippery slope to monetary union, a determination shared by her successor John Major. In the negotiations leading up to the Treaty of Maastricht, Major obtained a British opt-out on monetary union as well as the Social Charter. It was not enough to save him from the Eurosceptics. On Black Wednesday, 16 September 1992, speculation against sterling reached a point at which the Treasury raised interest rates first to ten per cent and then twelve per cent before admitting defeat and suspending British membership of the ERM. At a stroke, Major had lost both his economic and his foreign policy. In the House of Commons a band of somewhere between forty and sixty Eurosceptics fought tooth and nail against the bill to ratify the Maastricht Treaty. After months of bitter debate, the bill went through, but Major was a wounded and hunted beast for the rest of his premiership.

In place of the unitary British state which had reached its zenith in the 1940s, a three-tier Britain was taking shape. The first tier consisted of the devolved administrations in Edinburgh and Cardiff. Though still under fairly strict control from the centre, they were embryonic states with a momentum of their own. Following Labour's landslide victory in the general election of May 1997, referenda on devolution were held in both Scotland and Wales. The Scots were offered a legislative assembly with the option of additional, though modest, powers to vary the level of income tax by 2p in the pound. On polling day, 11 September 1997, 74.3 per cent voted in favour of a Scottish Parliament and 63.5 per cent in favour of tax-varying powers. The Welsh referendum had been fixed for a week later in the hope of persuading them to follow the example of the Scots. On a turnout of just over 50 per cent they voted by a hair's breadth margin of 50.1 per cent to 49.9 per cent in favour of a Welsh Assembly, which therefore owed its existence to one Welsh elector in four.[62]

The second tier of the new Britain was the old regime of Whitehall and Westminster, constantly visible and reported in the media; the third a secretive European Britain, conducted by ministers and civil servants behind closed doors and rarely reported except when the Commission committed some alleged outrage against British liberties.

The Long View

Taking the late 1950s as a personal benchmark, I have tried in this book to describe the transitions that led from Harold Macmillan's Britain to Tony Blair's. The Second World War had given us a Labour government, full employment, and a welfare state, but they were superimposed on a country that remained morally and culturally conservative. From the late 1950s onwards more radical changes ensued: the almost continuous rise in living standards, the slow but steady decline of the working class, the collapse of the post-war political settlement and the revival of free-market economics, the shift in attitudes towards gender and sexual morality, the emergence of a multiracial and multicultural Britain, the erosion of British national identity.

With a touch of hyperbole I have called the changes 'revolutions' to distinguish them from the type of gradual, incremental change that moves in a consistent direction. In overturning or subverting contemporary assumptions they were disruptive and highly controversial: paradigm shifts. As revolutions, however, they were incomplete. The working classes declined but they did not disappear. Many opportunities opened up for women but a glass ceiling limited their prospects for promotion. Free-market economics led to the privatization of major industries, but eighteen years of neo-liberal policies only succeeded in reducing public spending from 43 per cent of GDP in 1979 to 39.3 per cent in 1997. While the welfare state was pruned back in some areas, it expanded in others—in response, for example, to an ageing population. The devolution of power to Scotland and Wales fell far short of the break-up of Britain that some had predicted—and so on.

Qualifications, therefore, always have to be made, but the gulf between 1950s Britain and 1990s Britain was deep and wide, and this was particularly true of values and mentalities. Take one tiny fragment of evidence that helps us to measure the distance. In 1961 Keith

Waterhouse and Willis Hall submitted to the British Board of Film
Censors their script for the film adaptation of Stan Barstow's novel, *A
Kind of Loving*. The Secretary of the Board was John Trevelyan, deserv-
edly remembered as a great liberalizer who did much to relax the rules
governing censorship. 'We would not be prepared', he wrote in his
report on the script, 'to have any talk or action about the purchase of
contraceptives.'[1]

We have travelled a long way since then. From the late 1950s there
was, as Jerry Lee Lewis put it, 'a whole lot of shakin' goin' on', and it
was the concentration of so many different kinds of change within a
comparatively short period that gave the 1970s and 1980s their turbulent character. Competing ideologies heightened the sense of a society
in flux but the outcome was something of a surprise. In spite of a two-
party system based on the opposing philosophies of socialism on the
one hand and Toryism on the other, it was liberal ideas that proved to
be most enduring and effective: the economic liberalism of free-market
economics, the social liberalism of the 1960s (an umbrella term), and
the civic nationalism of the Scots and the Welsh.

In view of the fact that the last Liberal government ended in 1915,
the persistence of liberalism in British political culture is an intriguing
problem. It is arguable that beyond their attachment to the key elements of the welfare state, which itself owed much to the liberalism of
Beveridge and Keynes, the British in general were never converted to
collectivism, still less to corporatism. We also have to bear in mind the
growing Americanization of Britain (and indeed western Europe) after
1945. Liberal ideas in Britain were inspired to some extent by the variety of liberalisms in the United States: the Chicago school of economics, the civil rights movement, the libertarian counter-cultures of San
Francisco. At the level of everyday life, the constant emphasis of consumer society upon personal choice, and the new freedoms conferred
by the ownership of cars and homes and the expansion of air travel to
all points of the globe, were lessons in personal liberty that did not have
to be taught. There was, however, a notable gap in the liberalization of
Britain. The political class was reluctant to reform a political system
that increasingly concentrated power in the hands of a centralizing
state that deprived local government of its autonomy—and a European
Union whose decision-making processes were remote, obscure, and
unaccountable. Constitutional reform was a topic the politicians were

content to leave to professors whose proposals were often consigned to the waste paper basket. Sections of the white working class, therefore, were not the only great bastion of illiberal attitudes in modern Britain: the other was the bureaucratic state, steadily encroaching on local democracy and civil liberties.

While there was no clear-cut division of opinion along party lines, it was broadly true from the 1960s to the 1990s that social liberals tended to be on the left in British politics and economic liberals on the right. In his book *Capitalism and the Permissive Society* (1973) the economist Samuel Brittan argued that free marketeers and social liberals had much in common, since they were both seeking to do away with traditional constraints on the freedom of the individual. 'To the extent that it prevails', he wrote, 'competitive capitalism is the biggest single force acting on the side of what it is fashionable to call "permissiveness" but was once known as personal liberty. Business enterprise can, of course, thrive and prosper alongside a great deal of "moral" prohibitions and prescriptions, whether enforced by law or public opinion. But the profit motive will always be kicking against such restraints and seeking to widen the range of what is permissible—whether it is a 19th century publisher launching an attack on orthodox religion or a 20th century theatrical or film producer challenging conventional concepts of decency and decorum.'[2] In the short run his arguments were ignored. The Conservatives under Mrs Thatcher denounced the permissive society. Labour, under Michael Foot, reverted to the socialism of 1945 and proposed, logically enough, to withdraw from the capitalist Common Market. Both positions, undermined by changing realities, proved untenable in the long run.

Once they were in office the Conservatives, or at any rate the moral authoritarians among them, discovered that it was impossible to put the clock back. The party was not only divided over the issues involved, but embarrassed by them. The number of Conservative MPs involved in sex scandals suggested that the party's identification with 'traditional family values' was, to say the least, problematical. Cultural and generational change were also taking their toll on the values of stern, unbending Toryism. 'Few people under the age of fifty', wrote the journalist Peter Hitchens in 1999, 'now possess what could be described as a Conservative imagination. Their attitude towards sexuality, drugs, manners, dress, food, swear-words, music and religion has little or nothing in common with the traditional idea of Conservative behaviour.'[3] As for racial and sexual equality, the Conservatives did little to advance them and little (section 28 of the Local Government Act excepted) to retard them.

Meanwhile, under the leadership of Neil Kinnock (1983 to 1992), the Labour party's opposition to privatization and free-market policies was crumbling. John Smith, whose leadership of the party was cut short in 1994 by his untimely death, was a social democrat who believed strongly in a managed economy, the redistribution of wealth, and the public service ethic. At the same time he made strenuous efforts to reassure businessmen and financiers that Labour would pursue pro-market policies (the 'prawn cocktail offensive').

Exactly what line he would have taken as the leader of a Labour government is therefore a matter for speculation. His successor, Tony Blair, was much bolder in his embrace of the market. 'New Labour', of which he and Gordon Brown were the two main architects, marked a decisive break with tradition. A special party conference in April 1995 approved the removal of Clause IV of the party's constitution, which committed it to nationalization, and the substitution of a text that endorsed the market economy and spoke of putting power, wealth, and opportunity in the hands of the many instead of the few. Labour had already abandoned the cause of public ownership but the purpose of the conference was to publicize the change, and marginalize the remaining socialists within the party.

By the 1990s, therefore, the two main parties were both adjusting to the realities of a liberalizing society and a liberalizing economy. New Labour, however, proved to be more at ease with modernity than the Conservatives. This was partly because the Conservatives suffered from hang-ups over questions of national identity. They could not bring themselves to accept Scottish and Welsh devolution. They were deeply divided over Europe and plagued by a minority of Eurosceptics for whom the topic was a King Charles's head to be pursued at almost any cost to government and party. At the grassroots level the Conservatives were also an ageing party with a declining membership—an old-fashioned constituency out of touch with youth, pop culture, ethnic minorities, women's rights and so on. Labour, by contrast, had been the more socially liberal of the two main parties ever since the 1960s. Characteristically Labour introduced all-women shortlists in 38 constituencies in the run-up to the 1997 general election: 35 of the candidates were elected. Whereas the Conservatives put up 66 women candidates in 1997, Labour put up 156, of whom 102 ('Blair's Babes') became MPs.[4] The Conservatives, of course, could still claim to be more representative of the worlds of business and finance, but New Labour had narrowed the gap, embracing the market, the City, and the middle classes with all the fervour of a convert. Electorally, it was an ambitious, calculating and extremely successful attempt to broaden the social base of the party to the point where it was no longer identified with the working classes, but represented a cross-section of society. In all these respects New Labour stood at the confluence of all the main economic, social, and political changes that had taken place since the 1960s.

No one embodied this sense of modernity better than Tony Blair, the first charismatic leader of the Labour Party since Ramsay MacDonald at the height of his powers. Blair was more than an able politician and a fluent communicator. A consummate performer, he personified the youth and glamour of celebrity culture and harnessed it for political purposes. 'I am a modern man', he declared in April 1997. 'I am part of the rock and roll generation—the Beatles, colour TV, that's the generation I come from.'[5] A profoundly intuitive politician, impatient of ideological constraints, he was a magician in whose hands conflicts over doctrine and policy disappeared in a puff of smoke. 'We aim to put behind us', the Labour manifesto of 1997 declared, 'the bitter political struggles of left and right that have torn our country apart for too many decades. Many of these conflicts have no relevance whatsoever to the modern world—public versus private, bosses versus workers, middle class versus working class.' A protean personality on whom a great variety of hopes and expectations were pinned, Blair came to the leadership of the party at a time when Britain was entering the longest uninterrupted boom of the post-war period, and a feel-good factor was spreading. Upbeat, optimistic, and broadly in favour of aspiration and opportunity for all, he generated a sense of promise quite disproportionate to the modest scope of the programme on which he was campaigning. For a moment or two he lifted the British into a realm of the imagination far above mundane conflicts of interest but in the immortal words of Cole Porter it was 'just one of those things', and we soon came down to earth with a bump.

Ironically, it seems likely that the great unifier will always be remembered as the main protagonist of the war in Iraq, an act of foreign policy that divided the political nation as deeply as Munich or Suez. And whereas the Munich and Suez crises were over in a few weeks, the war proved to be the opening act of a long-running tragedy which has yet to run its course. How far the opposition to the war was fuelled by antipathy towards the domestic agenda of New Labour is one of those imponderables over which historians will speculate in years to come, but the impotence of New Labour's opponents at home may help to explain the ferocity with which they attacked the special relationship between a Labour government and a neo-conservative administration in Washington. However controversial his foreign policy, Tony Blair embodied and articulated a post-Thatcherite settlement at home that marginalized opponents on both Left and Right.

New Labour was sometimes described as nothing more than 'Thatcherism with a human face'. But the architects of New Labour retained a fervent belief in the welfare state that distinguished them from the Conservatives. Hence the massive investments they made in education, health, and some of the personal social services. Unlike Old Labour they did not believe in the levelling down of incomes, but they did attempt to level up the income of the poor through a statutory minimum wage, the Working Families Tax Credit, and kindred measures. Although, therefore, they did not reverse the economic inequalities of the Thatcher era, they prevented them from becoming more extreme. On the constitutional front, New Labour introduced devolution for Scotland and Wales, incorporated the European Declaration of Human Rights into United Kingdom law, and brought in a surprisingly effective Freedom of Information Act. True, they might have acted more radically and they sometimes behaved illiberally: the point is that, however much New Labour borrowed from 'Thatcherism', it was a more self-consciously liberal and progressive movement.

Under New Labour the notorious section 28 of the Local Government Act was repealed, the age of consent reduced to 16 for all, and Civil Partnerships introduced for same sex couples. With or without encouragement from the state, the rewriting of the rules of social morality continued apace. The number of couples getting married continued to fall as did the proportion who opted for a wedding in church. The proportion of children born to unmarried mothers, which had remained below the 10 per cent level from the 1940s to the 1970s, stood at over 50 per cent by 2010, though the proportion was higher in France: the 'permissive society' was a European rather than a British phenomenon. The gap between male and female earnings continued to narrow, but progress towards equality for women in the labour market was slow and there was no guarantee that it would continue. Racial discrimination was even harder to combat: like gender equality, racial equality was firmly embedded in official doctrine but quietly circumvented by some and openly defied by others. The ethnic composition of Britain was more varied than ever as a result of immigration from east European nations after their accession to the European Union. By the end of 2009 some 472,000 east Europeans were at work in Britain. Yet, for the most part, a diversity of ethnic groups lived peacefully side by side, and multiculturalism was practised in churches, mosques, and temples without bombs or riots. Meanwhile, in Cardiff and Edinburgh, devolved administrations were demonstrating that devolution worked by marking out new frontiers of policy and procedure that differentiated them from England.

At the core of this new social and political order lay the acceptance by virtually the entire political class of the rule of global market forces. Nowhere was the success of Mrs Thatcher and her allies more apparent than in the realm of ideas. The doctrines of economic liberalism, so passionately opposed by the Left in the 1970s and 1980s, had become the truisms and clichés of the twenty-first century. No mainstream politician claimed that the state could run the railways better than the private sector. None dreamed of arguing, as Douglas Jay had in *The Socialist Case*, that inherited wealth should be eliminated. Wealthy businessmen and bankers, whom socialists had once condemned as parasites who deprived workers of the fruits of their labour, were welcomed into the national pantheon as wealth creators and it was logical to suppose that the richer they were, the more wealth they had created. In New Labour thinking, they were the goose that laid the golden egg from which the welfare state could be financed, but it would no longer be a welfare state founded on a non-profit-making ethic of public service. Social provision too was to be privatized and the managers of social services incentivized by generous salaries and bonuses.

Economic liberalism, like social liberalism, had become an almost unexamined faith, accepted as one of the facts of life against which it was pointless to protest. Rational critics of the system supposed that the global financial crisis of 2008–9 had revealed its failings to all, and discredited the doctrines on which it was based. Only massive state intervention by governments around the world had averted catastrophe and kept the capitalist show on the road. On the Left, hopes were briefly raised of a revival of social democracy, but this was no more likely than a restoration of 'traditional' morality, or the Britishness of 1939 to 1945. Private profit and public policy were more closely allied than ever and there was, it seemed, to be no turning back.

Notes

Introduction

1 Kenneth Morgan, *The People's Peace: British History 1945–1989* (Oxford, 1990), p. 374.
2 Peter Hennessy, *Never Again: Britain 1945–1951* (1992), p. 40.

1 The Gentleman in Whitehall

1 Margaret Thatcher, *The Path to Power* (1995), p. 69.
2 Francis Beckett, *Clem Attlee: A Biography* (2000), p. 210.
3 Francis Williams, *A Prime Minister Remembers* (1961), p. 57.
4 C. R. Attlee, *The Labour Party in Perspective* (1937), p. 8.
5 Attlee, *Labour Party in Perspective*, p. 15.
6 The Labour Party, *Let Us Face the Future* (1945).
7 Douglas Jay, *The Socialist Case* (1937), p. 317.
8 His words were frequently misquoted by the government's critics as 'the gentleman in Whitehall knows best', a sweeping statement with which Jay, a moderate socialist on the Keynesian wing of the party, would certainly not have agreed.
9 I have taken this classification of controls from Alec Cairncross, *The British Economy since 1945* (1992), pp. 68–72, and added building licences, which he includes under the heading of controls over investment, and controls over production and design, which he omits.
10 Cairncross, *The British Economy since 1945*, pp. 57, 84.
11 Neil Rollings, ' "The Reichstag Method of Governing"? The Attlee Governments and Permanent Economic Controls' in H. Mercer, N. Rollings, and J. D. Tomlinson (eds.), *Labour Governments and Private Industry* (Edinburgh, 1992), p. 18.
12 *Economist*, 20 October 1945, p. 554.
13 Cairncross, *The British Economy*, pp. 46–7.
14 Peter Pagnamenta and Richard Overy, *All Our Working Lives* (1984), p. 228.
15 'Controls in Transition', *The Times*, 3 December 1945.
16 *The Times*, 26 September 1947, p. 2.
17 John Jewkes, *Ordeal by Planning* (1948), p. 220.
18 Ina Zweiniger-Bargielowska, *Austerity in Britain: Rationing, Controls and Consumption 1939–1955* (Oxford, 2000), pp. 163, 198–9, 202.
19 Rollings, ' "The Reichstag Method" ', pp. 18–19.
20 *Observer*, 10 August 1947, p. 4.
21 Bernard Crick, *George Orwell: A Life* (1981 edn), pp. 394–5.
22 Samuel H. Beer, *Modern British Politics* (1965), pp. 204–5.
23 Cairncross, *The British Economy*, pp. 46–7.
24 Richard Toye, 'Gosplanners v Thermostatters: Whitehall Planning Debates and their Political Consequences, 1945–49' in *Contemporary British History* vol. 14 no. 4 (2000), pp. 81–106.
25 Ben Pimlott, *Hugh Dalton* (1985), pp. 468–75.
26 Cairncross, *Years of Recovery*, pp. 337–8.
27 Martin Chick, *Industrial Policy in Britain 1945–1951* (Cambridge, 1998), p. 200.

28 Cairncross, *Years of Recovery*, p. 341.
29 TNA CAB/128/18 Cabinet conclusions 27 July 1950, p. 182.
30 Rollings, ' "The Reichstag Method" ', pp. 22–32.
31 TNA CAB/129/69, 'Legislation to Complete the Dismantling of the Defence Regulations', 23 July 1954.
32 *The Economist*, 14 August 1948, p. 261.
33 John Agar, 'Identity Cards in Britain: Past Experience and Policy Implications' in *History and Policy* (online).
34 Joe Moran, *Queuing For Beginners: The Story of Daily Life from Breakfast to Bedtime* (2007), pp. 62–3.
35 Zweiniger-Bargielowska, *Austerity in Britain*, p. 214.
36 Ibid., pp. 215–18.
37 J. C. R. Dow, *The Management of the British Economy 1945–1960* (Cambridge, 1970), p. 148.
38 Zweiniger-Bargielowska, *Austerity in Britain*, pp. 29–30.
39 Pearson Phillips, 'The New Look' in Michael Sissons and Philip French (eds.), *Age of Austerity* (Harmondsworth, 1964), p. 146; Alix Meynell, *Public Servant, Private Woman* (1988), p. 249; *The Times*, 26 September 1947.
40 *The Times*, 25 September 1947 (Jill Craigie); 29 September (Anne Scott-James); Phillips, 'The New Look', p. 147; Meynell, pp. 148–9.
41 Donald James Wheal, *White City* (2007), pp. 157–8.
42 Peter Hennessy, *Never Again; Britain 1945–1951* (1992), pp. 184, 203.
43 Chick, *Industrial Policy*, p. 78.
44 Christian Wolmar, *Fire and Steam* (2007), pp. 245, 264.
45 John Parker, *Labour Marches On* (Harmondsworth, 1947), p. 69.
46 Kenneth Morgan, *Labour in Power 1945–1951* (Oxford, 1984), pp. 110–27.
47 Julian Greaves, *Industrial Reorganisation and Government Policy in Interwar Britain* (2005), p. xiv.
48 William Ashworth, *The History of the British Coal Industry Vol. V: 1946–1982: The Nationalized Industry* (Oxford, 1986), p. 22.
49 Alec Cairncross, *The British Economy since 1945* (1992), p. 269.
50 Hennessy, *Never Again*, p. 211.
51 Paul Addison, *Now The War Is Over: A Social History of Britain 1945–1951* (1985), pp. 71–4.
52 Junichi Hasegawa, 'The Rise and Fall of Radical Reconstruction in 1940s Britain', *20th Century British History* vol. 10 no. 2 (1999), pp. 137–61.
53 Morgan, *Labour in Power*, pp. 303–5.
54 First Report of the National Parks Commission, PP 1950–1 (26), p. 2.
55 Michael Tichelar, ' "Putting Animals into Politics": The Labour Party and Hunting in the First Half of the Twentieth Century', in *Rural History* vol. 17 (2006), pp. 213–34.
56 John Stevenson, *British Society 1914–1945* (Harmondsworth, 1984), p. 226.
57 *Scotsman*, 22 January 1947, p. 6.
58 David Kynaston, *Austerity Britain* (2007), p. 599.
59 Julia Parker and Catriona Mirrlees, 'Housing' in A. H. Halsey (ed.), *British Social Trends: A Guide to the Changing Social Structure of Britain* (1988 edn), p. 375; Kynaston, p. 596.
60 Webster, *The Health Services*, pp. 133, 135.
61 Ibid., p. 261.
62 Brian Watkin, *The National Health Service: The First Phase 1948–1974 and After* (1978), p. 155.
63 Roderick Floud, 'The Dimensions of Inequality: Height and Weight Variation in Britain, 1700–2000', in *Contemporary British History* vol. 16 no. 3 (2002), pp. 20–1.

64 Paul Addison, *Now The War Is Over: A Social History of Britain 1945–1951* (1995 edn), p. 156.
65 Roy Lowe, *Education in the Post-War Years* (1988), pp. 43, 53; Rodney Lowe, *The Welfare State in Britain since 1945* (1999 edn), p. 213.
66 Lowe, *Education in the Post-War Years*, p. 51.
67 Martin Daunton, *Just Taxes: The Politics of Taxation in Britain 1914–1979* (Cambridge, 2002), pp. 213, 220–1.
68 John Colville, *The Fringes of Power: Downing Street Diaries 1939–1955* (1985), p. 644, diary for 22–3 March 1952.
69 Harold Macmillan, *Tides of Fortune 1945–1955* (1969), p. 491.
70 David Ellwood, *Rebuilding Europe: Western Europe, America and Postwar Reconstruction* (1992), pp. 217–18.
71 TNA CAB/129/94, 'Emergency Powers (Repeal) Bill, Memorandum by the Lord Chancellor', 18 July 1958; Emergency Laws (Re-enactments and Repeals), pp. 1963–4 (143).
72 Peter Hennessy, *Having It So Good: Britain in the Fifties* (2006), pp. 225–6.
73 *Time*, 17 January 1955.
74 Correlli Barnett, *The Lost Victory: British Dreams, British Realities 1945–1950* (1995), pp. 257–64; Correlli Barnett, *The Verdict of Peace: Britain Between Her Yesterday and the Future* (2002), pp. 135–6.
75 William Plowden, *The Motor Car and Politics 1896–1970* (1971), p. 333.
76 Barnett, *The Verdict of Peace*, p. 134.
77 Labour Party Research Department, *Twelve Wasted Years* (1963), pp. 34–7. The figures quoted by the Labour Party were from government sources.
78 Martin Daunton, *Just Taxes: The Politics of Taxation in Britain 1914–1979* (Cambridge, 2002), pp. 236, 243.
79 Cited in Keith Middlemas, *Power, Competition and the State: Vol. I: Britain in Search of Balance 1940–1961* (1986), p. 257.
80 Taylor, *The Trade Union Question*, p. 86.
81 Ibid., p. 87.
82 Webster, *The Health Services*, pp. 204–11, 389–90.
83 Sidney Pollard, *The Development of the British Economy 1914–1980* (1983), p. 277.
84 Lowe, *Education in the Post-War Years*, pp. 89–91.
85 Harriet Jones, ' "This is Magnificent": 300,000 Houses a Year and the Tory Revival after 1945' in *Contemporary British History* vol. 14 no. 1 (2000), p. 109.
86 Pathe News 28 January 1952, issue no. 7.03, 'New Homes to Solve Problem'.
87 Peter Weiler, 'The Conservatives' "Grand Design for Housing" 1951–1964', *Contemporary British History* vol. 14 no. 1 (2000), p. 126.
88 Hopkins, *The New Look*, p. 478; see also Paul Bridges and Rodney Lowe, *Welfare Policy under the Conservatives 1951–1964: A Guide to Documents in the Public Record Office* (1998), pp. 234–5.

2 Fair Shares for All

1 Ina Zweiniger-Bargielowska, *Austerity in Britain: Rationing, Controls and Consumption 1939–1955* (Oxford, 2000), p. 3.
2 Alec Cairncross, *Years of Economic Recovery: British Economic Policy 1945–1951* (1985), p. 29.
3 Mass-Observation file report no. 3073, 'Middle Class: Why' (1947), pp. 54–5.
4 Paul Addison, *Now The War Is Over: A Social History of Britain 1945–1951* (1995 edn), pp. 35–6; TNA PREM 8/506, Report on the Nutrition of the People of Britain in March 1947.

5 Alec Cairncross, *The British Economy since 1945* (1992), p. 66.
6 Pathe News 20 December 1945, issue no. 1173.16, 'Christmas at Peace'.
7 David Kynaston, *Austerity Britain 1945–1951* (2007), pp. 249, 252.
8 Peter Hennessy, *Having It So Good: Britain in the Fifties* (2006), p. 204.
9 J. C. R. Dow, *The Management of the British Economy 1945–1960* (Cambridge, 1970), p. 273.
10 B. C. Roberts, 'Industrial Unrest and the Wage Problem', in *Political Quarterly* vol. 25 no. 2, April 1954.
11 Zweiniger-Bargielowska, *Austerity in Britain*, pp. 56–7.
12 Harry Hopkins, *The New Look: A Social History of the Forties and Fifties in Britain* (1963), p. 414; Lawrence Black, *The Political Culture of the Left in Affluent Britain 1951–1964* (2003), p. 99. The first television commercial broadcast in the UK was for Gibbs SR toothpaste when commercial television was inaugurated, in the London area only, on 22 September 1955.
13 Mary Ingham, *Now We Are Thirty*: Women of the Breakthrough Generation (1981), p. 57.
14 A. H. Halsey and Josephine Webb (eds.), *Twentieth Century British Social Trends* (2000 edn), p. 449.
15 Joe Moran, *Queuing for Beginners: The Story of Daily Life from Breakfast to Bedtime* (2007), pp. 12, 14, 152. I am much indebted to this gem of a book.
16 'The Rise of the Supermarket in Britain' at *http://www.sabe.ex.ac.uk/research/consumer_landscapes/shopping/rise.html*. This is the web-site of a research project on the history of the supermarket, based at the Universities of Surrey and Exeter.
17 Quoted in David Kynaston, *Austerity Britain* (2007), p. 202.
18 Sean Glynn and Alan Booth, *Modern Britain: An Economic and Social History* (1996), p. 243.
19 G. Harrison and F. C. Mitchell, *The Home Market: 1950 Edition* (1950), pp. 41, 58.
20 W. G. Runciman, *A Treatise on Social Theory Vol. III: Applied Social Theory* (Cambridge, 1997), p. 233.
21 James Lansdale Hodson, *The Sea and the Land* (1945), p. 303, diary for 26 February 1945.
22 Ross McKibbin, *Classes and Cultures: England 1918–1951* (Oxford, 1998), p. 118.
23 Correlli Barnett, *The Verdict of Peace: Britain Between Her Yesterday and the Future* (2002 edn), p. 224.
24 Cited in Eric Hopkins, *The Rise and Decline of the English Working Classes 1918–1990* (1991), p. 105.
25 J. L. Hodson, *Thunder in the Heavens* (nd ?1949), p. 17.
26 William Ashworth, *The History of the British Coal Industry Vol. V: 1946–1982: The Nationalized Industry* (Oxford, 1986), pp. 677–8; Robert Bacon, George Sayers Bain, and John Pimlott, 'The Labour Force' in A. H. Halsey (ed.), *Trends in British Society since 1900* (1972), p. 121. The index for average weekly earnings rose from 221.0 in 1947 to 436.2 in 1957.
27 Ashworth, *British Coal Industry Vol. V*, pp. 162–4.
28 G. D. H. Cole, *The Post-War Condition of Britain* (1956), p. 48.
29 Special Enquiry: 'Health for the People'. Broadcast 28 December 1955. BBC Archives.
30 Harry Hopkins, *The New Look: A Social History of the Forties and Fifties in Britain* (1963), p. 114.
31 Alastair J. Reed, *United We Stand: A History of Britain's Trade Unions* (2005), pp. 338–9; Jim Phillips, 'The Post-War Political Consensus and Industrial Unrest in the Docks, 1945–55', in *C20 British History* vol. 6 no. 3 (1995), pp. 303–10.
32 John Bonham, *The Middle Class Vote* (1954), p. 170.

33 Zweiniger-Bargielowska, *Austerity in Britain*, p. 252.
34 Timothy J. Hatton and Roy E. Bailey, 'Seebohm Rowntree and the Postwar Poverty Puzzle', *Economic History Review* LIII, 3 (2000), pp. 517–43.
35 Joe Moran, *Queuing for Beginners* (2007), p. 101.
36 Richard Holt and Tony Mason, *Sport in Britain 1945–2000* (Oxford, 2000), p. 4.
37 Quoted in Harry Hopkins, *The New Look: A Social History of the Forties and Fifties in Britain* (1963), p. 298.
38 Stephen Wagg, '"Time Gentlemen Please": The Decline of Amateur Captaincy in English County Cricket' in *Contemporary British History* vol. 14 no. 2 (2000), pp. 31–59.
39 Hopkins, *The New Look*, p. 354.
40 Wolmar, *Fire and Steam*, p. 282.
41 G. Harrison and F. C. Mitchell, *The Home Market 1950*, p. 70.
42 'Middle-Class: Why?', Mass-Observation file report no. 3073, December 1948, p. 27. This file contains a number of unfinished drafts.
43 John Bonham, *The Middle Class Vote* (1954), pp. 129–31; David Butler, *British General Elections since 1945* (1989), pp. 11–13.
44 Bonham, *The Middle Class Vote*, p. 28, quoting Shinwell's speech of 7 May 1947.
45 *Report of the 46th Annual Conference of the Labour Party* (1947), p. 136, speech of 28 May 1947.
46 *The Economist*, 24 January 1948.
47 *The Listener*, 3 June 1948.
48 *Picture Post*, 4 June 1949.
49 Labour Party, *Let Us Win Through Together*.
50 Lord Beveridge, 'A Letter to Posterity', *The Listener*, 3 January 1952.
51 W. G. Runciman, *A Treatise on Social Theory Volume III: Applied Social Theory* (Cambridge, 1997), p. 203.
52 *The Times*, 27 February 1956.
53 John Burnett, *A History of the Cost of Living* (Harmondsworth, 1969), p. 303.
54 *The Economist*, 28 January 1956, pp. 278–80.
55 W. G. Runciman, *A Treatise on Social Theory Vol. III* (Cambridge, 1997), p. 221 fn 33, citing David Lockwood, *The Blackcoated Worker* (2nd edn, 1989), p. 104 fn 2.
56 Alistair Horne, *Macmillan 1957–1986)* (1991 edn), p. 62.
57 Quoted in David Cannadine, *Class in Britain* (2000), p. 152.
58 Irene Lovelock, unpublished memoirs, ch. 1, pp. 1–2; chs. 2 and 3.
59 Lovelock memoirs, ch. 7, p. 3.
60 The social survey organization founded in 1937 by the social anthropologist Tom Harrisson, the poet Charles Madge, and the documentary film maker Humphrey Jennings.
61 Kynaston, *Austerity Britain*, p. 115.
62 Simon Garfield (ed.), *Our Hidden Lives: The Remarkable Diaries of Post-War Britain* (2005 edn), p. 394, diary entry for 6 May 1947.

3 Victorian Values

1 The only sex education I ever received consisted of a single lesson at King Edward VI School. This was entrusted to the biology master, Mr Owen, a very popular teacher known for some reason as 'Bongo', who spoke with the authority of a young married man. Having drawn for us on the blackboard two rather puzzling diagrams of the male and female anatomy, Bongo explained to us that 'size does not matter,

so, Meakin, you can stop boasting in the showers'. More alarmingly he remarked that having sex was like 'lying on top of a horsehair mattress'.

2 David Kynaston, *Austerity Britain* (2007), p. 311.

3 A. D. Harvey, 'Not Fit For Our Eyes', *Independent on Sunday*, 31 July 1994, pp. 24–5.

4 Denis Gifford, 'Donald McGill' in *Oxford Dictionary of National Biography* (2004) *www. oxforddnb.com/view/article/55528*.

5 Noel Annan, *Our Age: Portrait of a Generation* (1990), p. 133.

6 *The Times*, 15 April 1948, p. 4.

7 J. L. Hodson, *Thunder in the Heavens*, p. 175, diary for 18 December 1948.

8 Kenneth Morgan, *Labour in Power 1945–1951* (Oxford, 1984), p. 62; *The Times*, 27 February 1956, p. 3.

9 Cited in Kynaston, *Austerity Britain*, p. 326.

10 Ceri Peach *et al.*, 'Immigration and Ethnicity' in A. H. Halsey (ed.), *British Social Trends since 1900* (1988), p. 602.

11 Peter Brierley, 'Religion' in A. H. Halsey (ed.), *Twentieth-Century British Social Trends* (2000 edn), p. 663.

12 Richard Hoggart, *The Uses of Literacy* (Harmondsworth 1958), p. 92.

13 Callum G. Brown, *Religion and Society in Twentieth-Century Britain* (2006), pp. 183–5.

14 Michael Young and Peter Willmott, *Family and Kinship in East London* (Harmondsworth, 1962 edn), p. 57.

15 Peter Brierley, 'Religion' in A. H. Halsey (ed.), *British Social Trends since 1900* (1988), p. 540.

16 Callum G. Brown, *Religion and Society in Twentieth Century Britain* (2006), pp. 188–95; Richard Weight, *Patriots: National Identity in Britain 1940–2000*, pp. 222–6.

17 Weeks, *Sex, Politics and Society*, p. 233. Could it be that anxieties about the use of birth-control by Anglicans, and the fear of a higher birth-rate among Roman Catholics, lay behind this pronouncement?

18 Thane, 'Population and the Family', p. 43.

19 Machin, 'British Churches and Social Issues', pp. 358–9.

20 Richard M. Titmuss, 'The Position of Women' in *Essays on 'The Welfare State'* (1963), pp. 91–2.

21 Thane, 'Population and the Family', p. 45.

22 Dolly Smith Wilson, 'A New Look at the Affluent Worker: The Good Working Mother in Post-War Britain', *20th Century British History* vol. 17 no. 2 (2006), p. 209.

23 Jane Lewis, *Women in Britain since 1945* (1992), p. 24.

24 Wilson, 'A New Look', p. 208.

25 Pat Thane, 'Women since 1945' in Paul Johnson (ed.), *Twentieth Century Britain: Economic, Social and Cultural Change* (1994), p. 394.

26 Dolly Smith Wilson, 'Gender: Change and Continuity' in Paul Addison and Harriet Jones (eds.), *A Companion to Contemporary Britain 1939–2000* (2005), pp. 252–3.

27 Roberts, *Women and Families*, p. 30.

28 Ibid., pp. 36–8.

29 Quoted in Elizabeth Wilson, *Only Halfway to Paradise: Women in Postwar Britain 1945–1968* (1980), p. 33.

30 Norman Dennis, Fernando Henriques, and Clifford Slaughter, *Coal Is Our Life: An Analysis of a Yorkshire Mining Community* (1956), p. 182. Featherstone is thinly disguised as 'Ashton' in the book.

31 Dennis, *Coal Is Our Life*, p. 183.

32 TNA WO 277/16 'Morale', War Office monograph by Lt Col. J. H. A. Sparrow (1949), p. 9.

33 Peter Howlett (ed.), *Fighting with Figures* (1995), p. 32.

34 *The People*, 1 January 1956.

35 G. I. T. Machin, 'British Churches and Social Issues 1945–1960', *20th Century British Social History* vol. 7 no. 3 (1996), p. 357.
36 Quoted in Annan, *Our Age*, p. 128.
37 Royal Commission on Marriage and Divorce, paras. 45–6.
38 Ben Pimlott, *The Queen: A Biography of Elizabeth II* (1996), pp. 237–8.
39 John R. Gillis, *For Better, For Worse: British Marriages 1600 to the Present* (1985), pp. 295–7.
40 'The Whitsun Weddings' in Philip Larkin, *Collected Poems* (1988), p. 115. The poem is dated October 1958.
41 *'Little Kinsey': Mass-Observation's Sex Survey of 1949*, in Liz Stanley, *Sex Surveyed 1949–1994: From Mass-Observation's 'Little Kinsey' to the National Survey and the Hite Report* (1995), pp. 132–3.
42 Lesley A. Hall, *Sex, Gender and Social Change in Britain Since 1880* (2000), p. 154.
43 Eustace Chesser *et al.*, *The Sexual, Marital and Family Relationships of the English Woman* (1956), p. 456. The survey was based on lengthy questionnaires distributed through general practitioners and completed by 6,034 women.
44 Hall, *Sex, Gender and Social Change*, p. 159.
45 Lorna Sage, *Bad Blood* (2001 edn), p. 3.
46 Chesser, *Sexual, Marital and Family Relationships*, pp. 397, 417.
47 Ibid., pp. 400, 404.
48 Ibid., p. 531.
49 Pat Thane, 'Population and the Family' in Paul Addison and Harriet Jones (eds.), *A Companion to Contemporary Britain* (2005), p. 50.
50 Stanley, *Sex Surveyed*, pp. 195, 199.
51 *The People*, 28 October 1956.
52 Geoffrey Gorer, *Exploring English Character* (1955), p. 86.
53 Peter Howlett, *Fighting with Figures* (1995), Tables 2.14 and 2.15.
54 *The Scotsman*, 18 January 1944.
55 Wilson, 'A New Look', p. 210.
56 Ibid., p. 212.
57 Paul Rock and Stanley Cohen, 'The Teddy Boy' in Vernon Bogdanor and Robert Skidelsky (eds.), *The Age of Affluence* (1970), pp. 294, 301, 304–5.
58 See below, p. 243.
59 Jon Savage, *England's Dreaming: Sex Pistols and Punk Rock* (1991), p. 50.
60 T. R. Fyvel, *The Insecure Offenders* (1961), p. 55.
61 Leslie T. Wilkins, *Delinquent Generations* (1958), p. 11. Brian Francis, Maria Giovanna Ranalli, and Keith Soothill, 'Delinquent generations: a statistical modelling approach to a classic criminology debate'.
62 Lord Boothby, *My Yesterday, Your Tomorrow* (1962), p. 40.
63 Ibid., pp. 239–40.
64 Annan, *Our Age*, p. 120.
65 Weeks, *Sex, Politics and Society*, p. 241.
66 Annan, *Our Age*, p. 138.
67 Anthony Howard, *RAB: The Life of R.A.Butler* (1988 edn), pp. 264–5.
68 Machin, 'British Churches and Social Issues', p. 363.
69 Roy Jenkins, *The Labour Case* (Harmondsworth, 1959), p. 140.

4 When British Was Best

1 The phrase 'Celtic fringe' derives from a speech by the Conservative Prime Minister Lord Salisbury in December 1890, when he spoke of 'the Celtic edges of both islands' and complained that they were over-represented compared to the rest of the

'Anglo-Saxon' population. See Colin Kidd, 'Race, Empire and the Limits of Nineteenth Century Scottish Nationalism' in *Historical Journal* vol. 46 no. 4 (2003), pp. 874–5.

2 Quoted in Richard Weight, *Patriots: National Identity in Britain 1940–2000* (2002), p. 10.

3 T. M. Devine, 'In Bed with an Elephant: Almost Three Hundred Years of the Anglo-Scottish Union', *Scottish Affairs* no. 57 (Autumn 2006), pp. 1–18.

4 Weight, *Patriots*, p. 414.

5 T. M. Devine, 'The Break-up of Britain? Scotland and the End of Empire', *Transactions of the Royal Historical Society*, 6th series vol. XVI, p. 171.

6 Richard Holt, *Sport and the British: A Modern History* (Oxford 1992 edn), pp. 258–9.

7 House of Commons Debates vol. 403, col. 2337, 17 October 1944.

8 Richard Holt, *Sport and the British: A Modern History* (Oxford, 1992 edn), p. 250.

9 John Davies, *A History of Wales* (2007 edn), p. 603.

10 On the initiative of then Secretary of State for Scotland, Michael Forsyth, the Stone was returned to Scotland in 1996 and installed in Edinburgh Castle on St Andrew's Day.

11 *Time* magazine, 20 December 1954.

12 Trevor Herbert and Gareth Elwyn Jones, *Post-War Wales* (1995), p. 34.

13 Stephen Broadberry, 'Employment and Unemployment' in Roderick Flood and Donald McCloskey, *The Economic History of Britain since 1700 Vol. 3: 1939–1992* (Cambridge, 1994), p. 201, Table 7.1.

14 Quoted in Jeremy Paxman, *The English: Portrait of a People* (1999 edn), p. 196.

15 Angus Calder, *The Myth of the Blitz* (1991), p. 196.

16 Robert J. Whybrow, *Britain speaks out 1937–87* (1989), pp. 39, 45, 55.

17 Geoffrey Gorer, *Exploring English Character* (1955), pp. 13, 17–22.

18 Cited in David Kynaston, *Austerity Britain 1945–1951* (2007), p. 347.

19 Andrew Rosen, *The Transformation of British Life 1950–2000* (2003), p. 19.

20 Edward Shils and Michael Young, 'The Meaning of the Coronation', *Sociological Review, N.S.3* (1953), pp. 67, 76.

21 Pathé News, 2 September 1948, 'The Clyde demands more steel'. British Pathé, *http://www.britishpath.com*.

22 Pathé News, 1 November 1948, 'The World Buys British Cars'.

23 Gillian Bardsley, 'Sir Alexander Constantine Issigonis', *Oxford Dictionary of National Biography* online edn; Peter Pagnamenta and Richard Overy, *All Our Working Lives* (1984), pp. 229–30.

24 David Bowen, 'Bigger is better for Britain's battered industry', *Independent on Sunday* 26 July 1992.

25 Ceri Peach, Vaughan Robinson, Julia Maxted, and Judith Chance, 'Immigration and Ethnicity' in A. H. Halsey (ed), *British Social Trends since 1900* (1988 edn), p. 571 table 14.4, p. 579 table 14.9.

26 Enda Delaney, *Demography, State and Society: Irish Migration to Britain 1921–1971* (Liverpool, 2000), pp. 162–4; Peach *et al.*, 'Immigration', p. 571.

27 Enda Delaney, *The Irish in Post-War Britain* (Oxford, 2007), p. 53. The rest of this paragraph is based on pp. 45–70.

28 Delaney, *The Irish*, p. 63.

29 Ibid., pp. 88–90.

30 Delaney *Demography, State and Society*, p. 193.

31 Peach *et al.*, 'Immigration', p. 575.

32 Delaney *Demography, State and Society*, p. 209, citing PRO, CAB 129/77, CP 102, 3 August 1955.

33 Ian Angus and Sonia Orwell (eds.), *The Collected Essays, Journalism and Letters of George Orwell Vol. IV: In Front of Your Nose 1945–1950* (Harmondsworth, 1970), pp. 276–7, 315.

34 William Ashworth, *The History of the British Coal Industry Vol. V: 1946–1982: The Nationalized Industry* (Oxford, 1986), pp. 152–3, 164–5.

35 Randall Hansen, 'The Kenyan Asians, British Politics, and the Commonwealth Immigrants Act, 1968', *The Historical Journal* vol. 42 no. 3 (1999), pp. 815–16.

36 Peach *et al.*, 'Immigration', pp. 594–7.

37 Ian R. G. Spencer, *British Immigration Policy Since 1939: The Making of Multi-Racial Britain* (1997), p. 22.

38 Spencer, *British Immigration Policy*, pp. 21–8.

39 Ibid., pp. 39–40.

40 Nicholas Deakin, *Colour, Citizenship and British Society* (1970), pp. 31–4.

41 *Manchester Guardian*, 24 June 1948; Peter Hennessy, *Never Again: Britain 1945–1951* (1992), p. 441.

42 *Manchester Guardian*, 24 June 1948.

43 Quoted in Wendy Webster, *Imagining Home: Gender, 'Race' and National Identity 1945–1964* (1998), p. 25.

44 Ben Pimlott, *Hugh Dalton* (1985), p. 577.

45 Hennessy, *Never Again*, p. 442; Andrew Roberts, *Eminent Churchillians* (1994), p. 217.

46 Peach *et al.*, 'Immigration', p. 590.

47 Harry Hopkins, *The New Look: A Social History of the Forties and Fifties in Britain* (1963), p. 465.

48 Peach *et al.*, 'Immigration', p. 591.

49 Mike Phillips and Trevor Phillips, *Windrush: The Irresistible Rise of Multiracial Britain* (1998), pp. 106, 163.

50 Phillips and Phillips, *Windrush*, pp. 112–13.

51 Ibid., pp. 116–17; Anthony H. Richmond, *The Colour Problem* (Harmondsworth, 1961 edn), p. 245.

52 Richmond, *The Colour Problem*, pp. 249–50, Phillips and Phillips, *Windrush*, pp. 136–7.

53 Robert Pearce, 'Cyril Osborne', *Oxford Dictionary of National Biography*.

54 Andrew Roberts, *Eminent Churchillians* (1994), p. 225.

55 Kenan Malik, 'A miracle no prince can perform', *Independent*, 27 June 1994, p. 14.

56 Harry Hopkins, *The New Look*, p. 466.

57 Anna Coote and Mike Phillips, 'The Quango as referee', *New Statesman*, 13 July 1979, p. 50.

58 George Orwell, 'The Lion and the Unicorn' (1941) in *The Collected Essays, Journalism and Letters of George Orwell Vol. II: My Country Right or Left 1940–1943* (Harmondsworth, 1970), p. 80; Richmond, *The Colour Problem*, p. 244.

59 John M. MacKenzie, *Propaganda and Empire: The Manipulation of British Public Opinion 1880–1960* (1984), p. 257.

60 George MacDonald Fraser, *Quartered Safe Out Here: A Recollection of the War in Burma with a new Epilogue: Fifty Years on* (2000 edn), pp. 264–5.

61 Henry Pelling, *Britain and the Second World War* (1970), p. 326.

5 Managing the New Britain

1 Anthony Sampson, *Anatomy of Britain* (1962), p. 637.

2 David Cannadine, *The Decline and Fall of the British Aristocracy* (1990), p. 666.

3 The last National Serviceman to be discharged was Lieutenant Richard Vaughan of the Royal Army Pay Corps, who was demobbed on 13 May 1963. See Trevor Royle, *The Best Years of their Lives: The National Service Experience 1945–1963* (1986), p. 224.

4 Alan Budd, *The Politics of Economic Planning* (1978), pp. 91–9.
5 Stewart Wood, 'Why "Indicative Planning" Failed: British Industry and the Formation of the National Economic Development Council (1960–64)', *C20 British History* vol. 2 no. 4 (2000), pp. 431–59.
6 John Ramsden, *The Winds of Change: Macmillan to Heath 1957–1975* (1996), p. 10.
7 TNA PREM 11/3930, 'Transcript of the Prime Minister's remarks to the Cabinet on May 28th, 1962'. I am grateful to Professor Peter Hennessy for this reference.
8 *Guardian*, 2 November 1959.
9 Peter Hall, 'Sir Colin Douglas Buchanan' in *Oxford Dictionary of National Biography*, online edn May 2006; Joe Moran, *Queuing for Beginners* (2007), pp. 131–3.
10 Deyan Sudjic, 'A Brum less humdrum', *Observer*, 30 March 2003.
11 Obituary in the *Newcastle Journal*, 28 July 1993, cited in Norman McCord, 'T. Dan Smith' in *Oxford Dictionary of National Biography* (2004).
12 McCord, 'T. Dan Smith'; Owen Luder, 'John Garlick Llewellyn Poulson', *Oxford Dictionary of National Biography* (2004).
13 Bruce Wood, 'Urbanisation and Local Government' in A. H. Halsey (ed.), *British Social Trends* (1988 edn), p. 331.
14 Christian Wolmar, *Fire and Steam: A New History of the Railways in Britain* (2007), pp. 280–2.
15 Ann Pimlott Baker, 'Richard Beeching' in *Oxford Dictionary of National Biography* (2004); Wolmar, *Fire and Steam*, pp. 284–5.
16 Pimlott, *Harold Wilson*, p. 304.
17 Callaghan, 'Industrial Militancy', p. 402.
18 Cmnd 3164, *Decimal Currency in the United Kingdom*, PP 1966–7, December 1966; Whybrow, *Britain speaks out*, p. 96.
19 Phillip Whitehead, *The Writing on the Wall* (1985), p. 53.
20 Ion Trewin (ed.), *The Hugo Young Papers: Thirty Years of British Politics – Off the Record* (2008), p. 12, lunch with John Biffen 24 March 1970.
21 Whitehead, *The Writing on the Wall*, p. 72.
22 Taylor, *The Trade Union Question*, p. 198.
23 Ibid., pp. 190–202; Whitehead, *Writing on the Wall*, pp. 70–80; Ramsden, *Winds of Change*, pp. 330–4.
24 Ramsden, *Winds of Change*, p. 352.
25 Quoted in Taylor, *The Trade Union Question*, p. 22.
26 Douglas Jay, *Sterling* (Oxford, 1986), pp. 147–52.
27 Ibid., pp. 155–6.
28 *The Hugo Young Papers*, p. 79, interview with William Armstrong, 5 February 1976.
29 Rodney Lowe, *The Welfare State in Britain since 1945* (1999 edn), p. 210.
30 A. H. Halsey, 'Schools' in *British Social Trends since 1900* (1988 edn), p. 254 and see Tables 6.13 and 6.14, pp. 250–1.
31 Nicholas Timmins, *The Five Giants: A Biography of the Welfare State* (1995), p. 239.
32 Celia Dodd, 'Holland Park: what's school got to do with it?', *Independent*, 9 June 1993.
33 Lowe, *Welfare State*, p. 241.
34 Susan Crosland, *Tony Crosland* (1983 edn), p. 148. Education in Scotland was the responsibility of the Scottish Office.
35 George Smith, 'Schools' in A. H. Halsey and Josephine Webb (eds.), *Twentieth-Century British Social Trends* (2000 edn), p. 199; John Vincent, 'The Thatcher Governments' in Peter Hennessy and Anthony Seldon (eds.), *Ruling Performance: British Governments from Attlee to Thatcher* (Oxford, 1987), pp. 276–7.
36 *New Statesman*, 29 August 1975.

37 Roy Lowe, *Schooling and Social Change 1964–1990* (1997), p. 91.
38 Roy Lowe, *Education in the Post-War Years: A Social History* (1988), p. 93.
39 Timmins, *The Five Giants*, p. 200.
40 This paragraph is based on Robert Anderson, *British Universities Past and Present* (2006), pp. 147–9. His book is a superb study of the changing roles and concepts of British universities since the eighteenth century.
41 Halsey, *British Social Trends since 1900* (1988 edn), pp. 274–7.
42 Ben Pimlott, *Harold Wilson* (1992), p. 513.
43 Pimlott, *Harold Wilson*, pp. 513–15; W. A. C. Stewart, *Higher Education in Postwar Britain* (1989), pp. 111–14.
44 Margaret Thatcher, *The Path to Power* (1995), p. 179.
45 Stewart, *Higher Education in Postwar Britain*, p. 118.
46 Paul Bridgen and Rodney Lowe, *Welfare Policy under the Conservatives 1951–1964* (1998), p. 216.
47 Lynsey Hanley, *Estates: An Intimate History* (2007), p. 121.
48 Timmins, *The Five Giants*, p. 187.
49 On Ronan Point and tower blocks in general see Hanley, *Estates*, pp. 105–22.
50 ITN Late Evening News 17 April 1963, News Film Online.
51 Lowe, *The Welfare State*, p. 191.

6 Great Expectations

1 Alistair Horne, *Macmillan 1957–1986* (1991 edn), p. 64.
2 Christopher M. Law, 'Employment and Industrial Structure' in James Obelkevich and Peter Catterall (eds.), *Understanding Post-War British Society* (1994), p. 93.
3 Taylor, *The Fifth Estate*, p. 32.
4 Sean Glynn and Alan Booth, *Modern Britain: An Economic and Social History* (1996), p. 251.
5 Peter Pagnamenta and Richard Overy, *All Our Working Lives* (1984), p. 144.
6 Ibid., p. 44.
7 Geoffrey Owen, *From Empire to Europe: The Decline and Revival of British Industry Since the Second World War* (2000), p. 230.
8 *Daily Telegraph*, 22 February 2003.
9 The Sainsbury Archive/Themes/Products/Product Range, Museum of Docklands web-site.
10 John K. Walton, *The British Seaside: Holidays and Resorts in the Twentieth Century* (2000), pp. 87–91.
11 This section on package holidays is based on a supplement to *The Economist*, 12 January 1974, pp. 59–70.
12 James Obelkevich, 'Consumption' in James Obelkevich and Peter Catterall (eds.), *Understanding Post-War British Society* (1994), p. 148.
13 Lawrence Black, *The Political Culture of the Left in Affluent Britain 1951–1964: Old Labour, New Britain?* (Basingstoke, 2003), p. 13.
14 Ibid., p. 75.
15 *The Times*, 31 October 1958, p. 7; 26 May 1962, p. 6; 15 November 1963, p. 6; 7 January 1971, p. 2.
16 Matthew Hilton, 'The Death of a Consumer Society' in *Transactions of the Royal Historical Society*, 6th series, XVIII (2008), p. 217.
17 Matthew Hilton, 'Michael Young and the Consumer Movement' in *Contemporary British History* vol. 19 no. 3 (2005), pp. 311–19.

18 John Hillaby, 'Total War on the Land', *Guardian*, 22 November 1960, p. 8.
19 Shirley Lewis, 'Whole Food and Nothing but Whole Food', *Guardian*, 7 November 1967, p. 6.
20 *Observer*, 22 June 1975.
21 W. C. Stevenson, letter to the editor, *Guardian*, 4 February 1975, p. 12. Stevenson was the landlord of the Laughing Cavalier at Stalybridge.
22 John H. Goldthorpe, David Lockwood, Frank Bechhofer, and Jennifer Platt, *The Affluent Worker in the Class Structure* (Cambridge, 1971), p. 22.
23 Ronald Pullen, 'Credit Cards: Discovering What the Future Holds', *The Times*, 8 December 1977, p. 23; for the launch of Barclaycard see *The Times*, 9 May 1966, p. 16.
24 *Social Trends 10* (1980), p. 35.
25 Trevor Blackwell and Jeremy Seabrook, *A World Still to Win: The Reconstruction of the Post-War Working Class* (1985), p. 83.
26 Quoted in John Hill, *Sex, Class and Realism: British Cinema 1956–63*, p. 11.
27 Mark Abrams, *The Teenage Consumer* (1959), p. 13.
28 John Savage, *Teenage: the Creation of Youth Culture* (2007), p. 465.
29 Richard West, 'Wise Old Morecambe', *New Statesman*, 8 August 1975, p. 168.
30 *The Economist* 16 May 1959, p. 601.
31 Michael Shanks, *The Stagnant Society: A Warning* (Harmondsworth, 1961), p. 67.
32 Ferdinand Zweig, *The Worker in an Affluent Society* (Heinemann, 1961), p. ix.
33 *The Times*, 10 October 1959; *Daily Telegraph*, 19 November 1959.
34 John H. Goldthorpe, David Lockwood, Frank Bechhofer, and Jennifer Platt, *The Affluent Worker: Political Attitudes and Behaviour* (Cambridge, 1971), p. 13.
35 Goldthorpe *et al.*, *The Affluent Worker in the Class Structure*, p. 179.
36 W. G. Runciman, *Relative Deprivation and Social Justice* (Harmondsworth, 1972), p. 336.
37 Goldthorpe *et al.*, *The Affluent Worker in the Class Structure*, p. 147.
38 John H. Goldthorpe, David Lockwood, Frank Bechhofer, and Jennifer Platt, *The Affluent Worker: Industrial Attitudes and Behaviour* (Cambridge, 1971), p. 84.
39 Samuel H. Beer, *Britain Against Itself* (1982), p. 81.
40 Ruth Glass, *London, Aspects of Change* (1964), p. xviii.
41 Joe Moran, 'The New Gentrifiers', *New Statesman*, 18 October 2007.
42 House of Commons Debates vol 875, 19 June 1974, col 628.
43 Richard Hoggart, *The Uses of Literacy* (Harmondsworth, 1958); Raymond Williams, *Culture and Society: 1780–1950* (Harmondsworth, 1958), *The Long Revolution* (Harmondsworth, 1965).
44 Richard Titmuss, 'The Social Division of Welfare' in *Essays on 'the Welfare State'* (1963 edition), pp. 34–55.
45 Brian Abel-Smith and Peter Townsend, *The Poor and the Poorest* (1965).
46 J. E. Floud, A. H. Halsey, and F. M. Martin, *Social Class and Educational Opportunity* (1956).
47 Stuart Laing, *Representations of Working Class Life 1957–1964* (1986), pp. 91, 185.
48 *The Complete Beyond The Fringe*, CD 7243 8 54045 2 8 (1996) Disc Two.
49 J. McIlroy, 'Notes on the Communist Party and Industrial Policy' in J. McIlroy, N. Fishman, and A. Campbell (eds.), *British Trade Unions and Industrial Politics vol 2: The High Tide of Trade Unionism 1964–1979* (Aldershot, 1999), p. 59, quoted in John Callaghan, 'Industrial Militancy 1945–79: The Failure of the British Road to Socialism?' in *20th Century British History*, 15, 4 (2004), p. 403.
50 Henry Phelps Brown, *The Origins of Trade Union Power* (Oxford, 1986), p. 164.
51 Goldthorpe *et al.*, *The Affluent Worker: Industrial Attitudes*, p. 177.
52 Ibid., p. 176.
53 Taylor, *The Trade Union Question*, pp. 151–4.

54 Quoted in ibid., p. 1.
55 Taylor, *The Fifth Estate*, p. 40.
56 Chris Wrigley, 'Trade Unions, Government and the Economy' in Terry Gourvish and Alan O'Day (eds.), *Britain since 1945* (1991), p. 73.

7 The Liberal Hour

1 House of Commons Debates vol. 755 col. 819, 1 December 1967. Stevas was opening a debate on the liberties of the subject.
2 *The Times*, 26 August 1967, p. 10; 25 September 1967 p. 2; 10 May 1968, p. 19. Corporal punishment in state schools was outlawed in 1986, in independent schools in 1999.
3 Colin Airey, 'Social and Moral Values' in Roger Jowell and Colin Airey, *British Social Attitudes: The 1984 report* (1984), p. 137.
4 D. A. Coleman, 'Population' in A. H. Halsey (ed.), *British Social Trends since 1900* (1988), pp. 72–3. For women the most common age of marriage was between 20 and 24. The marriage rate for this age-group reached a peak of 261.6 per cent in 1956–60, but the rates for 1961–5 and 1966–70 were only fractionally lower at 260.2 and 260.9. After this the rate fell sharply.
5 See Ch. 2.
6 Asa Briggs, *A Social History of England* (1983), p. 306.
7 Christie Davies, *Permissive Britain: Social Change in the Sixties and Seventies* (1975), p. 3.
8 Ibid., pp. 39–40.
9 C. A. R. Crosland, *The Future of Socialism* (1956), p. 522.
10 Lesley A. Hall, *Sex, Gender and Social Change in Britain since 1880* (2000), p. 25.
11 Ibid., p. 168.
12 Ibid., pp. 169–70.
13 Ann Pimlott Baker, 'John Trevelyan', *Oxford Dictionary of National Biography* (2004).
14 Quoted in David Hendy, 'Bad Language and BBC Radio Four' in *20th Century British History* vol. 17 no. 1 (2006), p. 77.
15 Colin Shaw, 'Hugh Carleton Greene', *Oxford Dictionary of National Biography* (2004).
16 Philip Whitehead, *The Writing on the Wall* (1985), p. 317.
17 Alan Travis, 'How Two Dames Saved Oh! Calcutta!', *Guardian*, 23 December 2000.
18 Tim Newburn, *Permission and Regulation: Laws and Morals in Post-War Britain* (1992), p. 62.
19 House of Lords Debates vol. 266, col. 644, 25 May 1965; vol. 257, col. 342, 21 June 1965. Boothby told the story, which may be too good to be true, in a filmed interview with Bernard Braden. *Then and Now: Lord Boothby* (1967), BFI In View, British Film Institute.
20 Richard Crossman, *The Diaries of a Cabinet Minister Vol. II: Lord President of the Council and Leader of the House of Commons 1966–68* (1976), p. 407, diary for 3 July 1967.
21 Jeffrey Weeks, *Sex, Politics and Society* (1981), p. 275.
22 Alan Travis, 'Navy Chiefs Ordered Secret Purge of Gay Sailors', *Guardian*, 31 October 2002; Michael Smith, 'Sacking all Gay Sailors would have Scuppered the Fleet', *Daily Telegraph*, 31 October 2002. Homosexuality was to remain banned in the armed forces until 2000.
23 Weeks, *Sex, Politics and Society*, p. 285; *The Times*, 19 October 1973, p. 7.
24 Mark Garnett and Richard Weight, *Modern British History: The Essential A–Z Guide* (2004), pp. 162–3.
25 Peter Thompson, 'Labour's "Gannex Conscience?" Politics and popular attitudes in the "permissive society" ', in R. Coopey, S. Fielding, and N. Tiratsoo, *The Wilson Governments 1964–1970* (1993), p. 137.

26 John Davis, 'The London Drug Scene and the Making of Drug Policy', *20th Century British History* vol. 17 no. 1 (2006), p. 30. The rest of this paragraph is based mainly on this article.

27 Christie Davies, *Permissive Britain: Social Change in the Sixties and Seventies* (1975), p. 168.

28 Newburn, *Permission and Regulation*, p. 144.

29 Davies, *Permissive Britain*, pp. 21–7.

30 Weeks, *Sex, Politics and Society*, p. 275.

31 Jenny Chapman Robinson, *Political Implications of Attitudes Towards Abortion 1967–1983* (Glasgow, 1985), p. 8.

32 Lesley A. Hall, *Sex, Gender and Social Change in Britain since 1880* (2000), p. 175.

33 Hall, *Sex, Gender*, pp. 175–6.

34 Gorer, *Sex and Marriage*, p. 62.

35 Ibid., pp. 74–6.

36 Lewis, *Women in Britain*, p. 47.

37 Eustace Chesser, *Is Chastity Outmoded?* (1960), p. 77.

38 Hall, *Sex, Gender*, pp. 171–2.

39 Michael Schofield, *The Sexual Behaviour of Young People* (Harmondsworth, 1968), pp. 32–3, 46, 109, 111.

40 Lewis, *Women in Britain*, p. 48.

41 Hall, *Sex, Gender*, p. 170.

42 *Guardian*, 11 October 1967.

43 Thompson, 'Popular Attitudes', p. 142.

44 Roy Lowe, *Schooling and Social Change 1964–1990* (1997), pp. 7–8.

45 Davies, *Permissive Britain*, pp. 65–6.

46 Gorer, *Sex and Marriage*, p. 214.

47 Cited in Thompson, 'Popular Attitudes', p. 142.

48 D. A. Coleman, 'Population' in A. H. Halsey (ed.), *British Social Trends since 1900* (1988 edn), p. 80; Jane Lewis, *Women in Britain since 1945* (1992), p. 45.

49 *Guardian*, 26 November 1967.

50 Edmund Leach, 'The cereal packet norm', *Guardian*, 29 January 1968.

51 *The Times*, 24 July 1967, p. 5.

52 Phillip Whitehead, *The Writing on the Wall: Britain in the Seventies* (1985), p. 310.

53 Anna Coote and Beatrix Campbell, *Sweet Freedom: The Struggle for Women's Liberation* (1987 edn), p. 5.

54 On the origins of the women's movement see Coote and Campbell, *Sweet Freedom*, pp. 1–16.

55 Jeffrey Weeks, *Sex, Politics and Society: The Regulation of Sexuality since 1800* (1981), p. 285.

56 Hall, *Sex, Gender*, p. 180.

57 William Plowden, *The Motor Car and Politics 1896–1970* (1971), pp. 456–7, 356–7.

58 Peter Catterall (ed.), *The Macmillan Diaries: The Cabinet Years 1950–1957* (2003), p. 556, entry for 3 May 1956.

59 Virginia Berridge, 'Post-War Smoking Policy in the UK and the Redefinition of Public Health', *C20 British History* vol. 14 no. 1 (2003), pp. 70–3.

8 National Identities

1 *The Economist*, 27 August 1966 p. 821.

2 T. M. Devine, *The Scottish Nation 1700–2000* (2000 edn), p. 580.

3 David Butler and Gareth Butler, *British Political Facts 1900–1994* (1994), pp. 332–3.

4 David Torrance, *'We in Scotland': Thatcherism in a Cold Climate* (2009), p. 49.

5 Kenneth O. Morgan, *Rebirth of a Nation: Wales 1880–1980* (Oxford, 1982 edn), p. 359.

6 Ibid., p. 384.

7 Devine, *The Scottish Nation*, p. 585.

8 Heffer, *Enoch Powell*, pp. 336–8.

9 Quoted in Richard Weight, *Patriots: National Identity in Britain 1940–2000* (2002), p. 453.

10 Hugo Young, *This Blessed Plot: Britain and Europe from Churchill to Blair* (1999 edition), p. 287. Richard Weight argues that popular hostility to the Common Market was grounded in deep-rooted aspects of British national identity but the evidence he presents seems to me inconclusive. See Weight, *Patriots*, pp. 332–8.

11 *Hugo Young Papers*, p. 11. Lunch with John Biffen, 24 March 1970.

12 Ceri Peach, Vaughan Robinson, Julia Maxted, and Judith Chance, 'Immigration and Ethnicity' in A. H. Halsey, *British Social Trends since 1900* (1988 edn), pp. 570–6.

13 David Butler and Gareth Butler, *British Political Facts 1900–1994* (1994), p. 328.

14 W. W. Daniel, *Racial Discrimination in England* (Harmondsworth, 1968), p. 9.

15 PP 1969–70 (309), Report of the Race Relations Board for 1969–70, p. 71.

16 PP 1966–7 (437), p. 15.

17 Mike Phillips and Trevor Phillips, *Windrush: The Irresistible Rise of Multi-Racial Britain* (1998), pp. 149–50, 209–10.

18 Humayun Ansari, *'The Infidel Within': Muslims in Britain since 1800* (2004), pp. 15, 139, 350–1.

19 Nicholas Deakin, *Colour, Citizenship and British Society* (1970), pp. 293–4, 296.

20 Daniel, *Racial Discrimination*, p. 47.

21 Ibid., pp. 59, 63, 65, 76.

22 Ibid., pp. 88–91.

23 Ibid., p. 155.

24 Ibid., p. 152.

25 Ibid., p. 196.

26 Deakin, *Colour, Citizenship and British Society*, p. 319.

27 Phillips and Phillips, *Windrush*, p. 315.

28 Ibid., p. 276.

29 *The Economist*, 6 September 1958, p. 723.

30 *The Times*, 4 September 1958, p. 10.

31 Whybrow, *Britain speaks out 1937–1987*.

32 Ian R. G. Spencer, *British Immigration Policy since 1939: The Making of Multi-Racial Britain* (1997), pp. 125–9.

33 Dennis Dean, 'The Race Relations Policy of the First Wilson Government', *20C British History* vol. 11 no. 3 (2000), pp. 263–5.

34 Dean, 'Race Relations Policy', pp. 267, 268–70.

35 Spencer, *British Immigration Policy*, p. 136.

36 PP 1964–5 Cmnd 2739, para. 32.

37 PP 1966–7 (437), Report of the Race Relations Board for 1966–7, p. 23.

38 Roy Jenkins, *A Life at the Centre* (1992 edn), p. 189. It was at the launch of the Race Relations Board that Jenkins set out the benchmark definition of multiculturalism already quoted in this chapter.

39 'Black and White Minstrel Show (1958–78)' BFI Screenonline, *www.screenonline.org.uk/tv/id/535195*, accessed 31.10.08.

40 Randall Hansen, 'The Kenyan Asians, British Politics, and the Commonwealth Immigrants Act, 1968', *The Historical Journal* vol. 42 no. 3 (1999), p. 831.

41 Ibid., p. 817. This paragraph is based on Hansen's article.
42 Simon Heffer, *Like the Roman: The Life of Enoch Powell* (1999 edition), p. 444.
43 Phillips and Phillips, *Windrush*, p. 249.
44 John Campbell, *Edward Heath: A Biography* (1993), p. 243.
45 Phillips and Phillips, *Windrush*, p. 247.
46 *The Times*, 22 April 1968, p. 11.
47 Patrick Cosgrave, *The Lives of Enoch Powell* (1989), pp. 252–3.
48 Ibid., pp. 252–3; Campbell, *Edward Heath*, p. 244.
49 Richard Crossman, *The Diaries of a Cabinet Minister Vol. 3: Secretary of State for Social Services* (1977), pp. 29–30, diary for 27 April 1968.
50 Campbell, *Heath*, p. 245.
51 Martin Walker, *The National Front* (1977), pp. 112–13.
52 Panikos Panayi, 'Immigration, Multiculturalism and Racism' in Francesca Carnevali and Julie-Marie Strange (eds.), *20th Century Britain* (2007), p. 249.
53 Phillip Whitehead, *The Writing on the Wall* (1985), p. 223.
54 Humayun Ansari, *'The Infidel Within': Muslims in Britain since 1800* (2004), p. 208.
55 This was the thesis of the book *Dark Strangers* (1959), a study of West Indian settlers in Brixton by the social anthropologist Sheila Patterson, who described herself as a 'Conservative with a capital C'. See also Michael Banton, 'Sheila Patterson' in *Oxford Dictionary of National Biography* (2004).
56 Roy Lowe, *Schooling and Social Change 1964–1990* (1997), p. 119.
57 Phillips and Phillips, *Windrush*, p. 284.
58 Ansari, *'The Infidel Within'*, p. 209.
59 House of Lords Debates vol. 320, 24 June 1971, col. 1060.
60 Ansari, *'The Infidel Within'*, p. 312.

9 Mrs Thatcher's Revolution

1 Rodney Lowe, *The Welfare State in Britain since 1945* (1999 edn), p. 309.
2 In a word search of *The Economist* the term first appears on 15 August 1970 in a context suggesting that its meaning was already well understood.
3 Tony Judt, *Postwar: A History of Europe since 1945* (2007 edn), p. 454. This paragraph is based on the discussion of the period in ch. 14 of the book.
4 Eric Hobsbawm, *Age of Extremes: The Short Twentieth Century 1914–1991* (1995 edn), p. 408.
5 Robert Taylor, *The Trade Union Question in British Politics: Government and Unions since 1945* (1993), p. 226.
6 Denis Healey, *The Time of My Life* (1990 edn), p. 369.
7 Taylor, *The Trade Union Question*, pp. 234–5.
8 Phillip Whitehead, *The Writing on the Wall* (1985), p. 149.
9 Ibid., p. 121.
10 Ibid., pp. 131–2.
11 M. Artis, D. Cobham, and M. Wickham-Jones, 'Social Democracy in Hard Times: The Economic Record of the Labour Government 1974–1979', *C20 British History* vol. 3 no. 1 (1992), pp. 44–5.
12 Taylor, *The Trade Union Question*, p. 237.
13 Artis, Cobham, and Wickham-Jones, 'Social Democracy', p. 46.
14 Richard Toye, 'The New Commanding Height: Labour Party Policy on North Sea Oil and Gas, 1964–74', *Contemporary British History*, vol. 16, no. 1 (2002), p. 93.
15 *The Economist*, 26 July 1975, Survey p. 5. The author of the article was Andrew Neil.
16 Taylor, *The Trade Union Question*, p. 248.

17 Geoffrey Owen, *From Empire to Europe: The Decline and Revival of British Industry since the Second World War* (2000 edn), pp. 108–11.
18 Ibid., p. 240; Whitehead, *Writing on the Wall*, pp. 264–5.
19 Ibid., p. 208.
20 *Social Trends No. 10: 1980 Edn* (1979), Chart 6.17, p. 146.
21 Taylor, *The Trade Union Question*, pp. 245–6.
22 Whitehead, *Writing on the Wall*, p. 282.
23 Ibid., p. 283.
24 Taylor, *The Trade Union Question*, p. 257.
25 Peter Hennessy, *The Prime Minister: The Office and its Holders since 1945* (2001 edn), pp. 379–80.
26 John Vincent, 'The Thatcher Governments 1979–1987' in Peter Hennessy and Anthony Seldon (eds.), *Ruling Performance: British Governments from Attlee to Thatcher* (Oxford, 1987), p. 278.
27 Sir Keith Joseph, 'Notes Towards the Definition of Policy', Conservative Research Department discussion paper, 4 April 1975, p. 1, Thatcher MSS (2/6/1/156), Thatcher Foundation website. The reference to choosing the path of consensus after the war appears to coincide with my own interpretation of the consequences of the war in *The Road to 1945*, which was published in October 1975.
28 Vincent, 'The Thatcher Governments', p. 274.
29 Hugo Young, *One of Us* (1989), p. 16.
30 *The Hugo Young Papers*, pp. 266–7, interview with Douglas Hurd, 27 October 1987.
31 Richard Vinen, *Thatcher's Britain: The Politics and Social Upheaval of the 1980s*, p. 290.
32 Ibid., p. 66.
33 Quoted in John Campbell, *Margaret Thatcher Vol. II: The Iron Lady* (2004 edn), p. 182.
34 Quoted in Campbell, *Margaret Thatcher Vol. II*, p. 530.
35 Margaret Thatcher, *The Downing Street Years* (1995 edn), p. 104.
36 Alec Cairncross, *The British Economy since 1945* (Oxford, 1992), p. 239.
37 Quoted in Samuel Brittan, 'The Thatcher Government's Economic Policy' in Dennis Kavanagh and Anthony Seldon (eds.), *The Thatcher Effect: A Decade of Change* (Oxford, 1991 edn), p. 23.
38 Douglas Jay, *Sterling* (Oxford, 1986 edn), pp. 165–6.
39 Thatcher, *The Downing Street Years*, p. 265.
40 Taylor, *The Trade Union Question*, pp. 292–3.
41 John Campbell, *Margaret Thatcher Vol. II*, pp. 356–60.
42 Alastair Hetherington, 'The Mass Media' in Dennis Kavanagh and Anthony Seldon, *The Thatcher Effect: A Decade of Change* (Oxford, 1991 edn), p. 292; Barrie Clement, 'Press Born again the Night Fleet Street Died', *Independent*, 22 January 1996, p. 7.
43 Robert J. Wybrow, *Britain Speaks Out, 1937–1987: A Social History as Seen through the Gallup Data* (1989), p. 135.
44 John Campbell, *Margaret Thatcher Vol. II*, p. 369.
45 Taylor, *The Trade Union Question*, pp. 304–5, 321–5.
46 Alastair J. Reid, *United We Stand: A History of Britain's Trade Unions* (2005 edn), p. 400.
47 Thatcher, *The Downing Street Years*, p. 687.
48 The unnamed minister (Norman Tebbit?) is quoted in Dennis Kavanagh, *Thatcherism and British Politics: The End of Consensus?* (Oxford, 1987), pp. 220–1.
49 David Butler and Gareth Butler, *British Political Facts since 1900* (2006), pp. 198, 206.
50 Christopher Warman, 'Critics of "Cut-Price" Sales Fail to Halt Steady Privatization', *The Times*, 17 December 1984, p. 4.

51 David Kynaston, *The City of London Vol. IV: A Club No More 1945–2000* (2002 edn), pp. 659–60.
52 Campbell, *Margaret Thatcher Vol. II*, p. 237.
53 Nicholas May, 'Privatisation in Action: A Comparison between British Telecom and the Electricity Supply Industry', unpublished undergraduate dissertation, University of Edinburgh (2001), p. 14.
54 Kynaston, *The City of London Vol. IV*, p. 724; Marr, *History of Modern Britain*, p. 431.
55 *Social Trends 22* (1992), chart 5.24, p. 102.
56 Marr, *Modern Britain*, p. 431.
57 Kynaston, pp. 696–7, p. 714; Margaret Reid, 'Mrs Thatcher and the City' in Kavanagh and Seldon, *The Thatcher Effect*, p. 49.
58 Nicholas Timmins, *The Five Giants: A Biography of the Welfare State* (1995), p. 508.
59 Josephine Webb, 'Social Security' in A. H. Halsey and Josephine Webb (eds.), *Twentieth-Century British Social Trends*, pp. 574–5.
60 Timmins, *The Five Giants*, p. 374.
61 Ibid., p. 392; Campbell, *Margaret Thatcher Vol. II*, pp. 171–2.
62 Arthur Marwick, *British Society since 1945* (1996 edn), p. 470.
63 Quoted in Timmins, *The Five Giants*, p. 453.
64 Royal Commission on the National Health Service, PP 1979–80, Cmnd 7615 (1979), Table 3.8, p. 23.
65 Timmins, *The Five Giants*, p. 467.
66 Charles Webster, 'The Health Service' in Kavanagh and Seldon, *The Thatcher Effect*, p. 182.
67 For a balanced and generally favourable assessment see Lowe, *The Welfare State*, pp. 331–3.
68 Timmins, *The Five Giants*, 352–3; *The Hugo Young Papers*, p. 151, *Sunday Times* lunch with Margaret Thatcher, 9 July 1980.
69 John Brown, *The British Welfare State: A Critical History* (1995), pp. 71–2; Lowe, *The Welfare State*, pp. 320–3.
70 Webb, 'Social Security', pp. 566–7.
71 Brian Simon, *Education and the Social Order 1940–1990* (1991), pp. 511–12.
72 Ibid., p. 540.
73 Margaret Thatcher, *The Path to Power* (1995), pp. 186–7.
74 Campbell, *Margaret Thatcher Vol. II*, p. 396.
75 Roy Lowe, *Schooling and Social Change* (1997), p. 42.
76 Campbell, *Margaret Thatcher Vol. II*, pp. 398–9; *The Times*, 30 January 1985, p. 1.
77 Alan Murie, 'Housing and the Environment' in Dennis Kavanagh and Anthony Seldon, *The Thatcher Effect* (Oxford 1989), p. 217. In 1989 the cumulative total of revenue from house sales since 1979 equalled 43 per cent of the combined revenue from the privatization of housing and all other privatizations.
78 Murie, 'Housing and the Environment', p. 216.
79 Andrew Dilnot and Carl Emmerson, 'The Economic Environment' in A. H. Halsey and Josephine Webb (eds.), *Twentieth-Century British Social Trends* (2000), p. 330; Anthony Sampson, *The Changing Anatomy of Britain* (1982), p. 202.
80 Michael Heseltine, *Where There's a Will* (1987), p. 136.
81 Paul A. Bull, 'The changing geography of manufacturing activity', in R. V. Johnston and Vince Gardiner (eds.), *The Changing Geography of the United Kingdom* (1991), p. 228.
82 Marr, *A History of Modern Britain*, p. 460.
83 Simon Jenkins, *Thatcher and Sons: A Revolution in Three Acts* (2007 edn), p. 132.
84 Thatcher, *Downing Street Years*, p. 645.

85 It could be argued, on the other hand, that all electors were contributing through direct or indirect taxes to the two-thirds of local government costs that were met by the Treasury.

86 *Observer*, 1 April 1990, pp. 1–2.

87 Borrowed from the title of Simon Jenkins's book, *Thatcher and Sons: A Revolution in Three Acts* (2007 edn).

88 Ibid., p. 259.

10 Haves and Have-Nots

1 The figures in this paragraph are taken from *Social Trends 22* (1992), p. 71 Table 4.4, p. 79 Table 4.23, p. 89, Table 5.1.

2 Ray Fitzpatrick and Tarani Chandola, 'Health' in A. H. Halsey and Josephine Webb (eds.), *Twentieth-Century British Social Trends* (2000), Table 3.1, p. 95.

3 A. H. Halsey, 'Further and Higher Education' in A. H. Halsey and Josephine Webb (eds.), *Twentieth Century British Social Trends* (2000), Table 6.4 pp. 228–9.

4 '*The Housing Act 1980* and its Scottish equivalent gave local authority tenants and tenants of other public bodies the right to buy their own homes, with discounts, if they had been a tenant for more than three years. This was subsequently reduced to two years by the *Housing and Building Control Act 1984*, which also increased the maximum available discount from 50 to 60 per cent. The maximum available discount for flats was further increased in January 1987 to 70 per cent.' *Social Trends 24* (1994), p. 8.

5 *Social Trends 22*, p. 148.

6 Peter Snow, *Oxford Observed* (1991), pp. 211–12.

7 *Social Trends 10*, p. 206, Chart 9.22.

8 *Social Trends 22*, p. 151, Table 8.16; *Social Trends 24* (1994), p. 115, Table 8.17.

9 Peter York and Charles Jennings, *Peter York's Eighties* (1995), p. 77.

10 *Social Trends 22*, pp. 113, p. 154, Table 8.22.

11 Joe Moran, *Queuing for Beginners* (2007), p. 155.

12 *Social Trends 22* (1992), p. Table 6.4, p. 108.

13 *Social Trends 10* (1980), p. 165, Table 7.11; *Social Trends 23*, p. 83, Table 6.4.

14 BBC Radio 4 'In Living Memory' Series 9 Episode 4, 17 December 2008.

15 Peter York, *Peter York's Eighties* (1995), p. 49.

16 *Time*, 9 January 1984.

17 Russell Ash, Marissa Piesman, and Marilee Hartley, *The Official British Yuppie Handbook: The State-of-the-Art Manual for Young Urban Professionals* (1984), pp. 44–5.

18 Moran, *Queuing for Beginners*, p. 143.

19 Alissa Goodman and Steven Webb write: 'The Gini coefficient is one of the most widely used summary measures of inequality and it varies between 0 (everyone has the same income) and 1 (one person has all the income).' It is based on the analysis of the total proportion of income held by each percentile or one per cent of the population, ranked in order of income. See note 32 below.

20 Quoted in Samuel Beer, *Britain Against Itself* (1982), p. 57.

21 R. J. Morris, 'Re-Using the 19th Century City: A View from the Year 2000'. Unpublished working paper, University of Edinburgh Department of Economic and Social History (2000); Robert Taylor, *The Trade Union Question in British Politics: Government and Unions since 1945* (1993), p. 379.

22 Rosen, *The Transformation of British Life*, p. 20.

23 Peter Townsend, *Poverty in the United Kingdom: A Survey of Household Resources and Standards of Living* (Harmondsworth, 1979), pp. 893–912.

24 'Policy for the Inner Cities', Cmnd 6845, PP 1976–7; *Social Trends 10* (1980), p. 39.
25 Jon Savage, *England's Dreaming: Sex Pistols and Punk Rock* (1991), p. 373.
26 Savage, *England's Dreaming*, p. 374.
27 Royal Commission on the Distribution of Income and Wealth, *Report No. 3: Higher Incomes from Employment*, PP 1975–6, Cmnd 6383 (1976), p. 895.
28 Tristram Hunt, 'Victory of the Middle Class', *Guardian*, 10 May 2002.
29 Roy Lewis, 'How the Middle Classes are being slowly taken over', *The Times*, 17 February 1975.
30 Harold Perkin, *The Rise of Professional Society: England since 1880* (1990), p. 440.
31 Anthony Heath, Roger Jowell, and John Curtice, *How Britain Votes* (1985), p. 32.
32 Alissa Goodman and Steven Webb, *For Richer, For Poorer: The Changing Distribution of Income in the United Kingdom, 1961–1991* (1994), p. 66.
33 Andrew Adams and Stephen Pollard, *A Class Act: The Myths of Britain's Classless Society* (1998), p. 89.
34 Bernard Alford, 'De-Industrialisation', *Refresh* 25 (Autumn 1977), p. 8; Alec Cairncross, *The British Economy since 1945: Economic Policy and Performance 1945–1990* (1992), p. 231.
35 *The Economist*, 29 September 1973, p. 5.
36 Ben Pimlott, *Frustrate Their Knavish Tricks: Writings on Biography, History and Politics* (1994), p. 177.
37 John Curtice, 'One nation?' in Roger Jowell, Sharon Witherspoon, and Lindsay Brook, *British Social Attitudes: the 5th report* (1988), p. 128.
38 *Britain in the Eighties: The Spectator View of the Thatcher Decade* (1991 edn), p. 103.
39 Andrew Adonis and Stephen Pollard, *A Class Act: The Myths of Britain's Classless Society* (1998 edn), pp. 73–4.
40 Eric Hobsbawm, 'The Forward March of Labour Halted?', *Marxism Today*, September 1978, pp. 279–86.
41 Tony Benn, *Against The Tide: Diaries 1973–76* (1990 edn), p. 4, entry for 25 January 1973.
42 Anthony Heath, Roger Jowell, and John Curtice, *How Britain Votes* (1985), pp. 32–3.
43 Duncan Gallie, 'The Labour Force' in A. H. Halsey and Josephine Webb (eds.), *Twentierh Century British Social Trends* (2000), p. 288.
44 Ian Bradley, 'You Can't Keep the Middle Classes Down', *The Times*, 8 February 1982.
45 *The Hugo Young Papers*, paras. 214, 278, interviews with Neil Kinnock 25 June 1985, 21 May 1988.
46 Roger Jowell, Sharon Witherspoon, and Lindsay Brook, *British Social Attitudes: the 1987 Report* (19087), pp. 12–13.
47 Muriel Nissel, 'What They Didn't Want You to Know', *Independent*, 26 January 1995.

11 The Permissive Age

1 Sue Bruley, *Women in Britain since 1900* (1999), p. 154.
2 A. H. Halsey, 'Further and Higher Education' in A. H. Halsey and Josephine Webb (eds.), *Twentieth-Century British Social Trends* (2000), pp. 228–9.
3 Duncan Gallie, 'The Labour Force' in Halsey and Webb (eds.), *Twentieth-Century British Social Trends*, pp. 296–7.
4 Bruley, *Women in Britain*, p. 171.
5 Dolly Smith Wilson, 'Gender: Change and Continuity' in Paul Addison and Harriet Jones (eds.), *A Companion to Contemporary Britain 1939–2000* (Oxford, 2005), p. 254.
6 Jane Lewis, *Women in Britain since 1945* (Oxford, 1992), p. 118; Sue Bruley, *Women in Britain*, p. 160.

7 Lewis, *Women in Britain since 1945*, p. 80; Sue Bruley, *Women in Britain*, p. 165.

8 A. J. P. Taylor, *English History* (Oxford, 1965), p. 166.

9 *Guardian*, 28 March 2000.

10 *Daily Telegraph*, 12 May 2009; Glyn Pursglove, 'James Kirkup', *Guardian*, 16 May 2009.

11 Callum G. Brown, *Religion and Society in Twentieth-Century Britain* (2006), pp. 278–9.

12 *Population Trends*, Summer 2000, p. 37, Figure 10.

13 Michael Young and Peter Willmott, *The Symmetrical Family* (Harmondsworth, 1984), p. 361.

14 See Chapter 7, 'The Liberal Hour'.

15 David Coleman, 'Population and Family' in Halsey and Webb (eds.), *Twentieth-Century British Social Trends* (2000), p. 58.

16 *Population Trends*, Summer 2000, p. 7.

17 *The Times*, 11 May 1981, p. 15.

18 *The Times*, 5 April 1984, p. 2, 19 November 1984, p. 13, 18 October 1945, p. 1.

19 *The Times*, 10 January 1985, p. 10.

20 *Social Trends 2000*, Table 2,17 p. 44.

21 Anthony Heath and Dorren McMahon, 'Changes in Values' in Roger Jowell, Lindsay Brook, Gillian Prior, and Bridget Taylor (eds.), *British Social Attitudes: the 9th report* (1992), p. 124.

22 David Coleman, 'Population and Family' in Halsey and Webb (eds.), *Twentieth-Century British Social Trends*, p. 62.

23 Tony Judt, *Postwar: A History of Europe since 1945* (2005), p. 377; 'The Marriage Savers', *Time* 19 January 2004, *Time* online archive accessed 24 March 2009.

24 Sheena Ashford, 'Family Matters' in *British Social Attitudes: the 1987 report* (1987), p. 124.

25 Ibid., pp. 126–7.

26 Michael Young and Peter Willmott, *The Symmetrical Family* (Harmondsworth, 1973), pp. 114–15.

27 Ann Oakley, *Housewife* (Harmondsworth, 1974), p. 222.

28 Catherine Hakim, 'Mummy, I *Want* to be a Housewife', *Times Higher Education Supplement*, 26 April 1996, p. 17.

29 Anna Coote and Beatrix Campbell, *Sweet Freedom* (1987 edn), pp. 95–6.

30 Roy Lowe, *Schooling and Social Change 1964–1990* (1997), p. 108.

31 Ion Trewin (ed.), *The Hugo Young Papers: Thirty Years of British Politics – Off the Record* (2008), p. 266, note of 27 October 1987; Margaret Thatcher, *The Downing Street Years* (1995 edn), p. 636.

32 Beatrix Campbell, *The Iron Ladies: Why Do Women Vote Tory?* (1987), pp. 160–5.

33 *The Times*, 22 November 1984, p. 3; 30 November 1984, p. 11.

34 Airey, 'Social and Moral Values', p. 137.

35 Simon Garfield, *The End of Innocence: Britain in the Time of Aids* (1994), pp. 44–5, 113–14.

36 Garfield, *End of Innocence*, pp. 117 and 128.

37 John Major, *The Autobiography* (2000 edn), p. 555.

38 Arthur Marwick, *British Society since 1945* (1996 edn), p. 251.

39 Ibid., pp. 251–2; House of Commons Home Affairs Committee, 'Misuse of Hard Drugs', PP 1984–5, HC 299-I, p. 4.

40 House of Commons Social Services Select Committee, 'Misuse of drugs', pp. 1984–5, HC 208, pp. vii–viii.

41 Social Services Select Committee, p. x.

42 Ibid., p. xii.

43 Margaret Thatcher, *The Downing Street Years* (1995 edn), pp. 629–30.

12 Uncharted Waters

1 Ian Spencer, *British Immigration Policy since 1939: The Making of Multi-Racial Britain* (1997), p. 146; Juliet Cheetham, 'Immigration' in A. H. Halsey (ed.), *Trends in British Society since 1900* (1972), p. 459; Ceri Peach, Vaughan Robinson, Julia Maxted, and Judith Chance, 'Immigration and Ethnicity' in A. H. Halsey (ed.), *British Social Trends since 1900* (1988 edn), p. 591; Ceri Peach, Alisdair Rogers, Judith Chance, and Patricia Daley, 'Immigration and Ethnicity' in A. H. Halsey and Josephine Webb (eds.), *Twentieth-Century British Social Trends* (2000), pp. 140–1, 157. Owing to the fact that the 1971, 1981, and 1991 censuses each adopted a different approach to the classification of race and ethnicity, while all classification is problematic in one way or another, there are no exact or indisputable figures. The broad trends are not in doubt.

2 Peach *et al.*, 'Immigration and Ethnicity', pp. 580–1.

3 Humayun Ansari, *'The Infidel Within': Muslims in Britain since 1800* (1988), pp. 253–4.

4 Peach *et al.*, 'Immigration and Ethnicity', p. 138.

5 Ruth Lupton and Anne Power, *Minority Ethnic Groups in Britain*, Case-Brookings Census Briefs No. 2 (2004), p. 1.

6 *The Economist*, 27 April 1974, p. 28.

7 House of Commons Debates vol. 914, cols. 1065–6, 5 July 1976.

8 TV Interview for 'World in Action', 27 January 1978, Margaret Thatcher Foundation website.

9 John Campbell, *Margaret Thatcher: Vol. 1: The Grocer's Daughter* (2001), pp. 399–401.

10 Kenan Malik, 'The Book-Burning that Changed Britain Forever', *Sunday Times*, 1 February 2009.

11 John Campbell, *Roy Jenkins: A Biography* (1983), pp. 162–3; *Annual Reports of the Commission for Racial Equality 1977–78*, HC 529, PP 1977–78; 1978, HC 128, PP 1979–80; 1979, HC 633, PP 1979–80; 1980, HC 397, PP 1980–1.

12 Andrew Marr, *A History of Modern Britain* (2007), p. 371.

13 Whitehead, *The Writing on the Wall*, p. 234.

14 This account of Newham is based on Francis Wheen, 'Where self-defence is an offence', *New Statesman*, 20 October 1978, pp. 492–3.

15 *Annual Report of the Commission for Racial Equality January to December 1978*, HC 128, PP 1979–80 (1979), p. 2.

16 Sarfraz Mansoor, 'The year rock found the power to unite', *Observer*, 20 April 2008; Jon Savage, *England's Dreaming: Sex Pistols and Punk Rock* (1992), pp. 241–3.

17 Dave Renton, 'Anti-Nazi League', dkrenton.co.uk.

18 Mike Phillips and Trevor Phillips, *Windrush: The Irresistible Rise of Multi-Racial Britain* (1998), pp. 357–65.

19 *Annual Report 1980*, p. 17.

20 'The Brixton Disorders 10–12 April 1981', PP 1981–2 Cmnd 8427, pp. 135–6.

21 Eric Hopkins, *The Rise and Decline of the English Working Classes 1918–1990: A Social History* (1991), pp. 257–8.

22 *The Stephen Lawrence Inquiry: Report of an Inquiry by Sir William Macpherson of Cluny*, Cm 4262-I (1999), para 6.34.

23 Jenny Bourne, 'The Life and Times of Institutional Racism', *Race and Class* 43,7 (2001), p. 8.

24 Andrew Rosen, *The Transformation of British Life 1950–2000* (2003), p. 99.

25 Ansari, *The Infidel Within*, pp. 350–1; Robert J. Pauly, *Islam in Europe: Integration or Marginalization?* (2004), p. 103.

26 Ansari, *'The Infidel Within'*, pp. 309, 317.

27 Ibid., p. 311.
28 Anthony Andrew, 'How one book ignited a culture war', *Observer*, 11 January 2009, p. 6.
29 Andrew, 'How one book…' p. 8.
30 *www.bobgeldof.info*; 'Live Aid 1985: How it Happened', *www.bbc.co.uk/music/thelive8event/liveaid/history.shtml*.
31 Whitehead, *The Writing on the Wall*, p. 237.
32 Richard Holt and Tony Mason, *Sport in Britain 1945–2000* (2000), pp. 86–7.
33 Spencer, *British Immigration Policy*, pp. 158–9.
34 *The Times*, 1 February 1977, p. 2; 'Scottish Politics: The Aalmanac of Scottish Elections and Politics', *www.alba.org.uk/home1.html*. This invaluable site, the work of Dr Ian Old, reproduces the results of the opinion polls carried out in Scotland by System 3 and published in the *Glasgow Herald*. For Scottish election results I have relied on Jessica Yonwin, *UK Election Statistics 1918–2004*, House of Commons Research Paper 04/61 (2004), p. 14. See also David McCrone and Lindsay Paterson, 'The Condundrum of Scottish Independence', *Scottish Affairs* no. 40 (summer 2002), pp. 54–75.
35 *The Times*, 15 October 1980, p. 2.
36 Andrew Marr, *The Battle for Scotland* (1992), pp. 139–40.
37 Hugh McIlvanney, 'A case of kamikaze in Cordoba', *Observer*, 11 June 1978, p. 11.
38 Alan Hamilton, 'Scots' Blood Pressure Rising as World Cup Approaches', *The Times*, 20 May 1978, p. 2.
39 Kenneth O. Morgan, *Rebirth of a Nation: Wales 1880–1980* (Oxford, 1981), p. 405.
40 Holt and Mason, *Sport in Britain*, p. 136.
41 Denis Balsom, 'The Three Wales Model' in John Osmond (ed.), *The National Question Again: Welsh Political Identity in the 1980s* (Llandysul, 1985), pp. 1–17.
42 Enoch Powell, *The Times*, 14 May 1982, p. 10.
43 Lawrence Freedman, *Britain and the Falklands War* (Oxford, 1988), pp. 94–9.
44 Margaret Thatcher, *The Downing Street Years* (1995 edn), p. 619.
45 *Scottish Economic Statistics 2001*, p. 133.
46 David Torrance, *'We in Scotland': Thatcherism in a Cold Climate* (2009), David Torrance, p. 167.
47 Campbell, *Margaret Thatcher* vol. 2, pp. 391–3; Torrance, *'We in Scotland'*, pp. 170–4.
48 Torrance, *'We in Scotland'*, p. xxiii.
49 See the profile of him in the *Observer Scotland*, 6 May 1990, p. 7.
50 Quoted by Eberhard Bort in 'Six Scots look at Margaret Thatcher', *Sunday Mail*, 26 April 2009.
51 John Osmond, 'The Dynamic of Institutions' in Osmond, *The National Question Again*, pp. 229–31; Davies, *A History of Wales*, p. 667.
52 David Butler and Uwe Kitzinger, *The 1975 Referendum* (1976), pp. 302–3.
53 *The Times*, 23 May 1974, p. 7.
54 Butler and Kitzinger, *The 1975 Referendum*, p. 293.
55 Ibid., p. 292.
56 Ibid., p. 259; Hugo Young, *This Blessed Plot: Britain and Europe from Churchill to Blair* (1999 edn), p. 296.
57 Butler and Kitzinger, *The 1975 Referendum*, p. 276.
58 This paragraph is based on 'European Legislation', House of Commons Research Paper SN/1A/2888 (2007).
59 *The Times*, 19 June 1985, p. 3.
60 Young, *This Blessed Plot*, pp. 347–8; Thatcher, *The Downing Street Years*, p. 743.
61 *Sun*, 1 November 1990.
62 Bogdanor, *Devolution in the United Kingdom*, p. 199.

The Long View

1 Tony Aldgate, *Censorship and the Permissive Society: British Cinema and Theatre 1955–1965* (1995), p. 147.
2 Samuel Brittan, *Capitalism and the Permissive Society* (1973), pp. 1–2.
3 Peter Hitchens, *The Abolition of Britain* (San Francisco, 2002), p. 1.
4 Richard Kelly and Isobel White, *All-Women Shortlists*, House of Commons Library Standard Notes N/PG/05057 (2009), p. 7; David and Gareth Butler, *British Political Facts since 1979* (2006), p. 121.
5 Hitchens, *The Abolition of Britain*, p. 1.

Further Reading

The following is a list of recommended further reading on the themes and topics discussed in this book:

Overviews of Britain since 1945

Andrew Marr, *A History of Modern Britain* (2007)
Kenneth Morgan, *Britain since 1945: The People's Peace* (2001)
Paul Addison and Harriet Jones (eds.), *A Companion to Contemporary Britain 1939–2000* (2005)

The State in Economic and Social Policy

Alec Cairncross, *The British Economy Since 1945: Economic Policy and Performance 1945–1995* (1995)
Nicholas Timmins, *The Five Giants: A Biography of the Welfare State* (1995)
Rodney Lowe, *The Welfare State in Britain since 1945* (1999)
Robert Taylor, *The Trade Union Question in British Politics; Government and Unions since 1945* (1993)
Martin Daunton, *Just Taxes: The Politics of Taxation in Britain 1914–1979* (2002)

Standards of Living and Social Structure

Arthur Marwick, *British Society since 1945* (1996)
Andrew Rosen, *The Transformation of British Life 1950–2000* (2003)
A. H. Halsey and Josephine Webb (eds.), *Twentieth-Century British Social Trends* (2000)
Andrew Adonis and Stephen Pollard, *A Class Act: The Myth of Britain's Classless Society* (1998)
Joe Moran, *Queueing for Beginners: The Story of Daily Life from Breakfast to Bedtime* (2007)

Sex, Marriage, and the Family

Lesley A. Hall, *Sex, Gender and Social Change in Britain since 1880* (2000)

Arthur Marwick, *The Sixties: Cultural Revolution in Britain, France, Italy and the United States c1958–c1974* (1998)

Ann Oakley, *Taking it Like a Woman* (1984)

Simon Garfield, *The End of Innocence: Britain in the Time of Aids* (1994)

Martin Durham, *Sex and Politics: The Family and Morality in the Thatcher Years* (1991)

Questions of National Identity

Richard Weight, *Patriots: National Identity in Britain 1940–2000* (2002)

Mike Phillips and Trevor Phillips, *Windrush: The Irresistible Rise of Multi-Racial Britain* (1998)

Humayun Ansari, *'The Infidel Within': The History of Muslims in Britain 1800 to the Present* (2004)

Tom Devine, *The Scottish Nation 1700–2000* (2000)

Christopher Harvie, *Scotland and Nationalism: Scottish Society and Politics 1707 to the Present* (2004)

John Davies, *A History of Wales* (2007)

Hugo Young, *This Blessed Plot: Britain and Europe from Churchill to Blair* (1999)

Specific Periods

Correlli Barnett, *The Lost Victory: British Dreams, British Realities* 1945–1950 (1995)

Peter Hennessy, *Never Again: Britain 1945 to 1951* (1992)

—— *Having it so Good: Britain in the Fifties* (2006)

David Kynaston, *Austerity Britain 1945–1951* (2007)

—— *Family Britain 1951–1957* (2009)

Brian Harrison, *In Search of a Role: The United Kingdom 1951–1970* (2009)

—— *Finding a Role? The United Kingdom 1970–1990* (2010)

Dominic Sandbrook, *Never Had it so Good: A History of Britain from Suez to the Beatles* (2006)

—— *White Heat: A History of Britain in the Swinging Sixties* (2006)

Mark Garnett, *From Anger to Apathy: The British Experience since 1975* (2007)

Richard Vinen, *Thatcher's Britain: The Politics and Social Upheaval of the Thatcher Era* (2009)

Copyright Acknowledgements

We are grateful to the following for permission to include copyright material in this book.

Extracts from Social Trends, Population Trends, and other Government publications and reports are reproduced under the terms of the Click-Use Licence No. 2009002680 with the permission of the Controller of OPSI and The Queen's Printer for Scotland.

Nicholas Deakin: maps from Nicholas Deakin: *Colour, Citizenship ad Society* (Panther, 1970).

The Estates of Michael Flanders and Donald Swann for 'Song of Patriotic Prejudice' (1963) words by Michael Flanders. Any use of Flanders and Swann material, large or small, should be referred to the Estates at leonberger@donaldswann.co.uk.

Institute for Fiscal Studies for figures from Alissa Goodman: 'Inequality and Living Standards in Great Britain: Some Facts', Institute for Fiscal Studies Briefing Note No. 19 (2001) and from Institute for Fiscal Studies 'Living Standards During Previous Recessions', copyright © Institute for Fiscal Studies.

Denis Balsom for map of 'The Three-Wales Model' from Denis Balsom: 'The Three Wales Model' in J. Osmond (ed.), *The National Question Again: Welsh Political Identity in the 1980s* (Gomer Press, 1985).

Motorway Archive Trust for 1964 and 1974 motorway maps, copyright © Motorway Archive Trust.

NI Syndication for facsimile extracts from *The Times*, 3 May 1952 and 3 May 1957, copyright © The Times 1952, 1957/nisyndication.com.

Palgrave Macmillan for figure from Guy Routh: *Occupation and Pay in Great Britain 1906–1979* (Macmillan, 1980).

PFD (www.pfd.co.uk) on behalf of The Estate of Arthur Marwick for table from Arthur Marwick: *British Society Since 1945* (3e, Penguin 1996), copyright © Arthur Marwick 1977.

Taylor and Francis Books UK for figure from Ian R. G. Spencer: *British Immigration Policy since 1939: The Making of Multi-Racial Britain* (Routledge, 1997), copyright © 1997, and map from R. J. Johnston and

438 Copyright Acknowledgements

Vince Gardiner: *The Changing Geography of the United Kingdom* (Routledge, for the Institute of British Geographers, 1991), copyright © 1991.

We have made every effort to trace and contact all copyright holders before publication. If notified, the publisher will be pleased to rectify any errors or omissions at the earliest opportunity.

Index